Traitors
&
Treason

A Startling and Factual Expose of the Treachery in a Great and Godly Nation Under Siege

By

Robert W. Pelton

Copyright © 2002 by Robert W. Pelton

All rights reserved. No part of this book shall be reproduced or transmitted in any form or by any means, electronic, mechanical, magnetic, photographic including photocopying, recording or by any information storage and retrieval system, without prior written permission of the publisher. No patent liability is assumed with respect to the use of the information contained herein. Although every precaution has been taken in the preparation of this book, the publisher and author assume no responsibility for errors or omissions. Neither is any liability assumed for damages resulting from the use of the information contained herein.

ISBN 0-7414-0955-0

Published by:

INFINITY
PUBLISHING.COM

Infinity Publishing.com
519 West Lancaster Avenue
Haverford, PA 19041-1413
Info@buybooksontheweb.com
www.buybooksontheweb.com
Toll-free (877) BUY BOOK
Local Phone (610) 520-2500
Fax (610) 519-0261

Printed in the United States of America

Printed on Recycled Paper

Published April, 2003

About the Author

The author is an informed, patriotic American; veteran of both the Korean and Vietnam Wars; a concerned father; and a Christian. Mr. Pelton contends that the Declaration of Independence is a timeless, divinely inspired masterpiece, given to mankind through the anointed pen of Thomas Jefferson.. He also contends that the U.S. Constitution is indisputably the product of Providential guidance and wisdom and not a document which evokes whimsical interpretations with the changing political climates. He further believes that all Americans have a *moral obligation* to stand up and be counted in these trying times. Mr. Pelton agrees with Abraham Lincoln who declared: "To sin by silence when they should protest, makes cowards of men."

Author Robert Pelton, is no shrinking "moderate". He has earned the right to his station through years of investigating, accumulating and organizing the material for those who slept through years of treason and treachery against America! Robert Pelton has issued his warning. **Traitors &Treason** contains voluminous, carefully documented evidence, that our Constitution has been and still is under organized attack by proponents of the socialist/communist New World Order in its quest for total control of our great nation through one-world government. Top priority in opposing that end should be to get the United States out of the United Nations and to abolish all of the unquestionably unconstitutional U.N. treaty commitments.

It can be truly said, argues Pelton, that through the Providential genius of our Founding Fathers, the *remaining remnants* of the original American Constitutional Republic -- even after decades of treason and treachery being allowed to run unchecked in our country -- still provides more freedom, opportunity, and abundance for mankind than is found in any other nation of the world. And that an informed and active, not a media brainwashed electorate, is the only antidote to further treason and treachery.

Contents
Preface

Part I — Massive Doses of Treason

CHAPTERS	PAGE
1. Arming America's Communist Enemies	1
2. Treason and Big Business	21
3. Financial Aid For the Reds	40
4. Trade With and Aid to America's Enemies	61
5. Illegally Importing Communist Slave-Made Goods	80
6. Vietnam—A Classic Example of Wholesale Treason	98

Part II — Are There Not Traitors Among Us?

CHAPTERS	PAGE
7. A Peek at Internal Security	119
8. Internal Security—the Supreme Court and the Presidents	140
9. Security Risks in the State Department	161
10. Misdeeds of the Subversive State Department	181
11. Those Close to the President	202
12. Presidential Words and Deeds	224
13. Miscellaneous Subversion in Government	245
14. The United States and the United Nations	266
15. Betrayal of the Prisoners of War – Korea and Vietnam	285
16. A Potpourri of Traitorous Acts and Treasonous Deeds	304
Epilogue: Communism's Inherently Evil Nature	331
References	350
Index	406

"Some are members of the Party, and some are not; but that is a formal difference. The important thing is that both serve the same common purpose."
Joseph Stalin

Patriotism means to stand by the country. It does not mean to stand by the President or any other public official save exactly to the degree in which he himself stands by the country.
Theodore Roosevelt

"Look at the means a man employs; consider his motives; observe his pleasures. A man simply cannot conceal himself."
Confucius

"Ye cannot drink the cup of the Lord, and the cup of the devil; ye cannot be partakers of the Lord's table and of the table of devils."
I. Corinthians. 10.21

Dedicated to The United States of America, the greatest country the world has ever known,

and to

True American heroes who, against seemingly insurmountable odds, risked everything in their courageous efforts to expose the infiltration of Communist espionage agents in government, as well as in other areas of American life. These patriots include such beacons of liberty as Senator Joseph Raymond McCarthy (R-WI); Historian Robert Welch; Senator William Jenner (R-IN); Senator William Knowland (R-CA); Congressman Martin Dies (D-TX); Congressman Francis Walters (D-PA); and Congressman Lawrence Patton McDonald (D-GA). Each, though ruthlessly maligned in his day, has already been vindicated by history.

Preface

"Treason against the United States shall consist only in levying war against them, or in adhering to their enemies, giving them aid and comfort."
U.S. Constitution. Article 111, Section 3.

What's your traitor-treason I.Q.? If you can answer the following questions, it's high. If you miss one or more, you should carefully read ***Traitors & Treason.***
* Which Secretary of State was identified as a Soviet agent?
* How many of the 17 Americans who helped create the United Nations were later exposed as Communist moles?
* Who allowed the head of the American Communist Party to have an office in the White House?
* Which President promoted a highly placed Communist mole after the FBI had exposed the man?
* Which major American university gave an honorary degree to a notorious Communist spy?

These are questions to which every American should rightfully have an honest answer! But, unfortunately, most do not. As the Honorable Ezra Taft Benson says: "The truth must be told even at the risk of destroying, in large measure, the influence of men who are widely respected and loved by the American people. The stakes are high. Freedom and survival is the issue."

Tragedy was carefully orchestrated by traitors in the Government and the media with regard to Cuba, Vietnam,

Laos, Cambodia, Rhodesia, China, El Salvador, Nicaragua and many other countries. Anastasio Somoza, former President of free Nicaragua, offered a startling insight: "I have factual evidence that the . . . betrayal of Nicaragua was not perpetrated out of ignorance, but rather by design."[1] Somoza was soon after assassinated. Earl E.T. Smith was the American Ambassador to Cuba when it was similarly delivered to the Communists. He makes this concise comment: "Nicaragua is Cuba all over again."[2] Is this not treason?

The answer to one of the initial questions is this: Henry Kissinger was named in sworn testimony as a Soviet espionage agent with the code name "Bor." This Kremlin mole was exposed by a top Polish intelligence operative, Colonel Michael Goleniewski, who defected to the West in 1961. Kissinger, while a U.S. Army sergeant right after World War II, was charged with being a member of a Russian spy ring called ODRA. He was at the time a counter intelligence interrogator and taught at the Military Intelligence School.[3] Are there not traitors among us?

John Lehman, Secretary of the Navy, made this shocking statement to the 1983 Annapolis graduating class: "Within weeks many of you will be looking cross just hundreds of feet of water at some of the most modern technology ever invented in America. Unfortunately, it is on Soviet ships." [4] Is this not treason?

Chevron-Gulf pays the Communist dictatorship in Angola over $600 million annually in taxes and oil royalties. This money buys new Soviet MiGs, tanks and helicopter gunships. And it pays Castro for supplying 35,000 imported Cuban mercenaries who keep the people enslaved.[5] Are there not traitors among us?

Stresses retired Brigadier General Andrew J. Gatsis: "Though aware of the Communist goal of world domination, the average U.S. Citizen refuses to believe . . . that the real threat comes from . . . governmental officials and their non-governmental confederates who secretly espouse the same objectives as the openly avowed Communists."[6] Anthony Sutton states: "We now have the formidable task of bringing these gentlemen to the bar of justice to publicly answer for their private and concealed actions."[7]

Traitors & Treason carefully examines the reasons for, and the Americans behind, the fall of freedom and the rise of tyranny throughout the world. Such a book won't win any accolades from the United Nations or the State Department. Nor will Harvard feel compelled to bestow an honorary degree upon the author. After all, Harvard Law School was the spawning ground for an incredible number of Red agents. Included were members of the first Soviet spy ring ever to be exposed in the government. Reed Irvine aptly comments: "Indeed, it has long been a joke among refugees from Eastern Europe that there are more Marxists at Harvard than there are in the Soviet Union, or Poland, or whatever Communist country the refugee called home."[8]

The definition of treason isn't difficult to interpret. It's not a murky gobbledegook of words. Treason is the *only* crime specifically mentioned in the Constitution. The description is crystal clear: "Treason against the United States shall consist only in levying war against them, or in adhering to their enemies, giving them aid and comfort."[9] Treason is still a most serious federal offense. U.S. Code, Title 18, Section 2381, forthrightly deals with those who commit treason; Section 2382 covers those who do nothing about it when they know of someone who commits treason.

Traitors & Treason is the product of years of intense research, data collection, and vast personal experience in intelligence. The evidence is irrefutable! The documentation is indisputable! The end result brings forth an inescapable conclusion—America has been subverted by many traitors in and out of government! America has been deliberately weakened by conscious acts of treason over a period of many decades from the Roosevelt Administration up to present day.

Traitors & Treason reveals the names of the players. It gives important facts about the game. Judge for yourself!

Part I

Massive Doses of Treason

"Whoever, owing allegiance to the United States, levies war against them or adheres to their enemies, giving them aid and comfort within the United States or elsewhere, is guilty of treason and shall suffer death, or be imprisoned not less than five years and fined not less than $10,000; and shall be incapable of holding any office under the United states."

U.S. Code, Title 18, Section 2381

"Whoever, owing allegiance to the United States and having knowledge of the commission of any treason against them, conceals and does not, as soon as may be, disclose and make known the same to the President or to some judge or the United States, or to the Governor or to some judge or justice of a particular state, is guilty of misprision of treason, and shall be fined not more than $1000 or imprisoned not more than 7 years or both."

U.S. Code, Title 18, Section 2382

Chapter 1

Arming America's Communist Enemies

Traitor: "A person who betrays his country . . . "
The American Heritage Dictionary

Treason: "Betraying one's government . . . revealing military secrets to the enemy."
Webster's Elementary Dictionary

Former Congressman John Breckinridge (D-KY) talked to Soviet First Deputy Minister of Defense N.V. Ogarkov while visiting Communist Occupied Russia in 1978. He was bluntly warned: "The United States has always been in a position where it could not be threatened by foreign powers. That is no longer true. Today the Soviet Union has military superiority over the United States and henceforth the United States will be threatened. You had better get used to it!"1

It's an acknowledged fact that Communist Occupied Russia is terribly inept when it comes to advances in science and technology. The backward Soviets couldn't possibly have become a major military power without the help of the United States. No one really believes that a dictatorship incapable of even manufacturing a common light bulb could possibly create and build its own sophisticated missiles and high-tech weaponry! No one really believes that a dictatorship incapable of producing an automobile could possibly create and build its own tanks, assault helicopters, and jet aircraft! America spends billions on defense in order to offset the USSR's advanced war-making capabilities. Ironically, the Soviets would possess little, if any, of this without U.S. technology transfers and arms sales.

There's absolutely no question about the correlation between American assistance and the military might of the "evil Red empire." There is ample reason to believe that Communist Occupied Russia, the slave bloc nations, and Communist Occupied China are deliberately being armed by the United States. American aid, trade, money, and business dealings are the only things responsible for the Red dictatorship's ability to flex its muscles! All of this is well known by the highest ranking leaders in Washington! Yet, these same officials go to phenomenal lengths to hide these facts from the American people. As Cicero once wisely advised: "A nation can survive its fools, even the ambitious, but it cannot survive treason from within."

All Americans should heed the words of retired Brigadier General Robert L. Scott, Jr.: "Our threat is not from abroad.... The danger is internal, and the solution can only be internal. Every American must . . . accept responsibility for what is being done in his name."[2]

Arming the Soviet Bloc

The Russians were promoted as the "good guys" when the U.S. began treasonously arming them many years ago. This was done under the transparent guise that there was a serious Chinese-Soviet split. If the U.S. assisted the Soviets, Americans were told, the geriatric despots who run the Red dictatorship would surely mellow. In case of war with the Communist Chinese "bad guys," the Soviet "good guys" would be America's allies.

So the United States injudiciously sold, traded, and gave the insatiable Russian Bear incredible amounts of weaponry and computers and factories. The Soviet Union became a first rate Made-In-The-USA military power. Have the Russians mellowed? Not in the least! Are they America's friend? Certainly not! Every Soviet dictator—up to and including suave American media favorite Mikhail Sergeyvich Gorbachev— has been unswerving in his commitment to one day conquer the United States! U.S. *News & World Report* observes: "Russia's leaders are shaping a military force as if they expect World War III to erupt at dawn tomorrow."

In 1930, Ford Motor Company contracted to build Communist Occupied Russia a state-of-the-art, mass-production vehicle factory. Ford and the Austin Company designed, advised, gave technical assistance, and furnished the equipment for a plant in Gorki, 250 miles east of Moscow. Gorki is a closed city, where important Russians who get out of line are banished into "internal exile" by Communist Party bosses. The factory was constructed with slave labor under the supervision of Albert Kahn, the builder of Ford's River Rouge complex near Detroit. The Gorki plant, one of the largest in the world, was designed to annually produce 140,000 cars, trucks, and buses. Ford specialists taught Russian forced-laborers the finer aspects of assembling mass-produced vehicles. Soviet engineers were even brought to America for training at the River Rouge plant. Yes, it can be truthfully said that Henry Ford established the Russian dictatorship's auto, truck, and bus industry! And Gorki was heralded as Russia's version of Detroit!*3*

Nevertheless, car production in today's Soviet Union is negligible. More autos are stolen annually in the United States than are produced in the USSR.*4* There are fewer privately owned automobiles in Communist Occupied Russia than there are cars owned by South African blacks.*5* Moreover, the average Russian citizen has little need for an automobile.

The entire country contains fewer paved roads and highways than does Massachusetts.*6* But all this trivia is beside the point! The Soviets *do not* use the Ford plant to mass-produce automobiles, commercial trucks, or buses! Instead, the assembly lines spew forth untold numbers of Red Army vehicles. These include GAZ-46 jeeps; GAZ-69

SHMEL rocket carriers; GAZ-56 and 62 trucks; GAZ-69A scout cars; GAZ-69 command cars; and GAZ-47 amphibious personnel carriers.

1930 was also the year Detroit's Arthur J. Brandt Company built their big ZIL factory for the Russians. C.P. Weeks, Vice president of Hercules Motor Corporation in Canton, Ohio, declared the factory was: "By far the largest and best equipped plant in the world devoted solely to the manufacture of trucks and busses."7 Not surprisingly, the Brandt factory *doesn't* make commercial trucks or busses. It produces Red Army BM-13 rocket launcher bases; ZIL-150 and 151 armored trucks; and howitzer tractors.

The William Sellers Company of Philadelphia received a contract from Communist Occupied Russia in 1938. They supplied Stalin's murderous dictatorship with the heavy machinery required to produce 12-inch thick armor-plate.8 In March 1939, Electric Boat Company of Groton, Connecticut, was selected to supply the blueprints, specifications, and construction services necessary to build the backward Soviet Union's first submarine.9

Red moles, other traitorous leftists, and immoral opportunists buried in the bureaucratic honeycombs of the government have for years been illegally arming Communist Occupied Russia. That criminal tyranny has been shipped a never-ending supply of strategic war-related goods. For example, the heavily Red infiltrated (Hiss, White, Abt, Pressman and cohorts) Democratic Administrations of both Roosevelt and Truman sent a combined total *10* Yet of between $11 and $12 billion in weaponry and other goodies to their Soviet comrades between 1942 and 1946. no one was ever arrested and charged with being a traitor! No one was ever prosecuted and sent to prison for treason' Why?

The array of military items given to the Russian enemy was phenomenal. Included were 219,000 tons of scarce copper cable and wire; over 400 destroyers and other combat ships; over 14,000 planes; nearly 500,000 jeeps, tanks and trucks; over 1,300 diesel engines for ships; well over 300,000 tons of explosives; vast quantities of special machine tools and industrial machinery—all necessary for the production of military goods.[11]

Finally, the Battle Act of 1951 was passed by Congress in a desperate effort to close the arms giveaway flood gates. A concise list of non-tradable military-related items was incorporated in the legislation.

Harold E. Stassen (CFR) became Eisenhower's administrator of the Battle Act and drastically revised the list of non-tradable items *downward* in 1954 to benefit America's many Communist enemies. The end result was a booming increase in strategic trade between the United States and the entire Soviet Bloc. The Communist war machine was now allowed to freely obtain machine tools, generators, and other highly strategic goods, including electronic equipment used on guided missiles and in the field of atomic energy. Many items of military importance yesterday, per Stassen's illogic, were somehow overnight no longer considered "strategic." As a direct result of these inexcusable, pro-Red arming activities, the military might of the Soviet Union was dramatically expanded.[12]

Paradoxically, Eisenhower began to arm Communist Occupied Yugoslavia (Chapter 10) and Red Poland—both miniature replicas of the Russian slave labor dictatorship! Despite massive assistance, Yugoslavia's Tito repeatedly pledged his undying allegiance to Moscow. He declared: "In peace as in war, Yugoslavia must march shoulder to shoulder with the Soviet Union."[13] Nevertheless, in 1956, Congress was warned not to stop military aid to America's "friend." Such action, said Secretary of State John Foster Dulles (CFR), with a straight-face, would force Yugoslavia back into the Russian camp! This was claimed despite the fact that Tito was, and always had been, firmly in the Soviet camp!

The treasonous arms giveaways continued non-stop through subsequent administrations! Even Ronald Reagan was afflicted with the infectious Militarily-Assist-The-Communists bug! He somehow came to the paralogistic conclusion "that furnishing of assistance to Yugoslavia . . . is vital to the security of the United States, that Yugoslavia is not controlled by the international Communist conspiracy, and that such assistance will further promote the independence of Yugoslavia from international Communism."*14*

During 1969—Nixon's first year in the White House—over seven million pounds of America's strategic stockpile of tungsten was shipped to Communist Occupied Russia. This metal is used for making armor-plating for tanks, assault helicopters, other military vehicles, and armor-piercing shells.

The Bryant Chucking Grinder Company of Springfield, Vermont, first tried to export 164 of their Centalign-B ball-bearing grinders to Communist Occupied Russia in 1961. The Reds claimed to need these highly sophisticated machines in order to build farm pump motors. Senator Thomas Dodd (D-CT) didn't buy the phony pitch and intervened to stop this questionable deal!*15*

President Nixon told C.L. Sulzberger: "The Soviets now have three times the missile strength (ICBM) of ourselves. By 1974, they will pass us in submarines carrying nuclear missiles."*16*

Why then did his Commerce Department grant an export license in 1972 for the shipping of these strategic ball-bearing grinders to Communist Occupied Russia? Without Nixon's authorization, the Centalign-B machines couldn't have been sold to America's deadly enemy. The disastrous deal was consummated at the insistence of identified Red espionage agent Henry Kissinger.*17* Nixon's subversive shadow put all his prestige and influence behind the sale to his Kremlin masters. These grinders produce precision micro-finish (25 millionths of an inch) ball-bearings which are used in the guidance systems of missiles and other space vehicles.

What did this advanced technology do for the criminal Russian dictatorship? Astoundingly enough, it actually allowed them to MIRV their missiles shortly after the sale! In other words, thanks to treasonable American assistance, Communist Occupied Russia could now fire missiles with multiple warheads—each programmed with a different target in the U.S.!*18* Respected consultant Dr. Miles M. Costick observed in 1976: "According to the intelligence estimates, by 1982, the Soviets will have at least 5,000 operational MIRVs aimed at the United States. Without American computer technology and machines for production of precision miniature ball-bearings, this would not have been possible."*19* Indeed, reports Senator Jake Garn (R-UT): "Not only have Soviet MIRVed ICBMs reached accuracies previously undreamed of by U.S. strategic analysts, but all Soviet military systems requiring precision inertial guidance have also reached a new level of accuracy and sophistication."*20* This is a classic case of dual treason—treason involving both the Nixon Administration and the Bryant Chucking Grinder Company! Says Dr. Susan L. M. Huck: "This particular bit of treason, alone, should have cost everyone involved his freedom, if not his life. But of course it hasn't."[21]

Where did the fiendish Red terrorists running Communist Occupied Ethiopia get their tanks and rocket launchers and planes? Who gave Comrade Mengistu Haile Mariam the guns he needed to stay in power and to commit terrible atrocities on his own people? The United States under Gerald Ford became Ethiopia's major weapons supplier during 1975 and 1976! This Marxist dictatorship was *given* more military hardware than Ethiopia had ever dreamed of getting as a non-Red nation!

Boeing rushed to get in on the help-the-Communists gravy train. This company eagerly arranged to provide Communist Occupied Angola with new jets. These aircraft were sold at terms extremely favorable to the People's Republic. In November 1988, Boeing officials acknowledged they'd agreed to sell three 767 jet liners to Communist Occupied Poland's Lot airline. The cost: $220 million—all of which, as could be expected, would be financed through Western banks! Polish leaders refused to name the banks![22]

Armored vehicles for the Red army were being mass produced, thanks to Gleason Works – which sold to Communist Occupied Russia the sophisticated gear grinding equipment needed for this task.[23]

The world's most advanced seismological (earthquake detection) equipment was approved for sale to the USSR by the Commerce Department. The Russians use this equipment to locate and track American missile-carrying submarines!

Inedible tallow doesn't at first seem important. The U.S. regularly ships tons of this to Communist Occupied Russia. The Soviets use inedible tallow to manufacture TNT![24]

Senator Jake Garn (R-UT) gives other concrete examples of incredible American duplicity—some would call it outright treason: "The Soviets obtained their shaped-charge technology used in war heads for antitank guided missiles from the U.S. oil-tool industry.... since the early 1970s the Soviets and East Europeans have legally purchased more than 3,000 minicomputers, some of which are now being used in military related organizations."[25]

Negotiations between Nicolae Ceausescu's oppressive Romanian slave state and United Aircraft were carried out for $100 million worth of heavy duty helicopters, much like those the U.S. military uses. Lockheed made a lucrative business deal to build and deliver helicopters for Communist Occupied Russia.26   Are these the devastating Mi-24 Hind/Assault helicopters the Soviets use in Nicaragua, Angola, Afghanistan, East Germany and elsewhere around the world? Or are the Mi-24 "flying tanks" built for the USSR by some other "patriotic" American company?

The AFL-CIO issued this belated warning "The list of recent Soviet acquisitions is enough to make Lenin's statement that the Western democracies would 'sell us the rope for their own hanging' seem like a prophecy." The AFL-CIO leadership stood virtually alone in its public acknowledgment that strategic war-related items could be utilized with "nuclear warheads, armor-piercing rockets, and submarine detection devices."[27]

The infamous Kama River truck factory (Chapter 2, 3) was built in the Tartar Autonomous Soviet Socialist Republic. This is the most spectacular example of America's treasonous assistance to Communist Occupied Russia to date. It was designed by Americans, built by Americans, and financed by Americans. The plant was officially sanctioned by the Nixon, Ford, and Carter Administrations. It's located in Naberezhyne Chelny, a small village with no more than a few thousand population. Where will the people come from to work in the factory and build the trucks? Try some of the slave labor camps found on the Kama River! Four of them are Chusovaya, Berezniki, Solikamsk, and Vishersk.[28]

In 1978, IBM sold Communist Occupied Russia computers worth $18 million for use in their Kama River truck plant. The foundry was thus equipped with the world's largest industrial computer system! This allowed the Reds to produce 250,000 diesel truck engines a year. They also mass produce tank turrets and an incredible array of other military items. The output of multi-axle 10 ton trucks at the Kama River plant surpasses that of all American truck builders combined!

The USSR dutifully promised to build only commercial vehicles. In spite of these promises, the very first trucks to roll off the assembly line were used in 1979 to carry Russian troops into Afghanistan![29] President Carter said his eyes were rudely opened by the shocking Soviet invasion and he temporarily embargoed further high-tech trade. Yet IBM was allowed to keep from three to twenty of their computer experts working at the Kama River plant. Here we find American citizens directly assisting in the production of Red Army vehicles!

In 1980, Soviet troops were methodically decimating the population of Afghanistan. Water supplies were poisoned and the earth scorched in an effort to defeat the tough little country. Carter reversed his short-term embargo and ordered the Commerce Department to approve the sale to Communist Occupied Russia of automated assembly line equipment. This high-tech machinery would double the output of the

Kama River factory. George P. Shultz (CFR), later Reagan's Secretary of State, bears a great deal of responsibility for the existence of the Kama River truck plant. So does Paul Volker (CFR), long-time Chairman of the Federal Reserve Bank. These men and their counterparts in other questionable deals with America's enemies are the ones Lenin referred to as "deaf mute blind men." They loan money, give away technology, and build the Communist military, all the while laboring towards suicide. Should not these and other American leaders have known better? Certainly! They were either incredibly misinformed, incredibly naive, incredibly crass— or they deliberately committed treason! It's certainly no secret that Red Army military vehicles have for decades been produced in American supplied Soviet auto and truck plants.

In 1980, the Dresser firm shipped to Communist Occupied Russia a $144 million factory to manufacture special petroleum drill bits for gas and oil exploration. Located near Kuibyshev on the Volga River, the completed plant was immediately converted to weapons production! It now produces armor-piercing shells designed to stop America's M-l tank. This treasonous sale included a computer operated electron beam welder. Such a high-tech welding machine is used in jet aircraft assembly and has a multitude of other military applications.[30]

It's puzzling to observe (or is it?) American politicians and government bureaucrats continuing unabated to develop Communist Occupied Russia's military-industrial base and equip their massive war machine. These traitors (or dupes) know the brutal Moscow-based dictatorship has saturated our government, media, industry, religious organizations, military, and other areas with massive spy networks. They also know the tyrants entrenched in the Kremlin have never once deviated from their publicly declared goal of destroying the capitalist system and conquering the United States! More than just a few of these people in and out of government are unquestionably important members of this conspiritorial group.

Some strategic items of distinct military application shipped to the Soviets have already proven disastrous. For example, Made in USA high-tech equipment—computers, radar and the missile firing guidance system—was used by the Russian fighter pilot when the Kremlin ordered him to bring down Korean Airlines Flight 007 on September 1, 1983 (see Chapter 12). Communist Occupied

Russia's most despised and feared anti-Communist, Congressman Larry McDonald (D-GA), was on that plane! And Larry is believed to be incarcerated in Russia to this very day as are most of the other 268 passengers who were on that plane.

It's impossible for highly advanced computers to have no direct military applications. Computer give-aways to the Soviet Union and other Red slave states are vital to their war-making potential! Such treasonous dealings are a most serious breach of America's national security! The Carter Administration allowed more than 300 new exemptions for exporting strategic goods to the Soviet Bloc. Included were Control Data Corporation's Cyber 73 master computer and the IBM 370. The Cyber 73 is presently hidden in the Ural Mountains beneath four miles of granite. From this location, it directs a satellite network of IBM 360 and 370 computers in place around Moscow. They in turn operate Communist Occupied Russia's ABM (anti-ballistic missile) defense system!

Executive vice chairman of the Control Data Corporation, Robert D. Schmidt, said: "We will never make our peace with right-wing individuals who oppose all trade with the Russians."*31* Schmidt's firm sold over $50 million worth of computers to Communist Occupied Russia during the 1970s alone. According to *Time:* "Control Data Corporation has delivered the largest Western machine in the Soviet Union, a model 6200 now at the Dubna Research Institute ...."*32* This computer is being used for the development of missiles and other exotic weaponry.

FBI Director J. Edgar Hoover pegged people like Schmidt well: "To me, one of the most unbelievable and unexplainable phenomena in the fight on Communism is the manner in which otherwise respectable, seemingly intelligent persons, perhaps unknowingly, aid the Communist cause more effectively than the Communists themselves. The pseudo liberal can be more destructive than the known Communist because of the esteem which his cloak of respectability invites."[33]

"Republicans pledge," said the Party platform of 1980, "to stop the flow of technology to the Soviet Union that could contribute directly or indirectly to the growth of their military power." Furthermore, the platform chided the Democratic Administration of President Jimmy Carter for allowing "the most extensive raid on American technology by the Soviet Bloc since World War II."[34] Apparently, these were no more than hypocritically hollow statements. The record speaks for itself!

It all boils down to one simple, inescapable fact. The Executive branch of the government treasonously provides military hardware, weapons, equipment, and training for brutal Communist police states! These inhuman Red dictatorships have all undertaken large-scale executions of their own citizenry. Each maintains dreadful concentration camps, which supply unending numbers of slave laborers. And they all, without exception, have a singular goal—the destruction of Western civilization, and especially the United States! Despite all of this, America continues to arm these tyrants and upgrade their weapons systems!

The genial appearing Mikhail Sergeyvich Gorbachev changed nothing. This ruthless dictator was simply Communist Occupied Russia's most cunning leader since Stalin. This chubby little Party functionary was Moscow's version of the great American showman, P.T. Barnum. He smiled, shook hands, and kissed babies, as if running for political office. Yet, the goals of his Communist regime remained the same. The murder, rape, torture, and naked Soviet aggression continue unabated!

Transfers of strategic American technology to Communist Occupied Russia are continually pushed by

America's leaders. These men are fully aware that, according to Anthony Sutton, "over 150 Soviet weapons systems are based on U.S. technology."*35* And: "What we have done is given the Soviets the industrial and military capacity to destroy us."*36* Solzhenitsyn warns: "They are burying us alive and you are selling them the shovels."*37*

Because the United States heavily arms the USSR, the Russians in turn can afford to heavily arm their surrogate slave dictatorships. Communist Occupied Nicaragua is a prime example. Defense Secretary Caspar Weinberger revealed that 23,000 metric tons of arms from the Soviets, East Germans, and Cubans were shipped to the Communist Sandinistas in 1986. The Pentagon said this included HINDS flying tanks (helicopter gunships), as well as "trucks and other vehicles, spare parts, communications equipment, armored vehicles, anti-aircraft guns, small arms, ammunition, and other military-associated cargo."*38*

"Years ago, when I was legal advisor to the [Soviet] Ministry of War Equipment, I spoke with many people who worked with the chief engineers and scientists," declares Avraham Shifrin, who spent 14 years in Soviet prisons for "anti-Soviet activities." "They openly told me that without American and European equipment, they absolutely could not work, because the calibrations and precision of Russian equipment were far too crude.... Their tanks are now standing on the threshold of Europe ... their missiles in Cuba, pointed in the direction of the United States . . . and their Embassies have proscription lists of the intelligentsia in your country marked for liquidation'."*39*

Dr. Edward Teller, father of the hydrogen bomb, was asked: "If the Soviets launch a surprise nuclear attack against the United States, what would be the result?" His candid response was: "The question is when.... In a few years, if present trends continue, it is practically certain that it will be the end of the United States. The United States will not exist . . . as a state, . . . a power . . . an idea. It is possible that, in a few years, we shall be at the mercy of the Soviet Union, unless present trends change."*40*

Ronald Reagan was asked his view on the long-heralded Soviet Red Chinese rift, while campaigning for the Presidency in 1980. He responded: "They were allies and the only argument that caused their split was an argument over how best to destroy us."*41* Asked if he would allow Communist Occupied China to obtain U.S. weapons: "No, because . . . they could turn right around and the day after tomorrow discover that they and the Soviets have more in common than they have with us."[42]

Mr. Reagan apparently had a short memory span. Soon after his election, America unhesitatingly jumped into bed with the world's bloodiest tyranny! Reagan proceeded to dramatically increase the arming of Red China, in an effort to boost the criminal regime to superpower level. Americans were now told they must—for reasons of "national security" and the advancement of "world peace,"—build the war-making capability of the despicable Red Chinese enemy. The United States must develop Communist Occupied China into a first-rate military power. Why? The same lame excuse as that used when U.S. leaders treasonously started militarizing the Soviets. The Red Chinese have somehow suddenly become the "good guys." They'll mellow, say the "experts," but only if America modernizes its military. In case of war with the Russian "bad guys," these new Chinese pals will side with America.

These "experts" must not have been listening to the late Chou En-lai. He couldn't have made it any clearer: "Some people may have thoughts of using Sino-Soviet differences to deal with China and the Soviet Union separately. Those with such ideas will certainly be disappointed. On the contrary, if any act of aggression

occurs against any Socialist country this would be an act of aggression against the whole Socialist camp. It would be impossible not to give support."[43]

As Commander-in-Chief of America's Armed Forces, Reagan supplied the totalitarian camp with at least two squadrons of American F-16 jet aircraft—among the most advanced fighter planes in the world. Keep in mind, Red

China is the gangster nation that sent hundreds of thousands of fanatical "volunteer" troops to Korea, when Americans were fighting and dying over there! Close to 1,000 American POWs were known to be still held in North Korea and Red China, when the Korean War ended in 1953 (Chapter 15)! Many were shipped to Communist Occupied Russia's slave labor camps, by the Korean Al Capones. Red Chinese soldiers were also sent into Vietnam to fight against and kill Americans in that no-win amphigory (see Chapter 16)!

Export licenses were approved for shipping $500 million worth of military items to Red China in 1982. In 1983, President Reagan amended the nation's export-control law. Unbelievably, Communist Occupied China somehow overnight went from "a nation hostile to the United States" to a "friendly, non-aligned country."[44]

Teng Hsiao-ping told the Third Session of the Chinese Communist Party Central Committee: "We belong to the Marxist Camp and can never be so thoughtless that we cannot distinguish friends from enemies. Nixon, Ford, Carter, and future 'American imperialistic leaders' all fall in this category."[45]

Nevertheless, the criminal giveaway of American military-related materials to the Chinese slave empire jumped to $740 million in 1983. America's Red Chinese-Advanced-Military-Technology Welfare Program was boosted to well over $1 billion in 1984. The treasonous upgrading of Peking's antiquated military is enthusiastically endorsed by numerous elected and non-elected U.S. officials. The same is also true insofar as selling this infamous Communist dictatorship America's most advanced military technology.

Senator Barry Goldwater (R-AZ) acidly commented: "These officials [might some be moles?] are so confident of the good faith and reliability of the Chinese Communist hierarchy and political system that they propose the United States Government should directly arm and modernize the military forces of a Marxist-Leninist regime founded on a one-party dictatorship . . . "[46]

In September, 1983, Secretary of Defense Weinberger (CFR) visited Communist Occupied China and offered America's avowed enemies a new selection of advanced military hardware! Zhang Aiping, head of Red China's of National Defense, paid a secret return visit to the Pentagon in March 1984. Discussions centered around weapon purchases.

Included were anti-aircraft missile systems, amphibious tanks and huge 18-inch naval guns. Tours of sensitive American defense plants were arranged so Aiping could do a little high-tech weapon window shopping!

James Gerstenzang wrote: "The United States has been trying for several years to help nudge the China military toward the 1980s. During his first visit to China as Defense Secretary in 1983, Weinberger initiated a military cooperation program...." One of the major items resulting from his trip?: "Letting China use American technology to produce large-caliber artillery shells more cheaply than in the past."[47]

"The United States delivered a $98 million ammunition plant capable of producing artillery munitions, explosives and other material."[48] This questionable venture was the first direct sale of military equipment and technology to Communist Occupied China by the U.S. government. Included in the deal were the plans and materials necessary to construct the large, ultra-modern munitions factory. This was done in an effort to improve the enemy's production time for making 155-millimeter shells.

Reagan was somehow able to rationalize that selling weapons and other military hardware to Communist Occupied China was in America's best interest. He said: "The furnishing of defense articles and services to the Government of China will strengthen the security of the United States . . . "[49]

How did America's newest pal and Red Chinese despot, Teng Hsiao-ping, feel about Reagan's statement? This diabolical monster gave ample warning: "Even though the American imperialists are the number one nation in scientific and technological matters . . . In the future she will have no way of avoiding defeat by our hands."[50]

Nevertheless, Aiping and other equally arrogant Communist Chinese thugs were again warmly welcomed to Washington in June of 1984. This time Aiping was prepared to make massive purchases of military hardware, with, of course, money borrowed at little or no interest from the United States! American leaders groveled at the feet of the Reds as they went on a "shopping expedition" for weapons.

Export licenses for shipments to Communist Occupied China skyrocketed under Reagan from 2,020 in 1982 to an incredible 8,600 in 1985! American exports to this corrupt slave labor dictatorship exploded to $5.5 billion—an increase of over 1,000 percent![51] Routinely approved for sale to the enemy were many high-tech military and military-related items. This included torpedoes, radar for jet fighters, telecommunications gear, scientific instruments, and equipment for manufacturing integrated circuits.

On December 16, 1985, restrictions on exporting strategic goods to Communist Occupied China were further relaxed. Strategic items suddenly became non-strategic with the simple stroke of a pen! America's most sophisticated computers, electronic instruments, precision machine tools, robotics, etc., could now be shipped to the Red Chinese with no restrictions.

Will Communist Occupied China leave Taiwan alone once they obtain enough U.S. military hardware to bring them into the Twentieth Century? The Red Chinese leadership have never tried to mask their intentions! Teng Hsiao-ping explains: "Once normalization between China and the USA is finalized, it will naturally be beneficial to us in resolving the problem of liberating Taiwan."[52] In other words, the Chinese Communist dictatorship fully intends to attack and conquer Taiwan as soon as they feel the time is right!

How did the President react? Incredibly, Reagan responded with an invitation for this bandit regime to move against Taiwan! He stated: "The problem between the

People's Republic and the people of Taiwan is one for the Chinese to settle between themselves. We will do nothing to intervene..."[53]

Communist Occupied China's plan for "liberating" Taiwan will follow a carefully scripted scenario. Their horrifying subjugation of Tibet gives an accurate picture of what may be expected. Offers James J. Drummey: "In their effort to exterminate the Tibetan race, culture, and religion, the Reds killed scores of thousands of people, destroyed more than 2,000 monasteries, imprisoned countless numbers of Buddhist priests and nuns, shipped children to Red China for indoctrination in Communist ideology, and virtually wiped the nation out of existence."[54] Yet, the President of the United States callously tells them *"We will do nothing to intervene!"*

In April 1986, Admiral James D. Watkins, Chief of Naval Operations, led a special delegation to Communist Occupied China. His assigned task of treason was to work out the details of yet another massive weapons and technology "sale" to America's Red enemies. Included in this particular giveaway package were sonar devices, anti-submarine warfare helicopters, and turbine engines, worth hundreds of millions.

May 1986 saw the arrival in Washington of the notorious General Yang Dezhai, Chief of Staff for the People's Liberation Army. The Red war criminal was treated like royalty, although he had personally led drug-crazed Chinese troops against American boys fighting in Korea. Despite his well known role in the Korean War, this Twentieth Century savage was actually wined and dined in the White House! Many U.S. leaders breathlessly shook Dezhai's hand, stained though it still was with American blood.

General Dezhai had private meetings with Defense Secretary Weinberger (CFR); Vice President George Bush (CFR); and Chairman of the Joint Chiefs of Staff, Admiral William Crowe (CFR). He had the audacity to ask that the U.S. participate with Red China in joint military exercises.[55]

What exactly did this bedlamite have in mind—to again use American servicemen for target practice, as he did in Korea?

This is the horrifying dictatorship the Reagan Administration sold hi-tech torpedoes to in 1986. Defense Secretary Weinberger said he was "making available to the Chinese navy an upgraded Mark 46 torpedo to improve the Chinese anti-submarine capability."*56*   Red Chinese sailors were to be trained in torpedo maintenance and use at the U.S. Naval Training Center in Orlando, Florida.[57]

The sale of "advanced avionics" equipment to Communist Occupied China was announced on April 8, 1986. These high-tech military items were innocuously described as "55 integrated avionics systems kits, support equipment, training, and system installation."*58*   They were to be installed on Red China's F-8 jet fighters. Included were airborne radar units, navigation gear, special computers and targeting panels. Defense Secretary Weinberger said "the improvement of the F-8s through the sale of $550 million worth of electronics and radar systems is considered particularly important."*59* Why?

The contractors selected to manufacture these high-tech items for the Communist Chinese were also to loan the Reds as many as 25 of their top engineers. These Americans would install the equipment and train their Chinese counterparts in its operation and maintenance. Lastly, five members of the *United*

States Air Force would be loaned to Red China for up to six years! They would have the unsavory task of training Chinese pilots.*60*   It's well worth remembering that some of the American flyers downed over Vietnam—members of the *same* United States Air Force—are still being held as POWs in barbaric Red Chinese prison camps!

"The sale of avionics technology to Red China should not be viewed as an isolated event, but as part of a continuing State Department strategy to 'solve the Taiwan problem,'" charges Senator Jesse Helms (RNC). "The 'Taiwan problem' is the refusal by the Republic of China (on Taiwan) to surrender its sovereignty and liberty to the

Communist regime on the mainland.... the transfer of military technology to Red China is an essential part of the strategy to sell out Taiwan."*61*

A spokesman for the Defense Department explained with a straight-face: "This sale will contribute to the . . . national security of the United States by helping to improve the security of a friendly country which has been an important force for political stability and economic progress in Asia and the world [as in North Korea, Vietnam, Laos, and Cambodia?]."*62* Politics being as they are, this same Defense Department secretly classified Communist Occupied China as "hostile to the United States."[63]

"We are at war," said Ronald Reagan, "with the most dangerous enemy that has ever faced mankind."*64* He was, of course, referring to the world-wide Communist menace. Why then did this President sponsor the sale of a $98 million ammunition plant to Communist Occupied China? How could this man allow the sale of advanced helicopters, tanks, missiles, and jet fighters to "the most dangerous enemy that has ever faced mankind?" What was his thinking behind letting Red Chinese soldiers take airborne training at Fort Benning, Georgia? Did Mr. Reagan have a change of mind on the way to, or upon becoming the President of the United States?

"There remains a final, supreme consideration for any American businessman who may still hanker after elusive profit from selling to the Communists," warns a *Barrons'* editor. "He must decide in his own private conscience whether the profit is worth the personal risk that someday, soon or late, on some near or distant battlefield, his neighbor's son or his own may be struck down by a weapon which his zeal for trade put into an enemy's hand."[65]

Chapter 2

Treason and Big Business

>   Traitor: "One who violates his allegiance and betrays his country."
>
>   The Century Dictionary
>
>   Treason: "The act ... of helping its [one's country] enemies."
>
>   The New Horizon Ladder Dictionary

An outwardly friendly, handshaking, smiling, but highly dangerous Russian fox visited the United States in December 1987. He glibly spoke to a gathering of American business entrepreneurs.

One trusting rabbit in the audience stood and enthusiastically vocalized: "You're a nice guy Mr. Fox! We really like you! We're going to enjoy doing business with you!" And the wily Red Fox hungrily licked his lips while his eyes glistened in anticipation.

This is the Mikhail Gorbachev who President Reagan said was "completely different from previous Soviet leaders."[1] It is the Mikhail Gorbachev who is running a brutal Communist dictatorship holding upwards of 15 million slave laborers in some 2,000 ungodly concentration camps. It is the Mikhail Gorbachev who still holds American POWs from the Korean War in some of these slave labor camps (Chapter 15)! And it is the Mikhail Gorbachev who, one month earlier in Moscow, had blandly stated: "In

October 1917, we parted with the Old World, rejecting it once and for all. We are moving toward a new world, the world of Communism. We shall never turn off that road."*2*

The dangers of doing business with Red dictatorships are obvious. A frightening torrent of American technology continues to flow to Communist occupied nations. These criminal regimes are shipped anything and everything they want. Complete turn key factories have gone to Russia. Nuclear power plants have gone to Communist Occupied Yugoslavia. Automated steel mills have gone to Red China. Such activity is clearly in the realm of treason. Yet an unbelievable array of American businesses greedily choose to illegally aid and abet the various Red slave states.

American companies sell Communist Occupied Russia and other satellite slave dictatorships machinery, complete factories, and other equipment. Maintenance contracts, service manuals, and training materials are included. Instructors are loaned to Communist tyrannies to teach the workers. Red bloc technicians and scientists are even trained in the United States. Dr. Miles Costick points out that as of 1976, the Soviets have been able to obtain from the West some 1,000 "turn-key" factories and plants.

PepsiCo's Donald Kendall wrangled a Pepsi-Cola monopoly from Communist Occupied Russia. Paul Austin got Coca Cola the same deal in Communist Occupied China. Here are a few of the culprits who have done (or are presently doing) business with Communist slave states: American Can; American Express; Atchison, Topeka & Santa Fe Railway; Atlantic Richfield; Avon Products; Bendix Corporation; Borg-Warner; Brown and Sharpe; Caterpillar Tractor; Chrysler Corporation; Firestone; The Hartford Insurance Group; International Harvester; IT&T; National Cash Register; Reynolds Metal; Sheraton International; Singer; Eastern, PanAm, and Trans World Airlines. There are many more!

Terrorist revolutionary Vladimir Ilich Ulyanov (pseudonym: N. Lenin) long ago correctly prophesied: "The Capitalists of the world . . . will close their eyes . . . and thus will turn into deaf, mute, blind men . . . giving us the materials and technologies we lack, they will restore our military industry, indispensable for our future victorious attacks on our suppliers.... they will labor for the preparation for their own suicide."*3*

Doing Business with Communist Occupied Russia

The marvelous Bolshevik achievements boasted about by American leftists in the 1930s were no more than a figment of the fertile "Liberal" imagination. Such glorified accomplishments were 100-percent nonexistent! They were pure propaganda, as are current tales about purported Soviet space triumphs and industrial growth! *Everything* was— and still is—the product of despised capitalistic ingenuity, money, and know-how. Every factory, every plant, every scientific advance, resulted from American and Western European technology transfers to Communist Occupied Russia. Few Americans realize that the USSR is still one of the world's most backward nations.

Larry Abraham was right on target when he stated: "Soviet economic, technological, and scientific achievements . . . are non-existent. Were it not for the West, the Soviet Union would be so primitive as to be the laughing stock of the world."*4*

Congressman John Ashbrook (R-OH) pointed out: "In order to enjoy the glories of the present Soviet system, we would have to abandon three-fifths of our steel capacity, two-thirds of our petroleum production, 95 percent of our electric motor output, destroy two out of every three of our hydroelectric plants, and get along on a tenth of our present volume of natural gas. We would have to rip up 14 of every 15 miles of paved highways and two of every three miles of our mainline railroad tracks. We would have to destroy 18 of every 20 cars . . . We would cut our living standard by three-fourths, destroy 40 million TV sets, nine out of every 10 telephones, and seven of every 10 houses; and then we would have to put about 60 million of our people back on the farm."5

Occidental Petroleum's notorious Armand Hammer (Chapter 11) has been a pal of various U.S. Presidents and patron of all Russian dictators from Lenin to present. His father was a personal friend of the goateed ghoul and a founder of the American Communist Party. This well-connected man went to the Soviet Union in 1921 with a large shipment of goods to help prop up the faltering Red dictatorship. Hammer's reward was a monopoly on the manufacture of slave-made pens and pencils in Communist Occupied Russia.6 Over a million dollars in blood money was netted the first year. He has since built huge chemical plants in the USSR and made many other treasonous deals with his Kremlin pals. Hammer's American Allied Drug and Chemical Company has the concession for mining asbestos in the Urals—another monstrous slave labor enterprise. His company was one of the first U.S. firms to open an office in Moscow.

Averill Harriman (Chapter 9) is another multi-millionaire American businessman who goes way back with his many Soviet buddies. In 1920, he founded W.A. Harriman & Company, a banking firm which immediately granted loans to Bolshevik leader V.I. Lenin, in order to keep the Communist terrorists in power. In 1925, this man paid the Kremlin bosses $3.45 million for the Georgian manganese concessions.7 He thereby obtained the exclusive right to mine and export manganese ore. How many men, women, and children were forced to dig out the ore in Harriman's Russian mines? How many slave labor deaths can be attributed to Ambassador Harriman's manganese mining venture?

Mack Truck sold $25 Million worth of heavy equipment for use in Soviet mining operations. How many slave laborers were forced to use Mack equipment? At least three million died from 1932 to 1954 in the freezing Kolymar region of Siberia, working in the Lena Goldfields Ltd. operation.8

Ford Motor Company sold 20,000 tractors and replacement parts to the Soviet Union between 1922 and 1926. Over 85 percent of all tractors and trucks in 1927 Communist Occupied Russia had been built by Ford in Detroit. Then, in 1929, the USSR purchased $30 million worth of Ford automobiles and repair parts.

The early 1930s saw U.S. firms stumbling all over themselves in an attempt to help shore up the floundering Soviet police state. Included were such American stalwarts as RCA, Ford, Douglas Aircraft, Westinghouse, and Dupont. A plant was designed and constructed by United Engineering to manufacture the aluminum sheets used in Russian planes.

Kharkov was the site where GE built Communist Occupied Russia a massive turbine electric producing facility. Its capacity is nearly three times that of General Electric's plant in Schenectady, New York.

A carbon copy of the Gary, Indiana, steel making complex was built in Magnitogorsk for Communist Occupied Russia. Employees of the Arthur G. McKee Company in Cleveland, Ohio, supervised the slave labor used to build the Soviet version!*9* The Koppers Corporation contracted to supply the coke ovens. This monstrous iron and steel complex is the world's largest!

During this same period, Standard Oil and other American firms supplied the Soviet Union with $37 million worth of equipment and machinery.*10* Tractor factories were built in Chelyabinsk by the John K Calder Company of Detroit.*11* Nitric acid plants were constructed for the Reds by Dupont.*12* Moscow was the site of the American built "MORNING" steel making complex.*13* Then there was the Stalingrad Tractor Plant. This factory was erected in the United States, disassembled, and shipped to Communist Occupied Russia. American engineers actually supervised the slave laborers assigned to reconstruct the plant in Stalingrad! Over 80 U.S. companies supplied equipment for this project.[14]

In 1966, Fiat of Italy agreed to build an $800 million auto plant in Russia. American companies supplied $50 million worth of machine tools and three-fourths of the equipment. These firms included Gleason, New Britain, and U.S. Industries.[15]

In 1967, Communist Occupied Russia's despotic Aleksei N. Kosygin visited the United States. He was asked: "With all the talk about friendship, peace, and 'building bridges,' does the Soviet Union still have as its primary objective the overthrow of capitalism?" His brazen response was immediate: "Of course!"[16]

Carl Gerstacker, Chairman of Dow, suggests that "an expansion of trade with Communist nations is 'highly desirable.' He also goes a step further and hints that Communist nations should be allowed to bid on government projects in the U.S."[17] American Cyanamid Executive Vice President Robert C. Swain agrees: "It is possible we will see a Soviet owned and operated plant on U.S. soil. It is also possible that the next generation of business leaders in the United States will be choosing sites in the Soviet Union for their plant operations."[18] Swain was right!

The Nixon-Kissinger team gave Most Favored Nation (MFN) trade status to Communist Occupied Russia in 1972. The Soviet enemy was thereby guaranteed an endless deluge of food, machinery, industrial plants, complete factories, and military goods.

Control Data Corporation signed a 10-year agreement with the Soviet State Ministry of Science and Technology in 1973. Included was an agreement to jointly develop a super computer! General Electric admitted their contract for electric power technology would bring "hundreds of millions of dollars worth of business."

In June 1973, Armand Hammer's Occidental Petroleum contracted with Communist Occupied Russia to run a 2,000 mile natural gas line across Siberia to Vladivostok. El Paso Natural Gas Company joined Occidental in this treasonous $10 billion project! Also grabbing a lucrative piece of the action was the Bechtel Corporation of San Francisco— the firm employing the men who were to become Reagan's Secretary of State and Secretary of Defense.

Irrefutable evidence proved Communist Occupied Russia's Siberian natural gas pipeline was being constructed with slave labor. At least 50 crude concentration camps were built by Finnish contractors. These "villages" were to house the slave laborers brought in to work on t

Despite this, another Soviet natural gas line was contracted to run from western Siberian gas fields to the port of Murmansk. "Project Northstar" was undertaken by three American firms—Brown & Root, Tenneco, and Texas Eastern Transmission. Charges William P. Hoar: "Western capitalists are helping to dig their own graves by making possible the largest East-West deal ever—the Soviet gas pipeline that will make Europe dependent on the Kremlin for energy." [20]

The United States faced a serious energy shortage in 1973. Nevertheless, the Nixon Administration traitorously peddled scarce oil drilling equipment to Communist Occupied Russia. America's enemies were sold, on credit, around a billion dollars worth—all financed by U.S. taxpayers. Some of the firms involved: International Harvester—$42 million worth of crawler tractors for pipeline construction; Kendall Polychem — thousands of tons of pipeline coating, Dresser Industries and Halliburton-Welex—$3.5 million worth of various exploration items.[21]

Business Week reported: "A severe shortage of drilling pipe and well casing" resulted in tens of thousands of oil wells not being drilled - in the U.S. even though there was an energy crisis.[22] Congressman John Ashbrook (R-OH) suggested with a tinge of sarcasm: "Perhaps after we have finished developing the Soviet economy, we can then turn to our own needs."[23]

The World Trade Center, also known as the "Traitor Inn" was paid for with American money and built in Moscow by the Bechtel Corporation (Chapter 3). Shadowy security risk, Armand Hammer, arranged the sweetheart deal, while Occidental Petroleum snared a lucrative $110 million contract for this monument to his KGB pals. Interestingly, all guest rooms were to be outfitted by Holiday

Inns of America. A few of the firms listed on the Building Directory are Control Data Corporation, 2006; Chase Manhattan Bank NA, 1709; Bank of America, 1605; Occidental Petroleum, 1409; Ingersoll-Rand Company, 1101; and Allis-Chalmers Corp, 901.[24]

U.S. News & World Report, described America's traitorous participation in building Communist Occupied Russia's Kama River truck factory (Chapter 1, 3). Referring to the spectacular 36 square mile conglomerate: "The plant contains more than 1 billion dollars worth of Western-made machinery . . . The list of the 40 U.S. companies that have had a hand in the project reads like a roll call of blue chip stocks. ... Without this U.S. participation, no one involved in the venture doubts that it would have remained on the drawing board for many years."[25]

The prime contractor was Swindell-Dressler of Pittsburgh, a subsidiary of Pullman Incorporated. They received a fat $190 million to design the arc furnaces and the foundry equipment. Swindell-Dressler was among the first U.S. industrial firms to open a he project.*19* Sparsely dressed men, women, and children were forced to work a 16-hour day, in below-zero weather. Engineering got a $30 million contract to supply molding machines. Ingersoll Milling Machine Company supplied the automated equipment needed to hone diesel engine blocks. Their take: $19 million. Also heavily involved in this treasonous project were Westinghouse, IBM, Honeywell, and General Motors.

The Commerce Department's Office of Export Control refused to identify the U.S. firms involved in the militarily invaluable Kama River venture. According to these bureaucrats, the names of participants must be kept secret. They claim it's a matter of "national security" per Section 7(c) of the Export Administration Act. Legal counsel William N. Letson said that making the names public "could lead to criticism and even economic pressure directed against specific private companies by persons who oppose the government's general policy on trade with Communist countries in non-strategic commodities." In other words, patriotic American citizens might just boycott such firms! And they just might view such outrageous activities as blatant acts of treason!

"The Soviets were allowed to acquire the most advanced American technology in computers, inertial guidance, semiconductors, high-propulsion, and wide-bodied aircraft," charges Major General George Keegan, retired Air Force Chief of Intelligence.*26* He reveals that the Commerce Department has destroyed official records on trade with Communist Occupied Russia and the Red Bloc slave states. Why else but to cover deliberate, massive acts of treason? The destruction of such records clearly indicates that the traitors are more than a little concerned! The leftists *know* they've committed treason! What else could it be called to assist enemy Communist dictatorships in building their military power?; to give them guidance systems to make their missiles more accurate?; to supply them with computers to run their missile defense system for protecting their cities?; to build them military truck and tank factories?; to sell them advanced jet fighters and to train their pilots to fly them?; and so and *ad infinitum.*

"The Soviet computer industry has always been a shambles," says Wade Holland, editor of Rand Corporation's *Soviet Cybernetics Review.27* The first American computer sale to Communist Occupied Russia took place in 1959. It was a Model-802 National sold by Elliott Automation, a British subsidiary of General Electric!*28* Sperry Rand Corporation is big on computer sales to Communist dictatorships. On April 15,1979, President Carter personally approved the sale of a

highly sophisticated Sperry Rand computer to *Tass,* the KGB controlled Soviet news agency.[29]

Honeywell has long been supplying computers to the Reds. IBM sold Intourist a computerized reservation system.*30* This was exactly what the government-run travel agency needed to assemble dossiers on foreign visitors. Computers used by the dreaded KGB are also American made. The Russians got them by saying they were needed by Aeroflot for ticket reservations.

Figures obtained from the Department of Commerce give a pretty good idea of how far American computer companies have gone down the treason road. From 1975 to 1979, U.S. firms sold Communist Occupied Russia $300 million worth of computers and related materials. In just one short six-month period, ending on April Fool's Day 1978, almost $43 million worth of American computer hardware was sold to the Soviet enemy.branch office in Moscow.

Other "patriotic" money-hungry American companies taking part in this questionable "non-military" project: Combustion

"How sickeningly ironical it would be if American computers would keep track of political prisoners," says Carl Olson, chairman of Stockholders for World Freedom, "or that American pipe-laying equipment would be manned by Vietnamese forced-labor gangs working on the Siberian gas pipeline [It is—see Epilogue]."[31]

Allis-Chalmers contracted to build a $35 million plant in Communist Occupied Russia for pelletizing iron ore. This factory is one of the largest of its kind in the world. According to UPI: ". . . the equipment to be used in the new Soviet plant will include some of the most advanced in the technology of converting iron ore into pellets, which are used for steel making."[32]

The C.E. Lummus Company of Bloomfield, New Jersey, agreed to build Communist Occupied Russia a huge petrochemical plant in the Ukraine. The cost: $105 million. The Soviets erected the building, using the usual slave labor crews. The Lummus Company provided the engineering design, supervision, and all the necessary equipment. Monsanto, also involved in the deal, sold the Soviets their latest technical data on the production of acetic acid.[33]

In December 1979, Armco Incorporated received a marvelous Christmas gift from America's atheistic "friends." They nailed down a contract to build a fully automated electrical steel mill in Communist Occupied Russia. The cost: $353 million![34]

"The military potential of the industrial plants which we are building for the Soviets should be obvious to anyone," offers Gary Allen. "Trucks, aircraft, oil, steel, petrochemicals, aluminum, computers — these are the sinews of a military-industrial complex. These factories, the product of American genius and financed by American capital, could have been built in the United States. Instead, they are constructed at the U.S. taxpayer's expense in the Soviet Union—a nation whose masters still keep millions in concentration camps and who have sworn to bury us."[35]

During Carter's peak years, over 60 American firms had lucrative but propitious science and technology transfer contracts with Communist Occupied Russia. Incredibly, these included three key U.S. defense contractors -- General Dynamics and Litton (both build nuclear submarines), and Union Carbide. Leading computer firms involved were Hewlett-Packard, IBM, and Sperry Rand. Bechtel was another—then run by Reagan's Defense Secretary Weinberger (CFR) and Secretary of State Shultz (CFR). The wiley Russians actually had America's major aerospace firms—Boeing, Lockheed, and McDonnell Douglas—in a building war to supply them with wide-bodied planes.

The Reagan Administration ignored the widespread Soviet slave labor practices and authorized a $90 million sale of 200 pipelaying bulldozers for use on their Siberian pipeline.[36] Soviet exile Mikhail Makarenko explained how slave labor was to be utilized on the 3,600 mile construction project: "They will be the ones who will clear the forests, build the roads and the first living quarters for the more skilled specialists who will put the pipeline in place.... It is going to be human bodies that will thaw this unbelievable tundra through which the pipeline will be built . . . Today in the Soviet Union you have 2,000 camps and prison; 150 are for women and children under two . . . Hundreds of other camps are for children from 11 to 18 years of age, and many of these prisoners . . . will be working on the pipeline."[37]

Senator Jesse Helms (R-NC) was against this sale. He charged that the special bulldozers "could be used to lay coaxial cable for hardened, underground communications networks for military command structures, ABM systems, etc."[38]

Howard Hughes was a vocal anti-Communist. He might well roll over in his grave if he knew the Hughes Tool Company was selling offshore exploration equipment to Communist Occupied Russia. This firm sold them $40 million worth of high-tech submersible pumps. On March 6, 1984, President Reagan approved the sale.[39]

We have already sent to the Soviet Union tremendously sophisticated machinery which," charges Senator Steven D. Symms (R-ID), "under their own system of suppressing individual ingenuity, would have taken years if not decades to develop. The flow of advanced technology from the United States to the Soviet Union has rapidly turned into a frightening torrent."[40]

Despite being aware of the Soviet Union's horrifying human rights record—unspeakable brutality, wholesale rape, mass murder, assassination, terrorism, slavery—40 Russian trade officials were cordially invited to the United States in May 1984. These Communist malefactors were to meet with American members of the US-USSR Trade and Economic Council (USTEC). The Soviet officials were told that American corporations were willing to ship Communist Occupied Russia such things as fertilizers, fuels, trucks, bulldozers, metals, and complete manufacturing plant packages.

The USTEC was organized in 1973 with the unqualified backing of Kremlin despot Leonid Brezhnev. It was conceived for one purpose only—to supply the Soviet enemy with the latest American technology. USTEC has hundreds of important supporters in the U.S. corporate community. Half of USTEC's board of directors is staffed by Russian government offficials. Senator Helms charges the USTEC with being "an arm of the Soviet Government, under KGB control, whose purpose is to subvert the U.S. economy."[41]

In early December 1985, 400 business leaders, representing 150 major American corporations, made a perfidious trek to

Moscow. Commerce Secretary Malcolm Baldridge arrogantly refused to reveal the names of the companies. Nor would he tell what kinds of technology and strategic goods these firms were selling to the Communists. No doubt the Commerce Secretary's greedy traveling companions welcomed his discretion, but surely these corporate leaders knew they were committing treason! Whether it's government sanctioned or not is beside the point. Treason is treason! But, their desire to participate secretly is understandable.

Infuriated at this bureaucratic secrecy, Senator Helms indignantly declared: "The Soviets know, the Commerce Department knows, and the Banking Committee knows. But nobody else is supposed to know, least of all the American people whose liberty and security may be at stake in this matter."[42]

A 1983 Heritage Foundation study unequivocally showed the Kremlin gaining the military edge over the U.S. This was caused by "a virtual hemorrhage of technology in the past decade," flowing steadily from America to Communist Occupied Russia.[43] The culprits include such companies as General Motors, Xerox, and Exxon—all of whom do big business with the Reds! The USSR has—with the treacherous assistance of America's leaders—come to a point where it can "zap" half the population in the United States more quickly than it took to declare ware in 1941, after Pearl Harbor was bombed!

Doing Business with Soviet Puppet Dictatorships

American fighting men in Vietnam were being maimed and murdered by North Vietnamese soldiers and Communist Vietcong terrorists. The North Vietnamese war effort was almost entirely subsidized by the United States and other Western nations through aid to Communist Occupied Russia and its numerous slave state satellites (Chapter 6). Yet, patriotic Americans were not to speak out against U.S. companies doing business with Red Bloc dictatorships. Nothing critical was to be said of those firms who were indirectly supplying weapons and war materials to the Vietnamese enemy with whom America was waging war. Indeed, subversives in the State Department made it appear that American businessmen who aided and abetted the enemy were patriots rather than traitors! At the same time, they tried to make the public believe that concerned citizens who protested such treasonous endeavors were guilty of un-American activities!

Private Boycotts vs The National Interest contained this ominous warning: "All American citizens should know that any American businessman who chooses to engage in peaceful trade with the Soviet Union or Eastern European countries [satellite Communist dictatorships] is following the policy of his government. So, too, is any American citizen who chooses to buy such goods . . . But any organization, however patriotic in intention, that undertakes to boycott, blacklist . . . any American business for engaging in peaceful trade with Eastern European countries or the Soviet Union, is acting against the interests of the United states."[44]

It was once illegal for American firms to sell advanced technology and strategic goods to enemy nations. Specifically prohibited were sales to Communist Occupied Russia and other Red slave dictatorships.

This dramatically changed under the Kennedy Presidency. The spigot for direct sales of high-tech/strategic goods was opened a crack and the dangerous giveaways began. The criminal policy of aiding and abetting the enemy was accelerated during Johnson's reign. It continued under Nixon, Ford, Carter, and Reagan. There's virtually nothing American businesses cannot now sell to the totalitarian enemies of freedom.

For example, in 1974, General Electric was preparing to build Communist Occupied Yugoslavia a nuclear power plant! The cost: $250 million! The United States even paid the bill![45]

A $75 million radial tire factory was constructed in Communist Occupied Romania by General Tire.[46] Other American firms making huge profits in Red Romania include

IBM, GE, Pepsi-Cola, and Phillip Brothers. General Tire was later doing business with the Marxists-Leninist Mafia in Communist Occupied Angola.

Corning Glass in upstate New York provided Janos Kadar's Red dictatorship with a light bulb factory. This automated plant can produce 1.5 million light bulbs daily, many of which are exported and sold to unsuspecting American consumers (Chapter 5).[47] The Corning people don't seem to be bothered by the fact that Communist Occupied Hungary openly deals in slave trade with their Soviet masters and with Communist China. According to a German church publication, troublesome able-bodied Hungarians are sold to Moscow like cattle for approximately $100 a head and to Peking for $150 each! The formal contracts call these slave laborers "specialized workers assisting in social reconstruction."[48]

Facts on File revealed: "The Dow Chemical Company, the first U.S. company to set up an office in East Berlin, signed a 10-year contract with East Germany...."[49] Malcolm W. Browne wrote of Czechoslovakia: "In the Bohemian town of Obernica, 11 American engineers and technicians of the Union Carbide Corporation have been . . . supervising construction of a polyethylene plant."[50]

The number of treasonous computer sales to Soviet puppet dictatorships has been absolutely astounding! During one six month period— from October 1977 through March 1978—American companies sold the Reds almost $50 million worth. And business has been booming ever since then. Here's the breakdown:

    Communist Occupied Bulgaria $1,188,421
    Communist Occupied Czechoslovakia $20,507,207
    Communist Occupied East Germany $2,195,770
    Communist Occupied Hungary $7,718,453
    Communist Occupied Latvia $249,720
    Communist Occupied Poland $10,805,896
    Communist Occupied Romania $6,158,730

"I'm profoundly opposed to the trade or transfer of scarce technology with military applications," declared Ambassador Jeane J. Kirkpatrick. "In my opinion that includes such things as oil drilling equipment as well as scarce computer technology.... There are laws against the transfer of certain technology to the Communist Bloc, and I think they should be enforced."[51]

Many companies play the Help-the-Soviet-Satellite-Game. Communist Occupied Poland appears to be a favorite of American business entrepreneurs. Swindell-Dressler contracted to build a huge $43 million foundry in General Jaruzelski's Red dictatorship.52 Westinghouse designed and equipped a $10 million electronics plant near Warsaw, for the Polish slave-labor tyranny.53 In 1979, RCA got a $68 million equipment and technology contract and began producing color television tubes in their Polish factory. RCA also operates a similar plant in the Soviet Union.

Control Data Corporation actually went into a business partnership with the Romanian Reds. CDC built a computer factory in Bucharest at a cost of $2.2 million. The Control Data people kept 45 percent interest in the venture.[54]

Angola was taken over by Moscow-backed terrorists in 1975. Chevron-Gulf immediately contracted with the barbaric Red dictatorship for exploration and production in the oil rich Cabinda Province. Many other stalwart American companies greedily grabbed a piece of the action! These include Cities Service, Texaco, Mobil, Exxon, Union, Marathon, Texas Petroleum, and Conoco. Nevertheless, Chevron-Gulf is responsible for about 90 percent of the oil pumped for the hostile Communist military regime.[55]

Westinghouse also scrambled to get in on the lucrative business opportunities soon after the Reds occupied Angola. This firm contracted to repair, modernize, and replace radar installations at Angolan airfields.56 Westinghouse people worked under relatively safe conditions, since combat-hardened Cuban troops were brought in to guard the areas.

In 1981, Chevron-Gulf announced its intention to invest $1 billion for oil exploration in Communist Occupied Angola, over a five year period.57 Here we have a unique situation: The Soviets supplied Red Angola with $2 billion worth of military equipment, guns, and ammunition in 1984-85 alone.58 Some of the biggest corporations in the U.S. paid for much of this with oil revenues!

Big business apparently intends to protect its profits at any cost. Howard Phillips points out: "Gulf's corporate executives have also been lobbying on behalf of the Soviet Union . . . urging Congress to reject U.S. aid to the UNITA [Angolan anti-communist] freedom fighters . . ."[59]

Westinghouse was still treasonously aiding and abetting the Red enemy in September 1981. With Free World financing and Westinghouse technology, Communist Occupied Yugoslavia's first nuclear power plant went operational.60 And General Electric sold Romania two nuclear reactors this same year![61]

Doing Business with Communist Occupied China

The succinct words of revolutionary Saul Alinsky apply here as elsewhere: "As for businessmen, I could persuade a capitalist on Friday to bankroll a revolution on Saturday that will bring him a profit on Sunday, even though he will be executed on Monday."[62]

President Richard M. Nixon and identified Kremlin spy Henry Kissinger*63* paid homage to China's genocide specialist Chairman Mao in 1973. While wining and dining in Peking, these men began doing business with one of history's worst mass-murderers. Suggests Gary Allen sarcastically: "Having carefully arranged to commit suicide by firing the Communist furnaces while our own are cold, to build Russian tanks and Russian planes and the Russian nuclear industry, and to feed the Russian bear, it is obviously time to provide for the Chinese dragon."[64]

There was absolutely no evidence in 1973 to lead anyone to believe Communist Occupied China's revolutionary goals had changed. Nothing even remotely indicated that the dogmatic Red Chinese were now to be accepted as America's friend and ally. Yet, the Nixon Administration allowed the criminal Mao regime to obtain Boeing 707 aircraft. Furthermore, Communist Occupied China's aviation industry was to be developed by Boeing.*65* Pullman company was given the green light to build ammonia plants worth $130 million—all on credit! A Pullman subsidiary contracted to construct eight large plants for the manufacture of synthetic fertilizer.[66]

The U.S. was going to help the arrogant Chinese Reds exploit their massive undersea oil reserves. Why? Robert S. Elegant reports: "Because only the United States possesses the deepwater technology and engineering hardware to sink wells in the 400-700 foot depths where most of the oil lies . . ."[67]

Standard Oil of Ohio was another money-hungry culprit. It agreed to supply these Marxist-Leninists with their secret process for making orlon, acrylics, and other fibers.*68* This was willingly done for a blood-thirsty Red regime with an unbelievable track record of terror, torture, devastation, and death.

Communist Occupied China has been allowed to make unlimited purchases of American aerospace, military, and industrial equipment. Much of this is paid for with American taxpayers money from the U.S. Export-Import Bank. Groveling in the wings and anxious to do business with these Red gangsters are such firms as Textron, McDonnell Douglas, Loral Corporation, Allied Bendix, RCA, Lockheed, and Martin Marietta.[69]

The savage Chinese dictatorship received diplomatic recognition and Most Favored Nation (MFN) status in 1979. None of this was really necessary, since American leaders had been quietly doing business with this tyrannical regime for years. All the Carter Administration did was legalize further unlawful plunder.

Private investment in Communist Occupied China exceeded $1 billion in 1986.*70* More than 250 American firms opened business facilities in Peking and elsewhere in

Red China.*71* Minnesota Mining and Manufacturing (3-M) agreed in 1983 to build a factory in the Red dictatorship. They were the first American company to take advantage of Communist China's low wages and slave labor. Their high-tech electrical items and telecommunications equipment parts are manufactured for sale throughout the free world.*72*

Motorola, Inc., according to chairman Robert Galvin, on November 14, 1988, is building two "world class" plants in Tianjin. Galvin said "multi-tens of millions of dollars" would be spent developing these factories. They'll manufacture mobile radio equipment, semiconductors, "transistors and integrated circuits" both for selling in Red China and for exporting.*73* No American firm can lose on these apostate, no-risk deals. Everything is insured by the Overseas Private Investment Corporation. In other words, American taxpayers are forced to pay off any company losses from an investment turned sour in the Red Chinese slave-labor state!

General Electric contracted with Communists Occupied China in August 1985 for five LM-2500 gas turbine engines. These were to be installed by GE on Red China's Luda-class destroyers.*74*

Red China produces AMC jeeps, courtesy of the American Motors Corporation. Peking just happens to be the District of Columbia's so-called "Sister City." Therefore, Mayor Marion Barry was given the first AMC Jeep Cherokee as it came off the Chinese assembly line, early in 1988.*75*

"It is bad enough when the news media see nothing but progress and light coming out of Red China and endow Deng Xiaoping with godlike qualities of leadership and wisdom," surmises Senator Barry Goldwater (R-AZ), "but now the [Reagan] Administration seems to accept the same distorted view . . . that Communist China can do no wrong and is a threat to no one."*76*

Lenin is attributed with saying that capitalists would go so far as to compete with one another to sell their deadly Communist enemy the rope with which they'd ultimately be hanged. Even Lenin probably never dreamed American businessmen would sell them the rope on credit!

Many elected and unelected U.S. officials have for years worked toward increased business dealings with Moscow, Peking, Belgrade, and all the other puppet slave states behind the impenetrable Iron Curtain. Greedy businessmen have sold unbelievable amounts of highly strategic merchandise to America's Communist enemies. Yet, no government official or American businessmen has ever been called to task as a traitor. Not one of these people has ever been prosecuted for treason. Why?

Chapter 3

Financial Aid for the Reds

Traitor: "One who betrays his country . . . one guilty of treason."
Webster's Collegiate Dictionary

Treason: "The betrayal of a trust . . . breach of faith, . . . treachery to one's country."
The American College Dictionary

    Highways, railroads, and dams in Communist Occupied Russia are constructed with slave labor and paid for with low interest American loans. Citrus growing in Red China is developed with slave labor and paid for with U.S. tax dollars. Communist Occupied Ethiopia's military is armed and uniformed and trained with money from low interest American loans. Communist Chinese universities are subsidized with U.S. tax dollars. Moscow's World Trade Center is paid for with low interest American loans. Steel plants in Communist Occupied China are paid with U.S. tax dollars. Machine tools for the Urus truck factory in Communist Occupied Poland are paid for with low interest American loans.
    Mexico extended a $55 million line of credit to Communist Occupied Cuba, using money loaned to them by the U.S.—at little or no interest! China, using borrowed American tax dollars, in turn loaned millions to Communist Occupied Nicaragua and Communist Occupied Yugoslavia!

Since 1956, American taxpayers have unknowingly provided the Yugoslavian tyranny with almost half its national income. Between 1981 and 1983, the U.S. Export-Import Bank gave $250 million in loans to this slave-labor dictatorship. Yugoslavia, using U.S. dollars, started its own foreign aid program to help prop up other Red dictatorships and to assist terrorists in overthrowing non-Communist governments. Representative Toby Roth (R-WI) reveals: "The West is supplying the Soviet Bloc roughly $1 billion every month in new loans. Every day, Western commercial banks send $33 million to the Soviet Bloc."1

Communist Occupied Romania grabbed a $230 million bonanza courtesy of the Export-Import Bank. The United States and other Western nations were Communist Occupied China's source for $4 billion worth of "loans" in 1986 alone. This oppressive police state (as well as all the others) makes no secret of how they perceive the United States. They're implacable foes of the American way of life! Each despises America. Each is virulently against everything America represents. Each spews out its anti-American invectives. Each promises America's ultimatedestruction. Yet, each has a hand outstretched for more and more American dollars. And the United States continues this thankless giving, with an unbelievable International Welfare Program!

Here are a few of the banking institutions that have been insidiously giving "aid and comfort" to Communist countries. The bank doing the most business with the Reds is Citicorp. It is followed by Morgan Guaranty Trust, Chase Manhattan, and Hanover Trust. Others who play the Help-the-Communists-Welfare-Game are: Detroit's City National; First National of Memphis; Hartford National; Indiana National; Industrial National of Providence; Republic National in Dallas; and Union Commerce, in Cleveland.

Financial Assistance to Communist Occupied Russia

It's fairly well known that Communist spies, under the direction of Moscow, penetrated and achieved positions of great responsibility in our government during Franklin Roosevelt's terms. Not so well known is the important part Harry Dexter White, Virginius Frank Coe, and other Kremlin moles played in developing the Bankrupt-America-Financial-Giveaway-Scheme.

Since 1946, the United States has given over a billion dollars in financial aid to Communist Occupied Russia. America also saved the Soviet Union's hide in World War II, when the Reds were given an incredible $11 to $12 billion in Lend Lease. No one remotely knows how much more was involved. It was all given to help save the Russian police state from Stalin's former Nazi friends! For example, the Russians were sent the plates, paper, and ink for making occupation currency in Berlin. The Reds in turn used this to print up untold billions of dollars in occupation money, which they redeemed for U.S. dollars! The Treasury Department's top Soviet spy, Harry Dexter White (Chapter 13, 14, 16), and Harry Hopkins (Chapter 11), Roosevelt's alter-ego and most trusted aide – finally exposed in 1990 as a Soviet spy by KGB defector Oleg Gordievsky -- were the key men behind the whole traitorous scheme.

How was America's generosity repaid? The Soviets perfected a method of "How-to-rip-off-America-and-get-away-with-it." The unappreciative Reds were allowed to wipe the slate clean by agreeing to pay a paltry $722 million by the year 2001.2 This was a bargain basement deal— less than seven percent of what the Russians actually owed. It's difficult to believe the United States would settle with any nation, especially a deadly enemy, for only $722 million, on a debt of over $11 to $12 billion.3 Even more incredible— Commerce Secretary Peter G. Peterson (CFR) let Moscow dictate the ridiculous terms! The U.S. had to also promise Most Favored Nation trade status for the Soviet Union. This, as could be expected, came to pass in 1972 under the direction of the Nixon-Kissinger team.

David Rockefeller (CFR) shuns any responsibility for the Russian occupation of Afghanistan. Yet, that invasion is directly linked to the immense Soviet truck factory his bank helped finance. In the early 1970's, Communist Occupied Russia came up with only 10 percent of the money it needed for the colossal Kama River truck plant project (Chapter 1, 2). The Export-Import Bank subversively loaned 45 percent of the money. Using this as their rationale, the Chase Manhattan Bank gladly loaned the USSR another 45 percent of the total. There is absolutely no question about it, but that by any stretch of the imagination, the invasion of Afghanistan was clearly made possible with American dollars!

William J. Casey (CFR), later President Reagan's CIA director, also had his hand in the pot. Casey, a close associate of the notorious Armand Hammer (Chapter 11), helped arrange the criminal financing for this Soviet truck factory. He was conveniently, at the time of the deal, Nixon's director of the Export-Import Bank. Here, as elsewhere, it appears that administration managers change, but the major players always remain in the game.

David Rockefeller is a 1936 Harvard graduate. He also attended the London School of Economics in 1938, a breeding ground for Communists and socialists. Harold Laski, a Red, was one of the schools most influential professors. Rockefeller worked for the Office of Defense under Soviet espionage agent Anna Rosenberg.[4] Born in Hungary, this subversive was a close associate of FDR intimate and Communist spy, Sidney Hillman (Chapter 11, 16). She was initially brought into the Defense Department—by her sympathetic patron, George Catlett Marshall (Chapter 9, 10)—as a manpower expert. Rosenberg, a close and trusted friend of President Eisenhower, was Assistant Secretary of Defense for four years in the early '50s. Here she selected key personnel for the entire Defense establishment![5]

As might be expected, Rockefeller's bank at One Chase Manhattan Plaza in New York was chosen by Soviet leaders to be the first American bank to have a branch in Communist Occupied Russia. It is located at One Karl Marx Square in Moscow. Says journalist Gary Allen: "Chase has been up to its gizzard in financing the Soviet military-industrial complex, while the U.S. spends hundreds of billions of the taxpayer's dollars on national defense to protect us from these same Soviets."6

Chase Manhattan is well-known for its scandalous loans to countries in captivity, under brutal Red dictatorships. David Rockefeller is a leading member of both the subversive Trilateral Commission and the Council on Foreign Relations (CFR). Both organizations, by their own admission, are working toward merging the U.S. and USSR "into a common culture, economy, philosophy, and despotism"7 —in other words, a socialistic (Communistic) one-world dictatorship! This is to be brought about "through an induced decline of the West and a parallel build-up by the West of Communist and Third World nations."8

Rockefeller tries to make light of conspiracy charges: "To some extremists [he means Birchites, McCarthyites, and other so-called "right wingers"], the Trilateral Commission is pictured as a nefarious plot by an Eastern Establishment Financial Aid for the Reds of businessmen in the service of multinational corporations, who will do almost anything including going into cahoots with the Kremlin for the sake of financial gain...."9   Sadly enough, the very capitalist-Communists business relationship he tries so hard to ridicule does exist. The Soviet 36 acre Kama River truck factory is but one example.

Despite the widespread use of slave labor in Communist Occupied Russia, the Nixon Administration underwrote a $36 million loan to build and furbish Moscow's massive World Trade Center (Chapter 2).10   The eager money lenders were the Bank of America and Chase Manhattan. Of course, as usual, no risk was taken by either of these commercial banks. The loans were guaranteed by American taxpayers!

In 1974, Richard Nixon authorized a $180 million loan for the Soviet Union, at a bargain six percent interest. This apostate giveaway was to pay for multi-millionaire Armand Hammer's fertilizer factory deal. The entire plant was to be transported to Communist Occupied Russia and constructed on site. This looting was done at a time when the United States was going through a severe fertilizer shortage. [11]

During 1973-74, the Export-Import Bank gave the Soviet parasites $496 million in direct government-to-government loans. In 1975, AFL-CIO President George Meany correctly noted that the Export-Import Bank was no more than "a welfare program for Russia!"

Victor Perlo was but one of the many Harvard law school graduates who turned out to be a Kremlin spy. He penetrated the Department of Agriculture with Alger Hiss, John Abt, Lee Pressman, and other Reds, back in 1933 (Chapter 13). Perlo is enraptured with the Export-Import Bank giveaways. He claims the government is finally using this bank "for its original purpose of financing trade with socialist [Communist] countries." This Soviet agent's comment should make every American think twice regarding the Export-Import Bank! If they understood its sinister goal, most U.S. citizens probably would legislate it out of existence!

In 1980, Communist Occupied Russia shipped 66,000 tons of weapons to their Cuban surrogate. In 1982—when Castro's economic problems became too severe—the Soviets gave their Red satellite $4 billion in financial aid. Managua's Madison Avenue mass-murderer, Daniel Ortega, was sent Russian army brigades, assault helicopters, tanks, and innumerable other costly military items. The Soviets also unload millions of dollars worth of weapons and military gear on Libya's predictably rabid Colonel Muammar Qaddafi. And the game still goes on and on and on!

"Has it not struck Western policy makers as odd that the Soviet Union, which has a total annual hard currency income of only about $32 billion from all sources (including arms sales), can sustain a global empire which can directly rival the Unites States?" asks Roger W. Robinson, Jr., formerly with the National Security Council. "More specifically, how does the USSR support such a vast array of third country commitments— many of which must be hard currency financed—with annual earnings equivalent to only about one-third of Exxon's annual revenues for 1985."[12]

Who does pay for all this? Where did the Soviets get the cash to feed and arm these anti-American satellites? Just look in the mirror! Between 1981 and 1983, the Export-Import Bank alone authorized loan credits to the Soviet Union for $620 million. And this is but the tip of the iceberg! Uncle Sam's cash spigot is never turned off! According to Jan Nowak: "This year, four leading American banks lent the Soviet Union $400 million, at unusually low interest rates, to buy American and Canadian grain."[13]

Ray Kerrison wrote: " . . . the First National Bank of Chicago led another consortium to extend a $200 million line of credit to the Soviet Union at less than 8.5 percent interest.... Why do American banks lend money to the Soviet Union at lower rates than to their own citizens? . . . The Soviets . . . have the worst record of human rights violations in the world. It's a gulag (slave labor camp) from one of its borders to the other."[14]

Dr. Miles Costick charges: "Seldom if ever has a country been able, as the Soviet Union has, to persuade the countries against whom most of the military build-up is directed to finance so much of such a build-up."15 But on the other hand, never has the country agreeing to undertake such criminal financing been so thoroughly infiltrated by agents in the employ of the Soviet Union. In many instances, the American bureaucrats making such decisions are evidently members of the enemy team! Over half a century ago, Kamanev boasted: "Foreign capital will fulfill the role Marx predicted for it . . . the foreign capitalists who will be obliged to work on the terms we offer them, will dig their own graves."[16]

Financial Assistance to Soviet Dictatorships

Government officials have absolutely no right funneling loans or giving away tax money or guaranteeing loans made by commercial banks, in order to prop up morally and financially bankrupt Communist dictatorships throughout the world. Nor is it their business to loan, give money, or guarantee the giveaways of commercial banks in support of Communist-led terrorists who are attempting to overthrow friendly anti-Communist governments. It's an indefensible act of treason when any leader of the United States deliberately gives or supports the giving of financial aid to those very Communist occupied nations which promise to one day conquer and occupy America.

Every Soviet puppet government matter-of-factly sanctions slave labor within its borders. This alone is reason enough for the United States to immediately terminate all forms of international welfare for these ruthless Russian mirror-images! Every shred of evidence clearly shows that financial aid to Red satellite dictatorships throughout the world is of *no* benefit to the United States. It only strengthens each Communist tyrant's hold on his enslaved people. None of these Captive Nations have *ever* achieved independence from Moscow, nor have they gained *any* viable measure of autonomy. These are the two stated reasons for such dubious financial dealings in the first place! The American cash give-aways, loans, and loan guarantees have merely served to relieve Communist Occupied Russia of any need to use their ever short supply of rubles to prop up their surrogate puppets. America's beguiled and America's traitors who control the money spigots in the United States willingly do it for them!

The Export-Import Bank guaranteed an astounding 29 loans to despot Janos Kadar's Communist Occupied Hungary during one period alone. Hungary has continually had a hand outstretched for more and more American dollars in order to purchase "commodities."[17] Despite so many cash giveaways, everything still went sour in this Captive Nation. Therefore, leftists in the U.S. government went so far as to fund a business school in Budapest. It's geared to teach desperately needed management skills to the Red leadership and the uninspiring Party bosses.

The Export-Import Bank guaranteed 21 loans to Communist Occupied Yugoslavia over the same time span. This money was said to be needed for machinery and equipment.*18*   Regular infusions of American financial assistance over the years was the only reason dictator Tito was able to stay in power. Nevertheless, Tito never failed to make it clear as to where he stood and who he stood with: "Yugoslavia, in time of war, as well as in time of peace, marches shoulder to shoulder with the Soviet people toward the same goal—victory over the enemies of Socialism."*19* Right after World War II, this Communist criminal ordered the execution of hundreds of American airmen who had been saved by the Yugoslavian anti-Communist underground.*20* Yet Tito was still given preferential treatment by U.S. leaders.

Through July 31, 1965, the Export-Import Bank guaranteed an incredible 32 loans to Communist Occupied Poland for food purchases.*21* The Polish Reds have been continually supported over the years with money donated by the United States. Neither Poland nor any other forlorn Captive Nation is able to feed its own people without American financial aid. When the Polish dictatorship needed cash to buy machine tools in 1977 for their state-owned Urus Truck factory, the Export-Import Bank, under Carter, loaned $7.9 million.*22*   Carter's disastrous White House years proved incredibly lucrative to the Reds worldwide. Bank loans to Communist countries quadrupled. The figure came to an astounding $68 billion!

"Mass resistance spirit against Communism has dropped to near nil, partly because the U.S. seems to be on Communism's side," reveals Robert Morris.*23* How else are the people to act when such unpopular police states are so consistently propped up with U.S. dollars? The Captive

Nation situation is one of discouragement, disillusionment, and desperation for the people in all Eastern European countries, so long under Russia's cruel yoke.

Gary Benoit offers this advice: "The way to free the captive nations is to stop supporting the captors. Cut off the pipeline of . . . U.S. loans and loan guarantees . . . to captors, and they will begin to lose their grip over their captives. Stop supporting Communism, and Communism will crumble."[24]

Satanist Samora Machel's Communist band of terrorists captured Mozambique in 1975. A murderous purge was initiated on the scale of that which took place in Cambodia. Machel signed a 20-year mutual cooperation pact with his Russian master. In poured the usual advisors and technicians from the Soviet Union, North Korea, Cuba, East Germany, and Bulgaria. Communist Occupied Rhodesia (Zimbabwe) sent 15,000 troops to help Machel stay in power. Russian doctors were brought in to conduct horrifying medical experiments on hapless Mozambique citizens.

What happened when Machel's Red dictatorship was securely entrenched in Mozambique? Incredibly, the United States funneled untold millions of dollars to the Soviet backed regime. Overt American financial aid to the terrorists in 1987 alone was $10.5 million. No one knows how much more was given covertly.

South Vietnam was a member of both the International Monetary Fund and the World Bank for almost two decades. This little anti-Communist country was *never* able to obtain a loan through either agency. Then, in 1976, Communist Occupied Vietnam became a member. The assistance was immediate and lavish! The *Mobile Register* revealed: "...the World Bank approved . . . a $60 million interest-free loan to Communist Vietnam for an irrigation program. The loan is the latest in what is becoming a steady flow of aid from international institutions to help Hanoi . . . The International Monetary Fund . . . gave Vietnam an interest-free loan of $30 million from a special fund for poor nations, raising to nearly $115 million the total IMF aid in the past three years."[25]

Barrons correctly charges the World Bank with making loans that foster "the spread of socialism and Communism."*26* So do all the other international lending organizations. For example, the Inter-American Development Bank (IMF-World Bank affiliate) loaned Communist Occupied Guyana nearly $50 million in 1978. The haven for Marxist-Leninist "Reverend" Jim Jones received $18.8 million from the International Monetary Fund (IMF). In January 1979, the International Development Association (World Bank affiliate) gave Red Guyana $20 million more. The United States government, over and above all this, provided another $20 million in direct financial assistance. Why?

The Bank of America saw fit in 1980 to grant Communist Occupied Poland a loan of $325 million. It's astounding how much money is so eagerly handed out

by commercial banks to these slave dictatorships. Not only are they all enemies of America, they're also the world's worst deadbeats! None of the Red tyrannies can even pay below market interest on *previous* loans. Despite this fact, U.S. banks compete viciously to lend them more and more money. But, then, it's readily understandable, since the government guarantees each loan. No bank, therefore, can possibly lose a dime if a Communist slave state defaults.

Romania needed steam turbines for their Made-In-USA nuclear power plants. Naturally, being a Communist dictatorship, they were flat broke. In May 1981, an Export-Import Bank loan for $120.7 million was approved by President Reagan.*27* This in spite of the fact that Cornmunist dictator Ceausescu lived in opulent luxury while his 23 million captives suffer constant hardships.

Communist Occupied Russia's army officers run the 100,000 strong Angolan military. Yet, who came through when despised Red dictator Jose Eduardo dos Santos needed money for an offshore oil development project? Reagan disingenuously allowed the Export-Import Bank to give Communist Occupied Angola a fat $85 million, low interest loan on July 8, 1981. [28]

A few days earlier, Chase Manhattan and Morgan Guarantee Trust led a consortium of American banks in lending totalitarian Angola $50 million. This was also for purchasing equipment needed on the same project.*29* There have been 45,000 soldiers from Communist Occupied Cuba stationed in this hapless country. The presence of Cuban troops, says Chase Manhattan's illustrious David Rockefeller, "has not interfered with our banking relations."*30* Citibank's in-house Benedict Arnold—Thomas Theobold—crassly comments: "Who knows which political system works? The only thing we care about is how they pay their bills!"*31*

Robert G. Mugabe is the blood-drenched murderer who runs Communist Occupied Rhodesia (Zimbabwe). This terrorist was interested in a new coal-mining venture. So naturally he looked to his hated American enemies for the money. This Soviet puppet easily obtained a $38 million loan in February 1981 from the Export-Import Bank.*32* Today, Mugabe's brutal Red slave state is just another typical Marxist-Leninist economic basket case. John F. Burns of the *New York Times* noted that Mugabe has the reputation "as a Marxist ideologue whose guerrilla forces, in their brutality against black and white civilians had few counterparts in modern warfare."*33* Nevertheless, David Rockefeller—Chase Manhattan's top man—liked Mugabe. He found Zimbabwe's fanatical Communist mass-murderer to be a "very reasonable and charming person."*34*

Zimbabwe is a prime example of how ridiculously easy Communist dictatorships can acquire American dollars for various and sundry projects. Although unable to feed its own people, this Russian colony could afford Soviet MiG-29 jet fighters. They could also donate 15,000 troops to Mozambique, in order to help that Red police state annihilate all anti-Communist opposition. North Korean soldiers (advisors) trained Zimbabwe military personnel to use the latest weapons supplied by Communist Occupied Russia. Apparently nothing the Reds did really made any difference!

The Reagan Administration continued authorizing the financial aid.

Free Rhodesia did better economically while under stringent world-wide sanctions than Communist Occupied Rhodesia did with $375 million in American aid.*35* However, massive infusions of dollars unquestionably supported the 140,000 Communist bloc soldiers keeping order in Zimbabwe, Angola, and Mozambique. These troops were sent by such tyrannies as Russia, Bulgaria, North Korea, Cuba, and East Germany. Even Libya and the Palestine Liberation Organization (PLO) are represented militarily. And the United States still smilingly pays the bills!

Lieutenant Colonel Mengistu Haile Mariam quickly reduced Communist Occupied Ethiopia to one of the world's poorest nations. The Ford Administration gave this Red dictatorship an incredible $135 million to purchase F-5E jet fighter planes and sophisticated M-60 tanks! The Communist tyranny got an IMF loan of $67.5 million in 1981 and was provided with $1 billion in financial aid between 1978 and 1982. Congressman Toby Roth (R-WI) asks: "Can you imagine that Ethiopia has Most Favored Nation status? This means they get loans at less interest than our local business people, farmers, or whoever in this country."*36*

Comrade Mariam spends much of his interest free booty on his 250,000 man army—the biggest and best equipped in all sub-Saharan Africa. This Communist despot—while his people were dying of starvation—wasted an incredible $200 million celebrating the anniversary of his bloody takeover. A half million dollars of borrowed money was blown on imported whiskey. Another $10 million was lavished on purchasing statues of his idols—Lenin, Marx, and Engels.

Colonel Chadli Bendjedid is in charge of the despicable Algerian police state. Innumerable "advisors" from Cuba and Russia actually run the Communist dictatorship. Prior to the Red takeover, Algeria was self-sufficient in food production! Under totalitarian rule, the country imports 70 percent of its food! This murderous despot needed two special furnaces for his government owned steel plant. Naturally, he had no money to purchase them. Alas, as with every other Marxist-Leninist earthly paradise, Communist Occupied Algeria was broke. Despite his mad dog rantings, in January 1982, Bendjedid's terrorist regime received a low-interest, $7 million loan from the Export-Import Bank.[37]

Communist Occupied Hungary is the worst credit risk of all the Red Block dictatorships. According to the *Wall Street Journal,* the Hungarian police state "has the highest per capita Western debt of any Eastern European country, with more than $700 owed for each of its 10.8 million people."[38] Janos Kadar's slave labor tyranny couldn't even pay the interest on its debts in 1982. The way the problem was solved? Communist Occupied Hungary joined the International Monetary Fund (IMF)! Soon thereafter, millions of dollars more in loans flowed from the West— all guaranteed by the U.S. government. Reagan went so far as to oppose a congressional amendment *prohibiting U.S.* dollars contributed to the Communist created IMF from being used to bail out Red slave state tyrannies.

The U.S. funded Inter-American Development Bank gave $134 million in loans to Anastasio Somoza's anti-Communist Nicaragua over a period of 19 years. The Moscow backed Communist Sandinistas were in power a mere 18 months and had already almost doubled the looting. They received $262 million![39] Communist Occupied Nicaragua was able to easily swindle another $34 million in 1982.

In December 1982, comrades entrenched in government arranged a $1 billion credit package for their comrades in Communist Occupied Yugoslavia. In March of 1983, Soviet dictator Yuri V. Andropov was warmly welcomed to Belgrade. The feared former KGB head told his Yugoslavian pals to expect long-termRussian economic assistance.

He also announced contracts for the construction of 24 new Soviet ships in Yugoslavia.[40]

Russian troops are permanently stationed in Communist Occupied Czechoslovakia. They're needed to keep the enslaved citizenry from revolting. Nevertheless, this totalitarian state was given a $50 million loan in 1983.*41* Comrade Gustav Husak's regime supplies, weapons, advisors, and technicians to various Red dictatorships throughout the world. For example, 2,000 Czechs were shipped to Communist Occupied Ethiopia. Their job? To assist the Bulgarians, East Germans, Romanians, Soviets, and Cubans in running the brutal police state. American tax dollars pay for all this!

The International Economic Summit was held in Williamsburg, Virginia, May 28, 1983. Astoundingly, President Reagan secretly pledged to contribute another *$50 billion* to the Communist created IMF.*42* This duplicity was exposed in the *London Financial Times,* but ignored by the American media. Why? Columnist Patrick Buchanan asked: "Why . . . would intelligent capitalists ship their wealth off the subsidize any Communist or socialist failure? If this . . . is a wise, prudent investment, let us fairly ask: How much of the personal wealth of these affluent international bankers is invested in such loans?"*43* The answer, of course, is none! Every dime is illegally confiscated from American taxpayers!

Don Conlan of the Board of Economists wrote about the IMF in the *Los Angeles Times:* "As I think about it, if I were a Marxist bent on controlling what really counts in an economy—its banks—I couldn't have written an slicker formula for getting it done—with help from the bankers." *44* The International Monetary Fund has "loaned" Communist Occupied Vietnam and Communist Occupied Ethiopia untold millions of dollars. The IMF regularly lends large sums of money to such Red slave labor dictatorships as Hungary, Yugoslavia, Poland, and China. And this same IMF was conceived in 1944 by Assistant Secretary of Treasury Harry Dexter White and his associate Virginius Frank Coe. Both were "moles"—Kremlin agents who had penetrated the government!

The Communists were ousted from the island of Grenada by U.S. Marines and Army Ranger in October

1983. Soviet and Cuban weapon and munition stockpiles were found. Discovered were a nuclear submarine base, an airfield, and a training facility for terrorists. The Communist occupation of Grenada had been partly financed by American taxpayers. How? The IMF had loaned the Red dictatorship $14 million.*[45]*

The Soviet Union totally dominates and is in unquestionable control of Angola. Sonangol, the state-owned oil company, and Chevron-Gulf were given a loan for $45 million by the Export-Import Bank in late 1983. Not ones to kick a gift horse in the mouth, Chevron-Gulf and Sonangol borrowed another $100 million for oil field development in October 1984.*(46)* To add insult to injury, Jose Eduardo's Communist Occupied Angola got another $227 million in loans early in 1986.*(47)*

Commercial banks reap huge profits, yet they risk nothing by granting sizable loans to Red dictatorships. American taxpayers unknowingly shoulder the burden since various agencies of the government guarantee these loans. For example, the Commodity Credit Corporation was created in 1933 and is presently buried deeply in the Department of Agriculture bureaucracy. Communist Occupied Poland was unable to pay off $71 million in delinquent loans owed American banks for grain purchases. In February 1982, the CCC announced it was going to pay off Red Poland's outstanding debt!*48* From May 1983 to March 1986, the CCC paid $18.8 million to American Banks when Communist Occupied Romania reneged on its loan payments. Why? Because these slave labor tyrannies had been given the money in spite of being worse than terrible credit risks! In order for Poland and Romania to initially get the loans, the Department of Agriculture agreed to co-sign the notes!

The Romanian tyranny employs one of every four citizens in its secret police terror network! Religious persecution is vicious. Nevertheless, more Export-Import Bank credits were given to this brutal regime in 1984. Why? So Romania, although her people do without most of life's basic necessities, could purchase General Electric's nuclear-power equipment!

"Trade is supposed to mean that I give you something and you give me something in return. But in our contemporary 'trade' agreements with the Communists," explains Herb Joiner, "our government first *guarantees* a loan made to the Communists to purchase the goods. If the Communists don't repay that loan, our government repays it for them—with your money! . . . Three parties benefit from this convoluted transaction: The Communists who get the products, the businessmen who sell them, and the bankers who make the loans. It's a cozy, risk-free transaction, and the taxpayer is forced to pick up the tab." [49]

Yugoslavia's brutal Communist dictatorship needed coal mining equipment in 1984. The Reds were broke as usual and had a worse than terrible credit rating. Naturally, American firms were reluctant to ship anything without up front cash. Nevertheless, the Export-Import Bank conveniently came through with a $23.3 million loan to cover the cost.[50]

"In 1984 alone," reveals Jan Nowak, "East Germany received $2.5 billion in Western credits."[51]   In March of 1985, American banks loaned *$1.1 billion* more to Communist Occupied East Germany.

"The Communist government of East Germany went shopping among Western banks last year for a $100 million loan," declares Ray Kerrison. "A consortium of three American banks and the Bank of Tokyo was happy to oblige. Heck, they told the East Germans, why mess with a paltry $100 million. Here, take $500 million. The East Germans accepted."[52]

East German Red leaders must have been convulsing in laughter as they walked off with the $500 million. They immediately loaned $20 million to Daniel Ortega Saavedra's Communist Occupied Nicaragua.[53] Ironically, the savage anti-American regime headquartered in Managua, was helped by its Communist comrades in East Germany, with money furnished by American banks.

Greedy bankers continue to traitorously lend money to Communist Occupied East Germany. Will all these cash giveaways draw the leaders of this concentration camp filled dictatorship away from their Russian masters and into the Western camp? Not hardly! When West Germany called for Germany's reunification, dictator Erich Honecker's unequivocal response was: "Socialism and capitalism cannot be united any more than fire and water!"

In 1985, Communist Occupied Afghanistan needed money. The U.S. funded Agency for International Development (AID) saw fit to help. Despite all the barbarianism and inhumanity, General Sayid Mohammed Najibullah's Communist regime in Kabul was given $3.4 million.[54]

Over half of America's $300 billion defense budget goes to subsidize NATO.55 A monumental portion of the defense budget is thereby used to protect Western Europe from the Red scourge. Ironically, this same Red scourge is also being subsidized by unlimited low and no interest loans which are taxpayer guaranteed!

In 1985, Communist Occupied Yugoslavia already owed a $19 billion debt. Nevertheless, the criminal Red regime was still able to get $300 million more in standby credit from the IMF. This simply allowed the deadbeat Red slave state to continue non-stop borrowing from the West.

In 1986, the all pervasive Hungarian secret police were jailing citizens who threatened "the internal order or the security of the state." Comrade Janos Kadar's harsh Communist regime was facing the specter of $16 billion in foreign debts. Nevertheless, this Red dictatorship was loaned hundreds of millions of dollars more though the IMF.[56]

Despite everything done by the United States, Communist Occupied Hungary stays in a never ending economic slump. The same is true of all the other Captive Nations, whether its Husak's Czechoslovakia, Castro's Cuba, Ceausescu's Romania, Chissano's Mozambique, Zhivkov's Bulgaria, or Garcia's Peru. Soviet exile Alexander Zinoviev's words are right on target: "An economically flourishing and democratic Communist country is as possible as a flying crocodile."

"What happens to cooperating Congressmen," asks Patrick J. Buchanan, "when Americans awaken to the knowledge that the 'non-aligned' dreck that treats their country like kitty litter at the UN is not only subsidized with our foreign aid, but is being carried on the books of our biggest banks? When the American people discover that the Soviet nuclear arsenal targeted on Europe and North America was underwritten with Western credit?" [57]

Financial Assistance to Communist Occupied China

Congress, under pressure from the Nixon-Kissinger team, removed the Wylie Amendment from the Export-Import Bank Act in August 1971. The Wylie Amendment specifically prohibited Export-Import Bank loans to Communist Occupied China. Now the Red Chinese dictatorship was also eligible for these low-interest give-aways. Congressman Chalmer Wylie (R-OH) argued: "We are talking about permitting . . . a bank . . . which is a creation of this Congress, and an agency of the United States, to make loans to improve the economy of countries which help finance the activities of a nation killing American boys."[58]

Communist Occupied China was granted diplomatic recognition and Most Favored Nation status by the Carter Administration in 1979. The Red tyranny was allowed to join the World Bank, the IDA, and the IMF, in 1980. The money spigot was immediately switched on and immense amounts of cash began to flow. In 1981, the IMF gave the genocidal-prone Chinese—who ravaged one-sixth of Tibet's population—a whopping $550 million in American taxpayer financed loans.[59] Senator Helms warns: "The West will rue the day that it did anything at all to strengthen China's Communist government."[60]

A multitude of negative things can be said about the long Red Chinese record of violence, deceit, terrorism, drug-dealing, and bloodshed. Solzhenitsyn charges the Chinese Red puppet regime in Tibet with being "more brutal and inhumane than any other Communist regime in the world."

A $200 million *grant* was given by the World Bank to improve the quality of university engineering and science programs in this violent dictatorship.*61* A student's "love of the Communist Party" is deemed more important than entrance test scores for admission in Red Chinese colleges. Then there was a $60 million loan for a desalinization project on slave labor farms in North China!*62* Lastly, the IMF generously made another incredible $450 million available for America's Red Chinese "friends."

The world's largest slave-labor dictatorship wanted money for power generating equipment in 1981. Reagan authorized the Export-Import Bank to give them $57.1 million American tax dollars. One year later, another $60.4 million "loan" was approved to pay for an ultra-modern, cold-rolling steel plant to be built in Baosham. At the same time, the Export-Import Bank guaranteed an $8 million private loan to the Bank of China.[63]

Red China's mortiferous tyrants were extremely successful in looting the U.S. treasury. By June 1983, Communist Occupied China had obtained huge money grants from the IDA, IMF, the World Bank, and the Export-Import Bank. Bloated with American dollars, they then decided to lend a few bucks to a comrade. Party Secretary Hu Yaobang visited Communist Occupied Yugoslavia. Although unable to feed its own starving people, China gave $120 million in foreign aid to the ever-needy Belgrade beggars.

American's newest Communist "friends" were loaned another $1.1 billion in 1984 by the World Bank. $400 million of this would be interest free from the IDA. The IDA then loaned $50 million more to Communist Occupied China in 1985, at an astounding one percent interest! This money was for citrus production and raising cattle on slave labor farms!*64* American taxpayers fork over a minimum of one-fourth of the IDA's lending assets.

Peking doesn't even have to pretend to like the United States in order to get cash. Red China was loaned $160 million by the World Bank on April 18, 1986. The IDA soon after granted Peking $70 million more in *interest free* credit! The World Bank was at it again in May, when it announced China was being given yet another multi-million dollar loan. This one had a 50-year pay back period—no interest and no payment due for 10 years!

In September of 1986, Communist Occupied Nicaragua got a $20 million interest free loan from Communist Occupied China! Here we find a paradox: America grudgingly gives millions of dollars to the anti-Communist Nicaraguan freedom fighters. This is purportedly to help them overthrow Madison Avenue Danny's murderous Communist regime. The United States eagerly approves loans through the Export-Import Bank for Red China. America also pushes for multi-million dollar loans to the Chinese Communists from the World Bank and the IDA. Communist Occupied China in turn, using American money, props up its Red pals in Nicaragua.*65* Few Americans even try to explain it!

"The International Monetary Fund announced a loan to China of $717 million to help pay for imports," reveals an AP dispatch. . . . the new loan will be . . . like a line of credit, that the Chinese dictatorship can draw over the next 12 months.... with an annual interest rate of 6 percent. *66* American taxpayers have to pick up the tab and make good on these high-risk loans when Communist Occupied China can't or refuses to pay them back. The Communist designed IMF bails out the commercial banks which make these ridiculous low interest loans to countries like Red China, who, in turn, are considered to be bad credit risks in the first place. Simply put, the IMF is the FDIC (used to insure depositors in American banks) for the entire world!

Chapter 4

Trade with and Aid to America's Enemies

Traitor: "One who behaves disloyally, one who betrays his country."
Oxford American Dictionary

Treason: ". . . consciously and purposely acting to aid its one's country] enemies."
American Heritage Dictionary

"The Communist ideology is to destroy your society," charges Soviet exile Alexander Solzhenitsyn. "This has . . . never changed . . . When there is détente, peaceful co-existence, and trade, they will still insist: the ideological war must continue . . . This is continued repetition of the oath to destroy the Western world. Just as, once upon a time in the Roman Senate, a famous speaker ended every speech with the statement: 'Furthermore, Carthage must be destroyed,' so today, with every act— détente, trade, or whatever—the Communist ['s] . . . repeat: 'Furthermore, capitalism must be destroyed.'" *1*

Vladimir Ilyich Lenin said: "When the capitalist world starts to trade with us, on that day they will begin to finance their own destruction." *2* And he also warned: Instead of using guns and tanks, we shall wage an industrial war .... As soon as we are strong enough to overthrow capitalism, we shall immediately seize it by the throat." *3*

One government agency stealthily wheedles away untold tons of grain to Communist Occupied Russia and other enemy Red slave state dictatorships. Shortages result and prices go up for Americans. Farmers are unable to get enough grain to feed their livestock in order to produce meat. Shortages again result! Another government agency turns around and purchases its beef from Romania (Chapter 5)—a Communist occupied country and enemy of the United States! The billions of dollars in international giveaways, and the amount of America's aid to and trade with Communist Bloc dictatorships—who in time of war would march with the USSR—is beyond comprehension.

That such mind boggling betrayal of trust has been allowed to take place, or even condoned, for so many years is incredible! Even more alarming is the fact that *all* of America's leaders are aware of the pervasive perfidy continually taking place in Washington. There appears to be a conspiracy of silence regarding aid to and trade with Red enemies of the United States!

Both past and present political leaders from the President on down, have every reason to be fearful should the American citizenry every obtain the untarnished facts.

Mikhail Makarenko spent eight long years in the Gulag Archipelago, Communist Occupied Russia's vast network of inhuman slave labor concentration camps. He was asked how the barbaric Soviet regime could continue to stand after decades of such terrifying brutality and oppression. His answer: "Western trade." *4*

James J. Drummey charges that "human beings have been systematically tortured and murdered in the Soviet Union for more than 60 years. More than 60,000,000 . . . have perished in these camps...."The murderers are now looking in your direction!" *5*

Made in the West media star Mikhail Sergeyvich Gorbachev is Lenin-Stalin-Khrushchev all rolled into one— the rough edges polished nicely and draped in an expensive Western suit. This violent Russian— despite the drooling, groveling, and awed posturing struck by America's most influential news, business, and political luminaries—came up through the Communist ranks as a ruthless protegé of Yuri V. Andropov, the monstrous head of the feared KGB. Marxist-Leninist dictators come and go with the passage of time, but the inhumanity, barbarism, and savagery always remain as a permanent fixture in the psyche of every Communist leader. Nevertheless, the West still aids and trades; lends and arms; and constantly does business with the most merciless enemy every faced by mankind.

Trade with and Aid to Communist Occupied Russia

Leftists in government have long advocated unlimited trade with the USSR. The idea of accelerated trade with America's deadly Communist adversary began to bear fruit during the Kennedy Administration. Washington subversives had a free hand to negotiate perfidious trade deals with the Soviets. Commerce Secretary Luther Hodges began to approve innumerable export licenses. Ridiculous long-term, low, and no-interest (but high-risk) loans were granted. Communist Occupied Russia's credit was even guaranteed by the government (Chapter 3). They used this money to pay for American wheat, chemicals, computers, factories, etc. (Chapter 1, 2).

The first attempt to justify such acts of treason was the 1960 *Ball Report*. This absurd rationalization was prepared under the direction of radical leftist George Ball (CFR) who was to become Kennedy's Under Secretary of State (Chapter 9). Ball claimed that unlimited trade with Communist dictatorships was "inevitable."[6] Other early proponents of heavy trade (in strategic goods) with America's Red enemies were socialist Vice President Hubert H. Humphrey (CFR), and two notorious security risks—Secretary of State Dean Rusk (Chapter 9, 10, 11) and National Security Advisor Walt Rostow (Chapter 11, 16).

Former Congressman Martin Dies (D-TX), for seven years Chairman of the House Committee on Un-American

Activities, says this about the liberal left: "When the 'Liberals' are accused of having been 'soft' on Communism, they go into hysterics and scream that their accusers are 'unfair.' The truth is that they *have* been soft on Communism from the very beginning, and they are still taking advantage of every opportunity to resume their policy of appeasing the Communists, whether it is by tacit approval of their physical crimes or by giving them reduced rates to buy our stores of foods and grains. This is a sore spot with the 'Liberals,' but it is true with the majority of the 'Liberal' leaders that they continue to accommodate the Communist enemy at every opportunity. That, after all, is what being 'soft' on Communism is all about."7

Six multinational grain dealers control all grain leaving the United States—Continental, Cargill, Andre, Bunge, Cook, and Dreyfus. Ninety percent of Continental Grain of New York is owned by one of the world's wealthiest families—the Fribourgs. When Jules ran the company back in the 1930s, he handled millions of tons of grain sales for the murderous Stalin regime. The entire grain crop had been confiscated from the peasant farmers, under a diabolical plan of mass starvation devised and executed by a neanderthal monster known as Nikita Khrushchev (Chapter 12). A famine was deliberately created (1932-1935), as a direct result. Roughly 14.5 million men, women, and children were methodically starved to death in the Ukraine alone. *8*

The Kennedy Administration wheat giveaways to Communist Occupied Russia in 1961 should have erupted into a national scandal. According to Congressman D.L. Latta: "officials of the U.S. Department of Agriculture and the Commerce Department agreed to sell surplus wheat to the Soviet Union for $.62 per bushel less than the baker who bakes your bread pays for it. *9* Some wheat shipped to the Soviets and their puppets is used to make ethyl alcohol. This in turn is used for manufacturing such war-related items as TNT, missile fuel, and poison gas!

In 1963, Communist Occupied Russia was sold $200 million worth of wheat. Senator Thomas Dodd (D-CT) later noted: "The wheat was not sold at the price which the government had paid the American farmer, but at the artificially low world price, so that the American government, in effect, was subsidizing the Soviet Union." *10* Dodd pointed out at the time of the wheat deal that "subsidized agricultural commodities should not be made available to the Soviet Union or to countries dominated by the USSR." [11]

"Sweetheart deals with the Reds are extensive and have been for decades," charges Joseph Mehrten. "In fact, so extensive is this U.S. aid that without it Soviet leaders not only could not pursue expansionist policies but would be powerless and overthrown." [12]

Continental was instrumental in selling $78.5 million worth of American wheat to Communist Occupied Russia in 1964. The Johnson Administration subsidized $24 million of this package—almost one-third the entire cost! Such a sweetheart deal enabled the USSR to purchase U.S. wheat at a price lower than could friendly nations. Cargill of Minneapolis sold $53 million worth of U.S. wheat to the same Soviet murderers. American taxpayer's again subsidized the sale—this time for $18 million. [13]

"I'm very much opposed to subsidizing imports or exports with the Soviet Bloc," says Jeane J. Kirkpatrick, "and I am very much opposed to the kind of credit advantages and guaranteed bank loans which constitute that kind of subsidization." [14]

In just a little more than a month in 1964, over 65 million bushels of subsidized wheat treasonously shipped to the Soviet slave empire. This was enough wheat to give a bushel to every third man, woman, and child in the USSR. *15* According to former Secretary of Agriculture Ezra Taft Benson, it cost taxpayers $42 million to subsidize this grain giveaway to our Communist "friends." [16]

In the meantime, Communist Occupied Russia shipped tons of subsidized American wheat to Cuba, Romania, and other satellite dictatorships! This was done in order to strengthen the USSR's grip on these Captive Nations. On the other hand, American grains and other food commodities were being traded or given away to some non-Communist nations, who in turn shipped them to the Reds! For example, in 1964, Nasser received $1 billion in grains and other agricultural products from the United States. The Egyptian government turned around and shipped 314,000 tons of these food commodities to Communist Occupied Russia, East Germany, Romania, China, Hungary, Cuba, and Bulgaria. Brazil pulled a similar stunt when (in 1965) they were given $61 million worth of free food commodities. The appreciative Brazilian government turned around and, using Russian freighters, sent eight thousand tons of American corn to Communist Occupied Cuba! [17]

The USSR is unquestionably history's largest food importer. Even in its best years, the Soviets produce far less food than does the United States. This is accomplished with 50 percent more land under cultivation and an incredible 1,000 percent more farm workers. An interesting point to consider is this: approximately three percent of the U.S. labor force farms, yet vast surpluses are continually produced. In Communist Occupied Russia, around one-fourth of the work force farms, yet they're still unable to produce enough food to feed the people. Charles R. Armour notes: "The premise that the Soviet Union is feeding its people, supporting its utopian society, creating its industrial, technological, and military capabilities, as a socialistic state, is the height of absurdity." [18]

1971 was another banner year for Americans supplying food to feed the Red Army! On November 5, the Department of Agriculture announced that Cargill and Continental Grain would sell another $136 million worth of heavily subsidized oats and barley to the USSR. [19] The Russians purchased them for less than half price—quite a bargain for an avowed enemy of the seller!

During the summer of 1972, identified Soviet espionage agent Henry Kissinger [20] and his old leftist friend, Helmut Sonnenfeldt, pushed hard to "sell" Communist Occupied Russia 400 million more bushels of wheat. [21] Sonnenfeldt was a serious security risk who had long been under investigation for spying. In fact, the FBI recommended that he be prosecuted under the espionage statutes. 22 He never was! Prices on this Great Grain Robbery were purposely kept low. Some $300 million in subsidies were paid to the exporting companies. The long-standing Needy Russian-Welfare-Program was still in full swing! Comrades in Washington gave their comrades in Moscow another $1 billion worth of American wheat at unheard of bargain-basement prices! [23]

The Commodity Credit Corporation "loaned" Communist Occupied Russia $760 million at 6-1/8 percent, so they could pay for the wheat they were stealing! Treasury had actually paid a higher interest rate to borrow the money than was charged to the ever needy Soviets. Taxpayers were forced to guarantee the $750 million Soviet loan. The Nixon Administration even agreed to deliver one-third of the Russian booty to Odessa, at American expense. U.S. shippers were paid a special subsidy of $12.95 per ton, or a total of around $80 million in this segment of the notorious Aid-to-Dependent-Communists-Program. Such treasonous grain transactions raised domestic prices of wheat from $1.63 to almost $4.50 per bushel. The Russians obtained incredible amounts of barley, rye, corn, oats, sorghum, soybeans, and approximately one-third of America's entire wheat crop. [24]

Food prices skyrocketed in the United States during the early 1970s! This was a direct result of the illegal commodity giveaways to Communist Occupied Russia and the Red Bloc dictatorships. Taxpayers were subsidizing bread at 11 cents a pound for Moscow housewives. The *New York Times* reported: "While [American] housewives are paying higher prices, Russian bread remains one of the biggest bargains in the Soviet Union."

The Great Grain Robbery also forced a scandalous jump in meat prices. $1.5 billion was added to the cost of meat purchased by American consumers. This was a direct result of grain shortages, which brought on the exorbitant cost of grain needed to feed livestock. Despite all this, the criminal food giveaways continued. Washington correspondent Paul Scott exposed the next facet of Nixon's Needy-Russian-Welfare-Program: " a massive new food and grain deal . . . provides for Russia obtaining U.S. food . . . for virtually nothing. Russia would pay for the grain in its own currency [worthless outside of Russia] which would have to be used on projects within the Soviet Union." [25]

Leonid Brezhnev, Moscow's answer to Howdy Doody, told the Soviet Politburo and the Warsaw Pact dictators in 1973: "We Communists have got to string along with the capitalists for a while. We need their agriculture and their technology. But we are going to continue massive military programs and by the middle 80's we will be in a position to return to a much more aggressive foreign policy designed to gain the upper hand in our relationship with the West." [26]

Ronald Reagan said: "I know of no leader of the Soviet Union since the revolution, and including the present leadership, that has not more than once repeated in the various Communist congresses . . . that their goal must be the promotion of world revolution and a one-world socialist or Communist state."[27] Despite such rhetoric, the *New York Times* noted: "The United States has agreed to nearly triple — *to 23 million metric tons* — the amount of American wheat and corn that the Soviet Union will be allowed to purchase in the next 12 months . . . The agreement set the stage for record purchases of American grain . . ."[28]

Secretary of Agriculture John Block was fully aware of slave labor usage on Russia's Siberian pipeline. In 1982, this leftist gave the Kremlin a new five year contract for subsidized, bargain-basement priced American grain. In this way, Block guaranteed the Red Army and the concentration camp guards wouldn't go without food. *29* How did the Soviets thank the United States? They brazenly assassinated or captured Congressman Lawrence McDonald (D-GA) and massacred or took prisoner 60 other Americans in the September 1, 1983, terrorist attack on Korean Airlines Flight 007 (Chapter 12).

How harmless to American security are such massive grain giveaways to the USSR? Soviet exile Mikhail Makarenko, warns: "Grain bought from the West is earmarked for the Soviet armed forces, not the people." Russian General Yevdokin Yegorovich Maltsev quotes Lenin: "The Red Army cannot be strong without great state reserves of wheat because without this the army cannot be moved about freely, nor trained as it should be. Without this one cannot maintain the workers who work for the army." [30]

Communist Occupied Russia was given another gift two days before Christmas 1985. Reagan's new Farm Bill created yet another loathsome grain giveaway program! A major portion of American wheat, corn and other farm products worth $2 billion went to dictator Mikhail Gorbachev's Soviet Union. [31]

August 1, 1986, saw a brand new facet of America's perfidious Communist Welfare Program at work. The Reagan Administration announced the most bizarre wheat deal to date. America's "friends" in Moscow were offered $52 million worth of free grain! This gift was supposed to induce Gorbachev's Red tyranny to purchase more wheat from the U.S. at the going world price.[32] Called "export enhancement," it was simply a phrase used to camouflage the donating of more subsidized wheat to the sanguinary Soviet adversary. In other words, taxpayers, whether they liked it or not, would actually *pay* the Russian gangsters to take U.S. wheat surpluses—wheat to feed their military, wheat to send to Communist Occupied Cuba or Ethiopia or Hungary.

These same Soviet "friends"—who feed their military with wheat and other farm products donated by the United States—are taking special precautions for the war they consider inevitable! Russia's Communist Party bosses—which include dictator Gorbachev—have carefully planned the assassination of every important American leader. This is to be undertaken by Spetsnaz or Special Purpose troops—elite commando units—who have been highly trained to successfully carry out their murderous assignment. Intelligence groups know of a great many Spetsnaz teams already in place throughout the United States. The government has made a concerted effort to keep this under wraps.

Trade with and Aid to Soviet Puppet Dictatorships

"Why has America built the world's most modern, most highly automated steel finishing plant for the Communist government of Poland?" asks the *Dallas Morning News.* "Constructed in Warren, Ohio, the plant was dedicated as the Lenin Steel Works . . . The American people 'lent' the Communists $2.5 million to pay for it."[33]

Strategic trade with Communist satellite nations started zooming upwards during the Kennedy White House years. Business leaders were pressured to get on the Red trade bandwagon. The *Baltimore Sun* reported: "The government is quietly encouraging American businessmen to expand their trade with the Soviet bloc." [34]

Eight million tons of scrap iron were loaded in Houston, Texas. The destination? Communist Occupied Czechoslovakia! 35 At the same time, scrap iron and steel worth $700,000 were shipped to Communist Occupied Yugoslavia! "Non-strategic" railroad equipment valued at around $2.5 million went to Communist Occupied Bulgaria. Says former Senator Frank J. Lausche (D-OH): "We are now indulging in the same evil practices of selling material to the Communist countries that we indulged in prior to World War II, when we sold scrap iron, which was a 'non-strategic material', to Japan." [36]

All these things were taking place during the 1961 Berlin crisis, when Nikita Khrushchev ordered the construction of the infamous Berlin wall. Communist Occupied Russia effectively sealed off East Berlin and stopped the massive exodus of enslaved citizens. Khrushchev, of course is the depraved mass-murdering beast who boasted: "The United States will eventually fly the

Communist flag . . . the American people will hoist it themselves!" [37]

In February 1963, the State Department announced that Communist Occupied Poland was getting $51.6 million worth of surplus farm products on long-term credit. This was to eventually be paid to the U.S. in worthless Polish zlotys, that could be spent only in Poland. At this particular time, American trade with Poland totaled $477.3 million. Such deals could be expected from the State Department while Dean Rusk (Chapter 9, 10, 11) was in charge. Rusk was never *identified* as a Communist mole, but he was an extremely serious security risk nevertheless.

In 1964, the Senate Judiciary Committee thoroughly investigated trade between the U.S. and Communist slave labor dictatorships. It actually took a Senate investigation to determine that American-Red Bloc trade *wasn't* conducive to the well being of the United States! The Senate report stated: "On the Communist side . . . East-West trade . . . [is] a matter of survival. The Communist bloc must have Western assistance not only in coping with its chronic agricultural crises, but also to cope with the chronic deficiencies of its industries." [38]

Tom Anderson was absolutely correct when he said: "The very survival of the Communist World rests upon the willingness and production of the Free World to support it."[39]

Congressman Ed Derwinski (R-IL) charged: "It is not the intention of the [Johnson] administration merely to permit expanded trade agreements with Communist governments, but it is the specific intention to subsidize that trade." [40]

During the Vietnam War, a phenomenal portion of America's national treasure was generously dumped on 99 different countries. Among the greedy recipients of the United States International Welfare Program, 95 either claimed to be "neutral", or they openly sided with Communist Occupied North Vietnam (Chapter 6)! This certainly doesn't speak well for the common sense quotient of the leftists permeating various echelons of government.

These "misguided" bureaucrats always excuse such traitorous giveaways with the illogical reasoning that America is buying the loyalty of these so-called "friends."

The Johnson Administration aided Todor Zhivkov's Communist Occupied Bulgaria by sanctioning the giveaway of platinum pellets. These special pellets are required for making high octane gasoline. The Reds actually paid nothing although the cost was $660,000. *(41)* The Soviet puppet was given long-term credit for the purchase as all Marxist-Leninist dictatorships have come to expect from America. Why does the U.S. do anything to aid this Bulgarian tyranny? After all, it is run by one of the harshest, most pervasive secret police organizations in the entire Russian Bloc!

Insanity or outright treason is evident when the United States enthusiastically transfers its most modern technology to Communist Occupied Russia and its Red slave state clones. These are the international Al Capones behind the murderous terrorist activities in the West. They're the same Communist criminals who organized the anti-war (actually anti-U.S.—pro-Hanoi) movements during the Vietnam era. They're the same revolutionary gangsters who were behind the no-win Vietnam War itself! They're the ones orchestrating the peace at any price (antiU.S.—pro-Soviet) movement today. And they're the ideological brothers of the zealots who coldly disemboweled pregnant women, bayoneted helpless babies, and blew the hands and feet off little children with boobytrapped toys in Afghanistan and elsewhere around the world!

During his 1968 campaign, Richard Nixon (Chapter 12) self-righteously protested the Johnson Administration's trade policies with Communist Occupied Russia and other satellite Red dictatorships. Once in office Nixon did an about face and advocated even more trade. He substantially increased the giveaway of strategic war supplies to these enemy nations. They in turn shipped arms, ammunition, and other war goods to Communist Occupied North Vietnam, to be used in slaughtering American troops (Chapter 6).

The Nixon Administration further opened the trade floodgates. Restrictions were deleted on shipments to Communist countries for an incredible "350 types of electronic instruments, machinery, transport equipment, 470 chemicals, and 300 classes of metals and metal products."[42] In 1971, over 1,800 more "restricted" items were deleted from the list of non-tradable goods.

In 1974, Richard Nixon deceptively allowed huge quantities of low sulphur coal tobe shipped to both Communist Occupied Yugoslavia and Communist Occupied Romania. Such clean burning coal was shipped to America's enemies despite the fact that it was desperately needed by the U.S. steel industry! As a direct result,many Americans found themselves out of work.

Syndicated columnist Victor Riesel had this to say: "So acute is Bethlehem Steel's need for this low sulphur coal, it is cutting back 'hot metal' production by a million tons in the next six months . . . the U.S. steel industry lies under a pall. Few have more than dangerously short supplies of this special coal." [43]

Many American POWs were abandoned in Laos (Chapter 15) when the Vietnam War ended with a humiliating but totally unnecessary negotiated defeat for the United States. All told, 569 airmen were downed in the jungles of Laos. Of the 311 known to have been alive at one time, none have ever been returned or even acknowledged as being held as a POW by the Communist Pathet Lao. Although the Laotian Reds ignore all requests for information on American POWs, Congressman Benjamin A. Gilman (R-NY) reported in 1980: "This year the U.S. government approved the sale of 10,000 tons of rice to Laos. Why give them any assistance until they have shown credibility and willingness to cooperate? "[44]

In 1981, Communist Occupied Romania became Eastern Europe's biggest market for American exports. As could be expected, Romania purchased all of these American goodies on credit. This is but another ingenious leftist method of giving one more Red enemy foreign aid through the back door. The United States gives aid to and trades with the Red dictatorship in Romania despite the fact that Nicolae Ceausescu vehemently finds any degree of free enterprise "incompatible with socialism."

Ambassador Zdzislaw M. Ruraz defected to the United States when General Wojciech Jaruzelski, the Polish dictator, declared martial law in 1981. Ruraz offers his expert view on East-West trade: "I know how absolutely necessary trade with the West is to the Communist bloc. Without it, they could not sustain their economies and they certainly could not continue to support the Soviet armaments built up that now threatens the entire world." [45]

In 1978, Soviet "advisors" and 20,000 Cuban soldiers were brought to Communist Occupied Ethiopia. Over 5,000 students were sadistically butchered in February of 1978 alone. Some as young as 12 years old were, according to Jeane Kirkpatrick (CFR), "immersed in hot oil, sexually tortured, or flung out of windows and left to die in the streets." During 1984, while the same sort of atrocities were still taking place, American leaders sent over 41 metric tons of food to the Ethiopian Reds. The cost—$22.7 million. During 1985, the United States donated another $127 million worth of humanitarian aid. Included were 223,000 metric tons of food. A ridiculous $12.40 per ton import tax was charged by the Marxist-Leninist dictatorship on all food unloaded from American ships—food donated to help alleviate the suffering caused by the despotic regime's *planned* famine program. [46]

The murderous Ethiopian leadership made it clear they were intentionally starving certain segments of their population. Despite this: "On November 2, 1984, the U.S. and Ethiopia agreed to a government-to-government humanitarian assistance program under which the U.S. is providing 50,000 metric tons of food *directly to the Ethiopian Government.*"47 (emphasis added).

Trade with and Aid to Communist Occupied China

Solzhenitsyn warns that U.S. leaders are making the same errors with Communist Occupied China that were made with the Soviet gangsters: "In 30 or 40 years you will read the Chinese Gulag Archipelago, and you will be stunned, you will say, well, we didn't know; but . . . you must know today what's going on.... By trusting China you will yield the other half of the earth . . . They are the same Communists, they use the same methods, and they use the annihilation policy." *48*

The diabolical scheme of supplying food commodities to America's Red Chinese adversary goes back many years. The administrative chief of the United States UN delegation, Louis Bohmrich, openly advocated a traitorous "Marshall Plan" for Communist Occupied China in 1966. In one lecture, this radical leftist said: "Every effort must be made to help China evolve . . . We must guarantee that China does not have to fight for food. It must be assured." *49* One simple question for all of the above—why?

Various Communist occupied countries have long been profitably looting the American food supply. The *Herald Examiner* revealed: "Congressional conferees Thursday tentatively agreed to authorize low-interest, long-term credit sales of food to Russia, China, Cuba, and other Communist countries. Repayment under such deals can extend 20 years with interest rates as low as 2 percent." *50* Was your Congressman a part of this treasonous activity?

Dr. Susan Huck expressed it perfectly: "The whole world dines at America's table. The trouble is, we get stuck with the check."

American citizens pay cash for their food, yet atheistic Communist dictatorships get theirs for virtually nothing. According to Washington correspondent Paul Scott: "Members of Congress and the nation's farm leaders are being privately told that if the Nixon Administration has its way, there will be no reversal of this policy of furnishing cut-rate and free food to Moscow and Peking." *51* Who's side was Richard Nixon and his leftist cohorts on anyway? How can the United States spend $300 billion a year to defend itself against Communist aggression, while it's also feeding the Communist aggressors?

There certainly was "no reversal" in Nixon's International Red Welfare policy! A news dispatch revealed the astounding amounts of three major food items Communist Occupied China was allowed to "purchase" from the U.S. on credit. These freebies were corn—630,000 metric tons; wheat—almost 127 million bushels (3.2 million metric tons); and soybeans—950,000 metric tons. *52* Soybean shipments to Japan—a paying customer and an ally—had to be embargoed in order to fill Mao's demands. Over and above these food commodities, this deadly dictatorship was given 775,000 bales of surplus subsidized cotton.*53* This equaled "the amount of cotton exported" to all nations in 1972. *54* And it tripled the price of cotton in the United States!

Communist Occupied China's Three Gorges dam on the Yangtze River is the biggest in the world. Amazingly enough, Reagan's Department of the Interior helped the despicable Red dictatorship build this 13 million kilowatt hydroelectric facility. It was originally designed for Chiang Kai-shek's Free China by engineers in the Interior Department's reclamation bureau, back during World War II. "The project was shelved in 1947" *(55)* when Mao's agrarian reformers" were instigating insurrection and terrorizing the countryside in an effort to violently Communize the country.

So impassioned is America's love affair with the murderous Red Chinese regime that trade blossomed to a new high of $8.1 billion in 1985. The United States exported $3.9 billion worth of goods to Red China— computers, ammunition factories, high-tech machinery, etc.*56* In return, the Communist Chinese slave-masters sent America $4.2 billion worth of merchandise—honey, cheap clothing, fire crackers, straw hats, Christmas decorations, wicker baskets, AK-47 assault rifles, nails, stuffed toys, alarm clocks, etc. (Chapter 5). None of these things were vital to national security or the U.S. economy. There's no question but that such trade practices directly aid and abet Communist Occupied China in the barbaric suppression of her enslaved people.

Senator Richard G. Lugar (R-1N), chairman of the Foreign Relations Committee, illogically commented: "I believe ultimately it is in our interests to cooperate with China and I am convinced that this . . . does not disrupt the current military balance between the People's Republic of China and Taiwan."[57]

President Reagan's Treasury Secretary James Baker paid a visit to Red China. While in Peking, he said the Administration was "eager to help China move forward to modernize and develop its economy in whatever way is mutually acceptable."[58]

Many American leaders refuse to listen to the Red Chinese criminals. In 1985, China's Communist Party Chief Hu Yau-bang claimed his country wasn't strong enough militarily to attack Free China (Taiwan). He said Red China could make such a move in four to eight years. According to Yau-bang "We have to wait until our economy is on the right track. Military power is economic power." [59]

Lugar, Baker, and many others evidently need to be reminded of a few pertinent facts. In Communist Occupied China, whole classes of people are thrown into medieval prisons and left to rot. Others are starved to death; summarily executed; tortured; or incarcerated in one of the thousands of disease-infested slave labor camps. Dr. David Rowe, Far Eastern specialist at Yale, explains: "Perhaps the most pervasive illusion underlying the U.S. China policy . . . is the belief that as of today Communist China has substantially changed . . . So Mao is dead, like Stalin, but have Teng Hsiso-ping and his clique abandoned Marxism . . . have they abandoned their basic war against capitalism? To both these questions we must answer with a resounding no." [60]

"The liberals hope you'll believe them when they tell you how anti-Communist they are. But they become alarmed if you really inform yourself on the subject of Socialistic-Communism," declares Ezra Taft Benson. "For after you inform yourself, you might begin to study the liberal voting record. And this study would show you how much the liberals are giving aid and comfort to the enemy and how much the liberals are actually leading America towards socialism itself. Communism is just another form of Socialism, as is Fascism." [61]

Vice Premier Yao Yilin of the Communist Chinese State Council, made an official pilgrimage to the Soviet Union in July 1985. Yao was the most important Chinese official to visit Moscow in 20 years. At this time, America's new found Chinese "friends" signed a $14 billion agreement with their Russian "enemy." Peking agreed to sell the Soviets raw materials, agricultural products, and various consumer products. Communist Occupied Russia would update 17 Chinese industrial plants and build them seven new factories. This certainly doesn't sound very antagonistic!

It's worth reminding American leaders from the President on down about Communist Occupied China's heavy involvement in illegal drugs. Intelligence specialist Frank Capell revealed: ". . . Red China's trade in narcotics has grown to more than double her official foreign trade, amounting to about $15 billion a year . . . 70 percent of the heroin in the United States comes from Red China . . . The U.S. Government has tried to suppress this fact."[62]

The Red Chinese dictatorship, according to leftist American leaders, *should* be sold nuclear technology. Their reasoning: Communist Occupied China can be used as a counterbalance to the military might of Communist Occupied Russia. Distinguished Senator Barry Goldwater (R-AZ) vehemently disagreed: "This ignores the insistence of Peking that it is not an 'ally' of the United States, and the argument is blind to the growing accommodation between the Communist giants."*63*

On July 23, 1985, President Reagan and Communist Occupied China's dictator Li Ziannian signed a nuclear accord. This agreement opened the door to the giveaway of more of America's highly guarded nuclear technology! Red China estimates it will have at least 10 American nuclear power plants operating by the year 2000. Their value? Around $2 billion!*64* Walter Kowalski asks: "How can our elected officials vote to stop America's nuclear breeder program and shortly thereafter vote to spend our tax dollars to help Red China with their nuclear program? *65* Good question!

Less than one year later, in March 1986, the Chinese-Russian "growing accommodation" noted by Goldwater surfaced more clearly. Red China's Vice Premier Li Peng announced that the two dictatorships would exchange nuclear technicians and engineers. On April 3, it was further revealed that nuclear power plants in Communist Occupied Russia were to be studied by Chinese nuclear experts. These two slave labor tyrannies also agreed to more closely cooperate in coordinating their state-planned economies.

W.F. Rockwell, Jr., Chairman of the Board of North American Rockwell stands out as a beacon of ethics in the greed-filled corporate community. He declares: "I don't agree that trade is feasible, as long as we are faced with fighting the Communist-Bloc countries.... I dislike losing business to foreign countries; however, at the same time, I hesitate selling materials to any country which eventually might prove to be instrumental in killing U.S. troops. *66*

". . . the United States continues to strengthen the Communists through aid and trade . . . in some instances, even military equipment and training," charges *The New American* in an editorial. "In fact, the aid that the United States has provided the Communists, beginning with the Bolshevik Revolution, is so massive that it is no

exaggeration to say of their Evil Empire: *Made in the U.S.!"*
[67]

Chapter 5

Illegally Importing Communist Slave-Made Goods

Traitor: "One who betrays a trust; especially one who commits treason.
The Reader's Digest Great Encyclopedic Dictionary

Treason: "betrayal, disloyalty ... sedition, treachery."
Roget's College Thesaurus

At least three slave-labor logging camps will be found on Communist Occupied Russia's Gusinobrodskoe Highway between Novosibirsk and Kemerovo. A former prisoner explained to Avraham Shifrin: "The hospital wards—barracks, in effect—were packed with sick people. It was cold and damp everywhere. A stench emanated from the overfilled rooms.... I witnessed dozens of cases in this 'hospital' of desperate prisoners driven to self-mutilation by the brutal working conditions in the logging camps. Instances of prisoners who had chopped off a finger, swallowed a nail, or stitched a dirty thread through the flesh of an arm or leg were common." *1*

Workers were needed in the Kolyma region of eastern Siberia to construct a port and build roads to the gold mines. Hundreds of thousands of slave laborers were packed in the holds of ships and sent on what Communist Occupied Russia called their "Dalstroy Experiment." These prisoners were forced to work in temperatures dropping to as much as 50 degrees below zero. They had no warm clothing. Few slept inside at night. Not even so much as a tent was provided by the inhuman Red tyrants. The casualties were enormous. Fewer than one out of every 50 slave laborers survived. The Russians just kept sending more shiploads of new slaves to replace those who died. The cycle was endless. 2

Despite authenticated stories like the above, slave-made imports from Communist Occupied Russia surpassed an astounding $200 million a year and they're still increasing! Yes, the United States illegally imports hundreds of millions of dollars worth of goods produced by slaves in concentration camps throughout Mikhail Sergeyvich Gorbachev's Soviet police state. Topping this figure is the illegal merchandise pouring in from Red China's brutal dictatorship and the barbaric Iron Curtain slave labor nations. These include East Germany, Romania, Hungary, Yugoslavia, Poland and Czechoslovakia.

Why do free people even consider buying slave made goods produced in the most repugnant tyrannies the world has ever known? How can Americans in good conscience purchase merchandise from merciless dictatorships where men, women, and children are held in bondage and forced to suffer under the vilest of conditions? Some of the responsibility must be shouldered by American political leaders! Some must be borne by members of the national news media! Both are well aware of the heinous Communist slave-labor system. Yet seldom, if ever, is it mentioned.

"And you must remember," suggests Chase Manhattan's David Rockefeller, "the Chinese . . . have a pool of cheap labor."3 Communist Occupied China certainly does have "a pool of cheap labor"—23 million slave laborers incarcerated in over 7,600 concentration camps throughout the country. Evidently, Mr. Rockefeller is looking to the future. Perhaps he can already envision the potential for reaping vast profits in a modern-day version of the early African slave trade. *Business Week* revealed: "China is getting ready to export what has long been its greatest asset— manpower. Battalions of [slave] laborers are being shaped up to be shipped overseas under contract. "

Such facts are ignored! There's a concerted effort to avoid offending the Soviets, Communist Occupied China, and the Red Bloc clones. Those in a position to do something, do nothing. Those in a position to say something, say nothing! Everyone simply pretends the problem doesn't exist.

Imports From Communist Occupied Russia

Alexander Ginzburg survived his harrowing stint in a Russian slave labor camp. He reveals: "We cut and polished glass for chandeliers. The room was full of abrasive dust. Men spat blood and got silicosis."[4]

Prisoners in Communist Occupied Russia are forced to do this dangerous work without wearing protective clothing. Face masks or a filtered breathing apparatus aren't supplied. Needless to say, slave laborers never live long under such atrocious conditions. They unwillingly face a slow, horrifying death from internal bleeding. These slave-crafted chandeliers are illegally imported by the United States for retailing to unsuspecting American consumers. They should rightfully be labeled: "Made in a USSR Death Camp."

Yuri Belov was arrested by the KGB security police in 1963 and charged with "anti-Soviet agitation and propaganda." He was convicted and sent to a slave-labor camp in Mordovia. Joseph Harriss tells a little of Yuri's story: "Here, 2,000 convicts each assembled 140 wooden chairs per shift, which were sent to a 'free' factory in Minsk. There, finishing touches were put on before the chairs were exported to the West. Thus the Kremlin could hypocritically claim the goods were made by 'free' workers."[5] The United States illegally imports vast numbers of these slave-made chairs each year. Check the bottoms when shopping for wooden chairs. If they come from a Russian forced labor camp, each will be stamped "Madein USSR" Every chair will each have the code number of the particular concentration camp where it was made.

A Heritage Foundation report confirms the widespread use of forced-labor in Communist Occupied Russia's wood industry: "Logging and wood processing is carried on in some 350 camps in the Urals, the Northwest, the Volga-Vyatka, and Siberia. Women fell trees around Kirov and Lake Baikal; children make shipping cases at Novaya Lyalya, in the Sverdlovsk region."6

Baltasi, according to Avraham Shifrin, is where "800 to 900 prisoners of a special, strict-regime camp work in a lumber mill." A former slave laborer from the Baltasi camp reveals: "Hungry people were herded ten or twelve kilometers to and from work on foot in both rain and snow through the forest. The prisoners were practically forced to run the whole way. Those who fell behind were beaten. The slightest retort would earn a prisoner a night on the naked cement floor of the isolation cell. Forced to run to work on an empty stomach the next morning, the prisoner would, together with other isolation-cell victims, be kept separate from the remaining inmates so no one could throw him a piece of bread."7

Everything from felling trees to milling lumber in the USSR is widely known to be accomplished using forced labor. Yet, vast amounts of Soviet slave-produced lumber are still brought into the United States at special low duty rates! Eighteen million board feet of Russian hardwood were illegally imported in 1982! Another $3.5 million worth of Communist Occupied Russia's wood products are also annually imported by America.8

Senator William L. Armstrong (R-CO) has long called attention to the Soviet Union's abominable slave-labor policy. Under Armstrong's continuing pressure, Undersecretary of State Lawrence S. Eagleberger *finally* acknowledged: "Soviet authorities still exploit forced labor on a large scale . . . forced labor . . . under harsh and degrading conditions, is used . . . to produce large amounts of . . . goods for . . . Western export markets."9

Here is a cross-section of Communist Occupied Russia's slave-made merchandise illegally imported by the United States: [10]

- Automotive: auto and farm equipment parts, tractors.
- Building Products: brick, tile, screens, plumbing equipment, lumber, plywood.
- Chemicals: ammonia, potassium chloride.
- Clothing: zippers, gloves, boots, buttons, coats.
- Electrical: electric cords and plugs, heaters, motors, pumps.
- Electronic: resistors, cathode ray tube components.
- Food: tea, caviar, crab meat, various fish products.
- Glass: chandeliers, camera lenses, glassware.
- Mining: limestone, gravel, coal, uranium, iron, gold.
- Miscellaneous: glass jar lids, wire fencing, mattresses, steel drums, barrels, peat, storage battery cases, watch parts, concrete products, woven bags, asbestos, cardboard cartons.
- Petroleum Products: gasoline, other motor fuels, engine oil.
- Wood Products: television and radio cabinets, fruit and vegetable crates, chess pieces, clock casings, furniture.

Senator Alfonse D'Amato (R-NY) correctly labels all of the above concentration camp items "products of misery" and the "obscenity of slave labor." D'Amato points out that "painted wooden figurines and chess pieces sold in some American stores were made by labor camp inmates in the Gulag who are forced to gather the lumber and carve the products."[11]

All gold in Communist Occupied Russia is mined using slave laborers. Even back in 1925, the United States supplied a giant dredge, six stories high, for use in the Russian gold mining business. Some of the brutally run gold mining camps are located in Muruntau, Artemovsk, Zeravshan, Taishet, Bodiabo, and Magadan.[12]

"Who else other than the Archipelago natives [slave laborers] would have . . . hauled on their backs the boxes of mined ore in the open gold fields of the Kolyma?" asks Alexander Solzhenitsyn. "Or have dragged out timber a half-mile from the Koin River . . . through deep snow on Finnish timber-sledge runners, harnessed up in pairs in a horse collar (the collar bows upholstered with tatters of rotten clothing to make them softer, and the horse collar worn over one shoulder)?"[13]

American leaders know full well that slaves mine Soviet gold. In 1978 alone, over $286 million in gold and $44 million in platinum-group metals were illegally imported by the U.S. These metals could have been obtained from South Africa orRhodesia at significantly lower prices. Both countries were once free! Neither condoned slave labor! Neither was a dictatorship! Neither was unfriendly towards the United States! Ross MacKenzie asks: "Why is it preferable to offend a country (South Africa) to which non-South Africans migrate to mine gold, for instance, yetnot to offend a country (the Soviet Union) whose regime is responsible for havingcaused an estimated 6 million deaths in 26 years in one mining region (theKolyma)alone?"[14]

Nikolai Sharegin survived 10 brutal years in hellish Russian slave-labor penal colonies and prisons. He reveals: "In the Kalinin region, prison inmates are producing Misha—the Olympic mascot teddy bear—and other souvenirs."[15] Such slave-made items were sold during the 1980 Moscow Summer Olympic Games and during the 1984 Winter Olympic Games held in Red Yugoslavia.[16]

Yes, Misha, the cute little official Olympic teddy bear was made by prisoners in 119 Soviet slave labor camps for women and children. Misha and many other items made by these same prisoners are shamelessly and illegally imported by the United States. Dr. Julius Margolin, a former inmate of Soviet slave labor camps offers this insight: "The prisoners live in primitive wooden barracks . . . About 100 prisoners live in one room, on plank beds arranged in two levels.... The mass of prisoners are dressed in stinking rags and present a pitiful sight . . . an indescribable hell . . . "[17]

At least $10 million worth of Soviet uranium is illegally imported by the United States on an annual basis! American leaders allow this immoral travesty to transpire despite the fact that the uranium ore is *always* mined using slave labor. The hapless workers aren't allowed to wear protective clothing while in these mines and radioactive contamination kills them off rather quickly. The Russian slavemasters *intentionally* work these people to death! Anyone sent to one of these concentration camps knows they'll never walk out alive. Such camps can be found at Novaya Borovaya and Zheltyye Vody in the Ukraine. A number of Siberian uranium mining death camps are located in Krasnoyarsk.[18] Despite having knowledge of these horrible Communist extermination centers, no one speaks out! Leaders in the U.S., the rest of the Free world, and the Communist dominated United Nations choose to see no evil, hear no evil, speak no evil!

Soviet slave-mined limestone worth $2.2 million was illegally imported by the United States during the first five months of 1983. Limestone is not something the country needs, yet the Russians shipped it halfway around the world and were allowed to dump it on the American market! Interestingly enough, the many mines in Siberia and elsewhere in the Soviet Union exploit hundreds of thousands of Vietnamese captives as forced laborers.

Check the label when purchasing caviar for your next party or other social event.All Russian caviar imported by the United States is illegal! Their red caviar is processed by 6,000 female slave laborers! These women barely survive the inhumane conditions of a concentration camp on Shikotan Island—Soviet occupied Japanese territory. Slave laborers process black caviar in the Lenin plant located in Gur'ev,

Kazakh S.S.R. *19* Shockingly, Russian canned crab meat was the *only* slave-processed or made item ever banned from the U.S. under the 1930 Smoot-Hawley Tariff Act. This was briefly done from 1951 to 1961. *(20)*

Lithuanian sailor Simas Kudirka tried to defect by escaping to an American ship. Instead he was forcibly returned to the Communists! This young man was sent to Siberia for the crime of wanting to be free. Kudirka later tells of his experience: "The camp was so hard to reach— so remote in the mountains—that there was no escape. Once there'd been a forest but they'd used women prisoners to chop it down. It was so well guarded even a bird could not get in. And the cold was so intense [temperatures dropped to 55 degrees below zero] that a sparrow would drop from the sky because it could not fly.... There was an entire complex of concentration camps spread out for kilometers on end. It defies the imagination to think how many men were in them."[21]

We know that in the Soviet Union people are rounded up by the millions on charges of hooliganism and sent to forced labor camps under conditions worse, in many cases, than those in Hitler's concentration camps," charges Colorado's Senator Armstrong. "For the United States to buy the goods produced in such camps makes us accomplices to that forced labor."[22]

Imports From Soviet Puppet Dictatorships

"Each year we renew our resolve to support the struggle for freedom throughout the world by observing Captive Nations Week," said President Reagan. "It is a week in which all Americans are asked to remember that the liberties and freedoms they enjoy are denied many peoples. With this observance we hope to inspire those who struggle against military occupation, political oppression, Communist expansion, and totalitarian brutality." [23]

Despite such moving rhetoric, nothing is ever done to rescue the poor souls enslaved in the barbaric Iron Curtain dictatorships! Instead, their cruel Communist masters are rewarded by America with Most Favored Nation trade status. This allows them lower duty rates when their slave-produced merchandise are illegally imported by the United States! Supermarkets and variety stores have been selling illegally imported Russian crab meat and Polish hams since the Kennedy years. The same is true of baskets illegally imported from Communist Occupied Hungary and Yugoslavia. [24]

Communist Occupied Nicaragua has an all pervasive secret police network set up and run by experienced East German, Cuban, and Russian murder and mayhem specialists. Hundreds of millions of dollars worth of military hardware have been shipped by the Soviet Bloc to Nicaragua since 1979. Nicaraguan passports have been issued to terrorists from Europe, the Middle East, and Latin America. Such passports enable these radicals to travel in the U.S. without anyone knowing their true identities. In spite of this, illegal slave labor imports from Communist Occupied Nicaragua into the United States—primarily bananas, coffee, and meat—total approximately $200 million a year.[25]

What should have been a $5 million typewriter scandal was announced in the *Washington Post:* "Since 1978, the East German made Optima typewriters, the cheapest on the market, have been selling like hot cakes to the Pentagon. The General Services Administration . . . [illegally] bought some $5 million worth of Optimas with most going to the Army. What's more, the Treasury Department [might Soviet agent Harry Dexter White's protégés still be in charge?] approves of the East-West typewriter connection."[26]

It's incomprehensible that the Pentagon would buy *any* typewriters manufactured in Erich Honecker's East Germany! It's even more incredible that U.S. Army personnel would be using slave-made typewriters, illegally imported from a brutal Red dictatorship! Surely the entrenched bureaucrats in the General Services Administration know of the 300,000 member dreaded East German secret police apparatus! Surely they know that the enslaved East German citizens are held in bondage by the presence of 380,000 Soviet Army troops! Surely they know that those East German secret police specialists, so diligently working with the Communists in Nicaragua, aren't typewriter salesmen!

Many Americans stroll through stores such as J.C. Penney, looking for winter clothing when it starts getting cold. The most difficult garment to find, unfortunately, isn't one made by slave laborers in a Communist country. Instead, it would be one with a label saying "Made in USA." Rack after rack of coats were checked in the women's section of a J.C. Penney store. These coats contained labels indicating they were made in Romania, Yugoslavia, or Hungary—each a Captive Nation. All are Iron Curtain dictatorships! All are clones of Communist Occupied Russia! And all contain innumerable slave labor camps!

A stylish tan, three-piece business suit was found in the Penney men's department. The label said: "By George for J.C. Penney." A closer scrutiny revealed a smaller label: "Made in Poland." The suit was selling for a price comparable to those made in the United States. This in itself is ridiculous! After all, the suit was made inexpensively by Polish slave laborers. And it was illegally imported at special low duty rates, since Poland has been given Most Favored Nation trade status.

Even some of the better hotels in the United States inadvertently take part in supporting slave labor in Red dictatorships. Communist Occupied Czechoslovakia is economically aided by Atlanta's super elegant Hyatt Regency Ravina, off 285 loop. Under "Beers of the World" on their "Fizazz" or drink list can be found "Pilsner Urguell— Czechoslovakian for $3.50 a bottle.

Is there such a demand for beer made and bottled in a Communist police state that the Hyatt Regency management feels obliged to keep it stocked? Are there not equal or better quality beers readily available from free nations throughout the world? Or is it simply considered to be more "continental" to offer an alcoholic beverage illegally imported from a totalitarian cesspool?

The Czech people live in perpetual bondage under Gustav Husak's dictatorship. They are kept in line by a virulent secret police organization backed by 80,000 Russian troops. The tyrannical Communist leadership openly sanctions terrorism against the West. Fanatical religious persecution in Czechoslovakia is matched only by that found in Communist Occupied Albania and Bulgaria. Many of the jobs reserved for Czech slave laborers are life-threatening. One such task is the grinding and polishing of crystal and jewelry. The forced laborers inhale the glass dust as they work. No face masks or other protective measures are allowed. Glassware, jewelry, and Christmas tree ornaments have been sold in the United States ever since 1962, when the Kennedy Administration allowed them to be illegally imported.

The people of Communist Occupied Bulgaria live in constant fear under the iron fist of dictator Todor Zhivkov. They are kept in line by the most savage secret police organization in the Red Bloc. Large amounts of unneeded tobacco are illegally imported from the Bulgarian slave state. This is true despite the fact that more tobacco is already grown in the United States than can possibly be used!

Although all Communist tyrannies brazenly use slave labor in their textile and clothing industry, America still illegally imports their wares! None of these arrogant police states have textiles the United States needs. Atheistic totalitarian Soviet puppet regimes, from which raw textiles and finished clothing are illegally imported, include Communist Occupied Yugoslavia, Hungary, Poland, Zimbabwe, Czechoslovakia, and Romania.[27]

Communist Occupied Ethiopia should be ostracized by all civilized nations, for their official genocidal policies. Little is heard about the mass slaughter of 1.8 million men, women, and children the first 10 years the Reds were in power. Typical slave labor concentration camps abound throughout this pitiful country. In 1977-78 alone, over 200,000 Ethiopians were wantonly murdered in the streets. Citizens are shot without warning if out after curfew. The

Marxist government actually requires that a fee be paid by relatives to "cover the cost of the execution," before a loved one's body can be claimed. Despite the overwhelming evidence of a modern-day holocaust, the United States maintains a thriving annual $200 million trade with Ethiopia. Many Americans are unknowingly drinking illegally imported Ethiopian coffee for breakfast, since this is one of their major export items![28]

The dictator of enslaved Communist Occupied Angola is Jose Eduardo dos Santos. This rabid Red despot is kept in power by the presence of 45,000 soldiers on loan from Communist Occupied Cuba. Large numbers of Russian and East German "advisors" actually run the dictatorship. Meanwhile, Communist Occupied Russia has supplied this Red slave state with around $4 billion worth of military goodies since 1976. Yet, the United States foolishly and illegally imports 35 to 40 percent of all oil produced in the People's Republic of Angola. Why?

An extremely poor quality Romanian alarm clock can readily be found in department and discount stores all over the United States. These manual clocks are made by slave laborers! Communist Occupied Romania has the largest secret police network (proportionate to its population) of any Red dictatorship in the world. Nicolae Ceausescu is the tyrant who forced the removal of "useless" elderly people from his cities. Why? So his Communist regime wouldn't have to provide medical services! Yet the United States still sees fit to illegally import alarm clocks, tobacco products, and many other things from this Red tyranny!

Bread is rationed in the Romanian people's paradise. It's a national crime to feed crumbs to birds. Five years in a slave labor camp is given to citizens who purchase more than one months supply of flour, sugar, coffee, rice, and other foods. Why the shortages? The *New York Times* revealed: "A large chunk of farm output is exported. The United States Army is a regular buyer of Rumanian meat."[29]

"Safe-T" light bulbs can be purchased in most variety, department, hardware, and other stores nationwide.

Distributed by Action Tungsram, Inc., of East Brunswick, New Jersey, these light bulbs are less than half the price of those made in USA? Why? Because they're manufactured (using slave labor) in Communist Occupied Hungary! Interestingly enough, these light bulbs were made in a factory provided by Corning Glass—a well known American firm (Chapter 2)—and paid for by American taxpayers!

We've all seen the "Yugo" on television commercials. Many consider it to be a sorry excuse for an automobile, promoted at a relatively tiny sales price. Why so inexpensive? Because it's manufactured using slave labor in Communist Occupied Yugoslavia. And because it's a lemon! *Consumer Reports* called the Yugo a "barely assembled bag of nuts and bolts."[30] The American who owns a Yugo should feel right at home wearing slave made clothing. Try "The Highlander Flannel by Bud Berma," a winter shirt labeled: "Made in Yugoslavia." These are the kinds of things illegally imported into the United States, despite the fact that Red Yugoslavia uses abundant slave labor in its industries. And at least four major anti-American terrorist training camps can be found within its borders!

Imports From Communist Occupied China

"Today Communist China has the worst human rights record of any nation on earth," charges Professor John F. Cooper. "It is estimated that there are 20 million political prisoners there. Estimates . . . go as high as 50 million."[31]

In January 1979, President Carter granted diplomatic recognition to the People's Republic of China. This murderous Communist dictatorship was also granted Most Favored Nation status. Imports of Communist Occupied China's slave-made goods began to illegally pour into the United States. Considering the actual cost of producing this Chinese merchandise—plus the break they get on import duties—someone down the line reaps a tidy profit off brutal Red Chinese slave labor.

A number of reputable American toy manufacturers have their products made by slave laborers in Red China.

Coleco is one of the culprits. Their popular "Alf" doll is duly noted on the box to have been made either in South Korea (a free country) or China (a Communist slave state). Coleco's "Cabbage Patch Talking Kids" are, per their box, "Made in Hong Kong, China, Taiwan, or elsewhere as specified within." How can an American shopper tell the difference? A consumer is forced to go to the trouble of opening the sturdy cardboard carton and scrutinizing the stuffed toy's label. This is the only way to avoid purchasing a Communist Chinese slave-made Alf or Cabbage Patch doll! Who has time for this during the normal rush of shopping, or especially over the Christmas holidays?

The company illegally importing the popular Teddy Ruxpin stuffed animals pulls the same nefarious duplicity. The box containing the toy says they are made in such diverse places as Hong Kong, Taiwan, Korea, Thailand, or China (Communist). A parent or grandparent never really knows for certain if a Red slave-made product has been purchased until it's opened at home by the child.

The well-known Mattel company also plays the illegal Red Chinese import game in a big way. Their "Baby Tender Love" doll is made in Communist Occupied China. Mattel's "Lady Lovely Locks Doll" is a blend of good and bad. "Doll and comb made in Hong Kong" reveals the note on the colorful box. "Hey, that's fine," you say, "Hong Kong isn't a Communist slave labor nation." But wait—read on! "Costume, shoes and barrettes made in China."

Hasbro's lovely "Moon Dreamers" doll and animal set are also made in Communist Occupied China. Playskool, a subsidiary of Hasbro, came out with the "Dolly Surprise." This Red Chinese slave-made doll is promoted as having hair that "grows right before your eyes." This is the same company that made a fortune off American kids with their patriotic GI Joe toys!

"The Talking Mickey Mouse Show" from the Walt Disney Company can surely be trusted to have been made in the USA. After all, the famous Disney characters—Mickey, Donald, Goofy—are as American as Mom, the flag, and apple pie. But incredibly, according to the eye-catching carton, even good old Mickey is now manufactured in Communist Occupied China! The Red Chinese slave-made version of Mickey Mouse can be found at such places as Toys R Us, Sears, K-Mart, Target, and Wal-Mart. Wal-Mart is, by the way, trying to offset the deluge of Communist slave-made products. Their stores are inundated with signs saying "Buy American" in colorful, eye-catching red, white, and blue.

Even the popular fast-food chains get in on the action! Hardees sold the California Raisin soft toys. Wendy's promoted a "Special Edition Furskin" for $2.49 with the purchase of a hamburger, fries, etc. Colorful cardboard signs sat on Wendy's counters with an attached sample of "This week's Furskin." Sadly enough, the cute California Raisin soft toys and the Furskins, both favorites of children, are made with slave labor in Red China and illegally imported by American businesses!

Arby's offers an "Adventure Meal"—a small Arby's sandwich, order of fries, and a Pepsi—packaged in a colorful lunch box. Children love the "Adventure Meal" because it always includes a surprise toy. One such gift was a rubber version of the well known cartoon character, Yosemite Sam. Another was Tweety Bird. Shamefully, both come in a sealed plastic bag, boldly labeled "MADE IN CHINA."

Furskins originated in Cleveland, Georgia, from the same individual who created Cabbage Patch dolls. Yosemite Sam and Tweety Bird have been around for as long as most people can remember. Why does Warner Brothers (they own the copyright) allow such thoroughly American toy products to be contaminated by the wholesale use of Red Chinese slave labor?

Cracker Barrel is a popular chain in the Southeast. Each family restaurant has an adjoining country store where customers can nostalgically browse among early American antiques. Old-time candies, country hams, slabs of smoked bacon and the like are available for purchase. Many of their craft items—baskets, man-made flowers, etc.—would naturally be surmised to be the artistry of local folks. They're not! The labels indicate that much Cracker Barrel merchandise is made with Chinese slave labor!

While enjoying the marvelous food at the Cracker Barrel, children can color a picture using a small package of crayons given to them by a waitress. Even these crayons are made in Red China! The same has been found to be true in a restaurant chain called Po-Folks as well as others. But this certainly doesn't have to be the case. Crayons for kids at Quincy's Family Steak House and the unique Darryl's Restaurant chain are made in the USA!

"Double Grip" nails can be found in many American hardware stores. These inferior quality nails are packaged in distinctive yellow and blue boxes. Such nails are needlessly and illegally imported from Communist Occupied China. They're made with slave labor in one of thousands of brutal work camps.[32]

Pic 'n' Save stores carry quite a variety of illegal slave-made imports from the Red Chinese dictatorship. A few of their consumer-could-just-as-well-do-without items include cheap wicker-baskets, trinkets, and stuffed animals.[33]

"Equity" manual alarm clocks and "Spartus Comet 111" electric alarm clocks can be found in many variety and department stores. Both are cheaply crafted by slave laborers in Communist Occupied China's concentration camps.

Realistic looking plastic wreathes are widely used for decorating over the Christmas holidays. Many of these wreathes are made by Red Chinese slaves. Or, how about "China" labeled Christmas tree ornaments and various items for sprucing up the house while celebrating the birth of Christ? Then there's "Holiday Trim"—strings of red, silver, and gold beads, which carry the word "China" on the label. Sounds innocent enough doesn't it? Yet these Christmas decorating items were made in atheistic Communist Occupied China—in slave labor camps.

Sears has the usual selection of clothing from the People's Republic of China. Unfortunately, the same can be found in most other department and clothing stores. For example, the Sears stylish "Classic Fashion" women's jacket carries a "Made in China" label. Such jackets, although cut and sewn by slave laborers, are essentially the same price as those made in the USA.

The label on that good looking men's long-sleeve shirt proclaims: "Christopher Hart Exclusive Apparel For Tall Men." The price is comparable to other similar shirts in the store. A closer peek at the fine print reveals the reason it shouldn't be! This shirt was "Made in China"—in some slave labor camp! Carefully check the label on those popular Jordache designer jeans — some are made in Communist Occupied China!

There's an over-abundance of honey produced in America and subsidized by the government. Yet, the United States still illegally imports tons of honey from Communist Occupied China. Honey can be produced in the United States for about 55 cents a pound. In Communist China, using slave labor, honey is produced for only 2.3 cents per pound. This brutal Red slave state sent over 664,000 pounds of the sticky sweet stuff in 1978. By 1982, the U.S. was illegally and unnecessarily importing 7.6 million pounds of Red Chinese honey, as well as huge quantities of their slave grown tobacco.[34]

In 1980, the Carter Administration substantially increased the quota of illegal clothing imports for Communist Occupied China's slave masters. Red Chinese slave-made clothing and textiles illegally imported by the United States jumped an astounding 55 percent during Reagan's first quarter of 1986. Incredibly, this is over 100 times the import increase allowed for Taiwan! In fact, textile imports from America's free Chinese ally are limited to a yearly growth rate of only 0.5 percent![35] Common sense warns the average citizen that American leaders are aiding and abetting a dangerous Red enemy, while alienating a friend. Why?

What Can be Done to Stop the Importing of Slave-Made Goods?

What can be done to stop this shameful avalanche of slave labor goods illegally being imported into the United States by American companies? Senator William L. Armstrong (R-CO) declares: "A good start would be to simply enforce the law already on the books."[36]

The law clearly states: "All goods, wares, articles, and merchandise mined, produced or manufactured wholly or in part in any foreign country by . . . forced labor . . . shall not be entitled to entry at any of the ports of the United States, and the importation thereof is hereby prohibited . . . "[37]

"According to the law, which is quite clear, the U.S. Customs Service is required to open an investigation when it is contacted by *any* citizen who suspects a violation of the prohibition against slave-labor imports," explains investigative journalist and author Gary Allen. "If available evidence 'reasonably' indicates a violation, Customs is to report to Treasury and the goods are to be impounded. The only way such goods can be released is by the importer producing a certificate from the foreign exporter attesting that no forced labor was used in any stage of production or any component of the merchandise."[38]

This law hasn't been repealed! Neither is it being enforced! No one in the Federal bureaucracy seems willing to rock the boat. Banning the importation of slave made items from the Soviet Bloc and CommunistOccupied China is sacrilege in leftist Washington circles. Political pragmatists, outright Reds, "liberals," and other leftists (in various government agencies) drag their feet on the issue. Sir John Harrington nicely capsulizes the problem:

> *"Treason doth never prosper;*
> *what's the reason ?*
> *Why, if it prosper,*
> *none dare call it treason."*

Chapter 6

Vietnam — A Classic Example of Wholesale Treason

Traitor: "One who betrays his country . . . one guilty of treason."
Webster's New Twentieth Century Dictionary

Treason: "Betrayal of one's country to an enemy."
Webster's New World Dictionary

Willfully Aiding and Abetting the Enemy

Marine Lieutenant Robert G. LoPresti had to use worn-out equipment in a field hospital near Pleiku. Spare parts weren't available and wounded marines died unnecessarily as a result. Upon returning to the United States, LoPresti found the Communists were being supplied massive quantities of the same spare parts and equipment needed in Vietnam by American forces! He reveals: "The same machinery I couldn't get, the same equipment that would have saved the lives of those marines, was declared 'non-strategic' and shipped to the very countries that supplied the rifles and bullets that are killing our men! . . . I remember visiting the Sixty-Seventh Evacuation Hospital in Qui Nhon. Walking through the intensive-care ward, I saw dozens of soldiers who had been maimed and mutilated. They had lost arms or legs, they were covered with plastic and swathed in bandages stained deep red by their own blood. Most were in agonizing pain or under heavy sedation. I knew that many would not live and others would be crippled and disfigured for life. Seeing this bitter fruit of our government's madness, I wondered how . . . our politicians would try to explain to these men about sending 'non-strategic' items to an enemy that has pledged to destroy us."*1* The "politicians" never bothered! Nor did any of them intend to!

A new era in treason was begun within weeks after Senator Barry Goldwater (R-AZ) lost his Presidential bid in 1964. The radicalized Johnson Administration officially sanctioned a traitorous trip to wheel and deal for expanded business behind the Iron Curtain. Allen and Scott reported: "More than 200 U.S. businessmen . . . made the journey to Moscow . . . a few U.S. firms with a big assist from the State and Commerce Department [sent] representatives for extended stays of one to three months,"*2*

The Honorable Ezra Taft Benson correctly charged: "in the waiting rooms of the Kremlin, American businessmen dream of personal gains and profits while thousands of American boys in Vietnam are slain by Communist bullets made in the USSR." *3*

Peter Stark is a Green Beret who lost both legs in combat against Communist Occupied North Vietnam. He charges: "We have assured . . . the Soviet Union and its satellite nations . . . who supply 80 percent of all the North Vietnamese was material, that we will not interfere in their shipment of war goods to the North Vietnamese enemy. At the same time . . . we have continued our policy of. . . sending strategic materials to the Soviet enemy. For example, in 1966, the United States sent the Soviet Union the entire technical specification that they needed to build a glycerol plant.... Specifically, in Vietnam, glycerol is used as a detonator in booby traps. Over 50 percent of all American casualties suffered in Vietnam have come from booby traps." *4*

Yes, while the war in Vietnam raged, the United States merrily aided, fed, traded with, loaned money to, and armed America's avowed Communist enemies throughout the world. American officials, from the President on down, knew all along that Communist Occupied Russia and her satellite clones were helping Ho chi Minh! The Communist *People's World* reported: "The dense AA gun and missile network and the sophisticated radar network . . . are all supplied by the USSR."5 According to Professor David Nelson Rowe, "The Russians supplied heavy weapons including surface-to-air missiles, tanks and artillery, as well as oil, all shipped into North Vietnam by ocean transport." 6 America's leaders also knew that four man teams of Russian Spetsnaz commandoes spent time in Vietnam testing a new 7.62 mm sniper rifle by shooting U.S. soldiers.

"The USSR is heavily committed to helping North Vietnam in its aggressive designs against South Vietnam" charged Congressman Glenard P. Lipscomb (R-CA)." . . . the Soviet Union has trained North Vietnamese pilots to fly the MIG-21 Russian jet fighter . . . Russian trawlers are . . . located off Guam to provide early warnings of B-52 strikes on Viet Cong concentrations in South Viet Nam [captured Vietcong boasted how they always had a two hour advance notice of a B-52 bombing attack] . . . Does it make any sense to help equip and feed the Soviets who are helping the aggressors kill our soldiers in Vietnam?" 7

Tons of food and equipment were being sent by ship to North Vietnam. Some of the supplies included "tractors, cables and paper, medical equipment and canned goods, flour . . . [as] part of the aid rendered by the Soviet people . . . "8 In addition, Communist Occupied Russia supplied Hanoi with trucks, road building machinery, small ships, transport planes, amphibious vehicles, machine guns, mortars, grenade launchers, rockets, helicopters and jet fighters.

Poland, Czechoslovakia, Romania, and other Soviet slave-state clones also supplied the North Vietnamese enemy with war goods. Their contributions included such things as rifles, ammunition, explosives, and missile launchers used to kill American military men. Senator Clifford P. Hansen (R-WY) warned: "American servicemen are dying this minute in Vietnam, killed by weapons which are the direct result of the various forms of trade that we have fostered and encouraged with Communist Satellite countries."*9*

Communist Occupied Russia was supplied with the technical data necessary to build three huge fertilizer plants. Meanwhile, our Soviet "friends" were shipping over 150,000 tons of fertilizer to Communist Occupied North Vietnam.*10* The Vietnamese Reds in turn were slaughtering American boys! Yet another outrageously criminal fertilizer plant deal (Chapter 3) was later consummated between the USSR and the Nixon Administration! All this was taking place while Russian dictator Leonid Brezhnev openly acknowledged his active support of the North Vietnamese gangsters! Brezhnev boasted that Hanoi would have been unable to keep up its heroic struggle . . . for so many years without the active and effective assistance of the Soviet Union, Poland and other Socialist countries."[11]

According to the Department of Commerce, there was a dramatic 44 percent jump in American trade with Communist Bloc dictatorships during the first half of 1966. These are the same criminal regimes who were supplying North Vietnam with better than 85 percent of their war-making capability! [12]

The Export-Import Bank guaranteed a $20 million loan to Communist Occupied Romania. Why? Because tyrannical slave master Nicolae Ceausescu wanted to buy an oil refinery! *13* Leftist Senator William Fulbright (D-AR) parroted the Kremlin propaganda line: "Romania has demonstrated its interest in improving relations with the United States."*14* Just the day before, on July 25, 1965, Red Romania publicly declared its support for the North Vietnamese and Chinese Communists who were killing and maiming American military personnel on the battlefield. According to Senator Strom Thurmond (R-SC): "the Romanian Communist Congress, meeting with representatives of Red China and Soviet Russia, passed a resolution condemning the United States 'acts of open wart in Vietnam."[15]

Johnson pushed hard to give Communist occupied Eastern European countries Most Favored Nation trade benefits. He also demanded fewer restrictions on exporting strategic military-related items. The President wanted more materials available for shipping to a variety of hate-America, slave dictatorships! LBJ made this treasonous statement: "I have just today signed a determination that will allow the Export-ImportBank to guarantee commercial credits to four additional Eastern European countries—Poland and Hungary, Bulgaria and Czechoslovakia.... We do not intend to let our differences on Vietnam or elsewhere prevent us from exploring all opportunities."[16]

"Our differences" noted by the Commander-in-Chief of America's Armed Forces just happened to be an undeclared war with over 200,000 American casualties! And each of the above mentioned Communist nations was vocally and materially aiding the North Vietnamese enemy! Dictator Todor Zhivkov bragged how "the Bulgarian government has extended and will continue to extend . . . material aid."[17] Hungary's despotic Janos Kadar declared: "We are fighting against U.S. aggression in Vietnam and will go on helping our Vietnamese brothers until their cause is crowned by ultimate victory."[18] Communist Occupied Czechoslovakia broadcast: "The entire [Communist] world has joined to provide Vietnam with all conceivable assistance."[19]

"After Congress had established a forbidden list of hundreds of items, nobody in America could ship to any Communist country sending supplies to the enemy," notes Senator Karl Mundt: "President Lyndon Johnson, on October 12, 1966, by Executive Order, in defiance of the expressed intentions and desires of Congress—opened up for unlimited and unlicensed shipment over 400 items of supplies to Russia and her satellites in Europe."[20] The list of crucial military supplies no longer classed as strategic was incredible! Cleared for export to enemy Communist regimes were such things as scrap metals, aluminum, grease, lubricating oil, diesel fuel, machine tools, tires and tubes, shipboard and ground radar, aircraft parts and navigation equipment, electric motors, synthetic rubber, steel tubing, copper cable, diethylene glycol (used to make explosives and liquid propellants for rockets), precision grinding machines, drilling machines, electrical machinery and diesel engines.

Communist Occupied Poland and Romania had previously been allowed special trade benefits by the Johnson Administration. Red Czechoslovakia, Hungary, Albania, Yugoslavia, Bulgaria and the Russians were all now to be recipients of the government's treasonous trade activities. The Commerce Department classed strategic items as "peaceful goods which may be freely exported [to enemy Red dictatorships] without any risks to the United States' national interest."*21* Here are more of the goodies made "non-strategic" with the stroke of the pen: rifle cleaning compounds, gasoline, petroleum drilling and production equipment, turbines, rocket and jet engines, generators, computers, ball bearings, rubber processing machines, railway equipment (trains, etc.), pipeline compressors, radiation detection instruments and radio beacon transmitters.*22* Soviet missiles directed by American computers downed many U.S. fighter planes and helicopters in Vietnam.

Such a thing during World War II would have been called treason in no uncertain terms! What exactly would you call it today?

Two weeks later, our new and favored trade partners were in the news again. According to the *New York Times:* "The Soviet Union and its allies agreed at the conference of their leaders in Moscow last week to grant North Vietnam assistance in material and money amounting to about one billion dollars.... Poland's contribution will be thirty million dollars."[23]

The *Chicago Tribune* had to this to say about America's Polish pal: "Weapons of the Polish armed forces are being shipped from Stettin harbor in Poland in ever increasing quantities to North Vietnam . . . While on one side of the Stettin harbor American wheat is being unloaded from freighters, on the other side of the same harbor weapons are loaded that are being used to kill American soldiers . . . The Poles receive the wheat from the U.S. on credit, and they in turn ship their weapons to North Vietnam on credit."[24]

Ambassador Averill Harriman was a long-term leftist and apologist for the Communists. He was America's first representative at the Paris-based Vietnam surrender negotiations in 1966. While there, Harriman made his views clear regarding aid and trade with Communist countries. He said that all foes of Red trade were "bigoted, pig-headed people who don't know what's going on in the world. "[25]

Former POW and Medal of Honor winner Rear Admiral James Stockdale notes: "It was Averill Harriman who insisted on keeping the torture evidence under wraps in the interest of furthering his 'delicate' negotiations on the prisoner's behalf, all of which came to nothing."[26]

Congressman Lipscomb revealed that the Johnson Administration had "clamped a tight lid on information showing just how much and what type of aid is being sent to Hanoi by the Communist bloc."[27] Why the big secret? Because by mid 1967, Communist Occupied Russia had contributed $2 billion worth of war materials to North Vietnam. Other Red bloc satellites are known to have sent at least $1 billion more in military aid.

There were nearly 10,000 Soviet-supplied anti-aircraft guns installed in North Vietnam. More than 30 Soviet-supplied SAM batteries, each capable of firing six surface-to-air missiles, were operational.[28] Not only did the Russians provide the weapons, they also trained the North Vietnamese military to more efficiently kill Americans. *The Reporter* disclosed: "The Soviet experts train their students in or near Hanoi, then go with them to the actual battle stations to see how they do under fire. More coaching follows on the spot, so it is almost inevitable that the Soviet officers actually man the radar screens and the missile launching devices." [29]

General John P. McConnell, USAF Chief of Staff, said North Vietnam's Russian-supplied air defense system was "the greatest concentration of anti-aircraft weapons that has ever been known in the history of defense of any town or in any area of the world."*30* Congressman Lipscomb has this to say: "Practically every American plant . . . shot down over North Vietnam has fallen victim to Soviet-made and Soviet-supplied surface-to-air missiles or anti-aircraft batteries. American planes have been tracked by Soviet [American] radar, American ground forces have been subjected to substantial casualties caused by Soviet and East European [American] equipment; and the Vietcong and North Vietnamese have been supplied in the South by trucks made in these countries [in American factories]."*31*

Ships from Communist Occupied Russia and Red Bloc slave-labor tyrannies off-loading in Haiphong Harbor were immune from being bombed or even fired upon! According to the AP wire service: "The Pentagon . . . has given North Vietnam official word that port facilities of Haiphong are safe from attack . . . *32* Their safety was *guaranteed* by President Johnson! Communist ships came at the rate of one every other day. Many of the Soviet ships bringing war supplies to North Vietnam were built by the United States! Among them were the *Tashkent, Bakuriani, Sevastopol, Voybou, Kubyshev, Ala-Tau, Suchan* and the *Kura.33* Five of these vessels were World War II Liberty ships! They had been loaned to Communist Occupied Russia under the Lend Lease program. The Soviets never bothered returning them!

On September 23, 1967, Communist Occupied Russia promised even more "aircraft, anti-aircraft guns, ground-to-air missiles, artillery pieces, small arms, ammunition, and also equipment, vehicles, products and other goods . . . "*34* Here we have American military men being slaughtered in Vietnam by enemy soldiers who are armed, fed, and trained by Communist Occupied Russia. This slave labor dictatorship was at the time being armed by the United States (Chapter 1, 2); obtaining loans from the United States (Chapter 3); being fed by the United States (Chapter 4); and being given preferential trade treatment by the United States (Chapter 5)!

Without monumental support from the Communist Bloc, North Vietnam's ability to fight a war would have collapsed! Without monumental American aid, trade, and loans to this same Communist Bloc, Russia and her Red-slave satellites' ability to assist North Vietnam would have collapsed! The United States was sending untold thousands of tons of strategic military goods to each and every one of these homicidal regimes!

In 1967, America's Polish "friends" were unable to even pay the interest on outstanding loans of $17 million. Johnson wanted to ease "the burden of Polish debts to the United States."*35* In other words, he wanted to let the Red slave labor dictatorship off the hook! On April 12, 1967, the State Department announced it had worked out a deal with the despots running Communist Occupied Poland to forgive their debts. Former Representative Paul Findley (R-OH) charged: "By relieving Poland of the need to pay the $17 million debt in dollars, our Government has thus enabled Poland to aid the enemy at a level it otherwise could not afford."*36* For example, also on April 12, 1967, Polish merchant ships were seen unloading military supplies in North Vietnam's Haiphong Harbor! At the same time, the Communist government of Poland announced a mammoth demonstration to show support of the Communist cause in Vietnam.[37]

Another traitorous activity was unearthed by Congressman Edward J. Derwinski (R-IL): " . . . U.S. Army engineers are working on a highway over which supplies could move from Russia to North Vietnam. More specifically, the highway in question is being constructed under the foreign aid program across Afghanistan and thus would be a link between Russia and North Vietnam."*38* The highway was designed by Americans! Its construction supervised by Americans! It was paid for using American dollars! Shockingly, this highway was actually built while Americans were fighting and dying in the dictatorship the highway was going to; in a war being managed and financed by the dictatorship the highway was coming from. And in December, 1979, Soviet troops invading Afghanistan were transported on this very same highway in military vehicles built in the American-designed-supplied-and-financed Kama River truck factory in Russia (Chapter 2, 3).

Dangerous security risk Nicholas deB Katzenbach (Chapter 9) was Johnson's Attorney General. Speaking in reference to trade with Communist dictatorships, which were arming North Vietnam, Katzenbach declared that such trade was "good business, good policy, and good sense."*39* The Communist-organized and-led street revolutionaries were closer to the truth than they realized with their slogan: "Hey, hey, LBJ! — How many boys did you kill today?"

Exports of strategic goods to enemy Communist dictatorships surpassed $100 million during the first six months of 1968. Around $20 million worth was food and clothing. The rest were highly sophisticated goods of a technical, military, and military-related nature. The kinds of military items sent to the Reds were protected by a "Top Secret" classification!

In 1968, America's extensive food commodity exports alone (to Communist Occupied Russia) were averaging an incredible $4 million per week.*40* A number of Congressmen, including Karl E. Mundt (R-SD), H. R. Gross (R-IA) and James B. Utt (R-CA) were against Johnson's treasonous giveaways to the Communists. Said Senator Peter H. Dominick (R-CO): "Administration pressures on Congress for trade expansion with the Communist-controlled countries of Eastern-Europe, including the Soviet Union, multiply day by day.... at the very time when our men in Vietnam are being killed by Soviet weapons."*41*

Johnson and Nixon both criminally undermined anti-Communist allies of the United States, while at the same time glorifying Red dictatorships. For example, friendly and free Rhodesia volunteered to send troops to assist the U.S. in Vietnam. The offer was rejected by leftist American policy makers! All trade with America's Rhodesian ally was barred by Johnson.*42* On March 17, 1970, Nixon further betrayed Rhodesia by shutting down the American Consulate! All during this time, LBJ and Nixon hypocritically expanded trade with Communist Occupied Russia and other Red enemies, who were openly supplying Communist Occupied North Vietnam.

Richard M. Nixon said as a Presidential candidate: "As all Americans bitterly know, the Soviets have been and still are the arsenal and the trainers of the North Vietnamese and have escalated this jungle battle into a major war."*43* In November of 1971, Nixon the President sent his Commerce Secretary to Moscow to work out the details of a $2 *billion* strategic trade deal with Communist Occupied Russia. According to Secretary of Commerce Maurice Stans: "We have eliminated some 1,800 items from the restrictions against sale to the Soviet Union, and that process is still continuing."*44* They could now be sold to the USSR and other enemy countries in the Communist Bloc. Included were even more priceless electronic equipment, tooling, and machinery that the Russian Bear desperately needed for the production of war goods!

After Vietnam—the Rewards

While campaigning for the Presidency, James Earl Carter said nothing about the POWs left behind in Southeast Asia, after Henry Kissinger (an identified Kremlin espionage agent) and his leftist cohorts had shut down the war. Nor did this pretentious "born again Christian" express any sympathy for the armless, legless, blind, or otherwise mutilated heroes who made it back and ended up in VA hospitals. Instead, he shamelessly declared: "During my first week in office, I would issue pardons to all Vietnam defectors."*45* Yes, the traitors and cowards who ran —and left their fellow Americans to fight, to die, to suffer capture by the bestial Communist enemy—were rewarded by this President Carter couldn't wait but a day. His first official act as President was to announce a "full, complete and unconditional pardon" on January 21, 1977 for all Vietnam draft-dodgers. He even went so far as to upgrade the discharges of military men who had not served honorably in Vietnam.

Jane Fonda's most despicable deeds took place during the summer of 1972. She visited Communist Occupied North Vietnam and made Tokyo Rose type broadcasts over Radio Hanoi.[46] USAF Colonel George E. Day charges: "When I was a prisoner of war in North Vietnam, Tom Hayden and Jane Fonda went on Radio Hanoi and called for American soldiers to throw down their weapons and stop fighting.... Clearly Tom Hayden and Jane Fonda committed acts of treason against the United States during a time of war."[47] Sam Johnson spent seven years in the infamous Hanoi Hilton, where many American fliers were incarcerated. This Texas State Representative will never forget hearing Fonda's "treasonous" broadcasts urging Americans to quit fighting. He speaks for many: "I don't think there's any apology that can make up for the things she did."[48]

Hanoi Jane sat at the controls of a North Vietnamese anti-aircraft gun. She peered through the sights while posing for propaganda pictures and expressed her "solidarity" with the Communist soldiers manning the weapon. The Benedict Arnold of Beverly Hills forced herself on American POWs and tried to get them to make statements in support of the Communist-led "peace" movement. POWs who refused to talk to Hanoi Jane were tortured and severely beaten. So were those who did listen but were not persuaded by her rhetorical garbage.[49]

Navy Lieutenant Commander David Hoffman revealed how the North Vietnamese used torture in order to force him to meet with Fonda. Accompanying Hanoi Jane was former Attorney General Ramsey Clark (Chapter 11, 16)! Hoffman recalls: "I had a broken arm. It was in a cast. I was hung by that broken arm several times and allowed to drop at the end of a rope from a table which was kicked out from under me."[50]

The *Trenton Times* tells the story of "a POW who had agreed to meet with some other Americans in the 'peace' movement. The 'peace' people commanded the POW to confess to war crimes. When he refused, repeatedly and adamantly, he heard a 'peace' person suggest to his captors that 'this young man needs to be straightened out in his thinking." "He was hung by his wrists until an arm pulled from its shoulder socket. . . . Other prisoners suffering similar abuse also were made to suffer Jane Fonda's voice: The North Vietnamese piped into the cells recordings in which she urged prisoners to actively oppose U.S. policy, and told the world how well the prisoners were being treated."[52]

Hanoi Jane Fonda returned from North Vietnam after two full weeks of socializing with her murderous hosts. This traitor and her husband, Tom Hayden, had deliberately betrayed America's fighting men and their country to the Communist enemy. Hayden blatantly lied when he claimed that American POWs weren't tortured. He declared: "They were the best treated prisoners in any war in history."[53] And Hanoi Jane blatantly lied when she agreed! Returning POWs contested this with firsthand experiences of brutality, torture, and murder. Hayden, speaking for himself and Hanoi Jane, called the POWs, "liars, hypocrites and pawns . . .."[54]

James Ray of Conroe, Texas, declared: "I would personally challenge that young lady to look at the scars still visible on my arms from the tortures and tell me to my face that I'm a liar and a hypocrite."[55] Chief Warrant Officer Roy E. Zeigler II spent five years in a North Vietnamese prison. He responded: "Liars, hypocrites and pawns are we? . . . Men died at the hands of their captors and you have the audacity to say we were the best treated prisoners in any war in history."[56]

Former Congressman Robert H. Steele (R-CT) nominated Oscar-winning Hanoi Jane for a special award: "The rottenest, most miserable performance by any one individual American in the history of our country.... Where does she get her colossal gall? I wonder if she would dare to make her charges to the faces of those men who were beaten with rifle butts in the jungle or to the captured airman who was tied down with wire while ants swarmed over his body until he thought he would be eaten alive?"[57]

"She and others like her were traitors," charges Lieutenant Colonel James Thompson, for almost nine nightmarish years a POW, "and I see no reason why she shouldn't be hung for it!"[58]

Congressman Robert J. Huber (R-MI) was outraged at the behavior of Fonda. He stated: "Examined from the evidentiary focus of a grand jury, the testimony of my colleagues establishes sufficient factual allegations to support indictments against Jane Fonda on the ground of conspiracy and under the Sedition Act (18 U.S.C. 2387)."[59]

But such indictments were never to come! Hanoi Jane got off scot-free! She was never even brought to trial. In fact, she wasn't even charged with anything! Why? How could she or anyone else do so much harm to her country and still get away with it? Her rewards? Over and above a Hollywood Oscar, in a personal affront to every American veteran, Hanoi Jane Fonda was invited to attend a White House reception on November 17, 1977. Carter honored her with this a little more than five years after she had pulled her traitorous shenanigans in Hanoi during 1972!

Newsweek, a magazine not unfriendly to Fonda, called her "a modern day LaPasionaria, if not quite yet a Mother Bloor."[60] This should give everyone a clue about Fonda's politics, should there be any question. LaPasionaria was a fanatical Red leader during the Communist insurrection in Spain—misleadingly called the Spanish Civil War. Ella Reeva "Mother" Bloor was a revered Communist during the 1930s in the United States. She was the mother of Harold Ware, an important Kremlin espionage agent. Ware had been sent to America by Stalin to direct the initial penetration of the government through the Department of Agriculture (Chapter 13).

Thomas Emmett Hayden is one of the few leftist revolutionaries in the United States whose record of treasonous acts and traitorous deeds exceeds those of his radicalized wife. Hayden was a founder of the subversive

Students for a Democratic Society, parent organization of the Weather Underground, a Communist anti-American terrorist group. Charged J. Edgar Hoover: "The aim of the SDS attack is to smash first our educational structure, then our economic system, then, finally our government itself."[61] One of Hayden's criminal cohorts was Bernadine Dohrn, an SDS official who called herself a "revolutionary Communist."[62] Jerry Rubin was another Red whose foundation was given a tax exempt status by the Nixon Administration to shelter his earnings.[63]

Hayden had been to Hanoi with Communist Party leader Herbert Aptheker and others, long before Jane Fonda had even heard of the place. Evidently well-connected, this radical moved about freely throughout the Red Bloc nations, while Ho Chi Minh's Communists were killing American boys. He was a professional agitator, who led the Communist-organized riots at Columbia University, in April and May of 1968; and directed the violent Red demonstrations at the 1968 Democratic National Convention in Chicago. Hayden was convicted under the anti-riot provisions of the Civil Rights Act. Although sentenced to five years in prison and given a $5,000 fine, his conviction was conveniently reversed by a federal judge.[64]

Tom Hayden would have been hanged for treason during World War II for doing the things he did while the Vietnam War raged. Both he and Fonda were unquestionably responsible for the further suffering and torture of American POWs. Says former POW, USAF Colonel George E. Day: "He's a traitor to this great nation and deserves to be treated as one."[65] Instead, "The radical bomb-throwing leader of the violent SDS"[66] was warmly welcomed by President Carter in the White House oval office, during February 1978. Hayden tells how Carter said "he was proud to meet me and started talking about the contributions that I had made to the country."[67]

Radical leftist Massachussets Senator John Forbes Kerry, who later was to hold sham hearings on behalf of the POWs, was at one time a leading activist with the ultraradical Vietnam Veterans Against the War. Kerry-led pro-Vietcong demonstrations welcomed "revolutionary Communists." According to the *Boston Herald Traveler,* the demonstrations were "characterized by an abundance of Vietcong flags, clenched fists raised [a symbolic Communist gesture], and placards plainly bearing legends in support of China, Cuba, the USSR, North Korea and the Hanoi government."68 When asked about Communist participation in his shameless anti-American efforts, Kerry said it was "not relevant." Nguyen khac Vien, a North Vietnamese propagandist, said this: "Our country has no capability to defeat you on the battlefield. But war is not decided by weapons so much as national will....We will win this war on the streets of New York."69 Kerry and his fellow radical leftist company saw to it that this was exactly what happened!

This shameful leftist appeared on "Meet the Press" and insultingly called American leaders "war criminals." Kerry falsely accused American fighting men of committing "all kinds of atrocities" in Vietnam. In 1984, this same anti-American misfit was amply rewarded by the voters of Massachusetts. He became their junior United States Senator. True to form, his subsequent traitorous support of the Red Sandinistas in Communist Occupied Nicaragua earned him the nickname, "The Senator from Managua." According to Senator Barry Goldwater (R-AZ), Kerry had violated the Logan Act by privately negotiating with the Communists.70 Yet he was never punished! Why?

Yes, the rewards for being an anti-American, pro-Communist Vietcong supporter were great! Many traitors who had treasonously aided and abetted the Communist enemy were well taken care of by the very government they so vocally despised. Just a few years before, these radicals were in the streets, leading treasonous demonstrations in support of the country's battlefield enemy! Shortly thereafter, these unkempt hippies were then cleaned up and were avidly recruited for important positions in the Carter Administration.

For example, President James Earl Carter's most influential advisor was British-born psychiatrist Peter G. Bourne. This radical was a promoter of anti-American causes from the time of his arrival in the United States, in 1957. Ironically, Bourne, a reputed drug user himself, became Director of the Office of Drug Abuse Policy and Special Advisor to the President for Health Issues. He took a leading part in Tom Hayden's Communist-run demonstrations, during the 1968 Democratic National Convention in Chicago. Carter's "closest friend in the world" was also a close pal of leftist John Kerry. He co-founded the violence-prone, pro-Vietcong Vietnam Veteran's Against the War. This Communist group undertook paramilitary operations and engaged in rioting during the Republican National Convention in Miami.

Mary King, Bourne's militant leftist wife was Carter's top female appointee. She had been "communications coordinator" for Marxist Stokely Carmichael's Student Non-Violent Coordinating Committee. This radical became Deputy Director of ACTION, under Samuel Winfred Brown.

Brown was a Harvard Divinity School dropout and an anti-American pro-Vietcong activist. This leftist openly declared in 1969 that he was all for a Communist victory in Vietnam. He worked hard for the defeat of his own nation! According to some authorities, Brown's efforts in behalf of the enemy, had the United States been in a declared war, would have resulted in his execution for treason! Yet, both the Constitutional definition of treason, as well as the Federal statutes, mention nothing about *only* in cases of "a declared war." Sam Brown was well rewarded for his enthusiastic support of Ho Chi Minh and the Vietnamese Reds. He became Carter's $52,000-a-year head of ACTION, an umbrella agency which ran the Peace Corps and VISTA. From here Brown proceeded to give outrageous grants to his various pro-Red cronies!

According to Margery A. Tabankin's resume: "She was also active in the anti-war movement, and visited American prisoners of war and government officials in North

Vietnam."*71* Tabankin took part in interrogations of American POWs who were imprisoned and tortured by the North Vietnamese Communists! Patrick Buchanan wrote: "Merge junketed to Hanoi at the height of the war, while American POWs were down the street at the Hanoi Hilton being tortured in Uncle Ho's prisons.... Today, this Axis Sally of the Vietnam War takes home a higher federal salary than almost all of the young American pilots accused of war crimes."*72* Tabankin's treasonous role in working on behalf of the North Vietnamese enemy should have warranted her execution for treason! And at the very least it should have prohibited her from *ever* holding a government job! Yet she was also nicely rewarded for her anti-American pro-Viet Cong efforts. One of radical Sam Brown's close activist pals, this traitor was placed in charge of ACTION education programs.

Quite a number of other anti-American, pro-Hanoi activists could be found implanted throughout the Carter Administration. Such radicals include Arabella Martinez, Assistant Secretary for Human Development in HEW. Another was James A. Joseph, Under Secretary of the Interior. While working for the Irwin-Miller-Sweeney Foundation, Joseph had channeled finances to Communist revolutionaries during the 1960s. Dangerous leftist Alex P. Mecure became Assistant Secretary of Agriculture for Rural Development. Mecure was once on the board of directors of the radical Center for Community Change, which gave birth to the anti-CIA *Counter-Spy* magazine. This publication was directly responsible for the exposure and assassination by Communist terrorists of CIA agent Richard Welch, in Greece (Chapter 16). Mecure's group also spun off the tax exempt Youth Liberation Project (once headed by Margery Tabankin) which trained young people in murder techniques and in the latest arson methods.

Harvard radical James M. Fallows, a coward, was editor of the leftist *Washington Monthly* magazine. He bragged about how he'd faked his draft-board physical "because . . . I was desperately afraid of being killed."*73* His leftist counselors had illegally advised him and his anti-war pals that "disruptive behavior at the examination . . . obstructed the smooth operation of the criminal war machine."74 Fallows proudly tells how many in his group "wore red arm bands and stop-the-war buttons . . . most chanted the familiar words 'Ho, Ho, Ho Chi Minh/NLF Is Gonna Win!'"75 These radicals did everything possible to disrupt the examinations, including throwing warm urine into the faces of orderlies! Here we find an *unprosecuted* Vietnam draft-dodger being rewarded with an influential, high-paying job, as Carter's chief speechwriter!

Hendrick Hertzberg was a contributing editor of *Win* magazine. This was a publication of the "socialist" War Resisters League, which works closely with the Soviet World Peace Council in support of Red terror groups worldwide. Hertzberg's Communist bias was clearly revealed in 1974: "It would be undeniably 'better' for the United States alone to be destroyed than for the Soviet Union, Europe and much of the rest of the world to be destroyed as well."76 In May 1976, while actively supporting the Communist enemy in Vietnam, he said: "I welcome their victory." Despite the horrible atrocities accompanying the Communist occupation of South Vietnam, Hertzberg said the Red takeover "was a moral victory" and "a victory for something honorable in the human spirit."77 Incredibly, this anti-American misfit was presented with a gift of $32,500-a-year to assist Fallows in writing speeches for the President!

Dangerous leftist revolutionary John Froines was one of the notorious Chicago Seven. He was a riot team pal of Communist Abbe Hoffman, Jerry Rubin, and Rennie Davis. They and Tom Hayden planned the violent disruptions at the 1968 Democratic National Convention. Froines boldly boasted to a mob of unwashed, anti-American, pro-Hanoi fanatics in the nation's capitol that he'd come to Washington to close down the government! This pro-Communist, Vietcong supporter also ended up with a soft job in the

Carter Administration. He was placed in charge of the Office of Toxic Substances at OSHA.

During the Vietnam War, radical leftist Senator Edmund Muskie (D-ME) audaciously defended the Communist-led, pro-Hanoi demonstrators who defiantly waved Vietcong flags. In March 1970, he said: "These people are not traitors! They are patriots!"[78] Ignoring the thousands of young Americans who had been butchered in Vietnam, he coldly commented that a Communist takeover "doesn't bother me." Muskie (CFR) was appropriately rewarded by Carter when he replaced another radical leftist, Cyrus Vance (CFR), as Secretary of State (Chapter 11).

The four leftists primarily responsible for the treasonous *Pentagon Papers* mess—Paul Warnke (Chapter 11), Daniel Ellsberg (Chapter 11), Leslie Gelb, and Morton Halperin—were all members of the Council on Foreign Relations. Ellsberg was a protégé of identified Soviet spy Henry Kissinger,[79] since his student days at Harvard. The respected Paris financial weekly, *Valaurs Actuelles* pulled no punches when they openly charged that Ellsberg also was a Communist espionage agent![80] On May 16, 1973, Warnke denied any involvement in Ellsberg's theft of the Papers. He was the compiler and later admitted that his copy was the one Ellsberg had. The *Pentagon Papers* were a collection of top secret military and intelligence data on the Vietnam War. Some highly sensitive portions were marked "For the Eyes of the President Only". Ellsberg's theft and release of these papers gave the Communists a virtual blueprint that would guarantee America's defeat in Vietnam. Along with such devastating information, the Red enemy was given the secret codes being used by the U.S. Interestingly, Soviet intelligence had copies of the *Pentagon Papers* almost a year prior to their publication in the *New York Times!* It's not difficult to guess where they got them! Nevertheless, Paul Warnke was nicely rewarded by Carter. This dangerous leftist became head of the Arms Control and Disarmament Agency and Chief SALT negotiator!

Part II

Are There Not Traitors Among Us?

"Whoever, owing allegiance to the United States, levies war against them or adheres to their enemies, giving them aid and comfort within the United States or elsewhere, is guilty of treason and shall suffer death, or be imprisoned not less than five years and fined not less than $10,000; and shall be incapable of holding any office under the United States."
U.S. Code, Title 18, Section 23[81]

"Whoever, owing allegiance to the United States and having knowledge of the commission of any treason against them, conceals and does not, as soon as may be, disclose and make known the same to the President or to some judge or the United States, or to the Governor or to some judge or justice of a particular state, is guilty of misprision of treason, and shall be fined not more than $1000 or imprisoned not more than 7 years or both."
U.S. Code, Title 18, Section 2382

Chapter 7

A Peek at Internal Security

Traitor: "One who helps the enemies of his country."
The New Horizon Ladder Dictionary

Treason: "The crime of giving aid or comfort to the enemies of one's government."
The American College Dictionary

"Since World War II, we have read and heard about the Cold War abroad. Few Americans realize that we are engaged in an even more desperate Cold War with Communism at home," declares the Honorable Martin Dies (D-TX), for seven years Chairman of the House Committee on Un-American Activities. "The extent of our losses abroad is enormous. But, whatever the state of our defeats beyond our borders, they are paled by the losses at home.... We are at least pretending to fight Communism abroad. At home there isn't even a pretense."[1]

J. Edgar Hoover made this observation: "The Communist threat from without must not blind us to the Communist threat from within. The latter is reaching into the very heart of America through its espionage agents and a cunning, defiant, and lawless Communist Party, which is fanatically dedicated to the Marxist cause of world enslavement and destruction of the foundations of our Republic."*2*

Intelligence specialist Frank Capell has this to say: "Before the election of Franklin Delano Roosevelt . . . Communists . . . were dealt with by the local police under state laws. They were prosecuted . . . and often deported. But, with the arrival of the New Deal, Communists were permitted to move into key positions . . . and began to help shape our national policies and programs. They had been given a new 'respectability'."*3*

During World War II, Communists running the War Department tried to destroy all files on fellow subversives held by the various branches of the military. In 1943, Naval Intelligence was directed to destroy their vital records on all known and suspected Communists in the United States. At least 100,000 incriminating file cards were methodically removed and burned.*4*

Alexander Barmine was a former Russian General and then advisor to the Office of Strategic Services. He was fired from the Communist infested OSS when, in October 1944, he wrote: ". . . tremendous pressure was exerted to bring about . . . a dismantling of those branches of the Army and Navy intelligence which dealt with the activities of Communists and Communist-fronters, and a destruction of their files. In the Third Naval District . . . the Navy had . . . extensive files on subversive individuals and organizations. So authoritative had this intelligence unit become that its weekly reports . . . went regularly to the FBI . . . Several months ago . . . the Washington Office of Navy Intelligence was partially dismantled, the New York 'desk' was virtually abolished and its trained experts sent to remote and unrelated assignments elsewhere."*5* Who behind the scenes masterminded and got away with this incredible anti-intelligence maneuver?

While Chief of Staff, General George C. Marshall enigmatically ordered the destruction of all Army counterintelligence data. These irreplaceable files covered years of intensive investigation of Communists in the United

States. The records were saved *only* because of forceful action taken by Senator Styles Bridges (R-NH).*6* Why would George Marshall even consider destroying the Army files on Red traitors in the first place?

David Emerson Gumaer charged: " . . . at the conclusion of the war [World War II] some *fifty thousand* security files on subversives known to be operating within the American military were *destroyed on orders from top officials in ourgovernment."7*

"In Leningrad the OGPU runs a mysterious school . . . the fine art of sabotage is taught to those who have passed an exacting screening," reveals former Communist Benjamin Gitlow. "Communist students learn how to dynamite a bridge, derail a train, set fire to a warehouse, seize and make use of existing telegraphic and radio communications.... These . . . Communist commandos form the iron core of resistance movements . . . They are kept in readiness in every European country. Given the signal, they will set Europe to the torch . . . put the whole continent under the hammer and sickle."*8* The same thing is now true in the United States!

Kremlin-trained commandos can now enter the United States at will! They move among us with impunity. They openly train domestic revolutionaries in guerrilla warfare! Julius G. Sourwine was former Chief Counsel to the Senate Internal Security Subcommittee (SISS). He reveals: "At least three intelligence networks—Russian, Czech, and Cuban—are actively engaged in acts of murder, sabotage and espionage within the borders of the USA."*9* In 1964, Boris N. Ponomarev—head of the Foreign Division of Communist Occupied Russia's Central Committee — issued this smug declaration from the Soviet Embassy in Washington: " The revolution in the United States has begun."*[10]*

On May 24, 1967, Lieutenant General Arthur G. Trudeau, Chief of Army Intelligence, appeared before the SISS. He warned that Communist Occupied Russia was using civil rights groups, radical student organizations, the peace movement, and anti-war groups to further the Soviet goal of world domination. Trudeau said that all of these groups are "honeycombed with Reds who take their orders directly from Comrade Ponomarev in Moscow."*11* One example is Tom Hayden's SDS (Chapter 15) which the FBI called the subversive leaders behind sabotage in America. SDS training programs in guerrilla warfare were held on campuses and elsewhere throughout the nation.

Back in 1969, FBI agent O.W. Nelson, Jr. revealed that the Soviet Union had developed a highly trained underground guerrilla army in the United States. Called "sleepers," they are Communists posing as ordinary American citizens in all walks of life. Nelson warns that they are actually "dedicated Reds who, when they are called, will do their jobs and do them well." These Communists have been thoroughly trained "to blow bridges, wreck trains and radio stations, wreck communications."[12]

Radicalized American college students were brought to Cuba by the chief of Cuba's secret police, Julian Torres Rizo.[13] Over 6,000 of these revolutionaries received terrorist and guerrilla warfare training from Cubans, East Germans, the Vietcong, Bulgarians, and others. Instructions, according to *Saga* magazine, were given "on how to make and use homemade explosives, such as grenades . . . bombs and incendiaries . . . Really tough militants . . . [were] sent to Prague, Czechoslovakia and even to Moscow for super courses in espionage, sabotage . . . "[14]

Former Congressman Dies speaks as an authority on this subject: "The Kremlin's most effective secret weapon is the Communist apparatus in the United States. It has always had an underground organization which is more important than its above ground apparatus . . . The underground organization is composed of men and women who are not only dedicated but who have received special training in revolutionary and conspiratorial methods. Most of them have been sent to the Soviet Union to receive graduate instruction in the schools which the Kremlin has maintained since the Red Revolution to train its agents in such subjects as sabotage, espionage, revolution, class warfare . . . "[15]

The battle to get rid of America's internal security safeguards is nothing new. For example, when John Fitzgerald Kennedy was a Senator, he sponsored legislation to repeal the loyalty oath provision of the National Defense Education Act. Lyndon Baines Johnson, an intimate of Communists his entire political life, killed critical legislation designed to restore the rights of states to punish subversives.

The Communist Party was outlawed between 1921 and 1928 and their records seized. The names of upwards to 10,000 card carrying Reds were found! Congressman Dies requested this information when he took charge of the House Committee on Un-American Activities. But alas, the membership list had somehow mysteriously disappeared! "Someone had destroyed them," charged Dies.[16]

The former Congressman asks: "Why is it that, at an early date the Dies Committee furnished the various government agencies with a list of 1,124 federal employees who were members of subversive organizations, the heads of these agencies refused to investigate them; even though Congress had passed a resolution requiring 'every department, agency, and independent establishment of the federal government' to 'investigate the employees' who are members of subversive organizations or advocate the overthrow of the federal government, and to report the findings to Congress."[17]

The American Civil Liberties Union—cited as being "closely affiliated with the Communist movement."[18]—started attacking the House Committee on Un-American Activities back in 1939. They later joined with the National Lawyers Guild, cited as the "foremost legal bulwark of the Communist Party." [19] Then came the National Committee to Abolish HUAC and the Emergency Civil Liberties Committee, a Red front founded in 1951 with the announced intent of abolishing the HUAC and the FBI.

Multimillionaire industrialist and financier Cyrus Stephen Eaton joined hands with the Communist Party and a multitude of Red Front organizations in viciously attacking the FBI and Congressional investigating committees. Eaton's theme consistently followed the usual Communist line: the U.S. is worse than Hitler's Germany because of the oppressive FBI; the U.S. has no Communists; etc., etc., *ad nauseam.20* On May 19, 1968, Francis E. Walter (D-PA) chairman of the HUAC announced that Eaton would be subpoenaed. His attacks were, said Richard Arens, Staff Director of the Committee, "typical of a campaign of vilification which the Communist conspiracy is promoting in the United States against our security agencies . . . to weaken our internal defenses."[21]

In April 1967 members of the Communist Party USA met in Chicago's Congress Hotel to plan their attack on the Senate and House internal security investigating committees. Frank Wilkinson, Carl Braden, Jack Spiegal, Jesse Prosten, and Abe Feinglass—all identified Reds—were there! Also present was former Congressman Robert F. Drinan (D-MA)![22] On April 24, 1968, Benjamin Spock, Roger Baldwin, and John C. Bennett joined Drinan in attacking the HUAC, the SISS, and the Permanent Senate Committee in Investigation. Each of these committees kept tabs on Communist revolutionary activities in the United States. Feinglass, noted above, serves on the Presidium of the World Peace Council—the major disarmament and terrorist-support organization of the KGB! He's also International Vice-President of the Communist-controlled Amalgamated Meatcutters and Butchers Workmen of North America.[23]

Drinan; Claude Denson Pepper (D-FL); Peter W. Rodino (D-NJ); Richard Bolling (D-MO); and radical pro-Communist Robert W. Kastenmeier (D-WI) all enthusiastically joined with the Moscow-directed Reds in their "Operation Abolition" program. Their battle cry was "Abolish HUAC!" John Conyers (D-MI) with the Communist National Lawyers Guild was another prominent team member. Radical pro-Communist Donald Edwards (D-CA), a virulent critic of FBI Director J. Edgar Hoover, aided the Red cause! And Phillip Burton (D-CA)—who in 1960 was part of the Communist anti-Committee mob in the documentary film *Operation Abolition*—did his part!

When the House Committee on Un-American Activities is destroyed," warned former Congressman Dies, "Marxism will have gained its greatest victory.... Clearly what the enemies of HUAC are after is the elimination of public exposure of Communism."[24]

Congressman Pepper was placed on the Internal Security Committee (the successor of the House Committee on Un-American Activities) as part of the radical left's vicious campaign to destroy it. Ironically, Pepper gained a seat on the very Committee whose files contained the sordid story of his extensive and unwavering Red-oriented activities! Never in the history of the Congress has anyone been more openly pro-Communist than Stalin's old friend. Another Harvard Law School graduate,[25] Pepper was a close pal and coworker of Soviet spy Alger Hiss!

Former Congressman Drinan is a radical leftist Jesuit priest and former vice-president of the Communist National Lawyers Guild. He was assigned to the House Committee at his own request, when first elected in 1971. Drinan boasted: "I am seeking to collapse it from within."[26] This Committee had already cited him at least three times for his Communist-related activities.

Drinan had viciously attacked the HUAC back in 1966, while supporting the National Committee to Abolish the Un-American Activities Committee. This Communist Front was founded in 1960 and run by Frank Wilkinson, a member of the Communist Party's elite security apparatus. Seven of its national leaders were Communists! Its chairman was Communist Aubrey Williams. This Red had been a close friend of Lyndon Johnson's since the Roosevelt era (Chapter 16) and Martin Luther King's from the Communist Highlander Folk School days (Chapter 12)! Dr. Robert McAfee Brown, a theologian from Stanford University and Baby Doctor

Benjamin Spock were sponsors. An interesting sidelight: This Communist organized and controlled Committee (300 members) included 63 purported "men of God."[27]

Were Congressmen Pepper, Drinan, Kastenmeier, Conyers, and others like them, Reds? No one but their Comrades would know, since Communists no longer carry cards. But if they weren't, then the Party was being cheated out of its rightful dues!

While America slept, these Congressmen and others working in unison with the Communist Party were ultimately successful in abolishing the House Internal Security Committee, on January 14, 1975. The Communists had achieved their 15-year goal! The House no longer had a reference source on Communist activities in the government and elsewhere in the nation. The Committee's files on dangerous anti-American subversives were sealed in the National Archives. There would be no further investigations by the House into traitorous Red activities within the United States. Interestingly enough, the end for this committee came suddenly! *It was quickly forced out of existence when it began to look into the Communist background of Henry Kissinger!28* Kissinger had been positively identified (in 1961) as a KGB agent, by a high ranking Polish intelligence officer who defected. Colonel Michael M. Goleniewski also revealed Kissinger's Communist code name—"Bor"*29* (Chapter 8, 11).

"The death of the House Internal Security Committee . . . was accomplished in a cloak and dagger operation . . . " wrote leftist Mary McGrory, in the *Washington Star News,* "the entire membership of the Democratic Caucus, under cover of voting on a package of rules changes in which the elimination of HISC was included, gave the coup de grace . . . the two daggers were Rep. Robert Drinan (D-MA), who joined HISC in order to destroy it from within, and Rep. Phillip Burton (D-CA) . . . who has hated HUAC and HISC with a genuine passion since 1949, when he undertook the defense of several of its targets [one typical "target" was Communist attorney John Caughlan]."[30]

A virulent smear campaign was also instigated against the Communists' deadliest enemy—the FBI; and their most dangerous adversary—Director J. Edgar Hoover. In a disruptive ploy, the Communist Party led a cacophony of leftist voices demanding an investigation of the FBI and that Hoover step down. Leftists in Congress—some blindly, others not so blindly—joined the hate-filled chorus! Congressman William R. Anderson (D-TN), for example, hypocritically claimed to deplore Hoover's use of "tactics reminiscent of McCarthyism."*31* This obscure politician was amply rewarded for unfailingly following the Communist line. An ego-boosting biographical sketch appeared in *Look.32 The New York Times Magazine* did a six-page photo spread and billed Anderson as an "ex-Navy Hero From Tennessee" who "attacked J. Edgar Hoover."*[33]*

House Majority leader Hale Boggs (D-LA) unfailingly followed the Communist line. This agitator, too, demanded Hoover's resignation. Boggs know better but rabidly charged the FBI was using "the tactics of the Soviet Union and Hitler's Gestapo."*34* A clue to Boggs' behavior may be found in his background. He was photographed giving the Communist clenched-fist salute while a student at Tulane University. Boggs was at the time head of a Communist front called the American Student Union.*35* Congresswoman Bella Abzug (D-NY)—another member of the Communist National Lawyers Guild—understandably demanded an investigation of the FBI. Senator George "Crawl to Hanoi" McGovern (D-SD)—to whom no sane or sensible person would listen—condemned Hoover time and time again on the floor of the Senate. And no one really paid much attention when leftist Senator Edmund Muskie (D-ME) emotionally joined in the Communist instigated fury.[36]

It was no secret who was directing the vicious smear crusade against Hoover and the FBI. An important Communist newspaper editorialized: "A furor over Hoover could implant serious doubts about the FBI in the minds of millions of brainwashed citizens.... we urge all left forces to get into it."[37]

Yale Law School professor Frank J. Donner runs the Communist founded ACLU's Political Surveillance Project. Donner had been a member of a Red cell comprised of

Communist attorneys employed by the National Labor Relations Board in Washington, D.C. The American Civil Liberties Union declared: "The ACLU has made the dissolution of the nation's vast surveillance network a top priority.... The ACLU's attack on political surveillance is being pressed through . . . litigation and legislative action."[38]

Dr. J.B. Matthews, chief investigator for the House Committee On Un-American Activities, had this to say: ". . . the Communist Party has never been able to do as much for itself as the American Civil Liberties Union has done for it."[39]

None of this should come as a surprise. A House Committee chaired by Congressman Hamilton Fish (D-NY) long ago clearly defined the subversive role of the ACLU: "The American Civil Liberties Union is closely affiliated with the Communist movement in the United States.... the main function of the ACLU is to attempt to protect the Communists in their advocacy of force and violence to overthrow the government."[40]

Communist Elizabeth Gurley Flynn was a member of the ACLU's Executive Committee in the beginning and she later become National Chairman of the Communist Party! The "Reverend" Harry F. Ward, was one of the top Communists in the United States for around 50 years. According to Joseph Zack Kornfeder—a founder of the Communist Party U.S.A. Ward paid visits to Stalin in Moscow, where together they planned the infiltration of churches in the United States.*41* This subversive was *Professor of Christian Ethics* at Union Theological Seminary in New York for 25 years. He served for 20 years as Chairman of the ACLU's Executive Committee! Ward was once asked about the slave labor camps in Communist Occupied Russia. He replied: "Those are not concentration camps. Those are personal rehabilitation camps, and they have done those people a world of good!"[42]

The subversive Institute for Policy Studies has been another leader in the Communist efforts to destroy internal security agencies in the U.S. Author Alan Stang charges:

"The IPS is the hub of a network of subversive organizations working to deliver our country to its enemies . . . the paramount goal of the network right now is the complete destruction of our nation's intelligence apparatus . . . Police intelligence squads across the country have been forced to destroy their files, and the present FBI apparently has retained about as much investigative capability as a team of meter maids.... our intelligence forces are being dismantled at the very same time that terrorism . . . is escalating to new heights."[43]

IPS founder and director Richard Barnet was one of many traitorous American guests of Hanoi during 1969 while the Red Vietnamese forces were torturing and murdering American POWs. Co-director Marcus Raskin and Arthur Waskow were intimately connected with radical leftist Tom Hayden's rather innocent sounding Students for a Democratic Society. SDS gave birth to the Weather Underground, a rabid group of deadly Communist terrorists. Peter Weiss, a major funder and chairman of the IPS board of trustees also belonged to the Communist National Lawyers Guild. His wife, Cora Rubin Weiss, was the daughter of the late Faberge perfume magnate and Communist Sam Rubin.

Congressman Larry McDonald (D-GA) had long been concerned over the lack of interest at the highest levels of government in internal security. He commented: "Our leaders do not care whether our defense secrets are stolen, sold, or given away. They do not seem to care if their mail is copied and forwarded to Moscow, or if American long-distance telephone calls are routinely listened to by the Soviet Embassy, or if Communist agents become staffers of the National Security Council."[44] McDonald introduced legislation to restore the House Committee on Internal Security,[45] but his efforts were derailed when he was *purportedly* assassinated as part of the Kremlin orchestrated Korean airline massacre (Chapter 12).

The immensely important Senate Internal Security Subcommittee was the last Congressional group concerned with investigating Communists and Communism. In 1977, its irreplaceable files on dangerous Communists in government and elsewhere were ordered destroyed. The order was methodically carried out!*46* "Liberal" Senator Edward M. Kennedy (D-MA) succeeded the retiring James 0. Eastland (D-MS) as Chairman of the Senate Judiciary Committee in 1979. He and Sen. Mark O. Hatfield (R-OR) were thereby able to scuttle the SISS.

"The campaign against our internal security was especially focused on the House Committee on Internal Security and the Senate Internal Security Subcommittee," offers investigative journalist John Rees.*47* The hearings, reports, and staff studies produced . . . were . . . scrupulously accurate sources of public information on . . . Communist political action, propaganda . . . espionage and counterintelligence. The appendices to the Hearings of these Committees remain the single greatest source of information on Communist . . . organizations available . . . "[48]

The Subversive Activities Control Board had the responsibility of deciding whether or not an organization under investigation was subversive. Senator Henry M. Jackson (D-WA) had long backed the Communist goal of abolishing the SACB. Its coup de grace was deliberately administered in 1973. The Bureau of Management and Budget simply stopped allocating operating funds. Why? Because President Nixon refused to request any![49]

Incidentally, when Senator McCarthy was exposing Communist spies in government, Senator Jackson was also one of his most vocal critics! McCarthy made it clear how he felt about such detractors: "I do not much mind the Communists screaming about my methods. That is their duty as Communists. They are under orders to do just that. But it makes me ill deep down inside when I hear cowardly politicians, and self-proclaimed 'Liberals' . . . parrot over and over this Communist Party line."[50]

The Civil Service Commission discarded all security safeguards in September 1976. Unbelievably, federal job applicants were no longer required to swear they weren't a member of an organization dedicated to the violent overthrow of the very government in which they were seeking employment! The Federal Employee Loyalty Program also ceased to exist. Government agencies were now prohibited from checking with the FBI regarding subversive affiliations of job applicants. M. Stanton Evans notes: "In a federal government that gives four million people security clearances, it is official policy *not to* ask a prospective employee if he is a Communist—because this would violate his civil liberties!"[51]

The Internal Security Division of the Department of Justice supervised investigations of Communists. It was also in charge of prosecuting Reds. The important division was absorbed into the Justice Department's criminal section in March of 1973. The number of employees assigned to internal security was greatly reduced and the special division was, for all practical purposes, abolished! [52]

Journalist Susan Huck talked to Department of Justice attorneys years before the Internal Security Division was eliminated. She was informed that they hadn't tried any cases involving Communist subversion for almost a decade! No one wanted to bother prosecuting Reds or the Communist Party because they knew beforehand that the Supreme Court would ultimately throw the case out! It's evident that the Internal Security Division of the Justice Department was effectively emasculated by pro-Communist Supreme Court decisions, long before it was actually abolished!

The Attorney General's list of subversive organizations was dropped by the Department of Justice in 1974. Person's applying for a federal position were previously required to check this list and swear they weren't and hadn't been members of any listed Communist and Communist front organizations. The Justice Department is now prohibited from keeping tabs on any government employee—even if the person is known to be attending secret meetings of a Communist cell.

Soon after J. Edgar Hoover died in 1972, the FBI stopped updating the Director's list of subversives and security risks. This extremely important list no longer exists!

What should have been one of Ford's most controversial appointments was long-time Communist fronter Edward H. Levi (Chapter 11)! The media deliberately ignored this notorious security risk's flaming "Red" background when he became Attorney General in 1975. As could be expected, FBI inquiries into Communist activities were severely curtailed under the infamous 1976 Levi "Guidelines for Domestic Security Investigations." The FBI could no longer investigate Communist Front organizations, Communist controlled groups (some unions, etc.), or Communist terrorist organizations, without "probable cause" that they had already committed a crime or were about to commit a crime within the next 48 to 72 hours.

Thanks to the apostatical Levi, the FBI was critically disabled, while rabidly anti-American Communist organizations were made relatively safe from exposure. Any FBI investigation of dangerous terrorist activities had to be completed and ready for trial within a 90-day period. If it wasn't, the case was closed. The FBI was then forced to open its sensitive files to the very Communist terrorist groups and individuals under investigation.

W. Raymond Warnell, the man in charge of FBI intelligence, disclosed that there are at least *1100 active subversive groups in place* throughout the U.S. Some *15,000 full-time anti-American revolutionaries* freely move around the nation! These organizations and individuals are extremely dangerous to America's internal security. Yet there are only some 800 FBI agents available to handle domestic intelligence! The Justice Department claims it can do nothing to correct this explosive situation!

The Trotskyite *Militant* boasted that Levi ordered the FBI to pull its 66 undercover agents out of the Communist-run Socialist Workers Party! This revolutionary group is dedicated to the "struggle against American capitalism and its overthrow." Its members are told to prepare for participation in "mass terrorism." *53* Yet, Levi pulled the FBI's undercover men out of the highly subversive SWP because he claimed it was *an invasion of their privacy!* He fraudulently stated that this subversive organization *was not* a threat to U.S. security!

So crippling were the radical Levi Guidelines that internal security investigations were all but disbanded! Investigations of subversives and subversion suffered an astounding drop from 9,814 to 147 in less than three years! Leftist organizations placed under surveillance dropped from 157 to 17! FBI agents assigned to internal security cases dropped from 788 to 143!

Ford chose Clarence Kelley to head the FBI. Kelley quickly purged the FBI of those agents in positions of influence who were loyal to J. Edgar Hoover. On July 7, 1976, he testified at the murder trial of two terrorist thugs with the Communist-backed American Indian Movement. They'd been accused of killing two FBI agents—Ronald Williams and Jack Coler. Although the FBI's *Domestic Terrorist Digest* clearly listed AIM as a terrorist organization, Kelley lied when he testified that the FBI didn't see AIM as "objectionable, subversive, or un-American."*54* The two revolutionaries were acquitted! This should give some insight as to the political orientation of the man placed in charge of the FBI under left-leaning Attorney General Levy!

William H. Webster, a Federal Appeals Court judge, was selected by Carter on February 23, 1978, as FBI Director for a 10 year term. This dependable but timorous leftist continued to strictly interpret and enforce the outrageously subversive Levi "Guidelines for Domestic Security Investigations." So harshly restrictive were these "Guidelines" that, upon taking over, Webster announced that the FBI was "out of the internal security business!"*55* Even Reagan as President made no effort to induce Webster to alter his anti-internal security stance! The so-called "peace" and "nuclear freeze" movements were thoroughly exposed as having heavy Soviet KGB penetration. Yet, Webster made a complete fool of himself when he ludicrously proclaimed there was *no* Soviet influence in these radical subversive groups.

Robert Morris, former Chief Counsel for the SISS is alarmed. He suggests: "Revise the FBI guidelines so that subversive organizations can be monitored, subversives kept under surveillance, and subversive organizations penetrated by the FBI....The FBI ... can no longer keep under surveillance people who are potential terrorists."[56] Incredible? Yes, but frighteningly true nonetheless!

"Committees of Congress have been prevented by intimidation from discharging their investigative duty to the country," charges the Honorable Martin Dies. "Our Congressional investigating Committees are given spacious offices, numerous patronage jobs for Committee members, and plenty of money for other purposes—but there is a tacit understanding that there shall never be a repetition of the fearless probe of Communist activity as that conducted by the Dies Committee on UnAmerican Activities."[57]

Ezra Taft Benson decries: "The smear seems to be the most widely used and effective tool of the Conspiracy to discredit and weaken any effective anti-Communist effort."[58] He's referring, of course, to what happened to Senator Joe McCarthy and so many other brave souls who exposed Communists in and out of government. The Reds and their leftist kneejerk liberal patrons and protectors were eminently successful in making it an unpardonable "sin" for anyone to expose Kremlin spies who are working toward the destruction of America! Susan Huck comments: "The mere idea of seeking out the enemy agents who are obviously at work . . . [is made] into a crime so heinous as to cause one to be vilified and ostracized as 'guilty of McCarthyism'."[59]

Former Party functionary Louis Budenz told why McCarthy was so viciously smeared, then methodically destroyed. It was simply "to intimidate any person of consequence who moves against the conspiracy. The Communists made him their chief target because they wanted to make him a symbol to remind political leaders in

America not to harm the Conspiracy or its world conquest designs."[60]

The Communist strategy worked well! Most Congressmen today show little or no inclination to fight Communist subversion. Members of the House and Senate continually face the spectre of what the Communists and their "liberal" friends were able to do to Joe McCarthy after he dared go after them. Few now have the courage to do battle with the Reds. The last one who did, Congressman Larry McDonald (D-GA), paid with his life. McCarthy rightly reminded those in Congress: "A Senator [or Representative] who is aware of treason but who refuses to expose the dangerous unpleasant facts for fear that he will be politically scarred and bloodied if he does, is actually guilty of a greater treason than the traitors themselves."[61]

"It is indeed appalling that some members of our society continue to deplore and criticize those who stress the Communist danger," said FBI Director J. Edgar Hoover. What these 'misguided' authorities fail to realize is that the Communist Party, USA, is an integral part of international Communism. As the world-wide menace becomes more powerful, the various Communist parties assume a more dangerous and sinister role in the countries in which they are entrenched. Public indifference to this threat is tantamount to national suicide."[62]

Gutless "liberal" political leaders, in various cities, were pressured to destroy their police intelligence data. State and local files on Communist subversives and subversion were burned! According to U.S. *News & World Report:* "Baltimore no longer keeps intelligence files . . . Eighty percent of New York City Police Department's data on 'public security matters' have been thrown out. Los Angeles junked nearly two million files it had on potential terrorists. "*63* As a result, internal security safeguards were devastated nationwide! Thousands of dangerous Reds now roam the streets of America's cities and no one in law enforcement has the foggiest notion as to who they are!

"If all the facts about KGB spying were known declares Senator Steven D. Symms (R-ID), it would probably blow the dome off the Capitol. KGB agents have an open door to the Capitol."*64* The presence of Soviet spies is so commonplace, charges former Senator James L. Buckley (RNY), that "well-known KGB types" can be seen regularly at Congressional committee hearings!*65* The fact is that the number of KGB agents in the United States has increased by 400 percent! Even White House communications are freely monitored from the Soviet Embassy in Washington!

Being under surveillance or having a dossier had a "chilling effect" on Communist revolutionaries according to the Red founded American Civil Liberties Union. The highly controversial 1974 *Freedom of Information Act* opened a new can of worms insofar as this aspect of internal security. Legal actions brought by the ACLU forced the release of many highly sensitive FBI and other intelligence agency files. Communist backed groups initiated lawsuits to ascertain how much intelligence agencies knew about the terrorist underground and to identify their sources of information. Leftist got injunctions to stop any further investigations of Communist infiltration and activities. Terrorists groups and enemy intelligence services use provisions of the law to identify FBI informants and to otherwise hamper investigations.

The Communist goal is to disrupt and/or end all internal security investigations! Friendly foreign intelligence agencies are reluctant to share their data with their U.S. counterparts. Domestic informants, as well as those in other countries, are afraid to feed sensitive data to American intelligence agencies. Former Senator Jeremiah Denton (R-AL) pointed out that in some cases, a simple "response to an FOIA request amounts to acknowledgment by the FBI that a file exists on a specific subject. As a result, hostile intelligence services are put on notice that an investigation is underway or has taken place.[66]

The *Hughes-Ryan Amendment to* the *Foreign Assistance Act* of 1974 gutted any semblance of secrecy from undercover activities of U.S. intelligence agencies. Covert actions could no longer be initiated without the President's approval! He in turn had to report to a congressional committee. This of course further jeopardized the secrecy of intelligence operations! The disastrous Senate Select Committee on Intelligence hearings, headed by radical leftist Frank Church (D-ID), followed soon after. As a result, Congress set up permanent committees to oversee intelligence agency spending. By 1978, six more congressional committees and over 70 Senators were involved—all privy to the most sensitive data involving security! Intelligence agencies could no longer safely conduct covert operations. Multiple leaks of highly sensitive intelligence data were impossible to plug.

Then there was the *1974 Privacy Act*. Incredibly, the FBI was barred from collecting press clippings containing informative or inflammatory statements made by Red terrorists or other Communists! Nor could the FBI maintain files of subversive newspapers, newsletters, or anything else, for that matter! So-called "First Amendment" activities of subversives were said to no longer be the business of the Federal Bureau of Investigation!

Senator Pat McCarran (D-NV) declared upon the passage of *The Immigration and Nationality Act (McCarran-Walter Act):* "Our present laws are shot through with weaknesses and loopholes. . . Communists . . . are even now gaining admission into this country like water running through a sieve."67 The 1952 legislation specifically bans Communists from entering the United States! Also prohibited are people who are closely affiliated with Communists.

The McCarran-Walter Act was circumvented in 1977 by Democratic Senator George McGovern's disgraceful amendment. McGovern's radical leftist ploy eliminated the ban on Communists and members of Communist terrorist organizations who wish to enter the United States! Automatic visa approval is now required for all subversives unless a full report involving a monstrous amount of paperwork is made to Congress. This report has to specify exactly why a Red terrorist or other undesirable alien should be banned as a threat to America's internal security. As a result, top secret intelligence sources would again have to be revealed.[68]

Red leaders from throughout the world are now freely admitted to the United States, where they openly organize and propagandize for the Communist cause! Under McGovern's outlandish legislation, Santiago Carillo, General Secretary of Spain's Communist Party, was allowed to come and lecture at Yale and Johns Hopkins. This treacherous fiend was a political commissar who executed helpless prisoners during the Spanish Civil War. Giorgio Napolitano, top Italian Party official came to lecture at Princeton, Harvard, and Yale! Italian Communist leader Guiseppe Pasquini was let in to take part in a promotional tour sponsored by Rich's Department Store of Atlanta!*69* Even Carlos the Jackal, the worlds most revolting Red assassin, would be welcome under McGovern's radical leftist legislation!

The Refugee Relief Act of 1953 and 1980 further weakened the *McCarran-Walter Act.* Under these laws, thousands of unscreened refugees flowed unchecked into the U.S. from the Communist Bloc and radical so-called "unaligned" Third World dictatorships. None were given background checks. None were questioned about their political convictions. Many of these aliens, according to all top security experts, are Communist espionage agents!

Carter's Attorney General Griffin Bell further hamstrung the FBI on April 10, 1978. Former Acting Director L. Patrick Gray and agents Edward Miller and Mark Felt were indicted! Their crime was over-zealousness in tracking down Communist trained terrorists in the Weather Underground. They were accused of violating the civil liberties of radicals who were contacts of these dangerous fugitive bombers. The Weather Underground boasts: "We are a guerrilla organization. We are Communist men and women . . . Our intention is . . . to attack from the inside . . . "[70]

The incredible action taken by Bell accomplished exactly what the left intended. The morale of the FBI was destroyed! Future investigations of Kremlin-trained terrorist groups were hindered. As a result, untold numbers of terrorist bombings and other violent Communist acts remain unsolved! The Department of Justice chooses not to prosecute the Communist gangsters whose goal is to install a Soviet dictatorship in America—a mirror-image of that horrifying tyranny found entrenched in Communist Occupied Russia! Prosecuted instead are loyal, anti-Communist FBI agents!

In 1978, the FBI was prohibited from investigating *any* Communist group or individual without first getting permission from the White House. Incredibly, the privacy of all Reds was now guaranteed by the President of the United States! According to Carter's Executive Order, no Communists could have their mail placed under surveillance! Terrorist groups couldn't be covertly photographed! Electronic surveillance equipment couldn't be used to monitor the anti-American activities of subversive groups!

The Foreign Intelligence Surveillance Act of 1978 was designed to further hamper FBI investigations of Communist terrorist groups. Per this radical legislation, the FBI had to obtain a court order before using electronic surveillance equipment while conducting a terrorist investigation. In order to tap the phones of any Communist organization, the FBI was required to first *prove* what was already common knowledge in intelligence circles—that the Red group had "substantial" backing or direction from outside the United States.

"For Moscow, Peking, and Havana, it is an incredible dream come true," explained Congressman Larry McDonald.". . . Campaigns teaming Communist operatives with big name 'Liberals' have destroyed the Subversive Activities Control Board, the House Committee on Internal Security, the Internal Security Division of the Justice Department, and . . . intelligence files of our local and state police. Nothing so silly could possibly happen in Moscow . .

. Only in Washington can you find a government so depraved that it helps its worst enemies to paw through and destroy our security files, or a Congress which spends the better part of a session pillorying the remnants of our security agencies, while yawning at the revelation that agents of the Soviet secret police have the run of Capitol Hill "[71]

Brigadier General Robert L. Scott Jr. warns: "History will repeat itself, if we refuse to learn its lesson. Ours would not be the first nation to be betrayed from within. More than two thousand years ago, Marcus Tullius Cicero faced a similar situation as he fought against the subversion of the Roman Republic."[72]

Chapter 8

Internal Security—The Supreme Court and the Presidents

Traitor: "One who betrays his country."
Webster's New World Dictionary

Treason: ". . . to deliver up, betray . . . breach of faith, treachery."
Oxford Universal Dictionary

"Traitors to the United States have no cause to fear a legal penalty as they go about mobilizing to take over the nation in a violent, bloody revolution," charges Dr. George S. Benson, President Emeritus of Harding College. "Read that statement again. It's true! The traitors know it's true. In Washington . . . one of the top legal minds of the nation, who is also one of the best informed men in America on the ramifications of the Communist conspiracy, told us that the United States Justice Department could not arrest traitors or halt acts of treason now prevalent throughout the country. Supreme Court decisions of recent years so shattered the security laws that there's no workable safeguard against the mobilization, arming and training of a massive revolutionary force which is determined to seize control."*1*

President Eisenhower, according to former Red Party member Maurice Malkin, was suffering from the virus of appeasing the Communists. He appointed, as a payoff for election favors, Earl Warren as Chief Justice of the Supreme

Court. Then followed the stoppage of prosecutions of the Communists under the Smith Act."2

Warren Court decisions had a major impact on America's internal security protection. Important internal security laws were systematically voided. No longer could Communist operatives—dedicated to the destruction of the United States Government—be made to name their associates under oath! The right of a congressional committee to investigate Communism and Communists was severely restricted! The Communist Party was no longer required to register as a subversive organization!

All these things came about despite the fact that the Supreme Court, under Earl Warren, reaffirmed in the mid-1960s that "the Constitution of the United States is not a 'suicide pact.' The Nation has the right and duty to protect itself from acts of espionage and sabotage, and attempts to overthrow the government by force."3

Nevertheless, the Supreme Court has by design placed many obstacles in the path of investigating and exposing Communism and Communists in the United States. M. Stanton Evans notes: "The Warren Court has laid level internal security statutes and regulations in almost every sector of American life.... The Court has erased from the books almost every sanction the United States has against the internal activities of the Communists."4

Martin Dies (D-TX) was for seven years chairman of the House Committee on Un-American Activities. He had this to say: "One by one the Court has destroyed every legal weapon which Congress and the states have constructed to defeat the treasonous activities of the domestic agents of the International Communist Conspiracy."5

"Where Congress and the states have legislated, the Court has invalidated," charges Dies, "where the FBI and the states' attorney Generals and our Bar Associations have moved to prevent sedition, the Court has remonstrated; where the Secretary of State and our Governors and loyal federal administrators have acted to remove Communists and subversives from vital positions in our government, the Court has reinstated."*6*

"The one area where there seems to be some predictability with respect to the Warren Court's action, is where cases involved the interests of the world Communist conspiracy and its arm in this country, the Communist Party, USA," suggested Senator James O. Eastland (D-MS). "It is moving . . . decision by decision, toward establishment of the Communist conspiracy in the United States as a legal political entity, with just as much right to exist and operate as any political party composed of decent patriotic American citizens. When suppression would help the Communist cause, the Court suppressed. When preemption would help the Communist cause, the Court has pre-empted. When invention would help the Communist cause, the Court has invented. When misstatement would help the Communist cause, the Court has misstated."*7*

"It would be extremely interesting to hear Mr. Justice Black try to explain how it was possible to believe that the Communists were right in *every one of* the hundred and two cases in which he participated," offers Revilo P. Oliver." . . . some members *of* it [the Supreme Court] have knowingly served the purposes *of* the Communist conspiracy, thus adding to the crime *of* judicial corruption the even greater crime *of* treason."*8*

Senate hearings were held in 1958 to create legislation to limit the Supreme Court's jurisdiction. SPX Research Associates, a highly respected group *of* intelligence experts, concluded that "decisions *of* the Supreme Court follow preestablished Communist lines." They further determined that "the United States Supreme Court is the most powerful . . . instrument of the Communist global conquest by paralysis."*9*

The Supreme Court handed down a multitude of disastrous decisions favoring the Communist Party and individual Communists. The nation's protective laws against subversives were either thrown out or rendered ineffective by the Court. No longer does America have adequate safeguards! Little can be done about those traitors who are systematically working towards the destruction of the Republic and the installation of a clone of Communist Occupied Russia in its place. Here are but a few of the many cases which clearly illustrate how far the Supreme Court has gone to aid and abet Communists and Communist activities in the United States.

In a 1941 hearing, Judge Charles Sears ruled that Harry Bridges, President of the International Longshoremen's and Warehousemen's Union (ILWU), *was* a Communist! He was identified under oath as a Red by at least 35 witnesses including his first wife! Sears further found that the Communist Party *did* advocate the violent overthrow of the United States Government. Attorney General Francis Biddle issued an order for the deportation of Bridges, an Australian alien. Then came a letter from the White House! Signed "Eleanor," it *ordered* that the deportation of Bridges be held up!*10* Meanwhile, the case was appealed. Incredibly, the Supreme Court said Bridges hadn't received a fair hearing regarding his Communist Party membership! Even more astounding, Justice Frank Murphy declared there wasn't "the slightest evidence introduced to show that either Bridges or the Communist Party seriously threatens to uproot the government by force and violence."*11* He then had the unmitigated gall to declare that "the Bridges case would stand forever as a monument to man's intolerance to man."[12]

The Immigration and Naturalization Service had most of the Communist Party ready for deportation in 1956. Over ten thousand *alien Communists* were going to be shipped back to their country of origin. In another obvious act of Communist appeasement, the Supreme Court stepped in and crippled America's immigration system! This was deliberately done to allow more Communists—and immigrants the Reds could control—to pour into the United States. At the same time, extremely dangerous alien Communists such as Australian Harry Bridges, were allowed to stay in the country! Maurice Malkin explains: "Next came the liquidation of the anti-subversive sections of I & N and the dropping of all deportation cases against Moscow agents in the United States. They were given a chance to regroup and reorganize into new fronts and penetrate civil rights and peace organizations.[13] Incredible? Yes, but true!

The federal government was unwilling and often now unable to prosecute Communists. Many states took it upon themselves to enact their own sedition laws, barring treasonous Communist activities within their borders. The Supreme Court moved post-haste to disarm the states in this regard! Communist Party leader Steve Nelson had been convicted in 1952 and sentenced to 20 years under Pennsylvania law. The Supreme Court overturned Nelson's conviction! This was no more than a ploy to free Communist criminals who had been convicted and imprisoned under sedition laws around the nation. The traitorous decision voided the sedition laws in 42 states.[14]

The Warren Court overturned the New York Supreme Court in favor of Harry Slochower, a Brooklyn College teacher. He'd been fired for pleading the Fifth Amendment when questioned regarding his Communist Party membership and Red affiliations. The Court deemed it unconstitutional for a school to dismiss a teacher who refused to discuss his Communist background. Brooklyn College was forced to reinstate Slochower and pay $40,000 in back wages. No longer could Reds be prohibited from teaching in tax-supported colleges and public schools. It was ruled to be a denial of academic freedom to fire teachers who taught and advocated the use of force and violence to overthrow the government.[15]

The *Summary Suspension Act of 1950* allowed the firing of federal employees "in the interest of the National Security of the United States." The Warren Court ruled it was not in the interest of national security to fire *anyone* for contributing services and money to Communist organizations! The only exception might be if the federal employee was working in a "sensitive position." The Court forced the federal government to rehire some 300 dangerous security risks!"[16]

Aliens have historically had a different status than citizens in the United States. An alien can't vote and can't be drafted. He or she is simply a foreign guest. Yet the Supreme Court ruled that the Attorney General can't even ask aliens if they've ever attended Communist Party meetings![17]

Rudolph Schware wasn't allowed to take the New Mexico Bar Examination. The Board of Bar Examiners ruled that Schware's past membership in and loyalty to the Communist Party made him a man of "questionable" character. The Supreme Court ordered the Board to let Schware take the examination despite his subversive background.[18]

"Lawyers are officers of the courts, and as such become an important and necessary part of our judicial system. It would appear unthinkable that we should admit Communists to become officers in our judicial system," declares former Congressman Dies. "When, therefore, the highest tribunal in our land denies to a Bar Committee the right to ask an applicant . . . whether he is a Communist, it deprives us of a safeguard against the infiltration of our judicial system by the enemies of our country."[19]

New Mexico union leader Clinton Jencks filed an affidavit in April of 1950, swearing he wasn't a Communist. He was prosecuted by the Justice Department and convicted for perjury. The Warren Court overturned the conviction. Why? Because Jencks wasn't allowed to see the FBI data used as evidence against him. This perverse ruling required that all reports by witnesses now be given to the disloyal, in cases involving Reds. The Communist defendant must be told precisely how the evidence was obtained. The Court ordered disclosures would reveal to the Communist leadership exactly who the informants were. Subversive revolutionaries are no longer prosecuted, because the information disclosed could cause more harm than would allowing the Communist to go free.[20]

Justice Tom C. Clark dissented: "Unless the Congress changes the rule announced by the Court today, those intelligence agencies of our government, engaged in law enforcement, may as well close up shop, for the Court has opened their files to the criminal and has afforded him a Roman holiday for rummaging through confidential information, as well as vital national secrets."[21]

As a result of the Jencks case, the Court of Appeals later ruled that the Communist Party was not required to register as a subversive organization, per the order of the Subversive Activities Control Board. Why? Because the FBI hadn't shown the Party their secret reports on its subversive activities!

"In 1948, for the first time since the 1920's, the Party found itself on the defensive when the Department of Justice initiated prosecution against its leaders," explains FBI Director J. Edgar Hoover. "The twelve members of the Party's National Board were indicted under the Smith Act . . . In a long trial, running through most of 1949, eleven members were convicted . . . In June, 1951, the Supreme Court upheld these convictions, and the government subsequently took prosecutive action against additional Party leaders. This government prosecution was a strong disabling blow against the Party. Many of its top leaders were arrested and convicted. Others lived in fear of arrest. As a result, the Party to a large extent went underground. . . "[22]

Attorney Roy Cohn describes the trial: "The display of bad manners and improper conduct by lawyers and witnesses for the defense was the worst this country has ever seen. The Communists did not fear conviction. Following instructions, they sought to turn the courtroom into a forum for their cause. The Party had instructed them that they were expendable and they accepted it . . . In the courtroom they laughed at us, at our judicial methods, at our judges "[23]

The Alien Registration Act (Smith Act) case handled by the Warren Court was a disaster for American internal security. The 1940 Smith Act simply prohibits any conspiracy that advocates the overthrow of the United States Government by force and violence.24 It was also unlawful for anyone to belong to a group advocating this. Lastly, the

Smith Act required the finger printing of all aliens in the United States.

Jack Hall was a well known Communist Party organizer. He worked undercover in the Communist dominated ILWU in Hawaii, on orders from Moscow. The Senate Internal Security Subcommittee disclosed: "By 1955, Communist political and economic control of Hawaii through Communist dominated unions was so great that the official Communist Party went out of existence. Since 1955, Communist propaganda and other activities have been conducted through the unions." *25* In 1953, Jack Hall was charged with conspiring to overthrow the U.S. Government by force. Hall was convicted of violating the Smith Act. But his conviction, as well as many others, was overturned in 1957 by the Warren Court.

The Supreme Court reversed two lower court rulings regarding the Smith Act. It was no longer a crime for a Communist to advocate and teach the violent overthrow of the government. Such activity was not illegal, even if there was "evil intent." said the Court, so long as this was "divorced from any effort to instigate action to that end."*26* New trials were ordered for nine convicted Communist Party leaders. Five others were acquitted!

J. Edgar Hoover revealed that every one of the 49 top Party leaders who had been imprisoned for advocating the overthrow of the government, were freed by the Supreme Court. Further prosecution of Communists under the Smith Act was stopped! A top Communist Party functionary described the ruling as the greatest legal victory the Party had ever received!

Congressional investigations were further emasculated by the Supreme Court, under the leadership of Chief Justice Earl Warren. The Court questioned whether or not congress had the right to investigate and publicize cases of Communist subversion. The Court ruled that this "involved a broad scale intrusion into the lives and affairs of private citizens." The conviction of John Watkins for contempt of congress was overturned. The Court held that a witness was not required to reveal the names of associates, even though he'd admitted to being involved in Communist activities.[27]

The Supreme Court ruled that a sovereign state had no right to ask a state employee questions regarding subversive activities. New Hampshire's Attorney General, said the Court, didn't have the authority to question professor Paul Sweezy, of New Hampshire University. Sweezy had refused to answer, when asked "Do you believe in Communism?" and "Did you advocate Marxism at that time?" The Court agreed that he had the right to do so.[28]

John Stewart Service was caught in the act of giving classified documents to Soviet espionage agents in 1945 (Chapter 10, 13, 16). He was finally fired six years later in 1951, under provisions of the McCarran Act, which gave the Secretary of State the responsibility of dismissing an employee in the interest of national security. Several lower courts refused to set aside this traitor's dismissal. End of story? No! The Supreme Court ordered Service reinstated, with back pay! This dangerous security risk's guilt was never challenged! Improper procedures were said to have been used in his firing. Service, obviously with the assistance of Comrades in high places, was ultimately assigned a diplomatic plum. He became American Consul in Liverpool, England.[29]

Another major victory for the Communist Party in the United States was realized on November 15, 1965. The Warren Court struck down the Internal Security Act of 1950! The Court ruled that it was unconstitutional (on the basis of self-incrimination) to force Communists to register with the Attorney General. In an eight-to-nothing decision, the Court said that "registration as a Communist party member and information asked on the registry form might be used as evidence in, or at least supplementary leads to, a criminal prosecution under the Smith Act of 1940 or other criminal statutes."*30* This ruling allowed the Red revolutionaries to proceed unhampered in their goal of ultimately overthrowing the government. The Communists no longer had to be concerned about being picked up and jailed during a national emergency.

Gus Hall, General Secretary of the Communist Party USA, was overjoyed. This fanatic said the decision would stimulate the "growth of the Communist Party now. It will be possible to be more openly active in all fields."*31* Hall's true bloodthirsty nature was shown when he said: "I dream of the hour when the last congressman is strangled to death on the guts of the last preacher—and since the Christians love to sing about the blood, why not give them a little of it?" *32*

Communist Archie Brown gained national notoriety in 1959, while leading the San Francisco riots against the House Committee on Un-American Activities. This Red was the underling of the notorious Communist union leader Harry Bridges. Brown had been convicted and sentenced to six months in prison for serving on the Executive Board of Local 10 of the Red controlled ILWU. It was a crime at that time for a Communist to be a labor union official. In 1965, the Warren Court ruled that such a law was unconstitutional!

Earl Browder—head of the Communist Party, USA— was provided an office in the White House by FDR! Here he kept close tabs on what American leaders were thinking and doing and he could assist in charting the course of government. So bold were those in power that no one even bothered keeping this fact a secret! Congressman John J. O'Connor (D-NY), Chairman of the House Rules Committee, noted that the Communist Party boss "had constant and immediate access, and was so close to the President that he could enter the White House, at any time, and through any door and with out any invitation."*33*

Subversive Harry Hopkins (many years later identified by a defector as a Communist mole) put together an "Elimination Committee" for Roosevelt, in an attempt to "purge" all anti-Communist elements from the Democratic Party. Congressman O'Connor again reveals a shocker: "During the years 1933-39, when I often visited the White House . . . I saw Browder there on several occasions. In fact, during the President's 'purge' of 1938, Browder directed purge operations from the White House, from which he telephoned instructions from time to time."[34]

"In a conference with President Roosevelt, I told him . . . there were spy rings or cells in every important department of our government . . . ," revealed former Congressman Dies. "I mentioned to him some of the names, including Alger Hiss, Harry Dexter White, Fuchs and others. I warned him that these spies were sending our most important secrets to their Communist masters in Moscow. The President treated this information and my warning as a huge joke. He laughed heartily and cautioned me to stop reading spy stories."[35]

Whittaker Chambers, former Communist spy and *Time* senior editor went to Assistant Secretary of State Adolph Berle on September 2, 1939. He gave Berle the names of two dozen Communists secretly implanted in government! Among them was the infamous Alger Hiss! Roosevelt again laughed when Berle presented him with this devastating information! Despite the fact that he was a known Soviet spy, Hiss was continually promoted within the State Department![36] He was glued to Roosevelt's side all during the Yalta betrayal (Chapter 12)! And he was an important figure involved in the UN founding and the writing of the charter (Chapter 14). Alger Hiss was finally exposed publicly nine years later in 1948 by the same Whittaker Chambers.

Roosevelt turned a deaf ear to all legitimate charges of Communist infiltration in his Administration. When Congressman Dies continued pressing, the President angrily retorted: "I have never seen a man who had such exaggerated ideas about this thing! I do not believe in Communism anymore than you do but there is nothing wrong with the Communists in this country! Several of the best friends I've got are Communists!"[37]

Evidently Roosevelt was telling the truth! The record shows he appointed Reds to a multitude of key government positions. He also prevented the FBI from conducting *any* investigations of Communists in the United States! FDR refused to listen to Dies and Berle, explains Malkin, because there were so many "leftist and Communists among his advisors and cabinet: Harry Hopkins, Albert R. William, Harold Ickes, Lauchlin Currie, Nathan Gregory Silvermaster, Harry Dexter White—not to mention his chiefs in the WPA, where Communists were in charge or control of the most important projects."[38]

President Harry S. Truman was another disaster to internal security! His treasonous promotion of Communist espionage agent Harry Dexter White from Treasury to head the International Monetary Fund (IMF) was done after he'd been repeatedly warned by J. Edgar Hoover that White was a Kremlin spy (Chapter 16). Another was his reaction to a telegram from Senator Joseph R. McCarthy (R-WI), after his famous Wheeling, West Virginia, speech on February 9, 1950. McCarthy reveals: "I wired President Truman and suggested that he call in Secretary of State Acheson and ask for the names of the 205 who were kept in the State Department, despite the fact that Truman's own security officers had declared them unfit to serve. I urged him to have Acheson tell him how many of the 205 were still in the State Department and why. I told the President that I had the names of 57. I offered those names to the President. The offer was never accepted. The wire was never answered."[39]

Truman brazenly issued an Executive Order in 1947 which protected from exposure those Communists who had successfully penetrated the government. The directive prohibited congressional investigators from obtaining personnel files on employees suspected of being Communist espionage agents. The order was expressly designed to thwart congressional investigations that threatened to expose Communists holding government positions.

Truman later initiated what was called the "Executive Fifth Amendment." This action further protected Communists already in place throughout his Administration and the carryovers from the malignant Roosevelt years. Officials in the executive branch had to first obtain permission from the White House before talking to Congressional investigating committees. The Order specified that information concerning the loyalty of federal employees "shall be maintained in complete confidence."[40]

Truman was terrified of Congressman J. Parnell Thomas (D-NJ), Chairman of the House Committee on Un-American Activities. He envisioned the man to be his political executioner! Truman was unsuccessful in strong arming Thomas to drop his investigations of Reds. All the Communists, pro-Communists, and fellow travelers in government and elsewhere were very nervous. Thomas had flatly rejected a $25,000 bribe to soft-pedal his findings of heavy Communist infiltration in Hollywood's movie industry! He was about to turn the spotlight on Moscow-directed subversives, inundated throughout the Truman Administration. HST treasonously ordered his Justice Department to stop the investigations at *any* cost. They did just that! Congressman J. Parnell Thomas was methodically destroyed by the left!

Why would a President go to such lengths to protect the enemies of his country? Were they all players on the same team? No doubt the nation's rising concern over Communist infiltration was seen by Truman (Chapter 11, 12) as a threat to his career! The exposure of "protected" Red agents in government would spell political disaster! After all, how could Truman admit he'd known of the dangerous problem all along, yet did nothing to rectify the situation?

While campaigning for the Presidency, Dwight D. Eisenhower (CFR) had promised to "clean out the State Department from top to bottom."[41] Taking over from the disastrous Roosevelt/Truman years, he did absolutely nothing to rid the executive branch of its infestation of Kremlin espionage agents. This President turned out to be yet another coddler of Communists! He let stand Truman's 1947 Executive Order banning congressional investigators from seeing the personnel files on federal employees suspected of being Red spies! He did nothing to circumvent Truman's 1948 directive prohibiting government officials from cooperating with congressional committees investigating disloyalty and subversion.

Senator McCarthy summoned leftist CIA employee William P. Bundy before his committee in 1953. When Harvard's Alger Hiss (CFR) was finally exposed as a Kremlin espionage agent, Harvard's Bundy (CFR) headed a fund raising committee and contributed hundreds of dollars for the traitor's legal defense. Bundy was the son-in-law of Truman's notorious leftist Secretary of State Dean Acheson (CFR), a man believed to have been a Communist espionage agent (Chapter 16). According to Bundy, Acheson felt it was an absolute necessity that his close Communist friend be cleared! So protective of dangerous security risks was Eisenhower that CIA Director Allen Dulles (CFR) was instructed to block the Bundy summons! Eisenhower blatantly defied the Senate's right to investigate subversives in government! During this period, untold numbers of Communist espionage agents were threatened with exposure due to McCarthy's courageous and unrelenting investigations. Many of these subversives were temporarily transferred to the CIA in a successful effort to protect them.

In 1953, the subversive tax exempt Ford Foundation gave a $15 million grant to start the subversive tax exempt Fund for the Republic. The Fund's purpose was twofold: one—to orchestrate a vicious attack on congressional committees investigating Communists and Communism! Two—to attack and destroy individuals like McCarthy who were investigating Communists and Communism! All such hearings and other antiCommunist activities were to be stopped! Earl Browder, former head of the Communist Party USA—and the Red who had his own office in Roosevelt's White House—was hired as a highly paid consultant![42]

Eisenhower did everything in his power to stop anyone from trying to expose subversives imbedded in government! He and his people worked desperately to cover up the vast Communist penetration of State, Treasury, Agriculture, etc. Ike sabotaged all investigations of this terribly serious problem! He was personally behind the Communist-staged vendetta to get Joe McCarthy. The patriotic Senator's *only* crime was his systematic exposure of Red agents in numerous federal agencies. Why then was this President so vehement in trying to block McCarthy's investigative endeavors? The Senator explained: "Too much was coming out and he had to stop the show!"*43* But why?

Henry Cabot Lodge (CFR) instigated Eisenhower's vicious smear campaign against anti-Communist Senator Robert Taft (R-OH), at the 1952 Republican National Convention. Lodge also worked closely with leftist Deputy Attorney General William P. Rogers (CFR), in the despicable 1954 attack designed to destroy McCarthy and end his exposure of the Communist enemy. McCarthy's revealing investigations had proven to be a time of anxiety for Reds and their patrons and protectors in the Eisenhower Administration. Rogers was no more than Ike's ruthless hatchetman! He spearheaded the vindictive campaign to destroy the Senator. If successful, the smears would discredit McCarthy and thereby halt further exposure of Reds buried in all levels of government.

"These Liberal voices would denounce Communism and then turn right around and parrot the Communist line," explains Ezra Taft Benson. "They claimed they were anti-Communist, but spent most of their time fighting those who were really effective anti-Communists. As I asked some of them at the time, 'Are you fighting the Communists or not? You claim to be fighting the fire, but you spend nearly all of your time fighting the firemen!'"[44]

Also participating in the planned destruction of a true American patriot, in order to protect Communists in government, were members of the White House Palace Guard. Included were Paul G. Hoffman (CFR), C.D. Jackson (CFR), and Sidney Weinberg. Others playing the "Destroy-McCarthy-Game" were Attorney General Herbert Brownell; White House aides Sherman Adams and Gerald Morgan: and Department of the Army counselor John G. Adams. These men gathered together on January 21, 1954, for an emergency meeting in the Attorney General's office. Something had to be done quickly about stopping Joe McCarthy! Word was out that the courageous Senator was planning to subpoena Army Loyalty and Screening Board members. These people were *known* to be giving clearances to dangerous security risks for sensitive federal jobs!

Here's how it all came to pass. Spies in the employ of Moscow had heavily infiltrated the Signal Corps' top secret radar laboratories at Fort Monmouth, New Jersey. The FBI had repeatedly warned the Army about this from 1949 to 1953. Absolutely *nothing* had been done to correct the problem until Senator McCarthy began an investigation in 1953. Then and only then were 35 serious security risks finally suspended by Fort Monmouth's Commanding Officer, Major General Kirke B. Lawton. Someone in the Pentagon was distressed over Lawton's cooperation with McCarthy! He was ordered to Walter Reed Hospital for an examination, confined to quarters for three weeks, then given a disability discharge! These actions were designed to get Lawton out of the way, to stop him from testifying before McCarthy's investigating committee.[45]

The Army Loyalty and Screening Board in the Pentagon eventually reviewed the 35 security risk cases. Incredibly, all but two of these dangerous subversives were *reinstated* with back pay! McCarthy rightfully demanded the names of the 20 civilians on the Loyalty Board! In January of 1954, he let it be known that they'd be subpoenaed. This action brought on the emergency meeting of top Eisenhower plotters on January 21, in the Attorney General's office. Here it was determined to stop McCarthy once and for all—whatever the cost! According to Senator Karl Mundt, Army Counselor Adams "made vigorous and diligent efforts" to block McCarthy's subpoenas of the Loyalty Board members.[46] Why? What exactly was Adams trying to hide?

Eisenhower's campaign slogan had been "Let's clean up the mess in Washington."[47]

Ike implied he was prepared to expose and fire security risks "in every department."[48] He did exactly the opposite! On March 5, 1954, the President sent a "Personal and Confidential" letter to each Cabinet head. They were ordered to "shield" their employees from congressional investigators looking into Communist infiltration. Why?

Army Counselor Adams inadvertently mentioned the secret January 21, 1954 meeting at the Justice Department, while testifying during the Army-McCarthy Hearings. Senator McCarthy and others were interested in hearing more but Eisenhower was determined to force a showdown!

The President perfidiously followed Truman's example and on May 17, 1954, ordered Defense Department employees not "to testify to any such conversations or communications or to produce any such documents or reproductions."[49] His directive was more far-reaching than had been Truman's. No information of any sort could now be supplied to congress! No executive branch employee could testify before any congressional committee, without having prior permission! This Presidential "gag rule" was better known as the "Eisenhower Black-out Order." It effectively put an end to investigations of Communist infiltration into various government agencies.

On June 2, 1954, McCarthy declared: "Communist infiltration of the CIA . . . disturbs me beyond words."[50] The Senator's past hearings had already terrified the paranoid Reds and their protectors on the "liberal" left! McCarthy's planned investigation of the subverted Central Intelligence Agency had to be stopped, so Eisenhower instructed Vice President Nixon to block his friend's efforts. Nixon followed orders and coldly betrayed McCarthy! It turned out that McCarthy was right all along. Such a CIA probe was certainly long overdue! It was discovered that Kim Philby, a high ranking Soviet spy, had successfully penetrated British intelligence. Philby had also been instrumental in initially setting up the CIA.[51] So pregnant was the CIA with Reds that it even bankrolled the Communist Party's *Daily Worker*.[52]

Congressional investigators were still turning up Communist spies and suspected Communists at all levels of government. Despite their questionable background and obvious disloyalty, these subversives had, for some obscure reason, been "cleared" by their superiors. To get around the problem, a new Eisenhower directive prodigiously placed all security files of executive branch employees "off limits" to congressional committees.*53* Had such an order been in effect earlier, Soviet spies such as Alger Hiss, Harry Dexter White and Lauchlin Currie would never have been exposed! Congressman Francis E. Walter (D-PA), Chairman of the House Committee on Un-American Activities, blasted the order as "incredibly stupid!"*54* Nevertheless, in a callous betrayal of his campaign promise, Eisenhower effectively stopped congressional committees from further investigating Communists in government!

In 1956, Vice President Nixon (CFR) *lied* when he credited Eisenhower with having eliminated security risks from the government! He *lied* when he said the issue of Communist subversion was now "out of the political arena!"*55* He *lied* when he charged that Communists imbedded in government were no longer a problem! And he *lied* when he claimed that McCarthy-type Congressional investigations were no longer necessary! Nixon deliberately ignored the findings of the 1951-1952 Senate Internal Security Subcommittee (Chapter 13). He stated: "The present security program resulted in 6,926 individuals being removed from the federal service."*56* This was another blatant lie! Nixon was merely trying to take the heat off the Administration and make it appear more antiCommunist! In fact, Civil Service Commission Chairman Phillip Young swore under oath that *not one* Communist of fellow traveler had been fired since Eisenhower took offfice!*57* Alan Stang may well have correctly concluded: "Nixon is lying whenever his lips move."*58*

William Rogers was richly rewarded for his behind the scenes dirty work, aimed at destroying Joe McCarthy. This Machiavellian political moiler became Ike's Attorney General in 1957. Rogers made no effort to rid governmental agencies of Reds, as Eisenhower had promised during his campaign. The exposure and rousting of Communists and other traitors in and out of government came to a screeching halt with the political demise of the anti-Communist Senator. Many men of stature (in and out of the political arena) objected much less to blatant subversion and outright treason than they did to where the investigations of such criminal activities might ultimately lead. The highly visible and well publicized destruction of Senator McCarthy had a purpose. He was made the example of what would happen to anyone who dared take on the Reds. The message was unmistakably clear!

Nixon again *lied* in 1959, when he declared: "Domestic Communism is no longer a political issue. The danger has receded a great deal in the last few years . . . mainly because we have become increasingly aware of it."*59* Could such an asinine statement have been made in ignorance? Hardly! A clue to the real Nixon surfaced when he deliberately ran a losing race for Governor of California in 1962. He campaigned hard against Proposition 24, a state-wide initiative to outlaw the Communist Party![60]

A concentrated drive to oust *anti-Communists* from government positions was initiated during the Kennedy Administration. JFK's leftist appointees allowed the wholesale penetration of all government agencies by security risks (Chapter 11). Known subversives were either left in place or promoted (Chapter 9). When men he wanted in his administration were denied security clearances by the proper intelligence agencies, the President and his left-leaning cronies merely overrode them and issued their own clearances.

In January 1961, Colonel Michael M. Goleniewski defected. This man was deputy chief of *Glowny Zarzad Informacji,* the Polish equivalent of the Soviet KGB! Here begins a phenomenal expose of a major penetration of the State Department, the CIA, and elsewhere! In fact, when the Colonel went to his initial debriefing meeting with top CIA brass, he found "one of my own agents sitting in front of me."*61* The importance of Goleniewski's knowledge can be seen in his expose of Henry Kissinger as a Soviet spy, with the code name "Bor"*62* (Chapter 7, 11). Goleniewski's incredible story has to date been ignored by the media and swept under the rug by those who run Washington. President Johnson and his subversive Secretary of State, Dean Rusk, did everything in their power to bury Goleniewski's revelations! They feared another Alger Hiss spy scandal in 1964, an election year.[63]

Richard M. Nixon had an atrocious pro-Communist record during his long political career. For example, candidate Nixon told the voters: "I want a Secretary of State that will join me in cleaning out the State Department . . . it has never been done . . . We are going to clean house up there!"[64] Nixon again lied! He had no intention of keeping his campaign promise! When this nefarious scoundrel finally became President in 1969, the problem of Communist subversion was conveniently ignored.

Nixon immediately announced that the maleficent leftist, William P. Rogers—the man in charge of destroying McCarthy for Eisenhower— was his pick for Secretary of State. Rogers ignored all evidence of Communist penetration and claimed the State department was in "excellent condition." Security risk Idar Rimestad was to continue as his Deputy Undersecretary of Administration. The subversive elements, so vociferously denounced while Nixon was running for office, were again safe from exposure!

Indeed, the President-elect paid a personal visit to State soon after taking office. He assured the many Soviet espionage agents that they needn't worry. There would be no "cleaning out" of the State Department! He announced: "When we talk about new leadership, that does not mean that all of those who have served in career positions in the old leadership should leave the service . . . Under no circumstances would I say to men who have rendered such distinguished service 'step aside' and put in completely inexperienced men in their places."[65] Nixon subsequently worsened the internal security problem with his widespread appointments of subversives (Chapter 9, 11).

True to form, Secretary of State Rogers also made it clear the Administration didn't intend to "clean house" as

Nixon had promised. Rogers joked: "You know, I come from a small town and to us a housecleaning was something that was done once a year. The wives freshened everything up, moved things around, got rid of things that weren't useful anymore—but they never threw out all the furniture."[66]

Rogers again showed his true colors when he personally blocked the reinstatement of anti-Communist Otto Otepka as head of State Department security. Otepka had been fired by notorious subversive Dean Rusk (Chapter 9, 10), for the crime of exposing dangerous security risks and blocking their placement in sensitive State Department jobs (Chapter 11).

Yes, it can be safely said that William P. Rogers never veered from his commitment to the Communist cause in America!

Why have traitors for so long had free reign in America? Why have these and other treasonous shenanigans been allowed to so consistently take place? Simply because it's not the policy of the government to fight internal subversion! It if were, the Hatch Act of 1939 could readily be enforced! One provision specifically bars federal employees from "membership in any political party or organization which advocates the overthrow of our constitutional form of government in the United States."[67]

Due to such massive infiltration over the years, the government appears to be a captive of the international Communist conspiracy and at this point nothing further can be done! The Department of Justice refused to enforce the Communist Control Act, a section of which effectively outlawed the Communist Party! This legislation was no anti-Communist figment of the imagination. It was the law of the land for many years, and it still would be today if not for the notorious Civil Rights Act of 1964, which overrode this important legislation. Here's the crystal-clear provision of the Communist Control Act:

"The Communist party of the United States, or any successors of such party regardless of the assumed name, whose object or purpose is to overthrow the Government of the United States, or the Government of any State, Territory, District, or possession thereof, or the government of any political subdivision therein by force and violence, are not entitled to any of the rights, privileges, and immunities attendant upon legal bodies created under the jurisdiction of the laws of the United States or any political subdivision thereof; and whatever rights, privileges and immunities which have heretofore been granted to said party or any subsidiary organization by reason of the laws of the United States or any political subdivision thereof are hereby terminated."[68]

Chapter 9

Security Risks in the State Department

Traitor: "One guilty of betrayal."
New Webster's Dictionary

Treason: "The action of betraying... treacherous action..."
A New English Dictionary

Secretary of State George Catlett Marshall was sent a confidential memorandum on June 10, 1947. The sensational document read in part: "It becomes necessary due to the gravity of the situation to call your attention to a condition that developed and still flourishes in the State Department under the administration of Dean Acheson. . . there is a deliberate, calculated program being carried out not only to protect Communist personnel in high places but to reduce security and intelligence protection . . .

"On file in the Department is a copy of a preliminary [100 page] report of the FBI on Soviet espionage activities . . . which involves a large number of State Department employees, some in high official positions. . . Should this case break before the State Department acts, it will be a national disgrace. Voluminous files are on hand . . . proving the connection of the State Department employees and officials with this Soviet espionage ring. . . " *1*

With his incredibly leftist background and previous pro-Communist track record, Marshall handled this explosive report exactly as could have been predicted. It was ignored, filed, and then forgotten for over two years.

The Senate Committee thereafter informed Marshall about a number of serious security risks in the State Department. It was pointed out that these people were "only a few of the hundreds now employed in varying capacities who are protected and allowed to remain despite the fact that their presence is an obvious hazard to national security."*2* Marshall also ignored this shocking report!

Before highly placed Communists and their radical fellow travelers were able to force him out, security evaluator Otto Otepka had reviewed the files of important State Department employees. Otepka subsequently testified with regard to 858 questionable cases: "It is necessary for me to stress that among the 858 cases there were allegations and evidence of actual membership in the Communist Party, actual membership in adjuncts of the Communist Party such as the Young Communist League, actual membership in Communist-front organizations . . . Actually there were 1,943 cases [almost 20 percent of the total State Department payroll] located during the 1955-56 investigation, of which 858 were the residue. Scott McLeod, as head of State Department Security, had called these 858 serious security risks to the attention of the Secretary of State." *3*

McLeod had his staff review Otepka's list. It was further trimmed to 258 "serious security risks." A secret June 27, 1956, memorandum listing these 258 State Department employees was prepared. William J. Gill revealed: "Approximately 150 were in high-level posts where they could in one way or another influence the formulation of United States foreign policy. And fully half of these 258 serious cases were officials in either crucial intelligence assignments or serving on top-secret committees reaching all the way up and into the National Security Council." *4*

No action was *ever* taken over the startling charges in the above reports. The Kremlin treason team was more firmly in control of the State Department than even the congressional investigators or Otto Otepka and Scott McLeod realized. The identical problem still exists decades later! State remains thoroughly infested by traitors in the employ of Communist Occupied Russia! A full scale investigation is certainly merited!

Reread this sentence from the Senate Appropriation Committee's secret memo: " . . . *there is a deliberate, calculated program being carried out not only to protect Communist personnel in high places but to reduce security and intelligence protection . . . "* 5

This is the answer, then, as to how so many Soviet espionage agents are able to commit treason, with such impunity. This is the reason so many traitors are able to move up in government positions, in spite of the fact that others are aware of their Red backgrounds. This is why so few Communists are ever rooted out of sensitive positions and publicly exposed. It is also the reason that the few who have been uncovered are merely dismissed but not prosecuted for their treasonous deeds. This is why Kremlin spies can still be working in the State Department for as many as 20 years or more after having been exposed. And it's the answer as to why so many traitors have consistently been given highly sensitive jobs, despite the fact that their atrocious Communist background is a matter of public record.

A classic example of such a protected subversive is that of Harvard man David Henry Popper. This notorious security risk was positively identified as a Soviet spy, by a defecting Russian intelligence agent. A high-ranking member of the American Communist Party was informed: "Popper is one of us and should be treated accordingly." 6

Here is part of the man's incriminating Red record: Popper had been on the editorial board of the Communist *Amerasia* magazine. He was deeply involved in the espionage scandal in which classified documents were stolen for the Russians (Chapter 16)! On the board with Popper were a number of other Communist agents—Frederick

Vanderbilt Field; Soviet-born managing editor Philip J. Jaffee; T.A. Bisson; Ch'ao Ting Chi, and Harriet Levine Chi. Owen Lattimore was there. He had also been reliably identified as a Communist, but he denied the charges.*7*

Popper was connected with Commonwealth College in Mena, Arkansas, a Communist training school! He worked for the radical Foreign Policy Association, cited as a "factory for propaganda to appease the Soviet Union and to apologize for its expansion in all directions."*8* His boss was Vera Micheles Dean, a dangerous subversive who was sent to the United States from Communist Occupied Russia in 1919. *(9)*

Popper held important policy-making positions from Truman to Carter, despite his atrocious Communist background! He was initially brought into government as a protégé of Soviet spy Alger Hiss in 1945. This Red was subsequently given an important position in the Eisenhower Administration, although he was widely known to have close connections with Soviet intelligence operatives. His name appeared on an official list of subversives compiled by State's Security Chief, Scott McLeod! The list was presented to Eisenhower's Secretary of State, John Foster Dulles. Dulles did nothing! *[10]*

This Soviet espionage agent became Kennedy's Senior Advisor to the UN on disarmament. As could be expected of any Communist clone, he called for the immediate unilateral disarmament of America. Popper was a member of Johnson's NATO delegation in 1962. He became Nixon's Ambassador to Cyprus and Ford's Chilean Ambassador. Popper never strayed from his anti-American subversion over the years. He was heavily involved in the Canal sellout to the Reds, as Carter's Chief of the Panama Canal Treaty Affairs. *[11]*

Popper worked closely with various Communists associated with the Institute of Pacific Relations. The IPR was a "vehicle used by the Communists to orientate American far eastern policy toward Communist objectives."*12* Intelligence agencies consistently brought Popper's Red background to the attention of the proper authorities. Instead of being publicly exposed and then fired, all reports on him were ignored. No effort was ever made to remove this suspected Red agent from government![13]

The astute words of Senator Joseph R. McCarthy (R-WI) certainly apply to David Henry Popper and all the other subversives to follow. He said: "There is no reason why men who chum with Communists, who refuse to turn their backs on traitors, and who are consistently found at the time and place where disaster strikes America and success comes to international Communism, should be given positions of power in government."[14]

A Few More Notorious Security Risks

Dean Rusk (CFR), was a protégé of suspected Communist agent Dean Achesont.[15] (Chapter 16). This radical leftist is one of the better known security risks in America! Back in 1949, Rusk and his pro-Communist pals (buried safely within State and Treasury) engineered the colossal betrayal of a loyal American ally. These traitors were responsible for disarming Chiang Kai-shek and then deliberately turning free China over to the Reds! Rusk and the other leftist "Old China Hands" dutifully spouted Stalin's "agrarian reformer" line, like a group of synchronized robots. Every one of these traitors, *without exception,* was closely tied to the subversive Institute of Pacific Relations. The IPR was much like an employment agency, which specialized in placing Soviet espionage agents in important government positions!

When Alger Hiss was exposed as a Kremlin spy and left the State Department in 1947, Rusk took his job as Director of the Office of Special Political Affairs. Hiss had used his position to place Communist agents in high paying UN jobs! Rusk continued this treasonous policy, until it was finally brought to light by a Senate Internal Security Subcommittee investigation. To say the least, many Communists were placed in influential positions at the UN, thanks to subversives like Hiss and Rusk.

As Truman's Assistant Secretary of State for Far Eastern Affairs in 1950, Rusk was directly responsible for America's treasonous "no-win" policy during the Korean War! This horrendous security risk recommended firing General MacArthur in 1951, for wanting to go after the retreating Red hordes and win the war. Rusk even wrote the letter of dismissal for Truman to sign. He was the man behind the disgraceful Korean Armistice, where the U.S. agreed in effect to shamefully surrender to the Reds and leave hundreds of American boys behind in POW camps (Chapter 15)!

So far to the left was Dean Rusk that when he spoke at the University of Pennsylvania in 1951, he compared bloodthirsty Mao Tse-tung to George Washington! The mass-murdering Chinese Reds were flatteringly described as "native revolutionaries in the American tradition!"*16* This dangerous subversive became Kennedy's most influential advisor (Chapter 11). He was instrumental in the incredibly callous betrayal of 1400 Cuban Freedom Fighters during the Bay of Pigs invasion on April 17, 1961. The invasion of Cuba and the downfall of Communist dictator Fidel Castro was contrived to fail from the beginning by Rusk and other subversives in government! It resulted (as planned) in the total destruction or capture of Castro's most feared anti-Communist opposition.

Rusk had a well-known record of unwavering commitment to the Communist cause! Yet this dangerous security risk was allowed to stay on as Secretary of State under Lyndon Johnson, after Kennedy was murdered by KGB-assassin Lee Harvey Oswald. Utilizing the same methods he'd previously employed so successfully against Chiang Kai-shek in China, Rusk supervised the systematic destruction of the pro-American, anti-Communist Laotian government. This subversive brazenly orchestrated the traitorous no-win war in Vietnam, as he had previously done in Korea! Dean Rusk's record of openly supporting Communists and Communism, over the decades, is absolutely astounding! Even more unbelievable is the fact that he got away with it!

How many Americans have heard of the virtually unknown subversive, Charles Woodruff Yost (CFR)? This radical leftist has been firmly imbedded in important government positions, starting with Franklin Roosevelt. Believed to be a Kremlin spy early on, Yost was still able to smoothly sail from one administration to another. This serious security risk was a close friend of Communist Alger Hiss and in 1935 worked with Communist agent Lee Pressman in the Resettlement Administration. He was also a ranking official in the Office of Arms and Munitions Control. This was conveniently during the time Hiss was legal counsel to the Senate committee, investigating the munitions industry!

Yost worked closely with Soviet spies Virginius Frank Coe and Michael Greenberg (later to become Truman's top White House assistant) and Nathan Gregory Silvermaster. Despite a damning record of association with top Reds, Yost was given the same top advisory job with Truman, at the calamitous Potsdam Conference, that his co-conspirator Hiss had with Roosevelt, at Yalta! Yost was a member of the subversive Institute of Pacific Relations, as was Dean Rusk and David Henry Popper. The FBI exposed the IPR as a Soviet spy ring.

Yost retired in 1966, after a lifetime devoted to the Communist cause. But so important a conspirator couldn't be left alone for long. He was brought back in 1969 to be Nixon's Ambassador to the very UN he'd helped Comrades Hiss and Pasvolsky to found. Yost had been identified as one of 258 extremely serious State Department security risks, by Otto Otepka, before the Senate Internal Security Subcommittee. He had always been given security clearances on the basis of "higher authority." When asked about Yost's incredible Communist background, Nixon responded with a straight face: *"There's no question about his loyalty to his country."* 17

Was Rusk a Communist? Was Yost? Such questions are moot when Stalin's definition is applied: "Some are members of the Party, and some are not; but that is a formal difference. The important thing is that both serve the same common purpose. [18]

Boris Klosson wrote the favorable 1961 report on Lee Harvey Oswald who, as a marine, had defected to Communist Occupied Russia from a U.S. base in Japan. Klosson's report enabled the assassin to return to the United States, after having renounced his citizenship. It reads: "Subject: Citizenship & Passports. Lee Harvey Oswald . . . twenty months of the realities of life in the Soviet Union have clearly had a maturing effect on Oswald. He stated frankly that he . . . has been completely relieved of his illusions about the Soviet Union and at the same time that he acquired a new understanding and appreciation of the United States, and the meaning of freedom . . . "[19]

Klosson had long been a member of identified Soviet agent Henry Kissinger's [20] inner circle. He eventually became the most important SALT negotiator for the United States. This subversive's name had once been found in a female Soviet agent's "contact" book! All of his character references were known security risks! Klosson was another dangerous leftist who had moved to the State Department from the Communist dominated OSS. He was Kennedy's Counselor for Political Affairs at the American Embassy in Moscow.

The State Department, true to its pro-Communist orientation, moved on the recommendation of Kissinger's friend Klosson—a sus*pected Communist* spy! They paid the travel expenses for a man FBI Director J. Edgar Hoover called a "dedicated Communist!" [21] They did the same for Marina, Oswald's KGB-connected spouse (Chapter 16). Yes, the State Department made it possible for Oswald to leave the Soviet Union —where he'd been carefully trained as an assassin—and return to the United States, where he would ultimately carry out his assassination of the President.

According to the syndicated Allen-Scott Report, there was substantial documentation to strongly indicate that Lee Harvey Oswald was not only a Soviet KGB agent, but a member of the Communist's secret army in the United

States.*22* Congressman John R. Pillion (R-NY) reveals a bit of little known information, not to be found in the public version of the *Warren Commission Report* (Chapter 16). But it *WAS* secretly included with the material deposited in the National Archives: "Immediately upon his arrival in the Soviet Union, Oswald voluntarily became associated with the Soviet secret police . . . the KGB provided a job for him in the sheet-metal shop of a radio factory in Minsk . . . This was a sham 'cover' job.

"The 1,400 ruble monthly income of Oswald was comparable to the salary of the general manager of the factory . . . The KGB provided Oswald with a scarce and comparatively luxurious apartment in Minsk for a period of more than two years," Pillion concludes. "The grant for a exit visa to Oswald and to his wife, Marina, is a most extraordinary Soviet act . . . There can be little question but that Oswald and Marina were considered by the KGB to be potential agents for either specific or future assignments. The KGB arranged to allow Oswald to engage in target practice and shooting [at a KGB training school] during his more than two years stay in Minsk. The use of a rifle and practice privileges in absolutely forbidden to foreigners in the Soviet." [23]

What has the media reported on these sensational revelations? Has John Chancellor (CFR) ever brought this story to his viewers? Or Robert L. McNeill (CFR) and Jim Lehrer (CFR)? Has James Reston (CFR) or Marquis Childs (CFR) reported on this to their wide readership? How about George Will (CFR), that presumptuous, pseudo-conservative? Or his boorish alter ego, William F. Buckley Jr. (CFR)? Unfortunately, none of these media super stars have had much to offer on the above story, nor will they in the future!

Dangerous subversive Louis Earl Frechtling was initially hired in 1942 by his friend and Soviet spy—Nathan Gregory Silvermaster! He was Roosevelt's Chief of the Near East Section of the Board of Economic Warfare. This leftist was brought into the State Department under Truman in

1946 and was still around during the Nixon Administration. Frechtling was formerly with the Communist-dominated Foreign Policy Association, as was David Henry Popper and a multitude of other subversives. He was also a member of the Communist-controlled Institute of Pacific Relations, which was cited as "an instrument of Communist policy, propaganda and military intelligence."*24* Although this security risk's Red background was known from the beginning, he always received security clearances by "higher authority."

Radical leftist Averill Harriman (CFR) went into government service (which government is open to question) during the Roosevelt years. He had, among many other treasonous deeds, assisted notorious Communist spy Alger Hiss in the sordid 1945 betrayal of Poland, at Yalta. Harriman (Chapter 2) was also instrumental in the sellout of pro-American, anti-Communist Laos, under Kennedy. This wealthy subversive was the architect of the infamous nuclear test ban treaty, in which every facet was designed to favor his friends in the Kremlin. Harriman was for decades one of Communist Occupied Russia's greatest benefactors, apologists, and appeasers. Over the years, his involvement in foreign policy has *always* resulted in disaster for America's best interests and has *always* greatly assisted the goals of the Reds!

Dr. Philip C. Jessup's record as a security risk was long and atrocious! He'd been on the Board of Trustees of the Communist dominated Institute of Pacific Relations. Jessup (CFR), Owen Lattimore, John Paton Davies, and Soviet spy, John Carter Vincent were all key State Department subversives involved in delivering China to the Communists. Harry Dexter White, Frederick Vanderbilt Field, and Lauchlin Currie were a few more of his close Moscow-directed Comrades. Another friend was John Stewart Service, who was apprehended while giving classified documents to Russian spies. Jessup, a protégé of subversive Dean Acheson, was found to have, to put it mildly, an "unusual affinity for Communist causes."*25* Truman ignored the damning facts, just as he did with Kremlin espionage agents Harry Dexter White and Alger Hiss. Ever loyal to his Red contacts, Comrade Jessup (Chapter 14) twice appeared as a character witness for his close friend Hiss.

John Fairbank (CFR), *Harvard professor*, was another of the "Old China Hands" in the State Department! He played a major part in Chiang Kai-shek's betrayal and the delivery of China to Communist Mao. This subversive was a trustee with the notorious Institute of Pacific Relations. The Senate Internal Security Subcommittee formally concluded: "Since the mid-1930s, the net effect of the IPR activities on United States public opinion has been pro-Communist and pro-Soviet . . . "*26* Louis Budenz, former editor of the *Daily Worker*, testified that, according to official Party reports, Fairbank was a Red! [27]

One of many serious security risks in the Eisenhower Administration was Jacob Dyneley Beam (CFR), who became Ambassador to Communist Occupied Poland in 1957. Beam covered for Edward Symans, one of his Comrades at the Warsaw Embassy. Symans was known to have been a Soviet espionage agent for *at least 18* years! This Communist spy *was not* prosecuted. He was instead allowed to retire with a fat government pension![28] The Ambassador had an affair with Madame Jerzy Michalowski, a Soviet agent and a member of the Central Committee of the Polish Communist Party! His record of Communist affiliations and appeasement spans decades. It goes all the way back to 1934, where he was on Ambassador William E. Dodd's staff in Berlin. So dangerous was Beam that the intelligence community was stunned when be became Ambassador to Communist Occupied Russia, under Nixon.

The man who initially recommended Daniel L. Horowitz for a federal job was Communist Lawrence Duggan. Duggan was a Soviet spy, who once headed the State Department's Latin American section (Chapter 10). Horowitz was often reported as a serious security risk! Both he and his wife have close associates among Russian espionage agents.

Horowitz had joined a variety of Communist Fronts, including the American Student Union. This dangerous subversive appropriately became a Special Assistant to Eisenhower's leftist Secretary of State, William Rogers (Chapter 8, 11).

Security risk Harlan Cleveland (CFR) was denied a clearance in 1961, when appointed Assistant Secretary of State under Kennedy. He got the job anyway, when subversive Dean Rusk intervened and waived the security check requirement. Cleveland immediately selected eight leftist cronies to work for him. Three had previously been on the personal staff of Soviet spy Alger Hiss. None were able to obtain clearances and State Department security chief Otto Otepka refused to grant them waivers. Cleveland simply hired his Comrades as consultants, thereby bypassing the normal security check requirements. In July of 1962, Cleveland rubbed salt in the wound, when he brashly queried Otepka: "What are the chances of getting Hiss back into the government?"[29]

Despite his extensive pro-Communist background, Cleveland became Ambassador to NATO under both Johnson and Nixon. He tried to obtain a clearance for another leftist friend, named Irving Swerdlow. Swerdlow had previously been fired as a security risk by another government agency. His subversive record was, according to one security investigator, "the rottenest I have ever seen."[30] No clearance was forthcoming. Swerdlow was subsequently cleared by "higher authority."

George Ball (CFR) started out in the Roosevelt Treasury Department from 1933 to 1935, as did so many other serious security risks. Despite his long subversive record, this radical leftist became Under Secretary of State for Dean Rusk, in 1961. Ball was instrumental in the treasonous betrayal of Katanga's anti-Communist leader, Moise Tshombe! In turn, he enthusiastically supported Communist Patrice Lumumba and his bloodthirsty UN savages in their terrorist subjugation of the Congo (Chapter 14).

Richard Barnet was but one of the multitude of clone-like security risks churned out by the Harvard Law School! This subversive was another pro-Communist State Department Arms Control official under Kennedy. He belonged to the Washington Chapter of the Communist National Lawyers Guild. The NLG was cited by the House Committee on Un-American Activities as "the foremost legal bulwark of the Communist Party . . . "*31* Barnet left the government in 1963 to found the Communist dominated Institute for Policy Studies.

Nicholas de B. Katzenbach (CFR) had an aversion for prosecuting Communists when he was LBJ's Attorney General in 1964. This subversive was later an Under Secretary of State. His wife's aunt was the notorious Russian-born Rose Pastor Stokes, a member of the Executive Committee of the Communist Party! Katzenbach (Chapter 11) was instrumental in bringing the despicable John Paton Davies back into government service, by waiving his security clearance requirement on January 13, 1969. Davies was okayed to work as a consultant on a highly sensitive disarmament research project, in the CIA's Center for International Studies at MIT! This was done with the consent of incoming Secretary of State William P. Rogers (Chapter 8, 11), a few days before Nixon took office.

John Paton Davies had been branded a serious security risk by a State Department Hearing Board in 1954. Ambassador Patrick Hurley believed Davies to be a Communist! He had Davies, John Stewart Service, and others recalled for their treasonous efforts to undermine Chiang Kai-shek and bring China under the control of Mao's Red terrorists (Chapter 10). Davies assisted many Communist friends and associates in finding government jobs. These included such identified Reds as Agnes Smedley, John K Fairbank, Anna Strong, and Edgar Snow.

Ellsworth Bunker (CFR) was on the Board of Directors of the American-Russian Institute for Cultural Relations with the Soviet Union. This organization was cited by Attorney General Tom Clark as "Communist."*32* Bunker was honorary president of the subversive Foreign Policy Association, known as a "propaganda" factory for Communist Occupied Russia.*33* He was also a trustee of the Marxist New School for Social Research. Bunker's public record of service to Communist causes spanned many Administrations. Despite this, Nixon kept him on as Ambassador to South Vietnam, where he helped to orchestrate the traitorous sellout of that nation to the Reds. Assisting Bunker in the sordid betrayal of war-torn South Vietnam was another serious security risk, Samuel David Berger. He was the notoriously pro-Communist Counselor at the U.S. Embassy in Tokyo, during Eisenhower's term! Berger was a protégé of Communist Harold Laski. He's but one of many subversives who started their long Red-aiding government career under Roosevelt.

Security risk Barbara Watson first joined the State Department under Johnson in 1966, with the powerful backing of Communist-connected Senator Jacob Javits (R-NY). She was a special assistant to leftist Deputy Under Secretary for Administration, William J. Crockett, who was forced to resign after being publicly exposed for trying to destroy anti-Communists in the State Department. Watson stayed on with Nixon and Carter despite the fact that, thanks to her, security at the State Department became even more of an international joke. This subversive relaxed passport restrictions on foreign Communists entering the United States and on American Reds freely traveling throughout the world. She was a friend of notorious Communist Fronter Mary McLeod Bethune and Eleanor Roosevelt, a woman who surrounded herself with notable Reds and who defended traitors like Hiss and Currie, when they were exposed! Watson belonged to a number of Communist Fronts herself and often hosted Communist dictator of Ghana, Kwame Nkrumah, in her home. This radical leftist received a distinguished service award from the Red government of Ghana.*34*

Another Harvard man, Leonard Unger, has a record of government service going all the way back to Roosevelt.

Unger was exposed in 1947 as a member of a Soviet spy ring operating in the State Department's European Affairs section! Others named with him were Robert W. Barnett (CFR), Edwin M. Martin (CFR), Livingston T. Merchant (CFR), Lawrence G. Vass, and Benjamin T. Moore (CFR).*35* Yet, Unger was still named Ambassador to Thailand under Johnson and Nixon, where he pushed for the betrayal of anti-Communists in both Thailand and Laos. A friend of identified Soviet agent Henry Kissinger*36* (Chapter 11), he was (almost insultingly) appointed as Ambassador to the Republic of China, on Taiwan—the perfect choice to assist in and help arrange the betrayal of anti-Communist Free China. Unger's name was found on State Department security chief Scott McLeod's list of 858 serious security risks. Nevertheless, this subversive was always given security clearances by "higher authority."[37]

Robert W. Barnett was considered to be one of the State Department's most dangerous security risks. He'd been exposed in 1947 as part of a spy ring in service to Communist Occupied Russia! Nevertheless, he could still be found working as a consultant in the Nixon Administration, almost three decades later! This identified Russian spy was a member of the Institute of Pacific Relations, in reality a Communist employment agency that regularly staffed the State Department. Barnett's wife, Patricia, also held sensitive State Department positions despite her atrocious subversive background. She worked for Nixon as an intelligence specialist, with a top security clearance! The Barnett's security files were classified "espionage," yet all efforts to remove these traitors from the State Department failed![38]

Edwin M. Martin (CFR) was shuttled over to the State Department in 1945—as was security risk Boris Klosson—from the thoroughly Communist infiltrated Office of Strategic Services (OSS). Although positively identified during the Truman Administration (in 1947) as a member of a Soviet spy ring,*39* Martin has consistently been one of the State Department untouchables! He was a member of the Red dominated Institute of Pacific Relations. As were

Leonard Unger and so many other highly placed moles, Martin was a member of the blatantly Red Washington Bookshop Association, a secret meeting place for Communists. This Communist espionage agent was an intimate friend of John Carter Vincent, another Soviet spy in the State Department. Martin's security file is so damning that the only way he could obtain a clearance was by some undesignated "higher authority." Also close to identified Kremlin agent Henry Kissinger,*40* Martin was named by his Moscow-directed Comrade in 1974 as U.S. Coordinator for the World Food Council.

German-born security risk Alfred Puhan was Nixon's Ambassador to Communist Occupied Hungary. So pro-Communist was he that Jozsef Cardinal Mindszenty refused to shake his hand when leaving Red Hungary, after 15 years of forced residency in the embassy. Puhan's atrocious subversive record goes all the way back to Roosevelt's Office of War Information, in the early 1940s. He was in charge of Voice of American programming under Truman in 1950. Otto Otepka had this to say: "An investigation of Mr. Puhan revealed . . . that he would not allow broadcasts . . . that were embarrassing to the Soviet Union; that he attempted to soften the anti-Communist tone of the Voice of America; that he purged individuals from the program who insisted on strong anti-Communist news broadcasts."*41* While on diplomatic assignments, Puhan consistently gave out erroneous data, to insure policy decisions in Washington which favored the Soviet Union. Puhan made a practice of deleting from his official reports any criticism of Red slave labor dictatorships!

Otto Otepka's 1955-1956 investigation resulted in a list of 858 security risks. According to Otepka: "The name of Alexander Johnpoll appeared on the list . . . Johnpoll . . . had made statements that the only war he would fight in would be to establish Communism in the United States. Mr. Johnpoll's brother was a member of the Young Communist League."*42* This subversive worked in government without interruption under various Administrations, including

Eisenhower, Johnson, and Nixon. He had intimate ties to blatant security risk, Alfred Puhan, and many others.

The security file of Daniel Franks Margolies carries the critical classification of "espionage."[43] Nevertheless, he still held a top secret security clearance under Nixon. Margolies was a close associate of notorious Communist espionage agent, John Abt—the lawyer requested by Oswald after he assassinated Kennedy. Margolies, Abt, and Hiss all worked with the LaFollette Senate Committee, some years ago. He belonged to a number of Communist Fronts, as well as the Red National Lawyers Guild. Margolies closest associates included Communist Eleanor Nelson, who infiltrated the Department of Labor; Harold Glasser, an identified Communist agent; and Communist Alan Rosenberg! Joe Panuch, a State Department security specialist, was unsuccessful in trying to get this dangerous subversive fired. Instead, Reds and their protectors in high places were able to turn the tables! Panuch was ousted while Margolies was promoted![44]

Notorious subversive William O. Hall joined the State Department in 1946 and worked for Kremlin agent Alger Hiss, in the Office of Special Political Affairs. Besides being a Hiss intimate, this security risk was also close to many other Soviet spies, including Harold Glasser and Frank Coe. Other associates were Rowena Rommel and Just Lunning, both fired for security reasons! Hall had first been identified as a serious security risk, in 1966. Yet, over two decades later he could still be found holding sensitive government positions.

Louis A. Wiesner is another security risk, who started in 1943, under Roosevelt, in the heavily infiltrated OSS. He quietly shuttled over to the State Department with no security check in August of 1944. Wiesner was affiliated with the American Student Union, a Communist Front! He actively supported the Young Communist League, attended Communist Party meetings, and applied for membership! Wiesner and droves of others with a like ideology were conveniently stationed in Saigon during the Vietnam War, where they could readily undermine American interests. These rabid leftists were a major factor in the betrayal of South Vietnam to the Communists! This subversive was still around during the Nixon Administration where his job was to disburse hundreds of millions of foreign aid dollars!*45*

Sam Fishback joined the State Department in October of 1945, under Truman. This dangerous security risk was closely associated over the years with numerous Communists. He was a Communist Fronter and a member of the Communist dominated Institute of Pacific Relations. Despite his subversive record, Fishback held a top secret security clearance. Senator Joseph McCarthy pointed out to the Senate that Fishback was recommended for his first government job by "an individual who was . . . a principal in a Soviet espionage case [a suspected Russian spy]. The record indicates he is running very closely with . . . Communists."*46* Fishback could still be found working in the Nixon Administration, for the State Department's Bureau of Intelligence Research. This department creates reports and makes recommendations on which foreign policy decisions are based!*47*

Evelyn Speyer Colbert penetrated the government under Roosevelt. Colbert, as did Wiesner and so many other subversives, transferred to State from the Communist-infested OSS! She has always maintained close associations and friendships with known Communists! Her name was found on security chief Scott McLeod's list of dangerous State Department subversives. Nevertheless, she could still be found working with fellow conspirator Fishback in Nixon's Bureau of Intelligence Research. Her husband, James—also a serious security risk—long had intimate contact with Soviet spies! He had initially been recommended for State Department employment by the notorious subversive Philip C. Jessup.*48*

Anton William DePorte came into the State Department under Eisenhower, using Communist Fronters for his references. DePorte joined the Communist Party as a University of Chicago student. He was an active member of a Red cell operating at the school. Nevertheless, DePorte was given a top level security clearance and assigned to intelligence! He was regularly promoted over the years in highly sensitive jobs. DePorte could be found in Nixon's Bureau of Intelligence Research, with fellow subversives Sam Fishback and Evelyn Colbert! He was also Carter's director of Research and Analysis for Western Europe!*49* Coincidence? Not hardly!

Jesse MacKnight was *positively identified* as espionage agent in the employ of Communist Occupied Russia! He provided Kremlin spy Judith Coplon with sensitive government documents. This intelligence operative was selected by Henry Kissinger, another identified Moscow man,*50* to head the State Department's Office of Security. Incredibly, Comrade MacKnight was actually placed in charge of granting security clearances! He's the subversive who cleared another Kissinger pal, Helmut Sonnenfeldt, even though the man was widely known to be a dangerous security risk! The Kissinger-Sonnefeldt relationship goes all the way back to when Kissinger served in Germany with Army Intelligence, during the 1940s. Sonnefeldt has been the subject of a number of espionage investigations!*[51]*

Dr. Walter Maria Kotschnig (CFR) was born in Austria, as were Henry Kissinger and so many other Comrades! This leftist was the protégé of an important German Communist leader. He was the featured speaker at the Young Communist League Conference in 1943. Joining the State Department under Roosevelt, in 1944, Kotschnig was Technical Assistant to Communist spy Alger Hiss, at the Dumbarton Oaks Conference. In 1945, he assisted his friend Hiss at the UN founding conference, in San Francisco. Kotschnig was one of the many dangerous security risks investigated by State's security chief Scott McLeod, in 1955-1956. Yet, on April 28, 1971, this subversive was presented with the State Department's Distinguished Honor Award!*[52]*

Victor H. Dikeos was in charge of security at the U.S. Embassy in Warsaw, Poland, when KGB agents were allowed free run of the place! He evaded questions and pleaded the Executive Fifth Amendment before the Senate Internal Security Subcommittee, when asked about his relationship with Soviet espionage agents! This subversive was promoted and placed in charge of State Department security, as a reward for his part in the shameful Polish Embassy coverup! This blatant security risk was later named as Carter's Deputy Chief of Mission in Panama.[53]

Royal Jules Wald was another subversive to be found in the Carter State Department who began his foreign service career decades ago. Wald was given a "top secret" security clearance, although he'd been a Communist while attending the University of Hawaii. He was also intimately involved in the American Student Union, an organization cited as "Communist and subversive." Wald was booted out of the Navy after his Communist connections were investigated. He was closely associated with Lieutenant Andrew Roth, who was indicted in the *Amerasia* magazine spy scandal (Chapter 16).[54]

Security risk Andrew Young (CFR) favored the "destruction of Western civilization," if necessary to "liberate" Third World countries.[55] Yet, this seditious radical became Carter's Ambassador to the United Nations. Young had been a top aide to subversive Martin Luther King (Chapter 12). He and King had been trained at Highlander Folk School —a notorious Communist indoctrination and training facility, in Monteagle, Tennessee. Young and his leftist successor, Donald McHenry, used identified Communist lawyer Stanley D. Levison as an advisor. Levison distributes the secret Kremlin funds used to finance Communist activities in the United States.

Philip C. Habib (CFR), a Marxist in his college days, joined the State Department in 1949, under Truman! He admitted to having attended Communist Party meetings. Some of his character references were Communist fronters. Habib contributed money to the Communist Party and maintained an ongoing association with many known Communists. He and his cohort, identified Communist spy Henry Kissinger,[56] negotiated the unconscionable betrayal of South Vietnam to the Reds! This notorious security risk was actually brought out of retirement in 1979 to be Carter's "troubleshooter" in the Caribbean.[57]

Was Abraham Lincoln a prophet when he said: "At what point shall we expect the approach of danger? . . . Shall we expect some transatlantic military giant, to step the ocean, and crush us at a blow? Never! All the armies of Europe, Asia and Africa combined . . . could not by force take a drink from the Ohio, or make a track on the Blue Ridge . . . At what point then is the approach of danger to be expected? I answer, if it ever reach us, it must spring up amongst us."[58]

Chapter 10

Misdeeds of the Subversive State Department

Traitor: "A person who betrays his country . . . one who commits treason."
The Merriam-Webster Pocket Dictionary

Treason: "The betrayal of one's country, esp. by giving aid to an enemy."
The American Heritage Dictionary

"The 'Liberals' ask what proof we have that Communists have been, and are influencing the policies of our government?" offers the Honorable Martin Dies (D-TX), former Chairman of the House Committee on Un-American Activities. "Our answer is: all the proof it was possible to obtain under hostile Administrations which actively smeared and persecuted every Committee of Congress which has tried to get the facts. . . No 'Liberal' will tell us what the eight hundred [actually 858] security risks named by Scott McLeod in 1956 are doing even now in our State Department, unless they are surrendering us to the Reds."[1]

Consider the years when Alger Hiss and his Communist cronies were running the show! How many more Red moles were Hiss and others of like ideology instrumental in bringing into the foreign service and elsewhere in government? The heirs of Hiss certainly didn't quit when their mentor, benefactor, and idol was imprisoned in 1950, for lying to a Grand Jury about being an espionage agent for Communist Occupied Russia! Hiss participated in a cornucopia of traitorous acts and treasonous deeds. Yet he was prosecuted only for being a liar, while under oath, and not a traitor! Why?

Carefully examine the State Department's past and present track record. When has State done *anything* resulting in something beneficial for the United States in foreign policy? Or rather, when has State done anything *not* favoring the global designs of America's dire enemy—Communist Occupied Russia? Look at the State Department's traitorous machinations with regard to Hungary, Cuba, the Congo, Yugoslavia, Nicaragua, and the rest of the Communist occupied slave labor dictatorships! Look at the State Department's traitorous machinations with regard to South Africa, Taiwan, South Vietnam, Laos, Rhodesia, and other anti-Communist American allies! All were either betrayed or are beingbetrayed to the forces of evil by conspirators in the United States government!

When was the last time Communist penetration of the State Department was investigated? Unfortunately, never! Both Eisenhower and Nixon promised during their Presidential campaigns to "clean out" the agency (Chapter 8)! Neither did anything of the sort! Nor did they intend to!

Even during the purported "conservative" Reagan years, the arrogant "leftists" were still untouchable entities! They insolently ran foreign policy contrary to the President's proclaimed goals and contrary to the best interests of America. This is especially appalling when, according to the *United States Government Organizational Manual,* the State Department's primary objective is supposed to be "to promote the long-range security and well-being of the United States."*2*

How the Subversion Game is Played

Some years ago, numerous highly placed traitors in the State Department deliberately undermined and brought down the government of Nationalist China! President Truman enthusiastically supported the betrayal of Chiang Kai-shek, long a dependable friend of the U.S. The country was treasonously relinquished to Mao's Red Chinese gangsters in 1949.. Yes, Free China was not so gently coerced into a Communist dictatorship—one of the bloodiest tyrannies the world has ever known! The Red terrorists looted the country, established their police state, orchestrated an unceasing murder spree, and proceeded to decimate the population.

Chiang Kai-shek's Nationalist Army was close to total victory over Mao's Communist guerrilla forces near the end of 1945. Truman rushed General George Catlett Marshall, a close friend of Eisenhower, over to China, *to stop the rout of the Reds!* Marshall gained a malodorous reputation in the Truman Administration as the official most responsible for Free China's betrayal to the Communists. Chiang Kai-shek, although clearly winning the war, was forced by Marshall to agree to a cease fire. Yet he balked at surrendering to the very Communist guerrillas he was so soundly defeating.

The United States was supposedly helping Nationalist China by sending them hundreds of millions of dollars worth of war goods. The anti-Communist forces desperately needed small arms and ammunition. So entrenched were Communists in the State Department that Chiang got nothing of any value! His supply depots were turned into military junkyards. According to Colonel L.B. Moody, who was there at the time, the anti-Communist forces got "billions of moldy cigarettes, blown up guns and junk bombs, and disabled vehicles from the Pacific islands . . . "*3*

America's free Chinese friends received machine guns with missing tripods, tanks with spiked guns, rifles with no ammunition clips and planes with no fuel!

Furthermore, explains Freda Utley: "President Truman took steps to prevent the National forces from obtaining arms and ammunition . . . On August 14, 1946, President Truman issued an executive order saying that China was not to be allowed to acquire any 'surplus' American weapons 'which could be used in fighting a civil war,' meaning a war with the Communists."*4*

George Marshall as Secretary of State, boasted: "As Chief-of-Staff I armed 39 anti-Communist divisions. Now with a stroke of a pen I disarm them."*5* Marshall clearly knew what he was doing! The Sell-Out China-Program went exactly as scripted by the multitude of Red traitors in the State Department.

Ambassador William D. Pawley blamed the tragic loss of China on the subversive machinations of Communist agents and pro-Communists solidly entrenched in the State Department. Included were Owen Lattimore, John Stewart Service, Philip Jessup, John Paton Davies Jr. John Carter Vincent, Dean Acheson, and O. Edmund Clubb.*6* A few more conspirators devoted to delivering China to the Reds were Communists Agnes Smedley, Frederick Vanderbilt Field, Alger Hiss, Maxwell Stewart, and Lauchlin Currie. All were either working for the State Department or for the Institute of Pacific Relations, cited as being controlled by a "small core of officials and staff members" who "were either Communist or pro-Communist."*7*

Ambassador Pawley was asked if the Red takeover of the Chinese mainland could possibly have been the result of "sincere mistakes of judgment." His unequivocal reply: "No, I don't."*8*

John Stewart Service (Chapter 8, 13, 16) was recalled to Washington in June 1945, at the insistence of the Ambassador to China. Patrick Hurley accused Service of passing secret information to the Reds! General Wedemeyer, for whom this subversive also worked, charged the man with supporting the murderous Chinese Communist forces! Reports written by Service, John Carter Vincent (a Communist), John Paton Davies, and many other conspirators never deviated from the Party line. Designed to discredit Hurley, these propaganda reports were regularly sent to Washington without the Ambassador ever having seen them!

A total of eleven leftist advisors were unloaded by Hurley. They included George Acheson, Jr., Raymond P. Ludden, Fulton Freeman, Edward E. Rice, Philip D. Sprouse, and Hungerford B. Howard. Hurley was shortly thereafter brought before the Chinese Affairs Board of the State Department. He explained: "I was called on the carpet, with a full array of the pro-Communists of the State Department as my judge and questioners . . . "*9*

Ambassador Hurley resigned in November of 1945, after learning that all the traitors he'd fired had been promoted. Most of these subversives were now his bosses. For example, Communist John Carter Vincent became a division head! Arthur Ringwalt became acting chief of the China Division! Two other security risks became Ringwalt's assistants. John Paton Davies, called a Communist by Hurley, was retained as a member of Dean Acheson's policy planning staff! He was later transferred to the Moscow embassy with another China conspirator, Horace Smith. John Stewart Service was assigned to General MacArthur's staff! To his credit, MacArthur refused to accept the traitor.

Hurley sacrificed his career in an attempt to warn Americans of the powerful Communist influence in the State Department. He vainly appeared before the Senate Foreign Relations Committee. His firsthand knowledge of Red penetration and domination was mindlessly ignored, ridiculed and labeled "absurd" by the illustrious Senators![10]

Louis Budenz, a former top Party leader, testified: "The Communists relied very strongly on Service and John Carter Vincent in a campaign against Ambassador Hurley."*11* A major push was initiated at this time to drive all *anti-Communists* out of the State Department. Budenz revealed that Communist Party members were given orders to force the resignation of anyone "considered to be against Soviet policy in the Far East."[12]

Professor Anthony Kubek reveals how anti-Communists, or "reactionaries" as they were labeled by the Reds, were methodically eliminated: "There was unloosed a barrage of insidious smear attacks and an all-out attempt to discredit the anti-Communists in the Department of State. This was done through Communist front organizations and by those liberal elements of press and radio who customarily promote the key Soviet objectives while pretending to oppose 'Communism.' . . . It is interesting to note that *in all cases the men singled out by the Communists* were removed. In effect, the hiring and firing of our State Department personnel was done in Moscow!"[13]

In this way, the Dean Acheson clique replaced anti-Communists with Communists and pro-Communists in all strategic State Department positions. Acheson was well rewarded as a result of his unwavering leftist policies. He became Truman's Secretary of State from 1949 to 1953. Here Acheson—believed to be a Red espionage agent (Chapter 16)— helped to hide the Communist background of Alger Hiss! He pushed Moscow's man up through the ranks, all the while knowing that Hiss was a spy, taking orders directly from the Kremlin!

* * * * * * * * *

The Voice of America began broadcasting programs about "freeing the captive peoples" and "rolling back the iron curtain." The people of Communist Occupied Hungary were led to believe the United States would come to their aid, if there were to be an uprising! As a result, they bravely revolted in October 1956 and drove out their Soviet masters! Even the Russian troops in Budapest turned on the Communist leadership and joined the freedom fighters!

Imre Nagy's newly formed anti-Communist government pleaded with the State Department for diplomatic recognition. The pleas of the heroic Freedom Fighters were ignored! What would have happened had the United States come through with the promised assistance? Soviet defector Oleg Penkovsky was in Moscow at the time. He explains:

"We in Moscow felt as if we were sitting on a powderkeg. Everyone in the General Staff was against the 'Khrushchev adventure.' It was better to lose Hungary, as they said, than to lose everything. But what did the West do? Nothing. It was asleep. This gave Khrushchev confidence. . . If the West had slapped Khrushchev down hard then . . . all of Eastern Europe could be free."[14]

On November 2, 1956, President Eisenhower completed the betrayal of Hungary's captive people! A treasonous State Department cablegram was sent to Tito, Yugoslavia's Communist dictator. It read: "The government of the United States does not look with favor upon governments unfriendly to the Soviet Union on the borders of the Soviet Union."[15]

This was the death knell for the Hungarian Freedom Fighters! The State Department had given its tacit approval for the Soviet tanks massed on the Hungarian border to invade. They did exactly that just 36 hours later! On November 4, Nikita Khrushchev, afterwards known as "the Butcher of Budapest," used thousands of imported Mongolian savages to crush the uprising.

On this sad day, the Hungarian Freedom Fighters broadcast their final words: "People of the world, listen to our call. Help us not with words, but with action, with soldiers and arms. Please do not forget that this wild attack of Bolshevism will not stop. You may be the next victim. Save us . . . Our ship is sinking. The light vanishes. The shadows grow darker from hour to hour. Listen to our cry. Start moving. Extend to us your brotherly hands . . . God be with you and us."[16]

The Freedom Fighters would wait in vain for the Americans to come! The incredible State Department treachery resulted in over 15,000 casualties in Budapest alone. Was this travesty no more than a series of mistakes in judgment? Hardly! It was all planned that way! The Eisenhower State Department obviously meant for Hungary's anti-Communist revolt to fail!

* * * * * * * * *

Senator Thomas Dodd (D-CT) said: " . in December 1958, what many people had considered impossible came to pass. While we stood by in confusion and disarray and apparent helplessness, a Communist dictator was installed on the island of Cuba, only 90 miles off our own shores."[17]

Consider carefully the implications of Dodd's words in reference to this portion of the 1956 House study, entitled *Soviet Total War*. Remember—this was issued over two years prior to Castro and his gangster group coming to power in Cuba: "Communist strategy teaches that there can be no successful revolution followed by the creation of Soviets in any Latin American country unless an internal revolution has been effected within the United States. The Comintern views the Western hemisphere as an integral unit in which the United States must first be rendered helpless before a Soviet-type government can be established in any other of the 20 republics in the hemisphere,"[18]

The Communist's own game plan tells us they couldn't install a Castro in Cuba, an Ortega in Nicaragua or a Red dictator anywhere else in our hemisphere *"unless an internal revolution has been effected within the United States"* and *"the United States must first be rendered helpless."*19 Has there been an internal revolution in the United States? Has the U.S. government been rendered helpless? Neither Fidel Castro or Daniel Ortega could possibly have brought Communism to Cuba or to Nicaragua without the aid, assistance, and direction of certain Communist and pro-Communist elements in the government and the media.

* * * * * * * * *

Robert Hill, former Ambassador to Mexico, testified before the Senate Judiciary Committee that the State Department, working hand-in-hand with the *New York Times,* delivered Cuba to the Communists!20 Earl E.T. Smith, U.S. Ambassador to Cuba during the Kremlin supported Communist revolution, makes some serious charges: "Castro could not have seized power in Cuba without the aid of the United States. American government agencies and the American media played a major role in bringing Castro to power. The State Department consistently intervened . . . to bring about the downfall of President Fulgencio Batista, thereby making it possible for Fidel Castro to take over the government of Cuba."[21]

Security risk William Arthur Wieland was one of the super stars in the game of Deliver-Cuba-to-Communist-Occupied-Russia! He had obtained his job without a security check and without even filling out an application. The Senate Internal Security Subcommittee reveals some pertinent facts about his background: "Before joining the Foreign Service during World War II Wieland lived in Cuba under the alias 'Arturo Montenegro'[22] . . . Wieland entered the Foreign Service when its Latin American Department was headed by a Soviet agent, Lawrence Duggan."[23]

Duggan (CFR), a close pal of broadcaster Edward R. Murrow,[24] was known to have "collaborated with agents of the Soviet intelligence apparatus."[25] This Communist spy was scheduled to testify before a Congressional investigating committee in 1948 but his life ended rather abruptly when he conveniently fell from a Manhattan hotel window. Not so strangely, many Communists have fatal "accidents" when their reliability becomes questionable. Kremlin spy Harry Dexter White's life also ended suddenly. He had a mysterious heart attack under similar circumstances!

The SISS findings continue: "As a reported 'protégé' of Sumner Welles, Wieland 'earned' four promotions in nine months and was assigned to Brazil in 1947 as press attache."[26] The American Ambassador to Brazil, William Pawley, informed Eisenhower as well as State Department officials of Wieland's leftist activities. His warnings were ignored! Wieland was again promoted and sent to Bogata, Columbia. While vice counsel in Bogota in 1948, Wieland, now recognized as one of the State Department's untouchables, continued his blatant pro-Communist endeavors.[27]

In May of 1957, career diplomat Wieland was in charge of the important Caribbean Desk. This security risk brazenly did pretty much as he pleased to deliver Cuba into the clutches of Communist revolutionary, Fidel Castro. According to the SISS: "From the time of his appointment to the key State Department post in May 1957, Wieland regularly disregarded, sidetracked or denounced FBI, State Department, and Military Intelligence sources which branded Castro a Communist and showed that his associates were Moscow-trained."[28]

In August 1959, Wieland 'wrecked' an intelligence briefing given to Dr. Milton Eisenhower by the American Embassy staff in Mexico City when it became obvious they were going to prove that Castro was a Communist . . . Wieland was denounced . . . as 'either a damn fool or a Communist'. Milton Eisenhower chose to ignore the incident."[29] This is the same radical leftist who as President of Johns Hopkins University, recommended that a plan be prepared for the gradual surrender of the United States to the Communists![30] The track record of American foreign policy clearly indicates that this has unquestionably been done!

The SISS notes that Wieland "never told his superiors officially or wrote in any Department paper . . . what he told friends as early as 1958 —or earlier—that Castro 'is a Communist' and is surrounded by Commies . . ."[31]

With Wieland's conscious assistance, Fidel Castro became Cuba's Red dictator on February 16, 1959. The SISS concluded: "Wieland is considered author of the fatal arms embargo which cut off munitions shipments to the anti-Communist Batista while Castro was being liberally supplied by sources in Florida and by Russian submarines surfacing off the Cuban coast . . . Similar State Department action ten years earlier had crippled Chiang Kai-shek's Army and permitted the Communists to come to power in China."[32]

Pawley wrote: "The deliberate overthrow of Batista by Wieland and Matthews, assisted by Rubottom, is almost as great a tragedy as the surrendering of China to the

Communists by a similar group of Department of State officials fifteen or sixteen years ago."[33]

Wieland was given a security clearance by "higher authority," when John F. Kennedy assumed the Presidency. The "higher authority" was none other than the traitorous Secretary of State Dean Rusk! Wieland was again promoted! Incredibly, his new job was to revise State Department *security procedures!* Kennedy was challenged over Wieland's questionable appointment to such a sensitive position. Reporter Sarah McLendon rightfully charged that the man was a dangerous security risk! The President responded by sternly rebuking McLendon and *not* the subversive in question! He personally vouched for Wieland's loyalty. Kennedy informed the press that both he and Rusk (himself a dangerous security risk) had checked Wieland's record.[34] They had determined him to be well qualified for the critical job! JFK said he "felt confident" Wieland could perform his duties "without detriment to the interests of the United States."[35] This nonsensical response wasn't even questioned by the other gutless reporters who were present or the media in general! Nixon did exactly the same thing in 1969 with Charles Woodruff Yost, another high ranking State Department security risk (Chapter 9), who was a close friend of Soviet spy Alger Hiss.

William Wieland was denied a security clearance by State Department security chief Otto Otepka. Otepka was fully aware of Wieland's treasonous role in deliberately bringing Castro to power, while knowing the Cuban terrorist was a Communist. He'd personally sent him hundreds of intelligence reports revealing Castro's Red background. Otepka testified: "Either Wieland did not read them, or if he did read them he deliberately misinterpreted them."[36] Even after his role was exposed, Wieland was rewarded well for his labors in behalf of the Communists! He was given a plum diplomatic post in Australia. As so many other notorious security risks have done, Wieland eventually retired with a sizable pension, courtesy of the very country he deliberately betrayed!

"The disastrous policies pursued, one after another, could not be viewed as mistakes, for if they were only such then by the law of averages we should have done something right once in a while," charges Bryton Barron, who was Chief of the Treaty Section for six of his 26 years in the State Department. "The perpetrators of disaster, themselves, never termed their acts mistakes: the 1949 *White Paper* on China openly boasted of a policy that brought the Reds to power in mainland China; and that Department official [Wieland] whose activities helped bring Castro to power was subsequently promoted."[37]

Dwight D. Eisenhower declared: "Only a genius and a prophet could have known for sure that Cuban Premier [dictator] Fidel Castro was a Communist in the 1950s."[38] Eisenhower was either grossly uninformed or he was a liar! Many people knew! For example, in September 1958, prior to the Red takeover of Cuba, Robert Welch declared: "The evidence from Castro's whole past, that he is a Communist agent carrying out Communist orders and plans is overwhelming."[39] That Fidel Castro was a Communist was known at least a decade earlier than this! According to the SISS, William Arthur Wieland and other subversives knew Castro was a Communist terrorist: "While the American vice counsel in Bogata, Wieland knew a young Cuban revolutionary, Fidel Castro.[40] . . . During the riots [in 1948] . . . U.S. officials heard him broadcast, 'This is Fidel Castro. This is a Communist revolution.' . . . Both Wieland and Roy Rubottom, Assistant Secretary of State and Wieland's superior . . . were in Bogota during the riots."[41]

* * * * * * * * *

In 1947, Lieutenant General Albert Wedemeyer was ordered to analyze the volatile Korean situation. The development of a strong South Korean military organization was recommended. Secretary of State Marshall buried the "Wedemeyer Report" and ordered the General to step aside. Marshall wrote Truman: "I think this should be suppressed."

The President's terse response was jotted on the letter: "I agree—H.T."*42* South Korea was deliberately left undefended in order to invite a military attack from the North!

Marshall was later accused of joining others in suppressing the Wedemeyer Report. He boldly asserted: "I did not join in suppression of the Report. I personally suppressed it!"*43* Senator Joseph R. McCarthy (R-WI) wrote: "If Marshall were merely stupid, the laws of probability would have dictated that at least some of his decisions would have served this country's interests."*44*

Dean Acheson further baited the North Korean Communists when he became Truman's Secretary of State in 1949. He announced to the world that the United States wouldn't defend South Korea! It was considered to be outside of "our defense perimeter." This was an engraved invitation for the North Korean Reds to attack. And attack the Communists did! Everything went exactly as anticipated by Marshall, Acheson, Truman, and their fellow subversives. In June of 1950, the United States became involved in its first "no-win" war of planned humiliation and demoralization. Truman kept telling the American people: "We are not at war." It was, he said, merely "a police action" against a "bunch of North Korean bandits."*45* The President knew better!

General of the Army Douglas MacArthur's forces were not allowed to chase attacking *Russian* MIGs back across the Yalu River! Nor could they fire on anti-aircraft guns clearly in view on the other side! Air fields and munitions dumps across the river had to be ignored! And only the Korean half of the bridges spanning the Yalu River could be destroyed! MacArthur charged: "I realized for the first time that I had actually been denied the use of my full military power to safeguard the lives of my soldiers and the safety of my army. . . It . . . left me with a sense of inexpressible shock."*46* Vietnam, a decade later, was like an instant replay of Korea!

USAF Lieutenant General Albert Stratemeyer recalls that the U.S. "had sufficient air, bombardment, fighters, and reconnaissance so that I could have taken out those supplies, those airdromes on the other side of the Yalu. I could have . . . stopped that railroad operating and the people of China that were fighting could not have been supplied . . . But we weren't permitted to do it. As a result, a lot of American blood was spilled over there in Korea."[47]

Thanks to the traitorous machinations of the Truman-Acheson duo, 50 thousand Americans were unnecessarily killed in the degrading, morale-breaking Korean War that America was forbidden to win. Joseph W. Martin Jr. (R-MA), House minority leader, was infuriated! He said: "If we are not in Korea to win, then this Administration should be indicted for the murder of thousands of American boys."[48] Martin was absolutely right! An identical charge would apply years later to Vietnam— yet many of the same traitors, along with a passer of newer ones, all got off scot free.

Truman shamefully fired MacArthur. America's premium military strategist was removed from his Korean command on April 11,1951. He was guilty of simply wanting victory, not defeat! His brilliant leadership was threatening to reverse the criminal no-win policy coordinated by Communists in the State Department, the UN, and the USSR. MacArthur almost won in Korea, despite the intimate ties between Comrades in Moscow and Comrades in Washington!

Secondly, MacArthur's recall came shortly after he'd demanded that traitors in the State Department and elsewhere be ousted by Truman. The General knew his military operation in Korea was being subverted by Communist and pro-Communist elements within the Administration. According to Willard Edwards of the *Chicago Tribune,* every message MacArthur sent to Washington during the Korean War was leaked to Moscow! Truman ignored the General's spy warnings! He was still defensive over the recent scandals involving Kremlin espionage agents Harry Dexter White and Alger Hiss. Charges of more Reds in his Administration, according to

General MacArthur, caused Truman "the deepest resentment."[49]

As unbelievable as it may sound, the United States actually protected Communist Occupied China from attack during the Korean War! The Seventh fleet was sent over with orders to guard the Communist coastline! America's friend and ally, Chiang Kai-shek, was stopped from invading Red China—yet Red Chinese soldiers were killing American boys! Chiang's soldiers on Formosa—six hundred thousand well-trained fighting men—volunteered to help in Korea. They were rejected! Owen Lattimore's traitorous 1949 plan was obviously being put into practice! This dangerous security risk had proposed, in a secret 1949 memorandum to the State Department: "The thing to do is let South Korea fall, but not let it look as if we pushed it."[50]

Communist Occupied Russia was behind the Korean War, just as it was the war in Vietnam! Despot Nikita Khrushchev admitted Stalin had personally "ordered North Korea to attack South Korea."[51] The U.S. had recently been victorious over the most advanced nations in the world — Germany, Japan, and Italy. Five years later the most powerful country on the face of the earth couldn't even defeat tiny North Korea and backward Communist Occupied China! The reason? The Communist enemy America was fighting also orchestrated America's side of the war through the United Nations (see Chapter 14). Senator Joe McCarthy was prophetic when in 1952 he said: "The war in Korea in only one of the stepping stones to Communist world conquest. Another stepping stone will be Indochina."[52]

* * * * * * * * * *

Aiding and abetting Communist Occupied Yugoslavia (Chapter 1, 2, 3, 4, 5, 6) has been the policy of the State Department under every President from Kennedy to Reagan. Yugoslavian dictator Josef Broz Tito was carefully trained in Communist Occupied Russia and sent to Yugoslavia by Stalin. No one except the Soviets knew who he really was or where he really came from. No one outside of the USSR even knew if Tito was his real name!

Despite overwhelming evidence to the contrary, Kennedy's State Department information officer in 1961 followed Eisenhower policy and declared: "Yugoslavia has remained independent, and has not participated in policies or programs to bring about the overthrow or subversion of legitimate governments by world Communism."[53] One can only surmise where Lincoln White obtained his information. It is, after all, no more than the official Communist line! But then, this is the same leftist who, as State Department press officer in 1950, *lied* in response to Senator Joe McCarthy's charges of Red infiltration. White's heated response: "We know of no Communist members in this department and if we find any they will be summarily dismissed!"[54] White was dead wrong! There had been hundreds of Communists found in the State Department. And they were protected and promoted rather than fired!

* * * * * * * * * *

Subversive Dean Rusk (CFR) became Kennedy's Secretary of State in 1961. He ignored normal channels and waived security checks on 152 questionable State Department employees. Security checks were also bypassed on over 600 more leftists, who were hired under a "blanket waiver" from January 1961 to May 1962. Security evaluator Otto Otepka questioned Rusk's alarming lack of security procedures and held up 150 promotions and job applications of subversives. The Secretary of State became incensed and initiated a vendetta to get rid of Otepka. Rusk's retaliation in the Spring of 1963 made Watergate seem like a Sunday School picnic! Otepka was harassed incessantly. His office was burglarized and illegally bugged. His phone was tapped and his safe was broken open. He was placed under constant surveillance as if some sort of criminal. No Communist under investigation had ever been treated so shabbily![55]

Rusk had Otepka transferred from security in June of 1963. He was denied access to his files, which contained damaging evidence on hundreds of subversives in high policy-making positions! Otepka was charged with conduct "unbecoming an officer of the Department of State." Rusk and his criminal cohorts were actually able to force an FBI investigation of Otepka! Word was leaked that he was going to be prosecuted for high crimes under the Espionage Act! Otepka had, according to State Department leftists, given classified information to the enemy! And who was the enemy? Kremlin spies? No! It was the *Senate Internal Security Subcommittee!*

A concerted effort to destroy what little was still left of the State Department's security program was culminated when Rusk fired Otepka in November of 1963. All this subterfuge was geared to destroy an antiCommunist patriot who (just five years earlier) had been given the meritorious service award. And to destroy a man described by his boss, Scott McLeod, as "the best security evaluator in government today."[56]

Regarding Otepka's firing, Senator Dodd, cited the law: "The right of persons employed in the civil service . . . to furnish information to either House of Congress or to any committee or member thereof, shall not be denied or interfered with."[57]

Dodd charged that the State Department, "by its action in the Otepka case, has in effect nullified this statute and issued a warning to all Government employees that cooperation with the established Committees of the Senate, if this cooperation involves testimony unpalatable at higher echelon, is a crime punishable by dismissal."[58]

The Senate Internal Security Subcommittee issued a report on State Department security in December 1967. Senator Strom Thurmond (R-SC) declared: "There are two issues of paramount importance . . . The first is whether a government employee loyal to his country can . . . furnish information confidentially to the appropriate congressional committees when he sees wrongdoing . . . The second . . . State was trying to hide a new policy of phasing out effective security procedures. The highest officials . . . no longer believed in . . . loyalty in employing personnel. Quite simply,

Mr. Otepka and a small band of associates were in the way."[59]

In 1968, anti-Communist Congressman John M. Ashbrook (ROH) said: "When you study the Otto Otepka matter, you are inclined to exclaim, *No wonder we are losing!* [60]

* * * * * * * * *

During a Ford-Carter Presidential debate, Jimmy Carter pledged: "I would never give up complete control of the Panama Canal. . . I would not relinquish the practical control of the Panama Canal Zone anytime in the foreseeable future."[61] Yet, once Carter became President, the State Department moved heaven and earth to surrender the American Canal in Panama. The recipient of this outlandish leftist ploy was Communist drug-pusher Omar Torrijos Herrera, a colleague of Fidel Castro!

Cuba's official news agency quoted Comrade Torrijos as saying Panama "might adopt the path of Ho Chi Minh to achieve national liberation"[62] should the United States not give up the Canal! Torrijos commanded no army, navy, or air force! His entire population wasn't 20 percent of that found in New York City! Yet State Department conspirators pretended to be afraid this preposterous little despot might actually wage war against the most powerful nation in the world!

State quashed all prosecutions of illegal drug smugglers close to top people in the Torrijos' dictatorship. Information about the intimate ties between Fidel Castro and Torrijos was suppressed! Conspirators in the State Department were determined to give away the Canal at any cost! The enormity of their role in this treasonous deed of September 6, 1977, can't be measured! In fact, not only did traitors in State authorize giving away America's Canal, but they arranged by treaty to pay the Marxist regime around $2 *billion* to take it off America's hands!

Meldrim Thomson declared: "I find it abhorrent . . . to witness an American President rushing to surrender the sovereign territory of the United States ."[63]

The former New Hampshire Governor was correct. There was absolutely no legal question as to who owned the Panama Canal! Panama didn't even exist as a country when the original deed was made! The United States *created* the Republic of Panama out of a province of Columbia. The Panama Canal Zone was as American as Hawaii or Alaska.

Dan Smoot explains: "In our 1903 agreement with Panama . . . We *bought* the Zone for 10 million dollars and a guaranteed annuity of 250 thousand dollars. This annuity was not a *rental* fee; it was a guarantee of revenue to keep the Panamanian government alive. We acquired full ownership and sovereignty . . . making the Canal Zone *United States territory forever.*"[64]

Panama's dictator was a leading member of the Communist People's Party! Torrijos' family members were prominent Reds in Panama! His parents founded a Communist cell in Veraquas Province! Key members of his government, including Manuel Antonio Noriega, head of his G-2 secret police, were all known Communists! Ambassador Henry J. Taylor revealed that Torrijos' "minister of foreign affairs and minister of labor . . . are . . . Communists . . "[65] The chief Canal treaty negotiator for Panama was Romulo Escobar Bethancourt, a close Castro pal and lifelong Communist Party member! His American counterpart, far leftist Sol Linowitz was, among other things, a registered foreign agent of Salvador Allende's Communist Government of Chile!

In no way could State's role in this subterfuge with the howling jackals who rule Panama not be considered treason! Carter's simpering betrayal of America's interests in the vital Canal was so serious it should have led to his immediate impeachment! The treason is compounded considering that the President and all the other conspirators were privy to the above information! State Department personnel deliberately ignored the damaging data and allowed the outrageous scam to continue. Everyone involved should be held accountable for their part in another horrendous sellout to Communist forces in this hemisphere! All those responsible, including the President of the United States, should be prosecuted for treason! To allow these people to continue to go unpunished is a moral travesty!

* * * * * * * * *

State Department subversives boldly engineered the ousting of anti-Communist Anastasio Somoza in Nicaragua! On December 27, 1978, Somoza was warned by American leftist not to go after the Communist terrorists in their Costa Rican "sanctuary". On June 15, 1979, the State Department enforced an arms embargo against this reliable American friend and ally! No weapons or ammunition shipments would be allowed for West Point graduate Somoza's pro-American government! This went into effect at the precise time Nicaragua (Chapter 12) was reeling under the attack of invading Communist forces from Costa Rica. Yes, dangerous security risks in the State Department deliberately allowed a Communist dictatorship to be installed in Nicaragua!

What the Sandinistas were was no well kept secret! The *Washington Post's* Ted Szulc reported more than a year before the Communist regime was placed in power: " . . . they would establish a revolutionary state . . . The guerrillas left no doubt about their admiration for the Cuban revolution, whose influence is powerful within the movement. . . "[66]

Four days after the Communists were forcibly installed in Managua—on July 24, 1979—diplomatic recognition was hastily bestowed on the Red barbarians. Kremlin agents in the State Department knew Thomas Borge, head of the dreaded secret police, was a convicted murderer and a Communist Comrade. They also knew all of the Communist Sandinista leadership had been trained in Panama, Cuba, Libya, Czechoslovakia, and other Red strongholds. Yet, the Carter Administration funneled an unauthorized $119 million to Communist Occupied Nicaragua immediately after the takeover. The loss of Nicaragua was not the result of an internal rebellion! It was totally external—a well organized invasion from Cuba, Panama, and Costa Rica! The undeniable fact is that subversives in the State Department had long planned to deliver Nicaragua into the hands of Communist Occupied Russia!

* * * * * * * * * *

It's evident that the State Department itself is a serious risk to the security of America! It's also evident that enemies of the United States are unquestionably in control of the foreign policy establishment! It's like a baseball game with *all* the players on the same team, or more specifically, with the American players on the Kremlin team! This problem isn't new. It's been there ever since Franklin Roosevelt opened the gates to a tidal wave of subversives and subversion, prior to World War II. There has been a covert Communist malignance stealthily sapping the vitality of the Republic ever since. Signs of this metastasizing disease are readily discernible in many federal agencies, but most notably in the bowels of State.

Nevertheless, even the most outspoken of Congressional and Presidential candidates dare not bring up or even acknowledge State Department domination by Communist espionage agents in service to the Kremlin. It is not just difficult but probably impossible to rid the State Department of Communists. No one dares initiate an investigation! None dare call a traitor a traitor! In fact, even 1988 Presidential candidate Pat Robertson would go no further than to cautiously refer to notorious Soviet spy Alger Hiss of Harvard as simply a "misguided young man."[67]

The Communist infested State Department continues to do as much as humanly possible to turn the United States into a toothless tiger. The ultimate goal of the conspirators is to do to America what they did to China, Angola, Cuba, Rhodesia, Nicaragua, and the rest. These traitors fully intend for the United States to become another satellite slave labor dictatorship, under the ever watchful eye of the gangsters running Communist Occupied Russia!

Consider the warning of Thomas Jefferson: "Single acts of tyranny may be ascribed to the accidental opinion of a day; but a series of oppressions, begun at a distinguished period, and pursued unalterably through every change of ministers, too plainly prove a deliberate, systematic plan of reducing us to slavery."[68]

Chapter 11

Those Close to the President

Traitor: "One who betrays; one guilty of treason."
Webster Handy College Dictionary

Treason: "Betrayal of one's country or ruler."
Thorndike Barnhart Comprehensive Dictionary

    Presidents come and go but the conspirators working quietly behind the scenes in each Administration often remain. Thousands of job slots are filled with each change of Presidents. With whom these openings are staffed largely determines whether or not the Administration follows or thwarts a President's objectives. A sizable number of positions in every Administration since Roosevelt—within State, Treasury, Agriculture, the CIA, etc.—have either been filled with outright Communists, suspected Communists or Communist sympathizers!
    Senator William Jenner's (R-IN) 1953 Senate Internal Security Subcommittee Report *1* revealed how Russian espionage agents penetrated the government many years ago. Soviet spies were able to obtain jobs all the way up to and including critical policy making positions! Once secure in a department, each Communist helped other conspirators find employment. They placed and promoted their Comrades and helped each other avoid exposure!
    Nothing has been done to date with any measurable degree of success to rid the government of these dangerous Moscow hirelings. Senator Joseph R. McCarthy (R-WI)

came too close for comfort! He was ruthlessly destroyed before his thankless task could be finished. Congressional hearings have come and gone! A very few traitors have been exposed! But little has been done to force the executive branch to take appropriate action.

A great number of serious security risks who began their shadowy careers in government under one President, can be traced through succeeding Administrations, whether Democrat or Republican! Many important subversives stay behind the scenes, to do the bidding of their Kremlin masters. They avoid controversy, work quietly in the background, and shun the media. They are often known only to intelligence agencies. Many names would not be at all familiar to the average American. And this is exactly the way it's preferred by a mole.

Owen Lattimore (CFR) was Roosevelt's Special Advisor to Chiang Kai-shek, when he headed the Nationalist Chinese government. According to former Communist and *Daily Worker* editor Louis Budenz, Professor Lattimore was a Communist! Budenz testified that Lattimore had been carefully selected by Soviet intelligence "to change the thinking here in Washington and in America on the Communist activities in China and its relations to the Soviet Union."[2] In fact, former Soviet General Alexander Barmine named this spy as *a member* of Soviet Military Intelligence![3]

Lattimore stayed on with Truman after Roosevelt died. Senator Joseph R. McCarthy (R-WI) first brought this security risk's Communist record to light in 1950. Abe Fortas (Chapter 13), a fellow subversive, was Lattimore's attorney! He would later be rewarded with an appointment to the Supreme Court by Lyndon Johnson! Lattimore was again exposed by Senator William Jenner's (R-IN) Subcommittee: "Owen Lattimore was, from sometime in the 1930s a conscious, articulate instrument of the Soviet conspiracy."[4] Lattimore was finally indicted by a Federal Grand Jury on seven counts of perjury—each for lying about his Communist activities! Incredibly, at the bidding of Fortas, the Justice Department quietly dropped all charges in 1955!

Despite his notorious Communist background, Owen Lattimore was kept on at Johns Hopkins and later unofficially welcomed back into the government in 1961 by John F. Kennedy!

Moscow directed labor leader Sidney Hillman (Chapter 16) was extremely close to Roosevelt. FDR's pat response to questions brought before him was: "Clear it with Sidney."[5] Hillman was a Communist spy who'd previously been deeply and personally involved in the Bolshevik takeover of Russia! This Kremlin espionage agent was the man who gave final approval to Harry Truman, as Roosevelt's 1944 running mate! What was a Russian revolutionary doing with an important White House job in the first place? What was a Russian revolutionary doing advising an American President? What traitors already in place were able to maneuver Hillman into this influential position?

Senator Joe McCarthy exposed John J. McCloy (CFR) for approving an order in 1944—while Roosevelt's Assistant Secretary of the Army — that allowed known Communists to become army officers! This Harvard security risk worked closely with such anti-American luminaries as Owen Lattimore, Alger Hiss, and Harry Dexter White, at the 1945 UN founding conference. Despite his extensive subversive record, McCloy was an advisor to nine Presidents, from Roosevelt to Reagan (Chapter 16). McCarthy rightly charged that this man's career was an "unbelievable, inconceivable, unexplainable record of the deliberate, secret betrayal of the nation to its mortal enemy, the Communist Conspiracy."[6]

Harold L. Ickes, FDR's radical Secretary of the Interior, brought innumerable Communists into government and he was a protector of those already there. Former Party bigwig Louis Budenz knew Ickes well: " To his dying day Mr. Ickes defended the 'rights' of the Communist conspiracy and assailed the prosecution of Red leaders under the Smith Act."[7] This security risk affiliated himself with numerous Red Fronts and spoke at rallies sponsored by the communist National Council of American-Soviet Friendship. His wife, Jane, was also heavily involved in Red activities. Among other things, she was on the National Committee of the Communist-founded ACLU.

Security risk David K Niles was another close aid and advisor to Roosevelt. This dangerous subversive was the White House contact for Soviet espionage agents.

Felix Frankfurter—believed to be a Communist agent *8* —was appointed by FDR to the Supreme Court! This subversive was a radical attorney who once filed charges against the Justice Department because of its anti-Communist activities. In 1917, Frankfurter became one of the "Insiders" in President Woodrow Wilson's "Braintrust". Former President Theodore Roosevelt stated that Frankfurter's attitude was "fundamentally that of Trotsky and the other Bolshevik leaders in Russia."*9* Frankfurter and the notorious leftist Roger Baldwin, along with Communists Elizabeth Gurley Flynn and William Z. Foster, founded the ACLU on January 12, 1920! He was the patron of leftist Democrat William J. Brennan, Jr., Eisenhower's choice for a seat on the Supreme Court! Frankfurter recommended his protégés for government service while he taught at Harvard. These included communists spies Harry Dexter White, Alger Hiss, Harold Glasser, and Lee Pressman! All were scholastically bright but intellectually stunted Harvard clones, who became Kremlin espionage agents!

So close was security risk Harry Hopkins (Chapter 3) to Roosevelt that he lived in the White House and slept in an adjoining bedroom! The President's Special Assistant, brought into government at Eleanor's urging, was, Russia's most valued mole in Washington during World War 11. This agent of the Kremlin conspiracy was publicly exposed in 1990 by a KGB defector named Oleg Gordievsky. Hopkins was a man who couldn't do enough to help Stalin. This subversive had authorized the delivery to Communist Occupied Russia of over half of the U.S. uranium supply, so they could develop their own atomic bombs! With this went cobalt, thorium, and cadmium—as well as top secret data from the Manhattan Project. Perhaps Hopkins believed his traitorous acts would never be exposed for he said in 1941:

"The people are too goddamn dumb to understand!"*10* The only reason Harry Hopkins wasn't indicted and tried for treason, at the time Congress investigated, was that he had died!

Subversive Assistant Secretary of State Dean Acheson's protégé, Lauchlin Currie (CFR), became the President's top Administrative Assistant. Currie was a high-ranking Soviet agent and a member of the Silvermaster spy cell. When this Comrade (Chapter 13) was called before the House Committee on Un-American Activities, his mentor Acheson stepped in as his defense attorney. Security risk Acheson is the same man who had previously vouched for the loyalty of Communist spies Alger and Donald Hiss!

In 1949, Acheson (Chapter 10) had the audacity to advocate that U.S. Army personnel train Chinese Communist troops! Chiang Kai-shek refused to allow Communist participation in his free Chinese government. Acheson was the man who advised cutting off further arms shipments! His program was designed to disarm the anti-Communist Chinese forces and set the country up for a Red takeover. Believed to be, (but never proven), a Communist (Chapter 16), Acheson was rewarded well for his traitorous pro-Red, anti-American labors. Instead of being charged with and tried for treason, this blatant security risk was named Truman's Secretary of State in 1949! Ambassador Arthur Bliss Lane had but one comment: "God help the United States!"

President Truman personally selected Michael Greenberg as his top White House assistant. Greenberg—a Communist from England's Cambridge University—was a member of a Soviet espionage cell. This spy had previously been Lauchlin Currie's personal assistant in the Roosevelt White House.*11* He was finally exposed as a Red espionage agent by Elizabeth Bentley.

"A Republican President will appoint only persons of unquestioned loyalty" proclaimed the Republicans in 1952.*(12)* Yet a subversive named Dr. Arthur Flemming became Ike's Secretary of Health, Education and Welfare!

He consistently decided in favor of identified Communists in government positions, while Civil Service commissioner under Franklin Roosevelt. One example was the notorious Nathan Gregory Silvermaster, who headed a Red espionage cell freely operating in Treasury. Flemming ruled that this Soviet spy could keep his job, despite the serious internal security ramifications!*[13]*

William P. Rogers' predecessor, Attorney General Herbert Brownell Jr., had declared: "... the evidence shows that the National Lawyers Guild is at present a Communist dominated and controlled organization fully committed to the Communist Party line ..."*[14]* Upon becoming Eisenhower's Attorney General in 1952, Rogers brazenly showed his leftist stripes when he reversed Brownell and blatantly dropped the Communist NLG from the Attorney General's list of subversive organizations. The NLG had been cited as "the foremost legal bulwark of the Communist Party..." Furthermore, the NLG "since its inception has never failed to rally to the legal defense of the Communist Party and individual members thereof including known espionage agents."*[15]* Rogers simply chose to ignore the evidence and charged that sufficient proof wasn't available. He lied! This subversive became Secretary of State in 1961, during Nixon's first term. He never veered from his commitment to the Communist cause in America (Chapter 8)!

The man responsible for Richard Nixon's selection as Ike's running mate in 1952 was notorious leftist Paul Hoffman (CFR). This security risk was a trustee of the Communist-controlled Institute of Pacific Relations. The IPR was cited as having been "considered by the American Communist Party and by Soviet officials as an instrument of Communist policy, propaganda and military intelligence.*[16]* Hoffman, a member of Eisenhower's Palace Guard, also took part in the conspiracy (Chapter 8) to silence Senator McCarthy, because he was so successfully exposing Reds in government.

Another Harvard leftist, Robert Strange McNamara (Chapter 16), brought in an array of security risks to traitorously and unilaterally disarm the United States under both Kennedy and Johnson. According to Admiral Chester Ward, McNamara (CFR) deliberately cut back "90 percent of our nuclear fire power."[17] McNamara's radical disarming program, charged Ward, would ultimately lead to a Soviet attack and national suicide. Robert S. Allen and Paul Scott reported: "Since McNamara became civilian head of the Pentagon in 1961, this country's all-important nuclear weapons stockpile has steadily decreased every year .... with the full knowledge and approval of the late President Kennedy and President Johnson, ..."[18] Daniel Ellsberg (CFR)—another Kissinger protégé and the thief who stole the *Pentagon Papers* (Chapter 6)—was one of the so-called McNamara "whiz kids" who was hired on the recommendation of notorious subversive, Adam Yarmolinsky. Despite everything, the media widely heralded McNamara as a "responsible conservative." Incredibly, even James Burnham,"former" Trotskyite Communist[19] and editor of Buckley's (CFR) *National* Review, Somehow saw leftist McNamara as a "conservative." Or did he?

Security risk Theodore C. Sorensen (CFR) was deeply involved in the treacherous Kennedy betrayal of the of the heroic anti-Communist Cuban freedom fighters, at the Bay of Pigs in April 1961! He avidly denounced all government loyalty and internal security programs; called for disarming America; and took classified documents from the White House without authorization! Sorensen advocated the dismantling of American's foreign intelligence gathering apparatus and he was in the forefront of the surrender-appeasement mob calling for a bombing halt and negotiations with Communist Occupied North Vietnam, which would allow them to more easily take the South! This subversive was bitter over the controversy brought about by Carter trying to install him as CIA Director. Taking the textbook leftist approach, Sorensen charged that he'd been smeared by "the extreme right wing." The man's atrocious pro-Communist record had simply been made public by Congressman Larry McDonald (D-GA)!

Another security risk clone out of Harvard, McGeorge Bundy {CFR), became Special Assistant for National Security Affairs under both Kennedy and Johnson. He was one of the leftist planner responsible for the American no-win surrender policy in Vietnam! He pushed for unilaterally disarming the U.S.; wanted to turn America's military over to the Red dominated United Nations; and advocated a merger of the U.S. with the Soviet dictatorship!

While Bundy headed national security, an avalanche of serious subversives were brought into government. Bundy opposed security checks on Federal job applicants, claiming they created "needless confusion and fear."[20] People with Communist backgrounds were instead "cleared on higher authority." Having a man like McGeorge Bundy overseeing the nation's security was as safe as hiring mass-murderer Theodore Bundy as chaperon for a high school prom! Bundy had the same job later held by identified Kremlin espionage agent Kissinger, under Nixon and Marxist Brzezinski, under Carter!

A protégé of suspected communist spy Dean Acheson (Chapter 16), Dean Rusk's disloyalty was never a secret! The "liberal" media had the audacity to label him a "hardline anti-Communist". Their absurd attempt to ignore this security risk's atrocious pro-Communist record (Chapter 9) was almost laughable! Rusk (CFR) brought a multitude of subversives into the State Department and purged it of anti-Communists. There is no question that Dean Rusk deliberately aided Communist Occupied Russia in expanding its extensive spy network throughout the government.

Otto F. Otepka (Chapter 10) of the State Department's security division, was pressured by both Rusk and Robert Kennedy (in 1961) to clear dangerous subversive, Walt Whitman Rostow (Chapter 16). Otepka adamantly refused! His decision was based on damaging reports from the FBI, CIA, and Air Force Intelligence. Two of Rostow's aunts were members of the Communist Party! His father had been a Russian revolutionary! Rostow (CFR) had already been denied a clearance in 1955 and 1957, because of his intimate ties to Soviet spies! Rostow couldn't be given a security clearance under the term of Executive Order 10450. This order required that if *any* question existed as to an applicant's loyalty, the doubts were to be resolved in favor of the United States—*not* the person in question!

JFK circumvented a security check by giving Rostow a job as Deputy Special Assistant to the President and later elevating him to Chief of the State Department's Policy Planning Council, in November of 1961. Rostow became Johnson's top advisor for National Security Affairs, in April of 1966, and headed the National Security Council. Ironically, Rostow couldn't even work for the NSC as a consultant a decade earlier, because of his pro-Communist background! Yes, Rostow was deliberately catapulted into the top echelons of the government, without any kind of security check! And one of the most dangerous subversives in America went on to traitorously orchestrate the disastrous no-win Vietnam War, from his White House office!

No one has been able to positively *prove* that Walt Whitman Rostow is a Communist. Reds don't carry cards anymore, nor are membership lists readily available. Whether he was or not is beside the point! The important question is this: What was anyone with such an astounding Communist tainted background doing, making foreign policy for the United States from 1961 to 1969? Equally as strange was the later Nixon-Rostow arrangement, exposed by columnist Paul Scott: "Rostow receives regular secret policy briefings on foreign and domestic affairs and has access to some of the most sensitive information in government."[21] Why?

Former boss of the subversive Americans for Democratic Action, Arthur Schlesinger, Jr. (CFR), joined President Kennedy's staff. This security risk's statement gives a clear picture of the man: "I happen to believe that the Communist Party should be granted freedom of political action and the Communists should be allowed to teach in universities."[22] Either Schlesinger's naive or he's on the enemy team! Either way he's equally as dangerous.

Communists and suspected Reds were now warmly welcomed to the White House. Included were Communist Linus Pauling and J. Robert Oppenheimer, who had his clearance revoked because of his Communist affiliations (Chapter 12). the White House social calendar included dinners and receptions in honor of brutal communist dictators, such as Yugoslavia's Tito and Sekou Toure, Guinea's own version of the horrid "Big Daddy" Idi Amin.

Security risk Arthur Goldberg (CFR) became Kennedy's Secretary of Labor. He'd worked closely with Robert Wirtz, Communist Party organizer and Secretary of the Illinois Communist Party.*23* Goldberg was past president of the Chicago chapter of the National Lawyers Guild. In this capacity, he worked under the direction of David J. Bentall and Isaac E. Ferguson—two important Reds who were involved in founding the Communist Party USA.*24* The NLG was cited as "the foremost legal bulwark of the Communist Party, its front organizations, and controlled unions."*25* Goldberg, despite his consistently subversive background (more probably because of it), was chosen to replace suspected Communist Felix Frankfurter*26* (Chapter 16) on the Supreme Court.

Willard Wirtz, another serious security risk, became JFK's new Labor Secretary, on the recommendation of leftist Goldberg. His previously mentioned brother, Robert, once headed a group collecting signatures in order to get the Communist Party on the ballot in Illinois. Feature columnist Ed Montgomery had this to say: "On this detail was a brother, William W. Wirtz. William is no longer known by that name. Today he is better known as W. Willard Wirtz, Secretary of Labor of the United States."[27]

Assistant Secretary of Labor was Esther Peterson. This woman was suspected of being a member of the Communist Party. Her security file revealed close associations over a long period of years with Reds and Red sympathizers.

One of LBJ's leftist friends, advisors, and Supreme Court appointees was security risk Abe Fortas (Chapter 13, 14). His notorious record of association with Communists, affiliation with Communist fronts, and questionable financial dealings forced him to resign from the Supreme Court in 1969. Says *Chicago Tribune* columnist Walter Trohan: "His best friends were members of one or another of the Communist cells which were fermenting under the care of Henry Wallace."*28* Fortas was a close friend of Communist spies Alger Hiss, Lee Pressman, John Abt, Harry Dexter White, and many others! He was subversive Owen Lattimore's attorney, when Lattimore was exposed by Senator Joe McCarthy (R-WI) in 1950. Lattimore was correctly branded two years later by Senator William Jenner's Internal Security Subcommittee as "a conscious articulate instrument of the Soviet conspiracy."*29* Fortas also assisted Lattimore in writing *Ordeal by Slander,* a thinly veiled attempt to smear and discredit the gutsy, anti-Communist McCarthy.

Lyndon Johnson had a penchant for nominating subversives to the Supreme Court! Thurgood Marshall was his second atrocious selection. Astoundingly, the Senate hastily confirmed this Harvard leftist in 1967. The media said nothing! Marshall was a member of the International Juridicial Association. So was Abe Fortas and his two Soviet spy friends from the Roosevelt days, Nathan Witt and Lee Pressman. The IJA was described thusly: "From its inception, the International Juridicial Association has specialized in the defense of individual Communists or of the Communist Party itself."*30* Many identified Communists were members of the IJA, including Joseph R. Brodsky, Leo Gallagher, David J. Bentall, Isaac E. Ferguson, and the notorious Cora Weiss King.

Marshall and Fortas were both on the Executive Board of the National Lawyers Guild. The SISS reported: "To defend the cases of Communist lawbreakers, fronts have been devised ... Among these organizations .. The National Lawyers Guild."*31* Marshall was one of the top ACLU officials in the Soviet controlled International Labor Defense, organized specifically to be the legal arm of the international Red conspiracy.

Congressman Martin Dies noted: "When the House Committee on Un-American Activities wrote ... in 1944 that 'there is not a single important Communist-front organization which does not have a substantial representation from the personnel of the International Juridicial Association, it surely did not contemplate that by 1966 the Supreme Court of the United States would be added to the list."[32]

Pro-North Vietnam, anti-American Ramsey Clark (Chapter 6, 15) replaced security risk Nicholas deB Katzenbach (Chapter 9) as Johnson's Attorney General in 1967. This radical leftist was with the KGB controlled International Association of Democratic Lawyers! The IADL was cited as being "One of the most useful Communist Front organizations at the service of the Soviet Communist Party".[33] Clark (CFR) refused to prosecute Reds and other traitors under the existing Trading with the Enemy Act and the Export-Import Control Act. Therefore, it wasn't a crime in the eyes of this subversive Attorney General to solicit supplies (blood, ammunition, money, food, arms, etc.) for the enemy, in Communist Occupied Hanoi!

Clark even refused to indict Communist terrorist Stokely Carmichael and Marxist race agitator Martin Luther King (Chapter 12) when they publicly urged defiance of the Selective Service Act! This law specifies penalties for *any* person "who knowingly counsels, aids or abets another to refuse or evade registration for service in the Armed Forces."[34] Despite this, Clark irrationally argued it would be a violation of their "free speech" to prosecute! Gary Allen charged: "Frankly, if Stokely Carmichael is not guilty of sedition, then the Communists have already destroyed our sedition laws. If Carmichael cannot be prosecuted for advocating draft-dodging, then the Communists have destroyed our laws against it. If he cannot be convicted for giving aid and comfort to the enemy, then there is no such thing as treason."[35]

Henry Fowler (CFR), Secretary of the Treasury, had been Virginia chairman of the Southern Conference for Human Welfare, cited as the South's top Communist front!

This subversive was responsible for getting Harry Magdoff—a Communist espionage agent and member of the Perlo cell—and influential government job. Kremlin spy Charles Flato mentioned Fowler prominently while testifying before the SISS. Red agent Irving Kaplan—also a member of the Perlo spy ring, as well as Silvermaster's—was asked when he knew Henry Fowler. The man replied: "I refuse to answer on the grounds that it may tend to incriminate me."

Wilbur J. Cohen was a self-professed Marxist, who drafted the original Social Security laws in 1935! Known as the "Father of Medicare," this subversive worked for two decades to force socialized medicine on America. According to former Congressman Martin Dies (D-TX), the passage of Medicare in 1965 was the most monumental advancement toward a Communist state in American history!*36* Cohen belonged to many Communist fronts and was close to top Red agents, over a long period of years. Dr. Marjorie Shearon has this to say about her former colleague: "Those investigating in Congress and the FBI were very close (in the 1950s). Men like Pressman, Stern and Kramer were confessing, or being proven, to have been Communists. These were the men Cohen had worked with and who had helped him in his legislative achievements."*37* Despite all the incriminating evidence, security risk Cohen was welcomed back in government by LBJ and made his Secretary of Health, Education and Welfare in 1968!

Stewart Udall was Secretary of Interior, under both Kennedy and Johnson. This leftist believed that private ownership of property was outmoded. He gave one of his idols, Communist Woody Guthrie, the Conservation Service Award for 1966! Udall also had the audacity to honor revolutionary Eugene V. Debs, by making his home a "national historic landmark!" Debs was an apologist for Lenin's ruthless mass murder of his countrymen. He was a subversive who was once tried and convicted for sedition! Ironically, under the Reagan Administration in 1988, landmark status was denied for the Maryland farm of *former* Communist Whittaker Chambers (Chapter 8, 13), who had been instrumental in exposing Alger Hiss and other Soviet spies![38]

Robert Weaver, another Harvard cloned security risk, became Johnson's head of Housing and Urban Development (HUD) in 1966. He started out in 1933 as an economic advisor to subversive Secretary of Interior, Harold L. Ickes, a notoriously rabid defender of the Red conspiracy. Weaver then became an Administrative Assistant to Russian spy, Sidney Hillman (Chapter 16), on the National Defense Advisory Committee. There are few people in government who were better qualified through experience to serve the interests of Moscow! Weaver was a leader at the second National Negro Congress in 1937, cited as "the Communist front movement in the United States among Negroes."[39] He was also a member of the Washington Book Shop Association, an organization "So obviously an enterprise of the Communist Party that it would have been impossible for any politically informed person to walk into it without perceiving its Communist character."[40]

Many security risks were brought into Government service under Richard Nixon. His choice for Special Assistant for National Security Affairs was the notorious Henry Kissinger (CFR), a man unknown at that time to most Americans! Kissinger had long before been named in sworn testimony as a Soviet espionage agent with the code name "Bor"![41] Top Polish intelligence operative, Colonel Michael M. Goleniewski defected to the West in 1961. He was carefully "debriefed" over a period of three years. *None* of the information Goleniewski gave was *ever* found to be inaccurate or untrue.[42] Yet none of the more than 2000 Soviet spies he exposed inside the U.S. Government and elsewhere were prosecuted.[43] Why? Goleniewski, unquestionably correct in his charges, noted that soon after World War II, U.S. Army sergeant Henry Kissinger was a member of a Russian spy ring named ODRA (Chapter 7, 8)! Kissinger at the time was a counter-intelligence interrogator and taught at the Military Intelligence School.[44] Despite these astounding revelations, Kissinger became Nixon's

Secretary of State in 1973! Has anyone heard Dan Rather (CFR) report on this shocking revelation? How about Tom Brokaw (CFR)? Or David Brinkley (CFR)?

Comrade Kissinger was almost single-handedly running American foreign policy, while at the same time he was accused of being one of Moscow's top operatives (spies)! In June 1974, a high ranking security officer warned nationally syndicated columnist Paul Scott: "Kissinger has opened the door for literally hundreds of homosexuals and security risks to move into the highest policy-making positions in government. Already there is a homosexual ring operating at the top level of the State Department with links in other agencies".[45]

Much of Richard Nixon's early political career was built on his undeserved reputation as an anti-Communist! He gained some measure of fame as a Congressman, in the sensational Communist spy scandal involving Alger Hiss. The notoriously subversive Dean Acheson—also believed to be a spy in the employ of Communist Occupied Russia (Chapter 16)—was constantly berated by Nixon over his radical leftist words and deeds. Yet on September 28, 1969, Walter Cronkite did a television special whitewashing Acheson's pro-Communist career. Acheson commented that he, too, was serving President Nixon as an advisor![46]

Nixon chose leftist Joseph E. Johnson (CFR) to be one of his Administration's talent scouts. Johnson was a close friend and chief State Department assistant of Kremlin espionage agent Alger Hiss. He had also been President of the pro-Communist Carnegie Endowment for International Peace. The subversive Carnegie organization had been headed by Soviet spy Hiss from 1946 to 1949, even though the trustees had known of his Communist spying activities *before* he was given the job.

Another of Nixon's major talent scouts was Harvard subversive Adam Yarmolinsky (CFR). This security risk had also helped select the entire Kennedy cabinet. Yarmolinsky (Chapter 16) was the son of two Communists! He once headed the Harvard Marxist Club and edited the *Yardling*, campus voice of the Young Communist League! This subversive told investigators: "The Young Communist league believed, and I was inclined to believe that a so-called Communist government was a desired end."*47* Despite all these things, Yarmolinsky became McNamara's top advisor and an influential behind-the-scenes policymaker! His Communist track record was reviewed by State Department Chief Security Officer Raymond A. Laughton, who refused to grant a security clearance. Laughton resigned when his decision was overruled by "higher authority." Yarmolinsky became one of security risk Paul Warnke's assistants on the Arms Control and Disarmament Agency under Carter. This subversive's career in government (since his Communist-oriented days at Harvard) reveals nothing to show that his views have changed one iota!

Radical leftist Elliot L. Richardson (CFR), Nixon's Under Secretary of State, laid the groundwork for the treasonous SALT negotiations. Security risk Yarmolinsky had been his close friend and Harvard classmate! Richardson was a protégé of Marxist Felix Frankfurter (Chapter 16) while at Harvard. In fact, the *New York Times* reported that Richardson was "a special favorite among his many proteges."*48* Among Frankfurter's other "favorites" were Communist spies Alger Hiss, Lee Pressman, Harry Dexter White, Lawrence Duggan, and Harold Glasser! Imagine, a security risk of this caliber becoming America's Secretary of Defense in 1973! Richardson left government and went to work for Communist Occupied China!*49*

Alexander Haig (CFR) was top assistant and highly polished protégé of identified Kremlin spy Henry Kissinger.*50* Interestingly, Haig said: "Over a period, Henry and I developed a special rapport. From my perspective, I found most of his views compatible with mine."*51* Not only was he the protégé of Comrade Kissinger, but of two other notorious subversives as well—Robert S. McNamara (CFR) and Cyrus Vance (CFR). This security risk had been heavily involved in running the treasonous no-win Vietnam war! He played an important role in the humiliating cut and run surrender of all Vietnam to the North Vietnamese Communists! Haig was the power behind the creation of the disastrous leftist Legal Services Corporation—"One of the most corrupt and pro-Left of all government agencies— nothing but a department for providing federal subsidies for our swarms of lawyers."*52* Despite his subversive background, Haig was selected to be Reagan's Secretary of State! Predictably and understandably, leftist Haig made absolutely no effort to clean security risks out of the State Department!

Communist fronter James Farmer became top assistant to the Secretary of Health, Education and Welfare. This subversive had been Vice-President of the Marxist League for Industrial Democracy! He was a board member of Tom Hayden's (Chapter 6) Communist led Students for a Democratic Society (SDS) and the Communist founded ACLU (Chapter 7)! Farmer's name could be found on the National Executive Board of the American Committee on Africa, a pro-Communist group which inexcusably supports Red terrorists and their murderous activities!

The establishment media led the American public to believe that Gerald Ford (CFR) was the most conservative man to occupy the White House since Grover Cleveland. Nothing could have been further from the truth! "The Accidental President's" first act was to announce that he would retain the dubious services of Moscow's shadowy Henry Kissinger! This identifed Soviet espionage agent *53* was going to be allowed to continue his service to the Kremlin as Ford's Secretary of State!

A reporter in Birmingham, Alabama finally had the courage to pose the question that no one else in the media had dared ask for over a decade after Kissinger's exposure. He began: "Mr. Secretary, we received a report that a Colonel General Michael Goleniewski, who was a Polish Army intelligence officer in World War II, had identified a list of KGB and GRU agents and officers who have since been arrested, tried and convicted. The General . . . also identified you, Mr. Kissinger, as having worked for a Soviet intelligence network—code name ODRA—headquartered in West Germany during World War II, at the same time you were a U.S. Army counter-interrogator and instructor in a military intelligence school . . . Is this true? And, if not, how do you explain your name being on General Goleniewski's list?"[54]

Henry Kissinger was known to be a man who flew off the handle when challenged in private by subordinates. But such reactions weren't allowable in public! So Kissinger, with no change of expression, covering his anger well, responded with a straight face: "I don't know who Colonel Goleniewski is, but I think he should be given the Pulitzer Prize for fiction."[55] What an absurd statement! How could the man in charge of national security *not* have heard of Colonel Goleniewski? Kissinger was plainly lying!

That was that! No media people questioned this subversive's ridiculously trite answer! The wire services ignored it all! The top news people on television dropped the story like a hot potato! And Comrade Kissinger was free to continue the pursuit of his subversion, sabotage, and sellout of America's interests!

Ford personally selected another identified Red to be his Vice President! CIA Director Walter Bedell Smith "warned Eisenhower that Rockefeller was a Communist"[56] in the 1950s. When Nelson Rockefeller was Assistant Secretary of State in 1944-1945, he was given incriminating files by the FBI, which proved Alger Hiss and Harry Dexter White were Soviet moles! Rockefeller is reported to have personally destroyed this irrefutable evidence, because he said that he and others in the State Department believed the FBI was "a Fascist organization in our own midst!"[57] We now know it was no more than a fellow Red protecting his Comrades! Ford was asked on November 14, 1974, about the most notable achievements of his first 100 days as President. He declared: "Number one, nominating Nelson Rockefeller!"[58]

Ford's Attorney General Edward H. Levi had been selected by two identified Communists—Henry Kissinger[59] and Nelson Rockefeller.[60] He was a member of the

National Lawyers Guild, which was founded by the Communist Party solely to defend Communists and Communist activities! While dean of the University of Chicago Law School, this subversive hired a Communist to head his law library—a man who'd been exposed as a member of the Silvermaster spy cell. Incredibly, a man who had been associating with and defending Reds for over 30 years was placed in charge of the surveillance of Communist spies; in charge of prosecuting espionage agents; and in charge of the FBI itself (Chapter 7)!

Coleman A. Young, *a Communist*, was chairman of Carter's 1980 Democratic Platform Committee. This Red espionage agent had also been a delegate in 1957 to the American Communist Party Convention. Detroit's subversive Mayor was a founder of the Communist National Negro Labor Council. He was identified before the House Committee on Un-American Activities in the early 1950s as a leading Negro Communist in the United States![61]

Harvard's Zbigniew Brzezinski (CFR)—a Marxist according to his writings—was appointed by Carter (CFR) to run the National Security Council! This is the same job identified Kremlin espionage agent Henry Kissinger[62] held under Nixon. An interesting correlation here is that Kissinger was a protégé of identified Moscow-man Nelson Rockefeller![63] Brzezinski was a protégé of Nelson's banking brother David (Chapter 3)! Both Kissinger and Brzezinski are foreign-born and became naturalized citizens. They were even classmates at Harvard graduate school. Kissinger has been named as a Kremlin spy![64] Alan Stang pulls no punches: "Zbigniew Brzezinski . . . is a Marxist."[65]

A devoted appeaser of the Communists, Brzezinski—possibly educated far beyond his ability to comprehend—believes Marxism to be an inevitable phase of man's development. This radical's Marxist orientation is readily exposed when he declares: "Marxism represents a further vital and creative stage in the maturing of man's universal vision.... Marxism is a victory of reason over belief."[66]

Investigative journalist John Rees charges that Brzezinski's books and articles indicate that "Marxism has not only been the major influence on [his] political thinking but that he accepts its basic principles."67 He advocates the abolishing of Congress and taking away the right to vote! Brzezinski openly calls for "a global taxation system" and a world dictatorship to be run by the intellectual elite! Is Zbigniew Brzezinski a Communist? Karl Marx would agree he is! According to Marx, in order to be a Communist, all one has to do is believe in Communism, and work toward its goals. Brzezinski unquestionably qualifies!

A major target of the KGB is the National Security Council. Whoever controls the NSC controls U.S. intelligence. Whoever controls U.S. intelligence controls America's ability to defend itself against Communists and Communism! At least four Brzezinski underlings in the NSC were intimately linked to Soviet KGB agent Orlando Letelier, at the subversive Institute for Policy Studies! Three of these KGB contacts were Gregory Treverton, Karl F. Inderfurth, and David L. Aaron (CFR). Aaron was the protégé of socialist Walter Mondale! The fourth KGB contact was Robert Pastor, son-in-law of subversive Robert S. McNamara, former Defense Secretary!

Sidney Harman, Under Secretary of Commerce, was formerly a trustee of the radical leftist Institute of Policy Studies! The staff of this blatantly pro-Communist think tank included a variety of Marxist-oriented misfits. There were Communist Party members, KGB operatives, Weather Underground terrorists, and leaders of the Trotskyite Fourth International! Other Carter people connected to the IPS include Peter Bourne, White House advisor and "the President's closest friend" (Chapter 6); Sam Brown (Chapter 6); Margery Tabankin (Chapter 6); and John Lewis.

Carter chose a *"former"* Communist to be his top economist! Lawrence R. Klein appeared before the House Committee on Un-American Activities in 1954 and admitted to having been a Party member. He claimed to have broken with the Communists because they were "dull" and said he'd rather work for "socialism" outside the Party. Klein also taught at important Red training schools in Chicago and Boston, which were cited as "adjuncts of the Communist Party."*68* Here we have a highly placed official in the Carter Administration who *claimed* to have left the Communist Party out of boredom! But he apparently remained a Communist! And he continued to work toward the goals of Communism! And this was acceptable to the President of the United States!

Security risk George Shultz (CFR), a carryover from the Eisenhower days, was named Nixon's Secretary of Labor in 1969. He was enthusiastically endorsed by dangerous subversive Willard Wirtz, who held that same position under Kennedy and Johnson! Shultz and identified Kremlin agent Kissinger*69* were close friends and mutual admirers! The applauding of Shultz by leftist Wirtz and his later unqualified support by Comrade Kissinger (as Reagan's Secretary of State) should certainly be enough to create some degree of suspicion! Shultz's track record is another cause for alarm. As could be expected, he made no attempt to remove Communist espionage agents from the State Department! Israel required their teachers on the West Bank to sign a loyalty pledge, renouncing support of the terrorist PLO. Shultz, aware that the PLO blows up entire schools full of kids, said such a demand interfered with "freedom of thought." His pro-Communist leanings became even more obvious when compared their action to "McCarthyism" in the U.S.

One of the most astounding security risks to be brought into the "conservative" Reagan Administration was the notorious Kremlin man, Armand Hammer. He was to be an unofficial "shuttle diplomat to work out a solution to the conflict" in Afghanistan. The Russians were losing and they wanted out of the war. So they arranged for a trusted comrade to be selected, to help save them the country for enslavement. A photo signed by Lenin hangs in his office. His idol wrote: "To Comrade Armand Hammer." This subversive's father, Dr. Julius Hammer, was a founder of the

Communist Party USA and an intimate of Lenin. Armand took tons of supplies to Communist Occupied Russia, in 1921, to help the new Red dictatorship get on its feet. He stayed until 1931. Hammer presently has an astounding number of business interests in the Soviet Union and is a key figure in the transfer of American technology to these avowed enemies of freedom (Chapter 2).

William J. Casey (CFR), named to head Reagan's CIA, was a bosom buddy of identified Soviet spy Henry Kissinger.[70] He was also a close friend of Armand Hammer, confidant of *every* Soviet dictator, including to Lenin. Casey was Nixon's director of the U.S. Export-Import Bank, where he helped build the Communist economy by wholesale looting of the treasury (Chapter 3). This wheeler-dealer was behind the largest single trade deal ever made between Communist Occupied Russia and the Untied States—Armand Hammer's $20 *billion* Occidental-USSR Fertilizer Exchange. Respected intelligence analyst Frank Capell described Casey: "Under the State Department security of the Otepka era it is very doubtful that William Casey would have been granted clearance. His past known associations with Communists . . . and his pro-Soviet outlook would have raised many questions . . . "[71]

Ronald Reagan appeared to be extremely critical of Henry Kissinger during his campaign and he wouldn't give a cabinet post to this longtime Communist espionage agent. But Comrade Kissinger was, nevertheless, secretly relied upon by the President as an influential foreign policy advisor! Reagan stunned his supporters by appointing this exposed Soviet mole[72] as chairman of the Latin American Policy Commission—thereafter known as the "Kissinger Commission." Did this not send a clear warning signal to all the anti-Communist leaders in Latin America? After all, as journalist Gary Allen concluded: "Moscow's most important man in Latin America is not Fidel Castro; it's Henry Kissinger."[73]

"When anything is said or written about Communist influence in our government," charged former Congressman

Martin Dies (D-TX), "the 'Liberals' are vehement in their denials—yet the Committee on UnAmerican Activities named not less than five thousand Communists on the federal payroll, and fifteen thousand working in defense industries . . . The Administration fired a few of these people . . . *all of them have been rehired* . . . We have yet to hear a satisfactory answer to what those five thousand Communists we found were doing in the federal government, unless they were stealing invaluable secrets and influencing our policies."[74]

Anyone attempting to unearth Reds in government today is still charged with "McCarthyism." Such courageous individuals are also derogatorily labeled "Birchites," "extremists," "rightwing fanatics," or part of the "lunatic fringe!" These Pavlovian scare words have been deliberately coined by Comrades of the very traitors being investigated! They are designed to elicit a conditioned response and force concerned, patriotic citizens to back off and leave the traitors alone. This technique has proved to be immensely successful for the Communists and their "Liberal" patrons, protectors, and friends!

Chapter 12

Presidential Words and Deeds

Traitor: "Person who betrays his country."
Thorndike Barnhart Comprehensive Desk Dictionary

Treason: "The betrayal of one's own country ... by consciously and purposely acting to aid its enemies."
Webster's 11 New World Dictionary

What's going on here? One President was photographed giving the symbolic Communist clenched fist salute! Another President wined and dined the greatest mass-murdering Communist in history! One President authorized a national holiday to honor a demagogue who proclaimed himself a Marxist! Another President presented a notorious security risk with a $50,000 tax-free award! One President delivered over 2,000,000 people to Communist Occupied Russia, for execution or incarceration in slave labor camps! Another President protected a Communist slave labor dictatorship from invasion!

Yes, what exactly is going on here? Thomas J. Anderson aptly concluded: "Ours is the only nation whose leaders could have done what they've done ... without being tried for treason."[1]

The Age of Treason began in the 1930s, with the advent of the Roosevelt Administration! Russian sympathizers and outright Soviet espionage agents were never in short supply in FDR's Administration. Franklin Delano Roosevelt knowingly allowed Red spies—many of them personal friends of his and Eleanor's—to freely infiltrate various agencies of the government! Former Congressman Martin Dies (D-TX), charged: "The Roosevelt Administration . . . had been compromised by their collaboration with Communists . . . and the employment of Communists in the government. The Administration felt that a fearless exposure of this sordid alliance would damage the Democratic Party."2

Roosevelt holds the unholy distinction of giving Diplomatic Recognition to Stalin's barbaric dictatorship in 1933! This single act gave legitimacy to a small gang of thugs in Communist Occupied Russia. He was well aware that Stalin's outlaw regime was personally responsible for murdering nearly 17 million of his own people! As pointed out by Representative Philip M. Crane (R-IL): "During the height of Joseph Stalin's reign of terror, more than 40,000 persons were being executed each month."3 Stalin himself had bragged to Churchill and others as to how he had dealt with 10 million kulaks. Most of these unfortunates died of forced starvation, under the iron fist of Stalin's henchman, Nikita Khrushchev! Such wholesale murder of Russia's most prosperous farmers didn't disturb Roosevelt in the least.

Nazi Germany and Communist Occupied Russia jointly invaded Poland in 1939. The Red Army rounded up and methodically butchered up to 15,000 unarmed Polish military officers! A huge pit was later discovered in the Katyn Forest, near Smolensk. Here were found 12 layers of corpses dressed in Polish military uniforms. Each man had a bullet hole in the back of his head. Roosevelt was aware of these deliberate murders but he covered for Stalin. George Crocker reports: "The gruesome facts of the Katyn massacre . . . had been laid on his desk . . . When . . . documents and pictures attesting Russian guilt in the cold-blooded atrocity were brought to Roosevelt in the White House, *he reacted with anger, not to the Russian murders, but at those who had collected the facts,* and he clamped the lid down tight."*4* (Author's emphasis)

An excellent example of Roosevelt's duplicity can be found in Poland's abhorrent betrayal! FDR assured exiled Prime Minister Mikolajczyk: "Stalin doesn't intend to take freedom from Poland. He wouldn't dare do that because he knows that the United States government stands solidly behind you.... I will see to it that Poland will not be hurt in this war and will emerge strongly independent."*5* The President was at the same time telling Stalin he could steal 70 thousand square miles of Polish territory! Everything Roosevelt promised Mikolajczyk was an outright lie!

In 1944, Molotov revealed: ". . . we agreed [at the November 28 December 1, 1943, Teheran Conference] that it would be best *not* to issue a public declaration about our agreement."*6* Roosevelt wanted his treasonous betrayal of Poland kept under wraps until after the 1944 election. He told Stalin that "there were in the United States from six to seven million Americans of Polish extraction, and, as a practical man, he did not wish to lose their vote."*7* The unbelievable concessions made to the murderous Stalin at Teheran were finalized by Roosevelt at Yalta and Truman at Potsdam. Betrayal and sellout to Communism became the accepted mode of action for FDR and *all* subsequent American leaders!

Roosevelt was sick and near death when the election was held in November 1944. Three months later, a much weakened President was manipulated into traveling around six thousand miles each way to attend the February 4-11, 1945 Yalta Conference! The meeting was held in Livadia Palace, built in 1911 as a vacation retreat for Czar Nicholas II. A dying American President was a virtual prisoner of his top advisors—the most influential being Kremlin spy Alger Hiss!

Roosevelt knew that Comrade Hiss had been Stalin's man since at least 1939, when Whittaker Chambers had informed A.A. Berle. Yet, here it was, six years later, and this traitor was more powerful than ever before! He was firmly glued to Roosevelt's side, constantly whispering advice in the incapacitated President's ear, taking care of all details, and handling all the paperwork. As the painful truth about Yalta slowly emerged, the extremely important role of Soviet espionage agent Alger Hiss was deliberately overlooked, denied, or played down! Hiss later commented on his part: "It is an accurate and not immodest statement to say that I helped formulate the Yalta agreement to some extent."[8]

Incredibly, the entire sordid Yalta sellout was agreed upon two *years* before Roosevelt and Stalin actually got together! Nicholas Baciu reveals how FDR wrote "Uncle Joe" on February 20, 1943, and promised the brutal Communist dictator all of the territories eventually annexed by the USSR!"[9] Communist enslavement over most of Eastern and Central Europe was guaranteed! At the end of World War II, John T. Flynn noted that FDR had "surrendered into Stalin's hands a whole collection of peoples, whose land comprised, along with Russia, almost two-thirds of the land mass of Europe and Asia."[10]

Roosevelt made a multitude of secret concessions to Stalin at Yalta. They agreed to divide Germany! The Russian mass-murderer was allowed the wholesale thievery of German industrial plants, factories, and other property! Millions of conquered Germans—men, women, and children—were to be shipped to Communist Occupied Russia, to finish out their lives in barbaric slave labor concentration camps!

Stalin demanded the return of millions of Hungarians, Poles, and others in Central Europe, who had fled since 1939! Their only "crime" was having escaped from Russian controlled areas. Roosevelt, charged Westbrook Pegler, "made a contract with Stalin to deliver millions . . . of European people . . . into Russian custody as salves . . . It was a foregone conclusion that many of them would be killed by firing squads. They were Soviet subjects who had surrendered to the Nazis . . . They knew Bolshevism. They thought nothing could be worse . . . "[11]

The diabolical plan was officially known as "Operation Keelhaul." General Dwight D. Eisenhower—a Roosevelt protege*12* "repatriated" these helpless men, women, and children against their will! Some of the men had actually served and fought with the U.S. Army. They, too, were rounded up at gun-point! Over *2,000,000* people were herded into boxcars and shipped, "prepaid" to the clutches of the monstrous Russian dictator! Many committed suicide rather than return to be shot, tortured, or to die a slower death in one of Stalin's slave-labor concentration camps.*[13]*

"This surrender to their enemy of millions of prisoners of war was a crime by established law," charged Pegler. "It was not a violation of one of the *ex-post facto* laws which monstrous Russians and monstrous Americans improvised against German generals and politicians for the gala hanging at Nuremberg. If any of those Germans deserved hanging how about Truman, Stalin, and Ike? That ought to be the penalty for dealing in slave trade!"*[14]*

Stalin had declared that he didn't want one additional inch of real estate "added to his empire" as a result of the war. Yet, charges John T. Flynn, the diabolical monster ended up grabbing *"some 725 million people,* which with the 193 million in Russia gave him dominion over 918 *million human beings* in Russia and 16 other European and Asiatic countries."*[15]*

Truman inherited a thoroughly Communist infiltrated executive branch. He made no effort to change this upon becoming President! It certainly wasn't that Truman was stupid! He'd long been aware of the powerful Communist presence under Roosevelt. And he knew about the multitude of subversives in his own Administration! Not only did this man inherit all of Roosevelt's Reds, he deliberately added a number of his own! Truman had an ongoing romance with the Communists, over a period of many years! They even openly endorsed him for the Vice Presidency!*[16]* In return, Truman the President showed complete "indifference to Communist penetration at home."*[17]*

HST went to Germany to attend the Potsdam Conference from July 17 to July 25, 1945. Here he was to wheel and deal with hard-nosed Joe Stalin in implementing Roosevelt's treasonous Yalta giveaways! Before leaving for Potsdam, Truman read a report prepared by 50 top Army intelligence specialists. They warned: "The entry of Soviet Russia into the Asiatic War . . . would destroy America's position in Asia . . . China will certainly lose her independence, to become the Poland of Asia . . . Chiang may have to depart and a Chinese Soviet government may be installed . . . "*18* He was then briefed by Owen Lattimore, identified as a Communist spy by former *Daily Worker* editor Louis Budenz and others. Truman ignored the Army intelligence report! He instead followed Lattimore's Communist-benefiting proposals and the Reds accomplished exactly what military intelligence said they would!

Alger Hiss was able to stay close to Roosevelt and Truman, even after they were repeatedly warned by Congressman Martin Dies and J. Edgar Hoover that he was a Soviet spy! When Hiss was finally publicly exposed as a Communist traitor, Truman, Eleanor Roosevelt, Felix Frankfurter (Chapter 16) and other leftists did their best to get him off the hook! During the 1948 election campaign, Truman charged the Hiss case was nothing more than a "red herring." He was lying!

"Red herrings" was also the phrase used by Truman to characterize the hearings of the House Committee on Un-American Activities, before which former Communists Whittaker Chambers and Elizabeth Bentley were testifying!

Truman knew he couldn't be re-elected in 1952, because of his consistent Made-In-Moscow-Policies. He'd been caught red-handed shielding Kremlin espionage agents! Known Communist spies had been promoted! All congressional investigations of Reds were blocked! Truman completed the delivery of Eastern Europe into Stalin's bloody grip! Chiang Kai-shek was driven out and China delivered to Mao's Red terrorists! Truman deliberately brought America into the Korean War, with no intention of winning (Chapter 14)! MacArthur was sacked for demanding victory! Sanctuaries were provided for the Communist enemy! There is much, much more, but suffice to say, Truman's sordid record speaks for itself.

In 1953, Eisenhower made his infamous "Atoms for Peace" speech. This marked the beginning of the treasonous giveaway of America's nuclear research data and materials to enemy Communist regimes! Eisenhower did more to give Communist Occupied Russia and other Red slave labor states nuclear capability than did the Rosenbergs and *all* other Soviet spies combined! The Rosenbergs were sentenced to death for their traitorous deed. Eisenhower was re-elected to another term!

On June 30, 1954, Eisenhower, ignoring his infamous role in the post World War II "Operation Keelhaul," hypocritically proclaimed: "I will not be a party to any agreement that makes anyone a slave."*19* Three weeks later, Ho Chi Minh was handed control of North Vietnam. Thirteen million Vietnamese people became slaves with the stroke of a pen! *Time* noted: "At Geneva the Communists got precisely what they sought; a vast slice of Indochina, and a stance from which to take the rest . . . "*20* Thanks to Eisenhower's treasonous act, America was fighting its second no-win war less than a decade later, this time in South Vietnam (Chapter 6). Ho Chi Minh, with the assistance of innumerable American traitors, *did* "take the rest!"

The astounding fall of Cuba to Castro's tiny band of Communist gangsters was carefully orchestrated by Eisenhower (Chapter 10). The choreographed leftist scenario went like this: Ike's subversive brother Milton (Chapter 13, 14) met with the Red terrorist leader in his Oriente hills guerrilla hideout in November of 1958! Castro's thugs captured Havana only six weeks later on January 1, 1959! Diplomatic recognition was hurriedly granted to the bandit gang a week later. Eisenhower *deliberately* gave Communist Occupied Russia a foothold in the Western Hemisphere!*21*

Thanks to this President, the Soviets were handed a base from which to expand their corrupt slave labor empire!

Nikita Khrushchev was invited by the President (in July 1959) to visit the United States, even though Ike was aware of the Butcher of Budapest's ungodly and bloody past. Hearings had been held and the documentation showed: "Khrushchev personally conceived and executed the mass starvation and liquidation of six to eight million Ukrainians in the early 1930's [including children] . . . Khrushchev was the chief executioner for the bloody Moscow purge trials in 1936 . . . Khrushchev, during a second two year reign of terror in the Ukraine in 1937-38, slaughtered another 400,000 people [including children]."[22]

Evidently, none of this mattered to Eisenhower! The "Red" carpet was dutifully rolled out at the White House, for a monster who had been Stalin's most trusted henchman! America's arch-enemy and the most despicable mass-murderer of all time was royally entertained at Gettysburg! Ike's grandchildren were photographed sitting on this ghastly killer's knee! The President called it a "heart warming scene."[23] He further declared: "Now, I don't think that Mr. Khrushchev is himself a cruel man... I'm sure he loves children.... Oh, he's very, very much of a family man that way. . "[24] Khrushchev's welcome conveyed exactly what it was meant to convey. It clearly signaled the death knell for the Captive Nations! The enslaved millions behind the Iron Curtain were unmistakably being told that they could no longer hope for help from America!

Despite his acknowledged enjoyment of this Communist neanderthal's company, Ike obviously didn't feel the same way about loyal American anti-Communists. Arthur Larson wrote: "Toward Senator Joseph McCarthy, President Eisenhower had a sense of loathing and contempt that had to be seen to be believed."[25] Eisenhower wrote that as President, I "yearned in every fiber of my being" to "smash" McCarthy.[26] Yet, Eisenhower would have done well to heed McCarthy's common sense warning "You cannot offer friendship to tyrants and murderers . . . without advancing the cause of tyranny and murder."[27]

Was Eisenhower a Communist? No one knows! Historian Robert Welch once drew a parallel to a politician-military man of another era— Alcibiades, the Athenian traitor: "Alcibiades, rich, famous, honored, and powerful, was the one man most Athenians would have found it most difficult to think of as a traitor."[28] The *Encyclopedia Britannica* description of Alcibiades could well fit Eisenhower: "Superficial and opportunist to the last, he owed the successes of his meteoric career purely to personal magnetism and an almost incredible capacity for deception." The point isn't whether Eisenhower was or wasn't an agent of the Kremlin conspiracy! Whether Ike's reasons for his actions were ideological, due to ignorance, or sheer political opportunism makes little difference! The end result is identical. The same is also true of every other President! And the law covering treason doesn't differentiate between ideology, ignorance, and opportunism!

Russian missiles and long range bombers were suddenly discovered to be in Cuba! Kennedy supposedly forced a much heralded "eyeball to eyeball" confrontation with Khrushchev. The Soviets were said to have backed down and meekly removed their missiles and planes. But this is highly improbably, for the Butcher of Budapest had previously met with JFK in Vienna and boasted: "I think that I have taught that young man what fear is!"[29] No one actually saw any missiles or bombers leave Castro's concentration camp island! Nevertheless, America-hating Marxist U Thant of the UN went to Havana during the crisis to take a look around. Conveniently, the man who idolized Lenin could find no missiles or big bombers! Taking Thant's word, JFK let Castro and Communist Occupied Russia conveniently slip off the hook!

No one knew it at the time, but Kennedy made a secret deal with the Russian tyrant in return for the purported missile removal! On October 27, 1962, he guaranteed that neither the U.S. nor any other nation in the Western

Hemisphere would *ever* invade Communist Occupied Cuba! The President of the United States officially made Castro's Cuba a protected Communist sanctuary! Unbelievable as it may sound, U.S. warships were sent to patrol the Caribbean! This was to protect the island from attack by anti-Communist Cuban exiles and refugees in the United States.

Senator Richard Russell (D-GA) recapped the disgraceful chain of events: "Three months ago we were pledged to see that Castroism in this hemisphere was destroyed. We have now been euchred into the position of baby-sitting for Castro and guaranteed the integrity of the Communist regime in Cuba. We don't know for a fact that the missiles and bombers have been removed . . . all we have seen is a box they said contained a bomber and a long metal container that they said contained a missile. We have not had on-the-spot inspection."*30*

Lyndon Baines Johnson was an ambitious, dishonest, and corrupt politician. This pseudo-conservative sounded like an English speaking Karl Marx in 1964. He bluntly declared his intent as President: "We are going to take all the money that we think is unnecessarily being spent and take it from the 'haves' and give it to the 'have nots' who need it so much."*31* Johnson had previously announced that he was "further to the left than Eleanor Roosevelt."*32* Evidently the American people weren't listening!

The much heralded "War on Poverty" was launched under LBJ's Presidency. Marxist Daniel P. Moynihan (CFR) and former Young Communist League member Adam Yarmolinsky of Harvard teamed up to write the Act that created the Office of Economic Opportunity! The agency immediately, *as was intended,* became a watering hole for Communist agitators and far-left radicals! Revolutionaries employed in the OEO distributed money to their revolutionary counterparts in the streets! Innumerable War of Poverty grants were used to finance their Communist directed activities! For example, New York's Black Arts Repertory Theater received a great deal of cash from the OEO. Run by black revolutionary Leroi Jones, his basement was the headquarters for black terrorists, who specialized in murdering other blacks! Pure and simple, Lyndon Johnson was guilty of treasonously financing Communist revolutionary activity in the streets of America!

In 1954, the Atomic Energy Commission pulled Dr. J. Robert Oppenheimer's security clearance and denied him access to classified government data. The AEC found that Oppenheimer, director of the A-bomb project during WW II, "was not a mere 'parlor pink' . . . but was deeply and consciously involved with hardened and militant Communists at a time when he was a man of mature judgment. His relations with these hardened Communists were such that they considered him to be one of their number."33 Oppenheimer had been on the Communist-founded ACLU's National Committee since 1948! His wife, mistress, and brother were all Communists! He regularly gave money to the Party and attended meetings! William L. Borden, former Executive Director of the Joint Committee on Atomic Energy concluded: "More probably than not, J. Robert Oppenheimer is an agent of the Soviet Union."34 In December 1963, Lyndon Johnson presented this subversive with the AEC's prestigious Enrico Fermi award. Oppenheimer walked away with a tax-free $50,000 check!

A month later, Johnson shamelessly honored the notorious Marxist, Roger Baldwin, on his 80th birthday. This subversive was a long-time Communist Fronter and a founder of the infamous ACLU! His wife, Madeline Doty, was a courier for the Bolshevists! Baldwin boldly testified before Congress that he upheld an alien's right to "advocate the overthrow of the government by force and violence" and to "advocate murder and assassination."35 Writing in a Harvard class reunion book: "I am for Socialism, disarmament, and ultimately for abolishing the State itself . . . *Communism is* the goal."36 The President hypocritically told this anti-American leftist: "Your unremitting fight against injustice and intolerance in this country . . . has earned you the warm gratitude of countless individuals . . .

you have shown a devotion to principle . . . which will long be remembered by your countrymen."[37]

Johnson never deviated from the Kennedy policy of banning the sale of arms and military hardware to South Africa—a free country, anti-Communist, and a reliable American ally! South Africa was treated as if it were a despicable slave state and a threat to U.S. security! This same hypocrite traitorously opened the floodgates to supply Communist slave labor dictatorships throughout the world with food and arms (Chapter1,2,4,6).

Nixon's Secretary of the Army, Stanley R. Resor, authorized a controversial directive on dissent, that went to all military commanders throughout the world. The directive[38] was so blatantly pro-Communist that it could have been composed by propagandist's working for Communist Occupied Russia's *Izvestia* and *Pravda.* Yet it's authors were instead employed at the Pentagon! Included were these points: Commanding officers *can't* punish military personnel who work on Communist projects off the post! Communist indoctrination centers, called coffee houses, *can't* be placed off limits to servicemen! Serviceman *can't* be banned from distributing Communist literature on base or off! The purchase or possession of Red literature on the base *can't* be prohibited![39]

Nixon deliberately ignored the Monroe Doctrine when Chile became another Communist dictatorship in this hemisphere! The leftist media offered no protest! Nixon deliberately ignored Peru when U.S. property was seized and the little country became a Marxist tyranny! The leftist media said nothing! Nixon deliberately ignored the Communist coup in Ecuador! The leftist media said little! Nixon made it "perfectly clear" that he had no intention of defending Panama, even in the event of a Soviet backed invasion! This, despite the fact that the Panama Canal Zone was, by treaty, made U.S. property "in perpetuity" as a condition for Congressional approval to finance the canal's construction (Chapter 10).

Nixon traitorously wrote off the Captive Nations in Europe and Asia! The treasonous "Nixon Doctrine" supported "the legalization of Communist control over all people and nations seized during and since World War II."*40* Nixon officially accepted the legitimacy of the Red slave states! He thereby abandoned millions of Europeans to a hopeless life of hardship and misery!

Ford was the President who *guaranteed* Communist Occupied Russia's permanent enslavement of the Captive Nations in Eastern Europe! This was accomplished in 1975 when he signed the European Security Agreement in Helsinki. By partaking of this treachery, Ford ratified the Roosevelt-Hiss sellout of Poland, Romania, Yugoslavia, and other countries! He also agreed that Russia would permanently occupy East Germany!

Ford continued the leftist Nixon programs and retained most of the man's radical appointees. He made it clear immediately after being sworn in, that there would be no changes in foreign policy. This, of course, simply meant a continuation of Kissinger's program of retreat, disarmament, betrayal, surrender, and humiliation! And Kissinger was a man who'd been exposed as a Communist spy in the employ of the Soviet Union.[41]

One of Ford's many serious betrayals was in dismantling America's $6 billion Anti-Ballistic Missile (ABM) system, one month after it became operational! Meanwhile, the Soviet Union installed their American-designed ABM system. It was run by computers supplied by Control Data Corporation and IBM (Chapter 1, 29.

The house organ of the Council on Foreign Relations— sounding like an official Communist propaganda journal— called for the "liberation" of Mozambique and Angola! Also demanded was a "swamp of blood" in South Africa!*42* Gerald Ford tried his best to accomplish all three! This leftist wouldn't consider liberating any of the Communist slave labor dictatorships, yet he avidly sought to destroy free anti-Communist nations! Ford completed the betrayal of Mozambique to Communist terrorists in late 1974! He eagerly delivered Angola to the Reds in 1975! And he allowed the Communist controlled Organization of African Unity to funnel American tax dollars to Red terrorist groups who were waging a brutal war against the free people of anti-Communist South Africa!

Ford did his dead level best to destroy anti-Communist Rhodesia —an ally and a friend of America—and turn it over to Red revolutionaries! He declared: "The United States is totally dedicated to seeing to it that the majority becomes the ruling power in Rhodesia." Ford was no more than a hypocritical meddler. He wasn't at all dedicated to forcing a similar majority rule on such Communist slave labor dictatorships as Russia, China, Cuba, Vietnam, Poland, Hungary, etc. Why?

Gerald Ford wanted, as did Richard Nixon before him, to treasonously give away the Panama Canal. The American-owned canal was to be turned over to the tinhorn Communist dictator in Panama. The treachery was to be culminated right after the elections in 1976. It *was,* but by Carter, rather than Ford (Chapter 10).

Carter was the only President to be photographed giving the Communist clenched-fist salute! His radical leftist behavior was noted at an Atlanta victory celebration: "Carter symbolically clenched his fist and held it high."*43* Every newspaper in the U.S. carried a photograph of KGB trained Kremlin Assassin Lee Harvey Oswald, giving an identical salute after he'd been captured! Such a gesture is universally recognized as the Communist sign denoting violent aggression.

Carter withdrew all U.S. agents operating covertly inside Communist Occupied Russia! Why? Immediately after taking office in January, 1977, Carter halted all SR-71 reconnaissance flights over Communist Occupied Cuba! Castro's island fortress was somehow determined to now be a "low priority" area, despite the fact that the Soviet Union was shipping their Cuban clone every imaginable kind of military hardware, including missiles! Carter treasonously suppressed the 1979 discovery of a Russian combat brigade stationed in Cuba! He even accepted Castro's Communist dictatorship as no more than "toleration of ideological diversity "[44]

Carter announced there'd be no proclamation honoring Captive Nation's Week in 1977! The gutless wonder didn't wish to offend Communist Occupied Russia by drawing attention to their string of slave labor tyrannies! Major General John K. Singlaub reminded Carter: "We in the Free World must recognize that the subjugated peoples of the enslaved and captive nations of the world-wide Communist Empire are one of the potentially most powerful forces in the world. They are, in fact, our strongest ally and constitute our greatest opportunity to bring the dismemberment of the Communist Empire without the risks of nuclear holocaust."[45]

Carter induced Somalia to break relations with Communist Occupied Russia and toss the Soviets out of their Berbera military base. Somalia, knowing no better, became an eager ally of the U.S. Prodded by Carter, they invaded Ethiopia in an attempt to overthrow the weak Communist tyranny. Carter then proceeded to betray the heroic little antiCommunist country! He refused to supply it with fuel, weapons, and military hardware as promised! The Somalian Army was soundly defeated!

Carter's National Security Council (under Marxist Brzezinski) (Chapter 11), adopted Presidential Review Memorandum No. 10. This memo advocated giving one-third of West Germany to Communist Occupied Russia, should they invade Western Europe.

Although Iran was of great geopolitical importance to the United States, Carter deliberately betrayed this long-time friend and ally. Political analyst Hilaire duBerrier declares: "Anyone who wishes to believe that Jimmy Carter destroyed the Shah of Iran out of naiveté is of course free to do so."[46]

When guerrillas from Communist Occupied Nicaragua (Chapter 10) and Red Cuba ferociously attacked Guatemala, Carter cut off military assistance to the Guatemalan anti-Communists! After all, he saw the Sandinistas as no more than idealistic and harmless "agrarian reformers." Tragically, this is exactly what the Red Chinese were wrongly called some years ago! In mid-September 1980, $75 million was given to the gangster leaders of the Nicaraguan police state!47 According to Carter, *no* intelligence data indicated that the Reds were exporting their violent revolution to other parts of Latin America. *The President lied!*

Representative William Young (R-FL), a member of the House Intelligence Committee, said: ". . . intelligence reports confirm in overwhelming detail that the Sandinista clique . . . is engaged in the export of violence and revolution. There is no disagreement within the Intelligence Community on the evidence."[48]

Daniel Ortega is the Kremlin stooge who ordered the execution of hundreds of thousands of his countrymen immediately following the July 1979 occupation of Nicaragua by Communist terrorists! His brother Humberto warned that enemies of the Red regime "will be hanging along the roads and highways of the country."[49] Despite this, the Georgia peanut farmer enthusiastically welcomed this corrupt little thug to the White House! Madison Avenue Danny came on September 24, 1979, and must have chuckled to himself upon finding such an abundance of groveling Carter people stumbling all over themselves to shake his bloody hand!

Carter absurdly made Ortega an offer to train his Communist soldiers on U.S. military bases in Panama. The designer sunglass-clad little dictator turned down this asinine proposal—probably in shock! After all, why should he bother sending his troops to train in Panama when Soviet, Cuban, and East German "advisors" were already training them in Nicaragua?

The unilateral disarming of the U.S. was continued by Carter! For example, hundreds of millions of dollars were wasted when Minuteman missile production was canceled! Incredibly, the facilities, as well as the tooling, were destroyed so the program couldn't be reinstituted! So rabidly was the Carter disarmament clique performing its task that retired Air Force General Ira Eaker couldn't recall the approval of any weapons recommended by the Joint Chiefs of Staff! Recommendations, on the other hand, coming from Russia's Howdy Doody look alike—Party boss Leonid Brezhnev—fared much better. According to Eaker, Brezhnev wanted Carter to cancel the B-1 Bomber program. Carter canceled! He wanted the U.S. to stop building a nuclear aircraft carrier. Carter stopped! The Russians meanwhile were aggressively pursuing their own shipbuilding program! He expressed dissatisfaction with the MX missile the neutron bomb, and the cruise missile. Carter delayed them all![50]

The Carter betrayal list is incredible! He praised Julius Nyerere, the barbaric dictator of Communist Occupied Tanzania. Carter fondly called this ghastly Red terrorist a "superb politician" who "recognizes that the structure of government can be used for beneficial purposes."[51] Was the President referring to Nyerere's one party police state, wanton torture and murder of all political opposition, or the slave labor camps set up to hold the "relocated" half of Tanzania's population?

Ronald Reagan campaigned for the Presidency as a fiery anti-Communist conservative in 1980. Yet, he did absolutely *nothing to* correct the critical lack of internal security safeguards (Chapter 7, 8) upon becoming President! He befriended and assisted and fed and armed Communist tyrants from Poland to Afghanistan, Yugoslavia to Angola, and Romania to Zimbabwe! He continued to make unreasonable demands of anti-Communist South Africa—a free country, reliable ally, and friend! And let's not forget, under Reagan's leadership, unarmed American marines were murdered by terrorists in Lebanon. These fighting men hadn't been allowed to carry loaded guns while on sentry duty!

Reagan did an astounding about face when he treasonously abandoned another staunch American ally, the anti-Communist Republic of China, on Taiwan! He instead recognized the Communist "People's Republic of China as the sole legal government of China."[52] Reagan made a pilgrimage to blood-soaked Communist Occupied China, as did Presidents before him. And following their lead, he proceeded to toast the greatest mass-murderers of our age! This purported anti-Communist President greatly expanded aid to (and trade with) the criminal Chinese Reds (Chapter 4). Reagan enthusiastically began to modernize the Communist Chinese military (Chapter 1). He approved of financing Red Chinese trade with low interest loans from the Export-Import Bank (Chapter 3).

The Communist Sandinista gangsters weren't placed in office by a popular vote of the people! Nor had their oppressive dictatorship been ratified by the people! Yet, leftists of every hue from pink to red complain that the U.S. is trying to overthrow the duly constituted government of Communist Occupied Nicaragua! By whom exactly was this Red tyranny duly constituted? Even Reagan refused to drive the Communists out of Nicaragua, although Ortega runs a hostile armed camp, only a two-day drive from the United States! The President made these incredible statements: "But let us be clear as to the American attitude toward the government of Nicaragua. We do not seek its overthrow . . . "*53* And, "We do not seek the military overthrow of the Sandinista government."*54* Why *not?* The Red dictatorship in Managua intends to eventually help overthrow the United States Government! That's the only reason there's conflict in Central America, in the first place!

Anti-Communist Robert d'Aubuisson wanted to set up a constitutional government in El Salvador, which was to be modeled after the United States. He wanted to govern El Salvador by implementing the 1980 Republican Platform. Incredibly, Reagan rejected him as a devious rightwing fanatic! Crypto-Communist Napoleon Duarte—a purported "socialist" was instead backed as a "moderate"! Reagan authorized a CIA expenditure of $2 million to buy the election for Duarte—an ally of the very Communist terrorists who were supposed to be his deadly foes!

The doors of the Reagan White House were thrown open to enemies of freedom, all over the globe. For example, Mozambique's Samora Machel was welcomed in September of 1985. Marxist Machel was wined and dined and toasted in Washington, despite the fact he was a notorious terrorist and *a practicing cannibal!* This contemptible criminal set up untold numbers of slave labor concentration camps, to keep his people in line!

Reagan became the epitome of the crass politician when he *signed* (rather than vetoed) legislation for a national holiday, commemorating the birthday of Marxist agitator Martin Luther King, Jr. Congressman John Ashbrook (R-OH), ranking minority member of the House Committee On Un-American Activities, charged that King had "done more for the Communist Party than any other person of this decade."55 King's top aid was radical leftist Andrew Young, later Carter's UN Ambassador and Atlanta's Mayor. King was trained, supported, and advised by known Communists! He and Young were both trained at Tennessee's subversive Highlander Folk School, cited as a Communist training facility and as "a meeting place for known Communists or fellow travelers."[56]

Might it not be late in the game, when a day is named in honor of a Red-associated demagogue?; a man unstable enough to have at least twice attempted suicide?;57 a notorious bedroom athlete; a leftist whose subversive record was hidden from the public by a January 31, 1977, court order?; a revolutionary who was an important cog in the conspiracy to replace the government of the United States with a Kremlin directed dictatorship?;58 a radical quoted by the FBI as declaring, "I am a Marxist!"; and a racist who may well have been a Communist espionage agent himself?

King's Southern Christian Leadership Conference was misnamed. Try Southern Communist Leadership Conference! It had been founded and run for years by *Communist* organizer Bayard Rustin, convicted in 1953 of sex perversion in Pasadena, California. The SCLC's Executive Director and close King advisor was Hunter Pitts "Jack" O'Dell. This Red was a Party organizer in New Orleans and on the National Committee of the Communist

Party USA! O'Dell later became "Reverend" Jesse Jackson's foreign policy advisor in the Presidential campaigns of 1984 and 1988! King's other trusted advisor was New York attorney Stanley David Levison. Andrew Young said Levison was "one of the closest friends Martin Luther King ever had."*59* Levison handled the distribution of cash subsidies provided by Communist Occupied Russia for the Communist Party in the United States! He was in frequent contact with KGB agent Viktor M. Lessiovski! For a time before he died, King's speeches were written by a top Communist Party functionary!*60* When King died, Levison became an advisor to both UN Ambassador Andrew Young (Chapter 9) and his successor, leftist Donald McHenry!

Reagan's reaction was shocking when a Soviet fighter plane deliberately shot down the Korean 007 airliner on September 1, 1983. Congressman Larry McDonald and 268 other civilians were *allegedly* killed in this calculated terrorist act! Here's an interesting sidelight to the story! According to Federal Aviation Administration spokesman Orville Brockman at FAA headquarters in Washington, D.C.: "Japanese self-defense force confirms that the Hokkaido radar followed Air Korea to a landing in Soviet territory on the island of Sakhalinska . . "[61]

The leadership of Communist Occupied Russia insultingly referred to McDonald as "a bush league McCarthy," and charged that he was "notorious for his virulent anti-Communism and strict tab-keeping on left and progressive organizations."*62* All McDonald did was regularly expose Communists and fellow travelers in his speeches, in committee testimony, and in the *Congressional Record.* Yet, Ronald Reagan, evidently fearful of offending the vicious Soviet Bear, avoided even mentioning McDonald by name in public pronouncements concerning the merciless attack! It was simply business as usual—arms giveaways continued non-stop, as did grain sales, unlimited loans, the building of factories, etc.

One moment Reagan blasted Communist Occupied Russia as "an evil empire."*63* The next he'd be joking with wiley dictator Mikhail Gorbachev and offering new trade agreements to give the enemy more food, technology, and weapons! He rightfully accused the Soviets of sponsoring terrorists and terrorism throughout the world. Without skipping a heart beat, he offered the Reds even more dangerous disarmament concessions!

In the Presidential campaign, Walter Mondale (CFR) promised to cut the defense budget by $103 billion over a three year span between 1986 and 1989. Once in office, Reagan reversed himself and greatly outdid his opponent! He okayed a defense cut of $124 billion over a two year period between 1986 and 1988!

Reagan stressed the need to rearm the United States. Instead, the dismantling of many weapons systems was *accelerated!* He cut back on building the Trident submarine. The Polaris/Poseidon nuclear submarine was delayed indefinitely, even as Reagan warned Americans of the dangerous Soviet military threat. Numbers of MX missiles were reduced! He refused to deploy the Minuteman III missiles! B-62 Bombers were deactivated.

Another of Reagan's reprehensible acts was the about fact he did on the United Nations Genocide Treaty. So controversial is this treaty that is has consistently been rejected since first being presented to the

Senate by Truman, in 1949! This dangerous treaty subjects Americans to trial and prosecution in international courts and by foreign tribunals, in violation of the U.S. Constitution! The treaty also places U.S. sovereignty and civil liberties at the whim of the anti-American, Communist controlled UN. Throwing the weight of the Presidency behind Senate ratification of this treaty, charges Clifford Barker, was "one of the most monumental acts of betrayal ever committed against the United States."[64]

President Reagan's dynamic conservative rhetoric notwithstanding, he essentially pursued the worn out socialistic New Deal policies of Roosevelt and Truman! Traitorous collaboration with Communist Occupied Russia was continued! Eisenhower's coddling of Reds in government continued! Kennedy's dismantling of U.S. defenses continued! Johnson's blatant arming of the enemy continued! Nixon's appeasement and surrender posture continued! Carter's unrelenting sellout of America's strategic interests continued! The "conservative" President's eight year record speaks for itself! Was Ronald Reagan a helpless captive of the establishment left? Or was he merely a cynical actor who all along unquestionably knew exactly what he was doing?

Chapter 13

Miscellaneous Subversion in Government

Traitor: "One who betrays, a deceiver . . . to hand over, deliver, betray."
An Etymological Dictionary of the English Language

Treason: "A breach of faith; treachery . . . betrayal."
The Reader's Digest Great Encyclopedic Dictionary

"Under the Nazi regime . . . a man worked making baby carriages.... the Nazi government would not let anybody buy a baby carriage," revealed Senator William Jenner (R-IN), back in 1954. "The man decided he would secretly collect one part from each department and assemble the carriage himself. When the time came he and his wife gathered up the pieces and assembled them. When they finished they did not have a baby carriage. They had a machine gun.
"Someone, somewhere, conceived the brilliant strategy of revolution by assembly line. The pattern for total revolution was divided into separate parts, each of them as innocent, safe and familiar looking as possible. But . . . when the parts of a design are carefully cut to exact size, to fit . . . perfect. . . in final assembly . . .," concluded the Senator. "The men who make the blueprints know exactly what the final product is to be. This assembly line revolution is like a time-bomb . . . The switch is not to be pulled until the American people are . . . convinced that resistance is

hopeless."*1* Communist Occupied Russia's espionage agents have successfully penetrated various departments of the government (Glasser, Peress, Kramer, Witt, Duggan, Abt, etc.). Such Kremlin moles are major participants in the Russian goal of world domination! But they're not the only conspirators working toward this same objective! Not all traitors or those guilty of treason are Communists, or at least they've never been exposed as Communists! Radical leftists in important leadership positions are quite often found to be members of the subversive Council on Foreign Relations. They're not ordinarily identifiable as Communist espionage agents, although quite a number have turned out to be (Alger Hiss, Henry Kissinger, Edwin M. Martin, Lauchlin Currie, Harry Dexter White, etc.)!

Far left CFR members are often as dangerous, if not more so, than Communist moles! They openly participate in running the government under an undeserved cloak of respectability (Zbigniew Brzezinski, Adam Yarmolinsky, George Shultz, Alexander Haig, Walter Mondale, Andrew Young, Robert McNamara, Sol Linowitz, Allen Dulles, etc.). It matters not whether those CFR traitors are Communist by name or socialist or whatever! Their methods of achieving the desired end result may vary (i.e. Communist—violent overthrow; socialist—gradual change). Whatever banner these masters of duplicity hide behind, their goals are identical! They *openly* declare their intention to replace America's Constitutional Republic with a socialist dictatorship! They *openly* write of merging the United States into a world federation of socialist (Communist) police states! This tyranny, according to their plan, is to be brutally dominated by the United Nations, an organization created by Communists for Communist purposes (Chapter 14)!

When Richard Nixon's (CFR) political star was on the ascendancy in 1952, he purportedly opposed both Communism and socialism! In this instance, he could well have been referring to the Council on Foreign Relations: "There's one difference between the Reds and the Pinks. The Pinks want to socialize America. The Reds want to socialize the world and make Moscow the world capital. Their paths are similar; they have the same Bible—the teachings of Karl Marx."*2*

A number of years ago, Congressman Hamilton Fish (D-NY) undertook a five-month investigation of Communist activities in 14 major American cities. The Fish Committee found a most serious situation: " . . . there are probably 500,000 to 600,000 Communists and active sympathizers in the United States . . . the Department of Justice has had no power or authority from Congress to obtain the facts regarding Communist propaganda and activities since 1925 . . ."*3*

There's more! The Fish Committee charged: "The American Civil Liberties Union is closely affiliated with the Communist movement in the United States, and fully ninety percent of its efforts are on behalf of Communists who have come into conflict with the law.... it is quite apparent that the main function of the ACLU is to attempt to protect the Communists in their advocacy of force and violence to overthrow the government, replacing the American flag by the Red flag and erecting a Soviet Government in place of the republican form of government guaranteed to each State by the Federal Constitution."*4*

Communist Occupied Russia secretly sent a special group of six loyal Reds to the United States in 1932. Both Lenin and Stalin must have read the words of Thomas Jefferson who said: "Were we directed from Washington when to sow and when to reap, we should soon want bread." Indeed, the assignment of these six Kremlin espionage agents was to initiate activities aimed at gaining control of and subverting American agriculture. Those in the delegation were:

John Barnett	Otto Ostram
Lem Harris	Henry Puro
Jerome Hellerstein	Harold Ware*5*

"The man who founded the first Communist cell in the United States Government was... Harold M. Ware," reveals a Senate report. "Ware's mother, the late Ella Reeva Bloor, was openly advertised by Communist officials as 'the First Lady of the Communist Party, United States of America.'... "6 In her autobiography, Bloor brags about how her son served in the USSR. Ware was a leader in the Soviet collective farm program under both Lenin and Stalin! Millions of Russian farmers were murdered! He was also a charter member of Russia's Communist Party and gained the personal praise of Lenin!7 Interestingly, almost the entire membership of the Ware cell were graduates of Harvard Law School!

Harold Ware was one of Stalin's most trusted Comintern agents! He had attended the Lenin School, where the top Communist spies are trained! Calling himself an agricultural engineer, Ware set up Farm Research Incorporated, as a safe meeting place for American Communists and Kremlin agents. From here he placed his espionage moles in the Department of Agriculture and elsewhere. Ware's job was to systematically create Communist spy cells wherever possible in government. He did his job well!

When Harold Ware died, Mother Bloor declared happily: "I find his boys and girls everywhere. It's my comfort."8 Ware's daughter, Hertha, married actor Will Geer who was identified as a Party member during the 1951 hearings of the House Committee on Un-American Activities! Geer went into oblivion after being exposed as a Red. When everything quieted down and the public had time to forget, he surfaced as "Grandpa" on *The Waltons!9*

Here's how the criminals in Communist Occupied Russia methodically organized and supervised the espionage game in America. Little was left to chance then, nor is it today! Edna Lonigan explains exactly how it works: "Directors of the NKVD sat with their maps of the 'terrain' of the Federal government, and moved their followers to one key position after another. Communists in government and the colleges were ordered to recommend their comrades for all desirable openings. They were told to locate the key jobs, to know when they would be vacant, and to pull the strings. Their people always had the 'best' recommendations.

". . . they put their people into jobs as personnel directors. Assistant directors proved even better for the purpose. These officials were never in the headlines. But they saw the incoming applications; they could weed out those with anti-Communist records; or 'expedite' those with key names and key experience to identify them . . . The duty of the ablest Soviet agents was not espionage. It was to win the confidence of those who directed policy. Their job was to attach themselves to higher officials or to the wives of these officials [e.g. Hiss, Currie, White, etc.]; to be ready day or night to take on more responsibility. So, each year, the network moved its men into higher and higher positions. When the war came (WW II) the veterans of eight years of conspiracy reached the highest policy levels."[10]

George N. Peek, head of the Agricultural Adjustment Administration, tells how the Kremlin's infiltration plan was actually put into operation: "A plague of young lawyers settled on Washington—in the legal division were formed the plans, which eventually turned the AAA from a device to aid the farmers to a device to introduce the collectivist system of agriculture into this country . . . most of that crowd . . . were Communists."[11]

Peek eventually resigned in opposition to the blatant Communist schemes! Today's total government domination of American farmers is certainly no accident! Neither are the socialistic policies of buying up surpluses; paying farmers not to grow; and severely penalizing those who don't cooperate! Nor is it an accident that Communist slave labor dictatorships around the world are treasonously given American wheat, soybeans, and other farm commodities, so they can better feed their armies! All these things and more can be traced to Agriculture's secret Kremlin cell, implemented by Soviet agent Harold Ware in 1933!

The costly and ruinous mess revolving around America's farmers and the nation's food supplies was brought about by Roosevelt's 1933 Agricultural Adjustment Act.*12* This radical legislation was challenged when it came before the House as being "more bolshevistic than any law or regulation existing in Soviet Russia."*13* Yet it was passed! The law was conceived and written by the "plague of young lawyers" mentioned by Peek! Among them were:

John J. Abt	Victor Perlo
Alger Hiss	Adlai Stevenson
Charles Kramer	Nathaniel Weyl
Lee Pressman	Nathan Witt

All of the above Harvard Law School graduates, except for leftist Stevenson, were positively identified as espionage agents in the employ of Communist Occupied Russia!*14* Abe Fortas (Chapter 11, 14), a Yale Law School graduate— later to become an Associate Justice of the Supreme Court under Lyndon Johnson—was Assistant Chief of the Agricultural Adjustment Administration's Legal Division. He was never identified as a Communist but his track record proves him to be a serious security risk, at the very least! At this same time Alger Hiss and Lee Pressman were, in the words of Hiss, "an Assistant General Counsel." Fortas and his many Communist cronies worked closely together over the years! Also identified as Soviet agents were:

Jessica Buck	John Herman
Bob Coe	Eleanor Nelson
Charles J. Coe	Henry Rhine
Henry H. Collins, Jr.	George Silverman *15*

Before their exposure as Communist spies, and having completed their subversive work in the Department of Agriculture, these moles and others fanned out and began to penetrate other important government agencies. They were immensely successful in gaining control of State, Labor,

Commerce, Treasury, the CIA, etc. In each instance, Red espionage agents (under the direct control of Moscow) were able to make official government policy.

Alger Hiss, destined to become one of the most influential of Communist moles—at least of those who were exposed—moved from Agriculture to a key job with a Senate Committee investigating the munitions industry! He also worked in the Justice Department for a time, before being smoothly maneuvered up the ladder as an important State Department advisor to Roosevelt and Truman! Hiss was the not-so-secret Red agent who was Roosevelt's subversive shadow at Yalta, where over 700 million people were bartered into Communist slavery and death (Chapter 12). And he was the powerful Communist spy who supervised the creation of the United Nations (Chapter 14). Lesser known Donald Hiss, Alger's brother, was also a Communist espionage agent! He worked for State and the Department of Labor.

Charles Kramer (aka: Krivitsky) was with the National Labor Relations Board (NLRB), then the Office of Price Administration (OPA)! This Kremlin spy was eventually employed by the Senate Committee on War Mobilization! Soviet espionage agent Nathan Witt was also moved over to the NLRB, where he became its top officer! Witt controlled all board employee appointments and made all decisions relevant to negotiations between labor and management. His influence on organized labor was virtually unlimited![16]

Moscow-man Lee Pressman moved up the ladder to become General Counsel to Roosevelt's Works Progress Administration! John Abt, another Russian spy, also shuttled over to the WPA! He was later employed by the Senate Committee on Education and Labor which investigated, of all things, the use of Communist agitators at steel plants! Abt finally rose to become the Attorney General's Special Assistant!

Henry H. Collins, Jr. was easily able to move from Agriculture to the National Recovery Administration! Collins, of English ancestry and a staunch New England background, was known as the aristocrat of the Ware cell. Whittaker Chambers testified: "The treasurer of the Ware apparatus, Henry H. Collins, Jr., Princeton and Harvard, and scion of a Philadelphia manufacturing family, was my personal friend."[17]

Soviet agents Victor Perlo and George Silverman moved over to Treasury, which, not so incidentally, runs the Internal Revenue Service! Comrade Perlo, considered to be the Communist Party USA's leading economic expert, left Treasury to work for the OPA and the War Production Board! Other Comrades then to be found in responsible, decision-making Treasury Department positions included:

Sol Adler	Irving Kaplan
Frank Virginius Coe	William L. Ullmann
Harold Glasser	Harry Dexter White[18]

Along with Alger Hiss, innumerable other Communist agents were deeply imbedded in various government agencies! Many were exposed as members of Communist Occupied Russia's espionage apparatus by both Elizabeth Bentley and Whittaker Chambers! All of the above well-hidden Soviet moles were instrumental in planning for and shaping the policies of the UN, when it was founded (Chapter 14).

Soviet mole Harry Dexter White (Chapter 14, 16) was Assistant Secretary of the Treasury under Truman! This subversive was promoted to head the International Monetary Fund *after* the FBI had repeatedly informed the President that he was an espionage agent![19] White had even been listed in 1942 as a "known Communist," by the Civil Service Commission.[20] Kremlin spy Virginius Frank Coe succeeded White as director of Treasury's Division of Monetary Research! Then he, too, was promoted by Truman and went on to the IMF with his traitorous Comrade! After being identified as a Red, Coe fled to Communist Occupied China, where he became an economist for Mao Tse-tung![21] Keep in mind that all this started in one government agency—the Department of Agriculture— under the direction of Stalin's trusted agent, Harold Ware, who came to the United States from the Soviet Union!

"Elizabeth Bentley . . . collected dues from secret members of the Party when she came to Washington as a courier of the Soviet espionage system," revealed FBI Director J. Edgar Hoover. "Among those from whom she . . . collected dues were officials of the Office of Strategic Services (OSS), Department of Commerce, the Air Corps, the Office of the Coordinator of Inter-American Affairs, the Treasury Department, and others. In some instances one person would collect dues for a group and hand them over to Miss Bentley. One such individual was Nathan Gregory Silvermaster, who, according to Miss Bentley, headed a group."[22]

Bentley first blew the whistle in 1945! She told the FBI of extensive penetration of the government by two large Soviet spy cells. One of these cells was run by Victor Perlo, who she identified as being a highly placed mole on the War Production Board! The other was run by an inconspicuous *Russian born* economist, buried deeply in the Treasury Department—Nathan Gregory Silvermaster![23] Both spies were supplying classified materials to Soviet couriers from their own agencies, as well as many others, including the Department of Justice, the Board of Economic Warfare, and the Foreign Economic Administration!

"I think the Communist conspiracy is merely a branch of a much bigger conspiracy!" said Dr. Bella V. Dodd, former high-ranking official in the Communist Party, USA. She was talking to Dr. W. Cleon Skousen, who summarizes the rest of their conversation: "Dr. Dodd said she first became aware of some mysterious super-leadership right after World War II when the U.S. Communist Party had difficulty getting instructions from Moscow on several vital matters requiring immediate attention. The American Communist hierarchy was told that any time they had an emergency of this kind they should contact any one of three designated persons at the Waldorf Towers. Dr. Dodd noted that whenever the Party obtained instructions from any of these three men, Moscow always ratified them. What puzzled Dr. Dodd was the fact that not one of these three contacts was a Russian. Nor were any of them Communists. In fact, all three were extremely wealthy American capitalists!"[24]

Here's a mysterious tale about one of these shadowy men of wealth, who made important decisions for the Communist Party USA. This sinister figure helped mastermind at least one Presidential campaign from his Waldorf Astoria suite! Frank A. Capell, intelligence specialist, has this to say: "The late Bella V. Dodd revealed that, when she was a member of the National Committee of the Communist Party USA, she attended a key Communist meeting at which an important policy decision had to be made. Earl Browder, General Secretary of the Party, sent a courier from the meeting to obtain advice for deciding the issue.... Browder's courier was sent to the Waldorf Towers. Dr. Dodd reported that the man who made the decision for the Communist Party was Arthur J. Goldsmith.

"It was to confer with this same Arthur Goldsmith that two Eisenhower brothers, Arthur and Milton [Chapter 12, 14], journeyed to New York, shortly before Ike was elected President of the United States," concludes Capell. "On July 30, 1953, Senator Ralph Flanders of Vermont, a fellow Republican, introduced Senate Resolution 301, calling for the 'censure' of Senator McCarthy . . . the speech made by Senator Flanders . . . as well as the Resolution itself, were written for him by the National Committee for an Effective Congress. Created by the late Arthur J. Goldsmith of the Waldorf Towers in New York City . . . One of its brochures contains a quotation from Senator McCarthy to the effect that it was the National Committee for an Effective Congress which took the lead in the drive to destroy his anti-Communist efforts."[25]

Louis Budenz was a high-ranking Communist who broke with the Party in 1945. This man had been Managing Editor of the *Daily Worker* and confidant of Party boss Earl Browder, who was provided an office in Roosevelt's White House (Chapter 8). Budenz told a Senate investigating committee that "thousands of Reds have infiltrated the Federal Government and that 'there have been several hundred in relatively important places."[26]

Leaders in the Soviet Union have always planned on starting a Communist revolution in the United States! These actions were being exposed before congressional investigating committees, as far back as 1949. FBI agent Herbert A. Philbrick surfaced after nine years of undercover work within the Party. He revealed how the Reds—while preparing to violently overthrow the government—have absolutely no intention of taking over a wasteland of destruction. A detailed blueprint for revolution was delivered to Communist leaders all over the United States! The chilling mode of action was clearly spelled out by Philbrick: ". . . the plan was to incapacitate . . . by knocking out power supplies . . . any facility which would render productive machinery useless to the governing authorities, but leave it essentially intact to be restored immediately by the revolutionary forces . . . The saboteurs would strive for complete paralysis . . . riots and fires will be started in industrial cities to dissipate the police and fire departments.

"While the police are busy trying to quell the riots . . . bands of guerrillas will seize radio and telephone stations to control communications. Bridges will be blocked or bombed to bring transportation . . . to a standstill. Power will be shut off, as well as gas supplies. The entire pattern is to create immediate panic. Special squads will capture the police department and will scan records to find out who has firearms. These people will be forced to give up these weapons, while guerrilla units will break into all stores selling guns and ammunition, seizing everything that might be used to quell the insurrection. Terror will be spread all through the night by the 'liquidation' of opposing units so that complete panic will reign by morning."[27]

Robert Stripling was chief investigator for the House Committee on Un-American Activities during the Whittaker Chambers-Alger Hiss hearings. He warns: "It is incontrovertible that every key point, strategically, in the

United States has been studied faithfully against the day when peaceful-looking American Reds ["sleepers"] will be called upon to come into the open and fight for Mother Russia."[28]

America's first Secretary of the Navy, James V. Forrestal, kept exhaustive diaries in which he methodically chronicled the extensive government penetration by Communist operatives in service to the Kremlin. David Emerson Gumaer charges that the unexpurgated diaries "would have blown the lid off Communist subversion in the government and the military."[29] Truman had them illegally confiscated and locked in a White House safe!

Forrestal is believed to have been murdered on May 22, 1949, by the KGB! He knew too much about Kremlin-directed espionage activities, at the highest levels of government. Strings were pulled to hold Forrestal incommunicado in the tower of Bethesda Naval Hospital for seven weeks. Just hours before his release, he was hurled out of a sixteenth story window with the belt of his robe knotted tightly around his neck! Medford Evans bluntly declares: "His enemies in and out of government had to kill him. He paid with his life for his 'premature' and too powerfully placed anti-Communism . . . He had been branded falsely as mentally ill. Now the same forces claim he was a suicide."[30]

Alger Hiss resigned from the State Department when he realized he was in danger of being exposed as a Communist mole! Assistant Secretary of State Dean Acheson (Chapter 10, 14)—believed to have also been a Soviet spy (Chapter 16)—was a man with an affinity for hiring, hiding, protecting, and promoting Communists! Acheson *knew* Hiss was a Kremlin espionage agent, yet he praised this spy as an ideal government official, at his farewell party! Hiss was well rewarded with the Presidency of the Carnegie Endowment for International Peace on February 1, 1947. This subversive had the solid backing of Acheson and John Foster Dulles, later to be Eisenhower's Secretary of State in 1953! This Moscow directed spy was given an honorary degree by the prestigious Johns Hopkins University!

Yes, Alger Hiss was warned of his impending exposure as a Communist spy! He resigned on the advice of his superiors! And he was nicely taken care of with the Carnegie job. Not so strangely, all of this took place under the direction of subversive Acheson, who had in his possession a copy of the 1945 security memorandum which revealed: "Bentley [former Red spy] advised that members of this group had told her that Hiss of the State Department had taken Harold Glasser of the Treasury Department, and 2 or 3 others, and had turned them over to direct control by the Soviet representatives in this country. In this regard, attention is directed to Whittaker Chambers' statement regarding Alger Hiss and to the statement by Gouzenko regarding an assistant to the Secretary of State who was a Soviet agent."[31]

Igor Gouzenko, a code clerk in the Soviet Embassy in Ottawa, defected with many top secret papers. These documents dealt with Russian espionage in Canada and the United States! A secret 51-page report of November 25, 1945, was placed on Truman's desk. In it Gouzenko said: "he had been informed by Lt. Kutakov in the office of the Soviet military attaché that the Soviets had an agent in the United States in May 1945 who was an assistant to the Secretary of State Edward R. Stettinius."[32] This Soviet "agent" was none other than Alger Hiss!

Whittaker Chambers was an important Communist agent for many years. He finally left the Party in 1948 and exposed Alger Hiss (CFR) as a top level Soviet spy. Hiss was considered a big fish in the Red conspiracy! Among many other things, he'd been Roosevelt's top aide at the Yalta sellout of Eastern Europe to Communist Occupied Russia (Chapter 12)! He also helped write the UN charter and was the first Secretary General (Chapter 14)! Little mention is ever made of what Whittaker Chambers did for a living. He has a $30,000 a year Senior Editor for Time magazine—a popular propaganda organ of the left![33]

Chambers also exposed Pressman, Witt, White, Abt, and other Communist moles before the House Committee on Un-

American Activities. Richard Nixon at the time, called Alger Hiss "an amazingly impressive witness."*34* Hiss boldly came forward, called Chambers a liar, and denied he was a Red! State Department documents, critical to national defense, were submitted as evidence. They had been stolen by Hiss and given to Chambers for transmission to Communist Occupied Russia!

The Communists throughout government, the media, and elsewhere were extremely influential. Despite such damning evidence, the Justice Department was being successfully manipulated to drop all charges against this dangerous Moscow-directed spy! Whittaker Chambers was to be severely punished by his former Comrades for having dared expose Hiss and many other Communist moles! Unbelievably, he (instead of Alger Hiss) was going to be indicted for perjury! Chambers then produced five rolls of microfilm containing many more purloined State Department documents. So staggering was this new evidence that there was no longer any way Alger Hiss could wiggle off the hook! Despite everything, he was still tried *only* for perjury and received a relatively light sentence for his crimes as a traitor! The mystery remains as to why Hiss wasn't tried under the existing espionage laws! Or better yet, why he wasn't tried for treason! No one has to date come forward with a reasonable explanation! Perhaps the answer is self-evident!

Alger Hiss and Lauchlin Currie (CFR) both came to government posts from Harvard Law School! Both were exposed before congressional committees as extremely important Kremlin espionage agents! Elizabeth T. Bentley was formerly a courier for a Soviet spy ring. She identified Currie and numerous others in the summer of 1948 as members of secret Communist cells. Currie had become Roosevelt's confidential personal secretary and Administrative Assistant for Foreign Affairs (Chapter 11). The President's wife reacted violently to the exposure of her Red friends! Eleanor was a rabid leftist, who had six-score Communist front affiliations. She declared: "Smearing good people like Alger Hiss and Lauchlin Currie, is, I think, unforgivable."*35* Such protectiveness for Communists was *not* unusual for this leftist First Lady!

Currie fled the country in 1949, rather than answer questions about his activities as a spy for Communist Occupied Russia! With the help of Comrades, he finally surfaced with a high government position in Bogota. Here Currie handled all Alliance for Progress money, provided by the Kennedy Administration for supposedly fighting Communism in Columbia! Said the *Chicago Tribune:* "It will be surprising if President Kennedy doesn't find out he has made an alliance for Communist progress in that country."[36]

Assistant Secretary of the Treasury Harry Dexter White was another spy in the employ of Communist Occupied Russia. Working with White in Treasury was Frank Coe, also a Soviet espionage agent. Solomon Adler, yet another Communist mole, was Treasury attaché in Chunking. These three highly placed Red agents were deeply involved in sabotaging Chiang Kai-shek and setting up Free China for a take over by the Chinese Communists! Chiang obtained a loan of $250 million in gold from the U.S. This was to be used for stabilizing his money, which had been deliberately destabilized by Communist Solomon Adler. White successfully stalled the delivery of the gold! Only $27 million reached Chiang Kai-shek over a three and a half year period. Congress authorized another loan, this one for $500 million. Not a cent reached Chiang, because of the delaying tactics used by White and his Communist cohorts! Threatened with exposure, Frank Coe fled the U.S. and went to work as an economist for his Comrades in Communist Occupied China! This traitor played an important role in arranging for another Comrade—identified Kremlin spy, Henry Kissinger—to meet with Chou En-lai, in order to set up the traitorous 1972 Nixon visit!

Elizabeth T. Bentley testified before a congressional hearing and identified a total of 37 Russian spies who had penetrated the government. She swore that "to her knowledge there were four Soviet espionage rings operating within our government and that only two of these have been exposed."*37* Bentley had been informed of these other spy cells by her Communist superiors. But she hadn't been told where they operated or who was in them. Whittaker Chambers also gave testimony in support of Bentley's. To date the two spy rings noted by Bentley, so many years ago still remain hidden in the bowels of government! Why?

Communist Occupied Russia's Colonel Ismail Ege defected to the West and made a startling revelation in October 1953. Ege said that he personally knew of not less than 20 Soviet spy cells operating in the United States, between 1941-1942, while he was chief of the Fourth Section of Soviet General Staff Intelligence!*38* Shockingly, not one member of these 20 Kremlin spy networks has ever been publicly exposed! Why?

Infiltrating and subverting a country are old Communist tactics, going all the way back to Lenin! General Secretary Georgi Dimitroff explained it this way, before the Seventh World Congress of the Communist International: "Comrades, you remember the ancient tale of the capture of Troy. Troy was inaccessible to the armies attacking her, thanks to her impregnable walls. And the attacking army, after suffering many sacrifices, was unable to achieve victory until with the aid of the famous Trojan horse it managed to penetrate to the very heart of the enemy's camp." Dimitroff suggested that Homer's famous tale be applied to modern day. "We . . . should not be shy about using the same tactics . . . ."[39]

The Senate Internal Security Subcommittee, chaired by William E. Jenner (R-IN), held 78 hearings during 1951-1952. Numerous witnesses were called to testify and hundreds of thousands of documents were studied. Thirty of these hearings specifically dealt with "Interlocking Subversion in Government Departments."*40* Did the Subcommittee feel there was no longer a problem of Communist subversion in government? Certainly not! The presence of Communists in the many government agencies was thoroughly and conclusively documented!

Intelligence specialist Frank A. Capell pointed out that these and subsequent hearings "proved not only that Senator McCarthy was correct, but that the situation was even more serious than he at first reported... that far from 'witch hunting' the McCarthy Committee had only scratched the surface."*41* A 2100 page report was issued. This most important document was ignored by the media! Among the Senate Subcommittee's alarming conclusions:

"The Soviet international organization has carried on a successful and important penetration of the United States Government and this penetration has not been fully exposed.

"This penetration has extended from the lower ranks to top-level policy and operating positions in our government.

"The agents of this penetration have operated in accordance with a distinct design fashioned by their Soviet superiors.

"Members of this conspiracy helped to get each other into government, helped each other rise in government and protected each other from exposure.

"In general, the Communists who infiltrated our Government worked behind the scenes—guiding research and preparing memoranda on which basic American policies were set, writing speeches for Cabinet officers, influencing congressional investigations, crafting laws, manipulating administrative reorganizations—always serving the interest of their Soviet superiors.

"Despite the fact that the Federal Bureau of Investigation and other security agencies had reported extensive information about this Communist penetration, little was done by the executive branch to interrupt the Soviet operatives in their ascent in Government until congressional committees brought forth to public light the facts of the conspiracy.

"Powerful groups and individuals within the executive branch were at work obstructing and weakening the effort to eliminate Soviet agents from positions in Government.

"Members of this conspiracy repeatedly swore to oaths denying Communist Party membership when seeking appointments, transfers, and promotions and these falsifications have in virtually every case, gone unpunished.

"Policies and programs laid down by members of this Soviet conspiracy are still in effect within our Government and constitute a continuing hazard to our national security."[42]

The State Department was found to have been seriously compromised by Soviet espionage agents in 1945. Thousands of employees from a number of war agencies— Office of War Information, OSS, Coordinator of Inter-American Affairs, Foreign Economic Administration, etc.— were absorbed by State. All of these agencies were heavily infiltrated by Communist spies![43]

J. Anthony Panuch, State Department official placed in charge of the transfers, testified in 1953: "the biggest single thing that contributed to the infiltration of the State Department was the merger of 1945. The effects of that are still being felt.[44]

The SISS Report charged: "It was apparent . . . that these agencies had no security safeguards whatever or else had no disinclination toward hiring Communists . . . In addition to the infiltration of the State Department through the medium of this merger the Subcommittee encountered still other penetration into the State Department."[45]

"What happened in the State Department happened in practically every important government department and agency," charged former top Red leader, Benjamin Gitlow. "The Communists and their army of fellow travelers and paid traitors entrenched themselves in government. They have kept their Communist ties a secret."[46]

W. Cleon Skousen, J. Edgar Hoover's top assistant in the FBI, talked to Senator Jenner right after the hearings were concluded. Jenner told him: "We were accused of seeing Communists under every bed, but that isn't true. What we saw were Communists *in* the bed of nearly every bureau in Washington!"[47]

Why, so many decades later, has *nothing* been done about this dire problem? Why have so many Soviet spies been left untouched in government positions? Why is no effort now being made to expose these subversives? Who's responsible for placing and promoting and protecting Communist espionage "plants" in various agencies? The simple fact is that *no one* had the courage to launch an investigation of Communist subversion in America since Senator Joseph R. McCarthy (R-WI) was so methodically destroyed in the 1950s! McCarthy's ruthless character assassination—exactly as the Reds had intended—still serves as a dire warning to others!

Nothing since has taken place to alter anything the SISS found! It's all still applicable today! Any semblance of internal security in the United States has been dismantled by subversive forces within and without the government (Chapter 7, 8)! Internal security laws have been shattered by decisions rendered by a dangerously leftist Supreme Court (Chapter 8)! Presidents have given clearances for dangerous security risks and have blocked investigations of known Reds in government (Chapter 9, 11)!

Senator Jenner held more hearings in which former top Communist Party functionary Dr. Bella V. Dodd gave eye-opening testimony concerning Communist activities in the United States. Consider her words carefully:

"SENATOR JENNER. What is your honest opinion as to whether or not the Communist Party is gaining, standing still, or losing ground in America? . . .

"DR. DODD. I think the Communist Party is gaining at an alarming rate. I think the Communist Party is not gaining under the label of Communist, but by having its operators operate under many different labels . . . the people who were known to me as either party members or associates of the party are mounting to important positions in policymaking, both on the industrial level, on the communications level, and on the governmental level. . . ."[48]

On January 12, 1969, Congressman Gordon H. Scherer (R-OH) warned Eisenhower of "potential espionage agents and saboteurs" working in American defense firms. He noted there were a minimum of *two thousand of* these subversives.[49] But nothing was ever done! No move was made to suitably resolve the problem! Scherer's warning was ignored by the media! It wee pushed aside by government officials!

The State Department's top security official, Scott McLeod, testified before the Senate Internal Security Subcommittee in 1961: "I think it is generally agreed among the security people in the Government that the testimony of defectors has pointed to the fact that we had at least three [four] spy rings in our Government, and to my knowledge we have only been able to identify two of these. So we must presume that the third [and fourth] still exists."[50]

"In the Soviet Union,. said Senator Malcolm Wallop (R-WY), "to assist the West endangers not only your own safety but that of your family . . . Here . . . the penalties are almost laughably lenient. We have no death penalty . . . and the families of traitors [as well as the traitors themselves] in government are still entitled to pensions."[51]

A case in point is high-ranking State Department employee John Stewart Service (Chapter 8, 10). Service was arrested by the FBI in June 1946 while passing classified materials to Russian spies (Chapter 16)! Shockingly enough, Service was never even tried for his crime! This security risk was allowed to honorably retire from the State Department almost 20 years later—in 1962. Imagine a pension for a career diplomat who was a major player in the State Department's Communist clique!

Is the consistent betrayal of friendly nations such as China, Rhodesia, Afghanistan, and Nicaragua to Communist slavery, over the past decades, mere coincidence? Who are the traitors who have been so consistently wrong in foreign policy decisions over the past 60 years? They were wrong, starting with the Roosevelt and Truman betrayals of Eastern Europe! They were wrong in bringing Communist Castro to power in Cuba and in arranging for the sellout of Hungary under Eisenhower. They were wrong in stopping American forces from winning in Vietnam, while supplying the enemy with arms under Johnson! They were wrong in shamefully and unnecessarily surrendering in Vietnam, while leaving

POWs behind under Nixon! They were wrong in helping Nicaragua become a Communist police state, under Carter.

Can these mistaken actions (and many more) possibly be the result of mere stupidity on the part of America's leadership? Hardly! Sheer ignorance? No! There can be only one other possible answer! And it does not take a genius to arrive at this conclusion—*subversion of a staggering magnitude!* The record speaks for itself. James V. Forrestal said it well, before the KGB silenced him: "Consistency has never been the mark of stupidity. It they [the policymakers] were merely stupid, they would occasionally make a mistake in our favor."[52]

The House Intelligence Committee published an FBI report in 1982, documenting how the Communist Party of the Soviet Union totally and unquestionably controls the Communist Party in the United States! The report stated: "The CPUSA continues to receive policy directives from the CPSU. During the last few years, the Soviets have instructed the CPUSA to place high priority on the issues of arms control and disarmament and the peace movement . . . The CPUSA has also directed its major front organizations to support Soviet foreign policy interests . . . the KGB clandestinely transfers funds to the CPUSA . . . Several KGB officers from the Soviet Embassy in Washington, D.C. and the Mission to the United Nations are in regular contact with the CPUSA. They monitor CPUSA activities and transmit guidance to CPUSA officials.[53]

William C. Bullitt was America's first Ambassador to Communist Occupied Russia. In 1936, this man sent a bitter dispatch to Secretary of State Cordell Hull from Moscow. It read in part: "There is no doubt whatsoever that all orthodox Communist parties in all countries, including the United States, believe in mass murder. It must be recognized that Communists are agents of a foreign power whose aim is not only to destroy the institutions and liberties of our country, but also to kill millions of Americans."[54] Bullitt's comments still apply today!

Chapter 14

The United States and the United Nations

Traitor: "One who betrays another's trust . . . one who commits treason."
Webster's Ninth New Collegiate Dictionary

Treason: "duplicity . . . breach of trust . . . disloyalty, treacherousness."
The Merriam-Webster Thesaurus

New York City is the home of two well known "houses." The one in the Bronx—Yankee Stadium—is called "the House that Ruth Built." It is as American as Mom, the flag, and apple pie! The other in Manhattan—the United Nations—is called "the House that Hiss Built." It is as Communist occupied as is Moscow, Minsk, or Riga! The glass enclosed stable for the Trojan Horse on the East River is a monumental welfare agency for Communist slave labor dictatorships, throughout the world! The United Nations headquarters could hardly be in a better place, from the standpoint of America's implacable Red enemies and their spying activities. Nor could it be in a worse place from the standpoint of America's national security!

For example, FBI Director J. Edgar Hoover said this (regarding Communist Occupied Russia's employees at the UN): "They are guests of the United States and are supposedly dedicated in the cause of international peace. But they are, in fact, carefully selected envoys of the international Communist conspiracy, trained in trickery and deceit and dedicated to the concept of fully exploiting the freedoms of the countries they seek to destroy."[1]

Punishment for espionage activities, while an employee of the UN, is nonexistent! Any Communist caught spying is simply sent back home and replaced by another spy! Columnist Henry J. Taylor offers: ". . . 865 Soviet-bloc personnel and more than 1,200 dependents, all with diplomatic immunity against arrest, and more of them accredited to the United Nations ... are stationed here.... about 80% of the Soviet-bloc personnel are intelligence officers and not diplomats at all. Nothing could be a heavier . . . blow to Red espionage than to put the UN headquarters elsewhere."[2]

Chiao Kuan-hua, one of Communist Occupied China's most important spies, headed Peking's first UN delegation! U.S. intelligence calls Huang Hua, Chiao's top aide, "a gifted saboteur and espionage artist."[3] Says columnist Paul Scott: "Espionage will be an even greater danger now that Red China has been admitted to the UN. Since the size of each country's UN delegation and staff reflects the size of the country's population, and since Red China has between 700 and 800 million people, she might be allowed 3,000 or more diplomats and staff members, each of whom would possess diplomatic immunity . . . The most obvious and practical solution to the drug and spying dangers to our country is to get the U.S. out of the United Nations and the UN out of the United States."[4]

The United Nations is no more than a Marxist-Leninist propaganda machine! It's a subversive international organization, conceived by Communists, designed by Communists, staffed by Communists, and permanently under the control of Communists! But is was all planned that way, from the very beginning! Arkady N. Shevchenko defected to the United States in April, 1978. This Russian was Undersecretary for Political and Security Council Affairs at the UN. He charges: "Soviet intelligence officers have become a Trojan horse behind the wall of the United Nations." Shevchenko further notes that New York City is the most important base of all Soviet intelligence operations in the world!"5

"There has never been any doubt about the United Nations importance as a global beehive of Soviet agents," suggests Hilaire duBerrier.6 The UN was headquartered in the United States because Communist Occupied Russia insisted it be placed on American soil!7 It operates solely to further the objectives and to achieve the goals of Communists and Communism! The public record speaks for itself.

Communist espionage agent Alger Hiss was the darling of the Roosevelts and the Washington "liberals." He moved with ease from Agriculture to Justice to State. On May 1, 1944, radical leftist Dean Acheson, Assistance Secretary of State under Stettinius, placed Hiss in charge of the Office of Special Political Affairs. He was to develop and coordinate all policy concerning the founding of the United Nations! This important Kremlin spy and his subversive underlings wrote *all* the crucial briefs used to guide each facet of U.S. policy. These papers were used by every American who attended the UN parleys! The Hiss group also recruited and placed members of the U.S. delegation to the UN, as well as personnel on the staff of the U.S. Representative to the UN! Let's take a look at the 17 Americans who were responsible for planning and directing policy leading to the creation of the United Nations! They were:

Dean Acheson	Victor Perlo
Solomon Adler	Abraham George Silverman
Virginius Frank Coe	Nathan Gregory Silvermaster
Laurence Duggan	William H Taylor
Noel Field	William L Ullman
Harold Glasser	John Carter Vincent

Alger Hiss	Henry Julian Wadleigh
Irving Kaplan	David Weintraub
Harry Dexter White *8*	

With the sole exception of shadowy, far-leftist Dean Acheson (Chapter 10), each of these men were identified as Soviet espionage agents. Acheson, although never proven to be a Communist spy, was believed to be one. (Chapter 16)! His loyal service to the Communist conspiracy began long before the Soviets had even gained diplomatic recognition. He was one of two American attorneys employed by Russia's horrific mass-murderer, Joe Stalin, to represent the interests of his despicable dictatorship in the United States. The other lawyer was Soviet spy Lee Pressman, of the Ware cell, to which Alger Hiss also belonged! *9* Acheson invited Communist Donald Hiss, Alger's brother, to join his prestigious Washington law firm. This took place *after* Donald had been identified as a Russian spy and was forced to leave the State Department!

Time enthusiastically announced: "The Secretary-General for the San Francisco Conference was named at Yalta but announced only last week—lanky Harvard trained Alger Hiss, one of the State Department's brighter young men . . . ."*10* This was frosting on the Soviet Union's cake! Serving as Secretary-General—the most powerful position at the UN founding conference—was none other than their own man, Communist agent Alger Hiss! The importance of this Kremlin spy cannot be overstressed.

On April 25, 1945, two weeks after President Roosevelt died, Hiss led the U.S. delegation to the UN founding in San Francisco. Abe Fortas (Chapter 11, 13), a Hiss friend from the early thirties—when they worked together in the Agricultural Adjustment Administration—went as an advisor! The *Chicago Tribune* reported that: " . . . Fortas helped Alger Hiss and Harry Dexter White, Soviet agents, to draft the United Nations Charter."*11*

Working closely with Hiss and the other 15 *known* Kremlin agents at the United Nations Conference on International Organization were over 40 members of the Council on Foreign Relations. This is an astounding figure in light of the fact that the entire U.S. Delegation numbered less than two hundred! These CFR people included such radical leftist luminaries as John Foster Dulles and John J. McCloy (Chapter 11, 16).

Dulles was instrumental in getting Hiss, a close friend, safely out of the State Department, when there was imminent danger of public exposure as a Soviet spy! Dean Acheson and McCloy were instrumental in obtaining diplomatic recognition for Communist Occupied Russia in 1933, McCloy was also the security risk who, while Assistant Secretary of War in the Roosevelt Administration, approved an order (in 1944) allowing Communists to be officers in the U.S. Army![12]

Also to be found was leftist and CFR stalwart Harold Stassen later to be Eisenhower's traitorous Battle Act Administrator. Stassen's criminal giveaways of strategic goods to America's Red enemies would have made any good Communist agent flush with pride (Chapter 1)! Identified Communist Ralph J. Bunche (CFR) was highly visible at the Conference, as a top Hiss assistant! This Red wrote the Charter provision on trusteeship for Hiss.

Extremely serious security risk, Philip C. Jessup (Chapter 9), was another CFR member in attendance! He had also been a leading member of the Communist-controlled Institute of Pacific Relations! This subversive organization was cited by Congress as being "considered by the American Communist Party and by Soviet officials as an instrument of Communist policy, propaganda and military intelligence."[13] This rampant subversive was later selected by Eisenhower to serve America's interests as a justice on the UN World Court.

John Carter Vincent, another IPR subversive, was there. This State Department heavyweight had been identified as a Red espionage agent by former Communist Party official Louis Budenz![14] Owen Lattimore (CFR), a member of the

IPR governing board, was also in attendance! This security risk was branded by the Senate Internal Security Subcommittee (in 1952) as "a conscious, articulate instrument of the Soviet conspiracy."[15]

Americans have deliberately been led to believe that the UN was created to be a peace-keeping organization. This simply isn't so! Nor was it every intended to be by those who were instrumental in giving it birth. The passage of time has proven beyond a doubt the not-so-peaceful intent of the UN! But prior to this, an astute international lawyer had already penned his succinct analysis.

In August 1945, before the ink on the Charter was even dry, Ambassador J. Reuben Clark charged: " . . . there is no provision in the Charter itself that contemplates ending war . . . The Charter is built to prepare for war, not to promote peace. . . The Charter is a war document not a peace document . . . [it doesn't] prevent future wars . . . it takes from us the power to declare them, to choose the side on which we shall fight, to determine what forces and military equipment we shall use in the war, and to control and command our sons who do the fighting."[16]

Interestingly enough, Alger Hiss had already worked closely with the Russians, in August 1944, as Executive Secretary of the Dumbarton Oaks Conference in Washington, D.C. He later was the top State Department advisor to a weak and dying Roosevelt, at the Yalta Conference (Chapter 12). Here Hiss and his Communist comrades had agreed on all the important facets of the UN structure and its preposterously deceptive Charter!

Russian-born Leo Pasvolsky (CFR) was called "the architect of the United Nations Charter."[17] Hiss and Pasvolsky worked closely together for a number of years on planning the international organization and drafting the Charter. Hiss was at the time a member of Harold Ware's espionage cell in Washington, of which almost the entire membership graduated from Harvard Law School! Pasvolsky's parents were both active Communists! This subversive penetrated the government in 1934 and eventually became Chief of the Division of Special Research in the State Department.

One would logically think the UN Charter would be modeled after a time-proven document, such as the United States Constitution. It, with the Bill of Rights, guarantees specific freedoms for everyone! But this was not the case when the Charter was "written" by the two American Comrades—Pasvolsky and Hiss! Rather than bothering to create a document of their own authorship, these Moscow-directed Charter authors simply plagiarized and produced one remarkably similar to the Constitution of the Soviet Union!

"The United Nations Charter was written by a State Department-Soviet Union coalition of strategists." charges W. Cleon Skousen, "who specifically designed the UN so that it could eventually override the sovereign independence of its member nations and subject them to the Marxist-dominated World Court and the Marxist-directed military forces of the United Nations . . . Anyone familiar with the Communist Constitution of Russia will recognize in the United Nations Charter a similar format. It is characterized by a fervent declaration of democratic principles . . . followed by a . . . limitation which completely nullifies the principles just announced!"[18]

The most shocking aspect of this entire situation is the undisputed fact that Alger Hiss and others were *already* known to be Communist spies, under the direct control of Moscow! Yet when intelligence reports were sent to their superiors, nothing was done to stop them! Or perhaps because such traitorous activity was openly condoned by the President of the United States, nothing could be done! As an end result, America was duped into joining and financially supporting a subversive organization, which was conceived, designed, and implemented by men in the employ of Communist Occupied Russia! There were the Reds in the Kremlin, on the one hand! And on the other, were their trusted, ideological Comrades secretly planted throughout the United States government!

Leftists of all stripes, who push the UN today, ignore the crucial roles that spies employed by Moscow played in the founding of this organization! They conveniently "forget" to mention the names of Hiss, White, Perlo, Adler, Silverman, and other important Reds! If such names are brought to light, simpering leftist apologists deliberately overlook the fact that these subversives were working for the Soviet Union! Or they try to play down the importance of such notorious Kremlin espionage agents.

For example, when President George Bush (CFR) was Ambassador to the United Nations, he parroted the typical apologist malarky. Bush unequivocally lied when he said: "Alger Hiss did not work on the Charter draft. He served in an administrative post at the San Francisco Conference . . . and was far removed from any policy-forming capacity . . . his duties were of a mechanical nature, such as scheduling of meeting rooms, supplying secretarial help, and similar functions."[19]

Of course Alger Hiss worked on the UN Charter! He admitted as much when testifying before a 1948 House hearing! Representative Karl Mundt (R-SD) pointedly asked Hiss about his role. The Kremlin spy replied: "I did participate in the creation of the draft that was sent by President Roosevelt to Churchill and Stalin, which was the draft actually adopted at San Francisco."[20]

Secretary-General Hiss alone was empowered to sign the credentials of every conference delegate allowed in the meeting hall! Absolutely no one could attend without this man's signature on his I.D. card. Using this prestigious position, Hiss channeled only trusted Comrades into key slots, in what was to become the Secretariat! Yes, Alger Hiss certainly held more than an insignificant "administrative post" as Bush implied! *Time* reported: "Alger Hiss will be an important figure there. As Secretary-General, managing the agenda, he will have a lot to say behind the scenes about who gets the breaks."[21]

Mr. Hiss most assuredly did!

Clamoring leftist voices still try to hide the traitorous machinations that transpired when the UN was founded. The United Nations must be a good organization, say the propagandists, because Stalin was against it from the start! The Moscow criminals, they claim, had to be arm-twisted into joining. Nothing could be further from the truth! After all, why should Communist Occupied Russia shy away from an organization their own people in Moscow and Washington conceived, created, and controlled?

Earl Browder (Chapter 8) was boss of the Communist Party USA and Stalin's top man in the United States. He said: "The American Communists worked energetically and tirelessly to lay the foundations for the United Nations, which we were sure would come into existence."[22] In fact the Constitution of the CPUSA contains a preamble which states: u . . . the cause of peace and progress require . . . the strengthening of the United Nations as a universal instrument of peace."[23]

Secretary of State Edward R. Stettinius Jr. (CFR) was in charge of the U.S. delegation to the San Francisco Conference. Wealthy Hollywood screenwriter Dalton Trumbo—another Hiss selection—played an important but little-known role. The speeches of Stettinius and other conspirators were ghost written by this Red! *24* Trumbo was one of the infamous Hollywood Ten cited for contempt of Congress during investigations of Communists in the film industry. He was identified as a Party member!

Another key figure at the Conference was Treasury's Harry Dexter White (CFR). This Red espionage agent was there to establish the World Bank, which uses American money to play Santa Claus to thankless Communist tyrannies around the globe. Being a part of this scam is, for the United States, like allowing Errol Flynn to take your teenage daughter on an unchaperoned boat ride, while you soak up some sun at the beach! William Ullman was White's chief lieutenant. This subversive was later exposed as a Kremlin spy by former Soviet courier Elizabeth Bentley!

Communists Hiss and White were also the creators of the United Nations Educational, Scientific, and Cultural Organization!*25* Former Communist Joseph Kornfeder warned: "UNESCO corresponds to the agitation and propaganda department in the Communist Party."*26* For example, UNESCO publishes and distributes propaganda world-wide which glorifies life in the Soviet Union! Such preposterous leftist dross blatantly asserts that Latvia, Estonia, Lithuania, and the other Captive Nations voluntarily became a part of Communist Occupied Russia's evil slave labor empire!*27* Nothing could be further from the truth!

An attempt was made to check on Americans employed in UNESCO. The SISS reported: "What appears . . . to be by far the worst danger spot, from the standpoint of disloyalty and subversive activity among Americans . . . is UNESCO . . . [there still exists in UNESCO] a clique of people who placed the interests of the Communists and Communist ideology above any service to UNESCO and above their own country . . . Seven employees of UNESCO who were dismissed after refusing to testify before the International Organizations Employees Loyalty Board appealed their dismissals eventually won decisions awarding them large indemities on the ground that the dismissils were improper"[28]

So badly did the Soviet Union want the UN Charter approved by the Senate, that they went all out with a fierce propaganda barrage. The official Party line was transmitted to American Communists through P*olitical Affairs:* "Great popular support and enthusiasm for the United Nations policies should be built up . . . The opposition must be rendered so impotent that it will be unable to gather any significant support in the Senate against the United Nations Charter and the treaties which will follow."[29]

The editors of *Life* magazine contributed to the unholy farce! Their "Picture of the Week" featured Soviet agent Alger Hiss, as if he were just another loyal American arriving in the nation's Capitol with a large package! The caption read: "At the conclusion of the San Francisco Conference the Charter of the United Nations was bundled off to a waiting plane and gingerly placed in a 75-pound fireproof safe equipped with a small parachute. Attached to the safe was a stern inscription: 'Finder— do not open! Notify the Department of State—Washington, D.C. Chief custodian was Conference Secretary-General Alger Hiss, shown here with the Charter at the end of the cross-country trip . . . "[30]

The Communist stage-managed acclaim for the UN Charter was eminently successful. It was carefully pitched to the powerful Senate Foreign Relations Committee by Soviet espionage mole Leo Pasvolsky, the brazen comrade of Alger Hiss! Only five days of testimony were required! The full Senate then shamefully ratified the Charter, sight unseen, with little debate on July 28, 1945. The vote was an astounding 89 to 2!

The *Chicago Tribune* described the Charter presentation: "The hearings in Washington started, appropriately enough, with a lengthy statement read by Mr. Stettinius, but apparently written by Mr. Pasvolsky. When the time came to ask questions Mr. Stettinius gracefully yielded the center of the stage to the same Mr. Pasvolsky, who knows all the answers.

"This is more than a little odd. Mr. Pasvolsky's expertism is said to result from the fact that he wrote the original draft of the treaty . . . Nobody has yet explained why the Department entrusted the drafting of this document to a foreign-born functionary . . . "[31]

Dr. Marek Korowicz was a member of Communist Occupied Poland's United Nations delegation, who defected to the United States. He reminds Americans: The Communist Party regards the UN as the most important platform of Soviet propaganda in the world."[32]

Russian General Bondarenko lectured future Soviet officers at the Frunze Military Academy in Moscow. His words support those of Korowicz: "From the rostrum of the United Nations, we shall convince the colonial and semi-colonial people to liberate themselves and to spread the Communist theory over all the world. We recognize the UN as no authority over the Soviet Union, but the United Nations serves to deflect the capitalists and warmongers in the Western world."*33*

Communist Occupied Russia demanded a "troika" when Swedish Secretary-General Dag Hammarskjold—a "socialist" supporter of world Communism—was killed in a 1961 plane crash! This was to consist of a neutralist, a Communist and a Western representative. Burma's U Thant, a dedicated Marxist, was widely acclaimed to be the "neutralist." Thant praised Lenin as "a man with . . . ideals of peace . . . in line with the aims of the UN Charter"*34*—a rather mild description for a despicable mass-murderer!

Thant was assigned two assistants to fulfill the balance of Russia's demands. One was his trusted KGB Comrade, Viktor Mechislavovich Lessiovski, from the Soviet Union! The other was Ralph Bunche, a protégé of Kremlin spy Alger Hiss! This revered and sainted American Comrade was positively identified as a Communist by two former top-ranking American Reds—Leonard Patterson and Manning Johnson! [35]

Yes, the Soviet Union was given their troika: The neutralist—a Marxist admirer of Lenin! The Communist—a KGB operative from the Soviet Union! The Westerner—a Red espionage agent employed by the Kremlin! But what else could be expected when the entire hoax was so carefully orchestrated between Washington and Moscow?

Secretariat posts reserved for each country are supposed to be filled by the Secretary General. Communist Occupied Russia insists that Moscow select their own nationals! This guarantees that the Soviets will have KGB agents in every position open to them. The presence of U.S. citizens on the staff does little to counter the presence of the KGB! Congressional investigations have shown that a great many Americans working for the UN are Kremlin spies.

Alger Hiss started it all by initially staffing U.S. positions at the UN with Communist espionage agents. Subversives running the State Department have since made a habit of obtaining jobs at the UN for government employees in danger of exposure as Red spies.*36* As a result, America's interests in the UN have been, and still are, directed by Americans who are subservient to the wishes of Moscow- and not Washington!

During the Korean War, a New York Federal Grand Jury uncovered evidence of serious Communist penetration of the American UN staff! A full-scale inquiry was initiated. Some two hundred American employees—to avoid testifying—resigned their positions. Here's the Grand Jury's post-investigation statement: ". . . startling evidence has disclosed infiltration into the UN of an overwhelmingly large group of disloyal U.S. citizens, many of whom are closely associated with the international Communist movement. This group numbers scores of individuals, most of whom have long records of federal employment, and at the same time have been connected with persons and organizations subversive to this country . . . "[37]

Due to this investigation and the resulting public clamor, the Secretary General—who had opposed the investigation— was forced to fire a number of American subversives! But a UN tribunal stacked with Communists and pro-Communists took good care of their own. They granted $250,000 in cash awards for their Comrades. Four security risks were actually reinstated with back pay! Seven others got nice fat payoffs! Jack Sargent Harris—a protégé of Communist espionage agent Ralph Bunche —pocketed $40,000! Harris was so serious a security risk that he was denied a clearance and couldn't even get a job with the State Department, while Communist spy Alger Hiss reigned supreme!

The publicity generated by the Grand Jury investigation brought on a Senate Judiciary Committee investigation. Senator James O. Eastland (D-MS), issued this statement: ". . . there is today in the UN among the American employees there, the greatest concentration of Communists that this Committee has ever encountered . . . almost all of these people have, in the past, been employees in the U.S. Government in high and sensitive positions.... the security officers of our government knew, or at least had reason to know, that these people have been Communists for many years. In fact, some of these people have been the subject of charges before Congress before and during their employment with the UN..."[38]

This was further verified by Joseph Kornfeder, another Moscow trained American Communist agent, who broke with the conspiracy: "How many Communists, fellow travelers and sympathizers there are among the UN employees, no one seems to know, but judging by their number among the American personnel, there can be no doubt that the Communists control the UN . . . most of the special agencies at UN headquarters are, in fact, operated by them . . . "[39]

"I realize that the United Nations secretariat cannot recognize Communist affiliations as a bar to employment of persons who are citizens of a Communist state," declared Senator Pat McCarran (D-NV), "but that is no excuse for allowing one disloyal person to contaminate the American group or misrepresent our ideals."[40]

The United Nations Charter makes clear provisions for an international militia. The UN Army is commanded by the Under Secretary-General for Political and Security Council Affairs. This super-critical post was secretly awarded to the Soviet Union by American traitors at the first UN London Conference, in January 1946! By this agreement, *only* a Russian could hold the position for the initial five years. Yet, since then, no one other than a Communist has been allowed to direct the so-called UN "peace keeping forces"! To this day not one American leader has even bothered to request that a non-Communist be given this key job! Shockingly, the USSR has always controlled the UN military arm, with Russian personnel—with the exception of one two year term! It was then run by a Red from Communist Occupied Yugoslavia, who still answered directly to his Kremlin masters!

If the above sound far-fetched, the facts are clearly confirmed by the UN's first Secretary General Trygve Lie, a fervent socialist from Norway and an idolizer of Stalin! Even this crypto-Communist was astounded that the United States would agree to such an absurdly dangerous arrangement! Lie had no idea that Alger Hiss—the man handling the negotiations on behalf of the U.S.—was in the employ of the Soviet international espionage apparatus. Referring to the first London Conference of 1946, Lie explains: "Mr. Vyshinsky . . . was the first to inform me of an understanding . . . on the appointment of a Soviet national as Assistant Secretary-General for Political and Security Council Affairs . . . Mr. Stettinius [U.S. Secretary of State] confirmed to me that he had agreed . . . The preservation of international peace and security was the organization's highest responsibility and it was entrusting the direction of the Secretariat department most concerned with this to a Soviet national that the Americans had agreed."[41]

Such incriminating evidence alone should be reason enough for the United States to abandon the United Nations. This anti-American organization should be allowed to sink into obscurity, under the weight of its bloated Communist bureaucracy. Simply pull the U.S. out of the UN! And direct the UN to get out of the U.S.! This conspiratorial group of anti-American misfits has certainly proven itself unworthy of any further U.S. hospitality.

The United States went to fight the North Korean Reds in what was no more than a pointless no-win slaughter! Thanks to the unforgivable machinations of Truman, Americans were forced to go to war under the UN banner. Here we have a patent absurdity—General Douglas MacArthur was commanding the predominantly American UN forces in battle against the North Korean Communists. Meanwhile, a Russian Communist sitting in the UN was MacArthur's immediate boss! Or to put it another way, Communist Occupied China's Mao Tse-tung was directing the enemy North Korean forces from Peking! Communist Occupied Russia's Konstantin E. Zinchenko was directing MacArthur's forces from the UN, in New York City! [42]

Not surprisingly, the North Koreans and Red Chinese both received top secret military directives from Washington and the United Nations before MacArthur did. MacArthur's battle plans were always given to the enemy (MacArthur's, not the United Nation's) in advance! Is there any doubt that the United States was *deliberately* humiliated in the eyes of the world?; that a no-win war was fought and *purposely* lost to the militarily inferior North Korean Reds?; that the U.S. was made to contemptibly surrender?; that POWs were shamelessly left behind to rot and die in the prison camps of the North Korean gangsters, Red China, and Communist Occupied Russia (Chapter 15)? Air Force General George Stratemeyer said this regarding one of the lessons learned by the U.S., after being defeated in the Korean War: "Don't ever fight under the United Nations. You will not be permitted to win!"[43]

And indeed there are other examples, as well. The United Nations eagerly, almost blithely, orchestrated the "peacekeeping" charade in the Congo, during the early Sixties! The UN action consisted of the savage butchery of unarmed men, women, and children! An incredible orgy of mass-murder, rape, and cannibalism was carried out, with the UN's blessing! The mayhem was directed against rebelling forces led by Katanga's President Moise Tshombe. Tshombe had three strikes against him when he tried to secede Katanga from the chaotic Central Congolese Communist dictatorship. He was anti-Communist, pro-American, and a professed Christian—all negative attributes from the standpoint of those who run the United Nations! Harlan Cleveland (Chapter 9) was one of the many dangerous American subversives who helped push the UN war against Tshombe!

Crazed Congolese troops, high on hashish and thirsting for blood were transported to Katanga, in American supplied transport planes![44] These maniacs used bazookas to deliberately blow up clearly marked ambulances enroute to and from hospitals! Red Cross markings on hospitals were used as targets for mortaring, bombing, and strafing practice! [45] UN mercenaries forced their way into hospitals in Elizabethville and sadistically machine-gunned and macheted helpless bed-ridden patients![46] Small children, babies, and the elderly were wantonly bayoneted by the unbridled savages![47]

Atrocities committed against the unarmed civilian population were extensive! Forty-six civilian doctors in Elizabethville sent telegrams of protest to President John F. Kennedy, Pope John, and 14 other world leaders. They implored them to "stop the terrorist bombardment of hospitals and civilian populations . . . .[48] Elizabethville's Catholic Bishop told how terrorist UN soldiers had deliberately murdered innocent men, women, and children and looted and destroyed churches![49] Nothing was done to put an end to the terrible punishment the UN was inflicting in the name of "peacekeeping." Tshombe, later a captive in Communist Occupied Algeria, was horribly tortured and subsequently executed!

It should come as no surprise that the UN *never* takes action against Communist acts of aggression and terrorism throughout the world! Communist Occupied Russia made a heinous practice of dropping plane loads of harmless appearing harmonicas, small red trucks, radios, plastic pens, and colorful birds in Afghanistan. These booby-traps would explode when picked up or accidentally stepped on by children! The Soviet toy-bombs were designed to blind kids and blow their hands or feet off, rather than kill them! The Russians see this as an efficient method of both terrorizing and demoralizing the people of Afghanistan. And they are also eliminating a future generation of anti-Communist Afghan Freedom Fighters!

What did the UN do? The UN did nothing! What did the UN say? The UN said nothing! In another instance, the UN even refused to pass a mere resolution condemning Communist Occupied China for its atrocious rape of Tibet! Nothing was done to stop the Communist Khmer Rouge's genocidal spree in which they murdered one-fourth of the Cambodian people! But their leaders did get a standing ovation at the UN for their deadly handiwork! No one at the UN ever mentions the naked terrorist aggressions witnessed in the Communist takeovers of Cuba, Rhodesia, Nicaragua, and other countries!

An article in the *Santa Ana Register* noted: "Most . . . folks . . . like the United Nations . . . on the grounds that the UN is a 'peacemaking' organization. Now, that simply isn't so . . . the method of the UN is to use armed might against any nation presumed to be an aggressor [with the exception of Communist dictatorships]. Its function is to make war . . . though it professes peace, it is obviously a war-making agency."[50]

The United Nations is far from mankind's last and only hope for world peace. Yet it's the *perfect* organization to bring about "world peace" by the Communist definition—the absence of opposition to Communism! It is *not* the only vehicle around which will prevent a nuclear holocaust— in fact just the opposite is the case! The UN isn't the epitome of man's unselfish aspirations! It isn't man's greatest triumph! Instead it's a monument to the greed of evil men.

The UN was brought about to foster traitorous, unilateral, disarmament in the United States! All American weapons, *including nuclear,* are eventually to be turned over to a Red controlled international "peacekeeping" Army. The UN was created to redistribute America's great wealth! The Marxist schemers plan to ultimately take from those who have and give it to the international have-nots, no matter how undeserving those have-nots may be!

The UN was formulated as a means to negate the U.S. Constitution and end American sovereignty—to do away with nationhood! It was (from the very beginning) to be the vehicle for eventually attaining a one-world dictatorship! The dream of the Communist schemers in the UN is to manage this global government from Moscow. The dream of the socialist schemers in the UN meshes with that of their Communist brothers! They claim to disagree *only* with the methods used (mass murder, terrorism, etc.) in achieving the desired end result. But even this difference is questionable!

Milton Eisenhower (Chapter 12, 13) couldn't have made it any clearer in reference to the UN: " . . . we should view our latest attempt to create . . . a true world government . . . every member is committed . . . to the sacrifice of *individual* sovereignty . . . commitment to limited sovereignty marks . . . a considerable advance in our progress toward . . . world government."[51]

The late Gary Allen charges: "Never before in recorded history has a nation permitted an avowed enemy openly to pursue its policies of conquest, on its home territory, within so vast a diplomatic sanctuary—a sanctuary supposedly dedicated to peace. At least Steuben should be employed to remodel the glass palace on the East River in the shape of a Trojan Horse."[52]

"Of all the good reasons to get the U.S. out of the UN . . . one of the very best is still the hauntingly laughable fact of its bizarre composition," declares Scott Stanley, Jr. "For the greatest nation on earth to sit down in a Byzantine parliament of man with mass murderers and dope pushers and assassins and terrorists and torturers and pathetic creatures in loin cloths . . . is as ludicrous on its face as the United Nations is sinister in its purpose. Equality of membership in the United Nations with such primitive societies is an absurdity of such ludicrous proportions as to make the anatomy of a giraffe seem reasonable."[53]

Stanley's point is well taken. For example, Gabon's first President, Leon M'ba, did time in a French prison for cannibalism and for selling human meat! Jean-Bedel Bokassa, President for Life of the Central African Republic, got into a controversy over his choice of cannibalistic bedtime snacks! Samora Machel of Mozambique practiced cannibalism while participating in Satanic Voodoo ceremonies! Mozambique's later President, Joaquim Chissano, also commonly eats human flesh during witchcraft rituals!

Sergeant Joseph Mobutu, Zaire's President for Life, changed his name to Mobutu Sese Seko Kuku-Ngbendu Wa-Za-Banga. Interpretation: "Mobutu the peppery, all-conquering warrior, the cock who leaves no hen intact![54] Equatorial Guinea's national anthem is "Let's Walk Through the Jungle of Our Immense Happiness!" Somalia executes men before a firing squad for "undermining the government's authority" by opposing a law giving equal rights to women! Tanzania citizens are flogged for wearing tight clothing!

Lastly, Zambia has its very own Minister of Space Research— Edward Mukuka Nkoloso. He applied for a $19.6 million loan for his space program saying "We are delaying our plans to plant the Zambian flag on the moon . . . My spacemen [they wear red and green Superman capes] demanded payment and refused to continue with our program of rolling down hills in oil drums and my special tree-swinging methods of simulating space weightlessness."[55]

Chapter 15

Betrayal of the Prisoners of War
Korea and Vietnam

Traitor: "One who betrays his country . . . one guilty of treason.
Webster's New Twentieth Century Dictionary

Treason: "Betrayal of one's country to an enemy."
Webster's New World Dictionary

Dwight D. Eisenhower campaigned for the Presidency in 1952 with a disarming boyish grin, a pledge of "peace with honor" in Korea, and a promise to "bring the boys home by Christmas."[1] This hollow campaign rhetoric was only superficially fulfilled. Close to 1,000 American POWs (and possibly many, many more) were abandoned in Korea! These brave fighting men were knowingly left behind! There they would be tortured and murdered and left to rot in the slave labor camps of Communist Occupied China, Communist Occupied North Korea, and Communist Occupied Russia. Eisenhower did absolutely nothing to rectify this terrible travesty! He readily admitted after the prisoner exchanges that "some prisoners are still left there."[2]

General Mark W. Clark commanded the United Nations fighting forces in Korea. He tells: "We had solid evidence after all the returns were in from Big Switch that the

Communists still held 3,404 men prisoner, including 944 Americans."*3* South Korea's President Syngman Rhee said: "Thousands of Americans and ROK soldiers are still held by the Communists."*4*

Acting Assistant Secretary of State for Congressional Relations, Robert E. Lee, later wrote this regarding these 944 American POWs: "Neither the Department of Defense nor the Department of State has ever received any reliable information or intelligence to indicate that any of the men listed as unaccounted for may yet be alive and held prisoner by the Soviet Communists, the Chinese Communists, or the North Korean Communists . . . "*5*

Mr. Robert E. Lee was either terribly misinformed, covering up, or he's an unconscionable liar!

Retired U.S. Army Captain Eugene Guild explains that there's *never* been a lack of concrete evidence! He points out: "Repatriated POWs saw hundreds of Americans traveling North toward Soviet Manchuria in open trucks instead of south toward the exchange site . . . At least 389 other servicemen have been seen alive from days to months after capture by the North Koreans and Chinese. Freed POWs told of speaking to them in prison camps. Red Chinese and North Korean broadcasts repeatedly mentioned them by name and serial number."*6*

Lieutenant Colonel O'Wighton Delk Simpson was the American Air Attaché in Hong Kong in 1955. General John Singlaub tells how Simpson "had an extraordinary meeting with a young émigré newly arrived from the Chinese mainland. The émigré, of Polish-Russian extraction, had been working at the railway station at Manchouli, where the Chinese rail system links up with the Soviets' Trans-Siberian Railway. According to Colonel Simpson, the émigré said he had 'observed uniformed prisoners being unloaded [enroute to the Soviet Union] on the station platform while the train's undercarriage was changed. He said they were Americans from the Korean War and described their uniforms, even with a drawing of the chevrons. He never before had seen anyone with black skin and this drew his particular attention.

He said that he had been quite close to the individuals and had heard them speaking English. The number of prisoners he estimated to be about 700 . . . ."7

John H. Noble was incarcerated in a Russian slave-labor concentration camp from 1945 to 1965. He writes: "Laborers coming to Vorkuta from camps in Taishet, and Irkutsk and Omsk in Siberia and Magadan in the Far East told me there were American G.I.s and officers . . . working as slaves in their camps. They had been taken prisoner by the Reds during the Korean War *and shipped to the Soviet Union.*"8

These heroic young men sacrificed everything to fight for their country! If alive, they're still POWs today! Captain Guild was told by reliable underground agents of "hundreds of young Americans working in Siberian slave camps."9 Isn't it more than a little odd that the identical thing transpired over two decades later as a result of identified Soviet espionage agent Henry "Bor" Kissinger's (Chapter 11) dishonorable surrender negotiations in Vietnam!

The Betrayal of Prisoners of War in Vietnam

Shades of Rambo! Yes, shades of Rambo! Not many Americans realize it, but the Stallone classic, *Rambo II,* quite accurately portrayed an important POW rescue mission! The *only* difference was that, in the real life case, it wasn't a heroic Medal of Honor winner—a Special Forces veteran—bringing the POWs out. It was several much less colorful Communist Pathet Lao defectors!
Here's exactly how the sensational story developed. Contact was made in December 1972 with a Laotian, in the capital city of Vientiane. He had discovered the locations of a Pathet Lao POW compound. A number of the Communist prison guards wanted to defect and they offered to help some American POWs escape! All they wanted in return was a promise of political asylum in the United States! The plan was to sleep by day and travel by night in order to avoid capture by the Pathet Lao forces. The long and hazardous

jungle trek would all the while be heading for northern Thailand.*¹⁰*

Finally, in mid-February 1973, a Lao courier told Reverend Paul Lindstrom that *nine* American POWs had successfully made their escape from an underground prison! Accompanying them were the defecting Pathet Lao guards. The courier also revealed the remote jungle location of the fleeing prisoners. Personnel at the American Embassy in Vientiane were informed. Plans for a helicopter rescue mission were carefully drawn up by Assistant U.S. Army Attaché, Major John B. Wilson. Embassy officials waited until the last possible moment before *scrubbing* the rescue attempt in early March 1973! The mission was aborted on the day the pickup was to be made! No explanation was given then, nor has one been offered since! Nine American POWs were once again betrayed and left to rot in the steaming jungles of Southeast Asia!*¹¹*

Also in 1973, Lindstrom was given important data on other American POWs, while he was visiting a U.S. military base in Southeast Asia. An officer in military intelligence supplied information on over 200 American POWs known to be alive in Communist Occupied Laos, Vietnam, Cambodia, and Red China! Laotian prison camps pinpointed on a U.S. Air Force map were Sieng Su, Tam Bai, in a cave near Houie Talet, and Ban Pat. Pows were being held at map coordinates VH-0158—a cluster of buildings referred to as French Villas, and WJ-9989—a compound used to segregate highly skilled POWs. Americans were also known to be incarcerated in primitive slave labor camps just over the Laotian border, in Red China's Yunan Province. North Vietnam's Tham Moung Tin Khuang was another town known to be holding POWs! In Cambodia, there is one pinpointed at map coordinates 124045-N and 1061000-E, another at 122044-N and 1052732-E!*12* And there are others to be found throughout Southeast Asia!

Astounding reports continued to surface regarding American POWs still being held by the Vietnamese Reds! One of these focused on Hanoi's Ly Nam De Prison: "A

Vietnamese national was interviewed by U.S. government officials in October 1982, about his eyewitness account of five American POWs he had seen in Hanoi in August 1982. Looking down into an enclosed courtyard, he saw several Caucasians congregated around a cistern . . . He further provided information which led him to feel certain that these men were American prisoners. This source was twice polygraphed and both times showed 'no deception'."[13]

Congressman Robert C. Smith (R-NH) reveals: "Another subsequent report came from Robert Garwood, the collaborator who came out in 1979, who said that he saw them there [in 1977] on Ly Nam De Street in a cistern . . . So we went to Vietnam. We took with us a map from Garwood, who drew the inside of the compound. He told us, go in the gate, go down this way, there's a barracks here, turn right, go through a little passageway and there's the cistern . . . When we got there [Congressman William] Hendon, myself, three or four other members of the delegation and a camera crew . . . ran down the street to this compound. We pushed the gate open and got inside . . . we rushed into the compound, followed Garwood's map through the compound, turned right, ran through the opening which Garwood had described, and *there* was the cistern!"[14]

Congressman Smith returned and charged that the Defense Intelligence Agency's failure to act on legitimate reports of American POWs in Southeast Asia was *"deplorable"*. He noted: "They are there! I've seen the evidence! . . . There's no garbage about deciding whether live Americans are there or not! That's not the issue! They are there!"15 Congressman Frank McClosky (D-IN), another member of the delegation to Hanoi, had this to say: "We have moved from an opinion to a certainty! We are convinced beyond the shadow of a doubt."[16]

The Vietnam War ended for the people of the United States and for the 591 POWs who came home, when Kissinger worked out a humiliating surrender agreement with North Vietnam in 1973. But no such accord was ever signed with the Laotian Communists who openly admitted they were holding large numbers of American POWs! Referring to American prisoners of war left behind in Laos, retired Navy Captain and former POW Eugene "Red" McDaniel explains: "We lost 569 airmen there of which 311 were known to be captive at one time, acknowledged by our government to be so. None of those 311 have ever been returned! *Not* one."[17] According to the *New York Times,* "officials believe that the number of prisoners held by the Pathet Lao guerrillas is possibly substantially higher."[18]

Yes, 591 POWs came home from North Vietnam in 1973. *None* were released by the Laotian Reds. There's indisputable evidence that many U.S. fighting men were abandoned in North Vietnam, Cambodia, and Laos! Many are alive and still there today—held as captives in inhuman Communist slave labor camps! Others have been reported to be confined in the infamous gulags of both Communist Occupied Russia and Communist Occupied China! They were taken to Russia and China for intelligence reasons and to be used for hard labor when needed.

Robert C. McFarlane was one of Reagan's top National Security Advisors. He offers his view: "I think there have to be live Americans there! . . . There is quite a bit of evidence given by people who have no ulterior motive and no reason to lie, and they are telling things that they have seen . . . There is more that we ought to be doing than we are."[19]

McFarlane is one man who should know! As assistant to identified Kremlin intelligence operative Henry Kissinger, he was instructed to bribe the North Vietnamese with $100 million worth of medical supplies. These supplies were offered in trade shortly after Operation Homecoming, in 1973, for the *rest* of the American POWs still known to be held by the Reds! Hanoi officials laughed in McFarlane's face and refused the offer. They insisted, instead, on the *billions* not millions of dollars secretly promised by Nixon at an earlier date![20]

On February 1, 1973, the Communist North Vietnamese revealed the contents of a letter to Pham Van Dong from President Nixon. The amount of the POW bribe offered by the President was $3.2 billion! Spokesmen at the White House were forced to own up to the existence of this treasonous document! Yet Nixon claimed Executive Privilege and refused to make the damning letter public!*21* Yes, Nixon, Kissinger, Harriman, McFarlane, and a multitude of others all knew, from the very beginning, that American prisoners were being left behind!

Who's to be blamed for this horrifying situation—for American POWs still being held by the Communists? The ultimate responsibility must be placed squarely on the shoulders of the men who allowed two unnecessary no-win wars to be fought: Presidents Truman and Eisenhower in Korea! Presidents Kennedy, Johnson, and Nixon in Vietnam! And especially the two men who allowed peace-at-any-price surrenders to be negotiated with the militarily defeated Communist opposition: President Eisenhower in Korea and Nixon in Vietnam! Such agreements were signed, all the while knowing that innumerable American POWs were being abandoned!

J. Thomas Burch served in Vietnam as a marine officer. He now coordinates the National Vietnam Veteran's Coalition. Burch charges bureaucrats in the DIA, the CIA, the State Department, etc., with unquestionably knowing that live POWs were abandoned in Southeast Asia! Says Burch: "The DIA has a list of these people and where they are, right down to their toenails . . . that is a very strong statement but exact."[22]

Retired Colonel Earl P. Hopper's son has been missing since 1968, when his plane was downed over the Laotian-Vietnamese border. Hopper testified: "It is my personal opinion that American prisoners of war, servicemen and civilians who were left behind are still being held today against their will in Southeast Asia by the Communist governments of Vietnam and Laos!"[23]

Hopper presented CIA and DIA documents proving "beyond a doubt that the Central Intelligence Agency knew American prisoners were in Laotian camps" in the early 1970s. Colonel Hopper explained how "these reports give the number of American prisoners held at specific locations in Laos! More significant, however, is the CIA's designation of these camps as confirmed prison camps! . . . in order for a prison camp to be confirmed, it must be reported by two or more independent sources." Hopper then asked: "Why weren't these prisoners returned and where are they today? Someone knows the answer to these questions! The burden of responsibility to obtain answers rests squarely on the shoulders on the United States government. To date, it has not fulfilled that responsibility"[24]

The United States government has been unwilling (not unable) to "bring the boys back home"! Why? Captain "Red" McDaniel spent 2,110 brutal days (six years) as a POW in Southeast Asia. He charges: "The U.S. Government seeks to obscure their existence because it doesn't want veterans and current military personnel to know their comrades in arms were abandoned! Armed with that knowledge, these fighting men might come marching down Pennsylvania Avenue demanding action!"[25]

Scott Barnes was part of an ex-Green Beret team which, in October 1981, went into Northern Laos to search for American POWs. Two were located and photographed near a prison compound. Barnes and the group reported their sensational progress. Orders came down to *"liquidate"* the POWS![26] Such callousness startled even these combat-hardened ex-Green Berets. They refused! The group was soon after disbanded. Barnes and the others involved have since suffered terrible character assassination and their lives have been threatened!

Is this so difficult to believe of a government that betrayed *nine* escaping POWs in the jungles of Laos, by denying helicopter pickup in February 1973? Is this so difficult to believe of a government that ordered the murder of American POWs in Laos and tried to thoroughly discredit the 1981 rescue efforts of Scott Barnes and his ex-Green Beret team? Is this so difficult to believe of a government that betrayed three more POWs, who were ready to be taken out of Laos in 1984? The latter case involves the incredible story of U.S. Army Major Mark Smith and Sergeant First Class Melvin McIntire, who were with the Special Forces Detachment in South Korea (SFD-K) from 1981 to 1984.

Major Smith and Sergeant McIntire were assigned the task of collecting data on living American POWs being held in Southeast Asia. They obtained concrete evidence of a significant number. McIntire testified: "I learned of approximately 200 living Americans in Laos who were prisoners of war. I was being provided information in detail sufficient to identify the number of American prisoners of war being held in the general vicinity. I was also being told of the conditions under which they were being held."*27* But Smith and McIntire fast came to realize an astounding fact of life: important intelligence, military, and political officials don't want *any* live POWs to be found! Official policy is to bury or destroy all information leading one to believe there are live American prisoners in Southeast Asia!

"I received the code word from a general officer in Thailand that there were three American prisoners of war available to be taken out of Laos in May 1984,*28* offers Major Smith, himself a former prisoner of war. In April 1984, he prepared a briefing paper on the Laotian POW situation. This sensitive material was passed on to Major General Kenneth C. Leuer, later to be Fort Polk's commanding general. In a sworn statement, Smith explained: "After reading the two cover letters, the general turned white, handed the briefing back to me and said: "This is too hot for me to handle, big guy!' I told him at that time, 'If you as a Major General can't handle this, what am I supposed to do with it?' I was told that if I was smart, what I would do was to put the briefing through a shredder and forget the entire issue! I demanded authorization to go to Washington, D.C., and see another general in the office of the Deputy Chief of Staff for Operations . . . I was given a direct order not to have any more contact with that officer in Washington!"[29]

Major Smith wasn't allowed to arrange a rescue mission for the three POWs! General Leuer ordered that any further work on the POW/MIA issue was "unauthorized and terminated. . . I was told that if I wanted to be a Lieutenant Colonel in the Army, I should forget about the POW/MIA information which had been reported to intelligence channels for the past three years! I was told in no uncertain terms that I should forget the matter! The conclusion I reached . . . is that the production of intelligence on American prisoners of war was determined by some agency of the U.S. government to be unacceptable!"[30]

There were over 800 eyewitness reports of American POWs within a recent two year period! Congressman William M. Hendon (RNC) notes that "over 100 of them [relate] to prisoners in a captive environment, in prison, in chains, in caves, in cages . . . these witnesses have passed lie-detector tests on top of lie-detector tests. [They have] no reason too lie, nothing to gain . . ."[31]

Retired USAF Lieutenant Colonel A.D. Shinkle is a highly decorated veteran. He served as an intelligence officer for nine years in Southeast Asia. Fluent in Laotian, much of his intelligence work was done while closely working with Laotian agents. Shinkle's testimony gave an embittered picture of POW efforts by the U.S. government. The CIA was accused of virtual criminal neglect: "The most important intelligence collection objective sought by my USAF unit was information about the fate and disposition of U.S. airmen downed in Laos. The single greatest obstacle to collecting this information was not the enemy; it was the CIA! It is my personal opinion that the primary reason there were no U.S. airmen returned from Pathet Lao POW camps and the primary reason why we have so little information about those unreturned men is almost solely due to the failure of the CIA to perform its assigned mission in Laos and secondarily, their steadfast refusal to let U.S. military intelligence mount a viable and effective intelligence collection system inside Laos!"[32]

Lieutenant Colonel Shinkle told of the Thai CIA mercenary who had been captured by the Pathet Lao. The man was put in a "POW camp, where he stayed for several months, prior to his escape and return to Thailand. He was imprisoned in an above ground cage, constructed of bamboo and slender logs. He observed his Pathet Lao captors play with up to ten U.S. flying helmets. The Pathet Lao soldiers used them as soccer balls. He saw six to ten U.S. flying uniforms hanging on clothes lines or being worn by Pathet Lao soldiers! Several times he saw white men brought from a sealed-off cave and made to run outside his cage, seemingly for exercise. The men wore tattered shorts, they all wore beards, and they all wore a large hardwood hobble on one leg. The Thai said all white men looked much the same to him so he couldn't be sure how many different individuals he saw. He was questioned thoroughly and we concluded there were six to eight different individuals in that cave.[33]

"When the Thai escaped and returned to Thailand he reported to his CIA supervisor and told him of his capture, his imprisonment, and his escape. The CIA supervisor did not ask . . . if there were any Americans in the prison. You would have to understand in depth the Thai culture to understand why the Thai didn't volunteer information about having seen the Americans. In Thai culture it was up to the CIA supervisor to ask his subordinate questions and not for the subordinate to try to push information onto his supervisor.[34]

"It was only after one of our curious USAF case officers heard of the Thai who had escaped from the Pathet Lao prison, sought him out, and interviewed him in depth—as his CIA supervisor should have done —that his observation of U.S. POWs became known . . . As a matter of policy CIA/Laos didn't give a tinker's damn about POWs, even U.S. POWs!"[35]

A spokesman for the Department of Defense *lies* when he claims: "There is no credible evidence of any Americans still in captivity over there."[36] Actually, there is no credible evidence there are not! According to innumerable refugee and other reliable reports, there are many American military men still being held as POWs in Southeast Asia. Astounding enough, there have been over *6,000 POW* sightings reported since the Vietnam War ended in 1973!

For example, one refugee told how American POWs were hidden in underground tunnels, until U.S. troops were pulled out of Vietnam! Another refugee saw American POWs on Vietnamese Government television! She heard the commentator say: "We must punish these imperialist criminals until their government pays off our country all war damages caused by the destructive bombings."*37* American POWs were seen building a jungle prison barracks in 1978 on the Ca Mau peninsula! An eyewitness described them as "gaunt, skeletal, sad-looking men."[38]

In October 1978 over 25 American POWs were observed doing hard labor, 90 miles out of Saigon!*39* A Laotian refugee had a December 1978 encounter with five American POWs he described as "emaciated figures"!*40* Marine Private Robert Garwood was court-martialed for cooperating with the North Vietnamese, while a POW. He saw from 129 to 170 other American POWs in various areas of Vietnam, as late as 1979!*41* Eight American POWs were seen near the port city of Vung Tua, by two former school teachers. They were chained like animals and being loaded onto a truck![42]

A refugee was shown a list of over 50 American POWs by a Red officer, before she left Vietnam! The man told her that he "would turn the list over to the Americans if they would help him escape."*43* People who regularly re-supplied a Laotian prison camp told Major Mark Smith and Sergeant First Class Melvin McIntire of 14 American POWs held there!*44* A 57-year old Vietnamese refugee named Nguyen says he personally saw two American POWs in Hanoi, during October 1983. He believes there are at least 50 others in the same city!*45* A group of men were recently seen working under heavy guard by a West German diplomat in Laos. He asked who they were. His guide sneered: "They are American POWs left over from the war!"[46]

Kham-Mou Boussarath was director of intelligence for free Laos. After the withdrawal of U.S. military forces, his people "in the field identified many American POWs! The lists were given to American officials at the Vientiane Embassy and other agencies."*52* Now Supreme Commander of the Laotian freedom fighters, Boussarath's forces are still trying to locate and liberate American POWs! Kirk Kidwell writes: "Indeed, the American government is not merely failing to take action to bring home American POWs, but is actually seeking to suppress the efforts of the Indochinese to rescue them."*53*

After a careful review of the evidence, reporter Bill Paul concluded: "Hundreds of American prisoners . . . are scattered throughout the Communist world." Paul accuses govern"There are certainly still live Americans in Southeast Asia who have been left over from the Vietnam War," declares New Hampshire Congressman Robert Smith. ". . . the evidence is overwhelming . . . conclusive . . . if the American people could ever see those live sighting reports that are strictly classified in the Pentagon, they'd be utterly outraged! And God forbid if the families ever saw them . . . We've got absolute, unequivocal proof. . . "*47*

"The Americans . . . are held in small groups, anywhere from two to 12 . . . They are chained together and are forced to do slave labor by day and to sleep in bamboo cages at night," offers former Congressman John LeBoutillier (R-NY), who served on the House Task Force on POWs and MIAs. "They are moved around, as in a shell game, to prevent a rescue attempt and to keep the local population from having contact with them.*48* Recent reports by native refugees (all checked by lie-detector) tell a story of stark brutality! Starved and clad only in filthy rags, American soldiers and airmen are . . . made to work like animals pulling heavy plows, forced to toil from daybreak to nightfall in steaming tropic heat, kicked and beaten constantly just for their guards' amusement!"*49*

Cynthia V. Ward charges that "in their haste to cleanse themselves from the shame of defeat in Vietnam, our politicians abandoned hundreds of our men to live out their lives—to die—as desperate captives in that Communist Hell

. . . the evidence grows stronger that *hundreds* of Americans are still alive in Communist captivity! And, according to many who have studied this matter most closely, our government knows their location and in some instances their names."[50]

The government officially acknowledges that approximately 2,500 Americans are missing in action. The government refuses to acknowledge 2,000 to 2,500 more men that came up missing when they disappeared on secret missions! The actual number of MIAs then is closer to 5,000 rather than 2,500! This fact is the reason for the continued high number of sightings being reported of American POWs still enslaved in Laos and Vietnam. Researcher Yvonne Becker points out: "If officials devoted as much effort to extracting prisoners as they ment bureaucrats of "lying that there is no proof these prisoners exist."[54]

Syndicated columnist Jack Anderson makes this candid observation: " . . . we've spent years investigating whether American prisoners are still alive in Vietnam, Cambodia and Laos . . . We are convinced that some Americans on the missing-in-action list have actually been held in bondage by their Communist captors for more than a decade."[55]

Admiral Jerry Turtle headed the Defense Intelligence Agency's POW/MIA branch. He declares unequivocally: "There are definitely American POWs held against their will . . . maybe up to 100 or more! There is no doubt about it . . . there are many of our men still held over there!"[56]

Former Defense Intelligence Agency Chief James Williams testified: "If I were to show you Congressmen a map depicting the reported locations of Americans, it would look like Southeast Asia had an outbreak of the measles!"[57] Congressman Hendon adds: "I have seen that map and it's devastating!"[58] Congressman Smith volunteers: "Believe me, if members of the press and the public ever saw what Bill Hendon, and I, and a few other Congressmen have seen in those DIA briefings, I guarantee you there would be a public outrage!"[59]

General Singlaub offers this: "One of the most credible accounts concerning American POWs in Vietnam was provided by a recent high-ranking defector from Hanoi . . . The defector, identified as Hoang Huu Quynh, a 37-year old former Communist official, said he had not personally seen any POWs but that it was 'common knowledge among the party's cadre that an undetermined number of Americans were being held for possible use in future bargaining with the U.S. for aid, trade and diplomatic recognition."[60]

The Honorable Meldrim Thompson observes: " . . . the North Vietnamese have (unofficially) advised our government people that what they want in exchange for *all* surviving *POWs* and the remains of our MIAs is (1) a sizable sum as war reparations; (2) formal recognition of the Hanoi Government by the United States; (3) a favorable trade agreement with the United States; and (4) a seat in the United Nations."[61]

Hanoi made it into the United Nations without giving up one American POW! Nor could a whimper of opposition be heard emanating from anyone in the Carter Administration! In fact, on September 25, 1977, Samuel Winfred Brown (Chapter 6), a top Carter appointee, again made a public display of his pro-Communist leanings. He and former Attorney General Ramsey Clark (Chapter 6, 11, 16)— another notorious pro-Vietcong leftist—attended a "celebration and welcome" gala to honor the Red delegation from Communist Occupied Vietnam to the UN. Brown applauded mightily and said he was "deeply moved" by seeing and hearing his Vietnamese comrades![62]

As is obvious, there's more than ample evidence that American POWs are being forcibly held in Southeast Asia by the Reds! The Communists have a policy of keeping prisoners long after a war is over. Take for example the 30,000 French soldiers who were left behind when France pulled out of Vietnam in 1954. Yes, over *30,000* French military personnel were listed as MIAs or POWs! Over 10,000 were taken prisoner at Dien Bien Phu alone! France was given 11,706 POWs in the official prisoner exchanges when *their* Vietnam War was over; and they signed *their* humiliating surrender agreement in Geneva, on July 20,1954! Another 1,500 were eventually released, long after the Red North Vietnamese bandits claimed they had returned all French POWs. A few of the men captured at Dien Bien Phu were returned, but only after 16 long years had passed! Over 16,000 others were never returned, never accounted for by the North Vietnamese Communists!

Congressman Hendon made a number of secret visits to Vietnam and Laos for President Reagan. These trips and an intense survey of the POW problem convinced him that there were at least 200 POWs still alive in Southeast Asia! Hendon told of his last visit: "the Vietnamese admitted the possibility of Americans still being held alive. Their Deputy Foreign Minister, Hoang Son, told me, 'there could be Americans living in mountains and caves.' That immediately brought to mind the French POWs who were left behind when the French forces withdrew after their conflict with the Vietnamese. The Vietnamese denied the existence of POWs for a long time, but eventually over a thousand were returned to France!"[63]

Congressman LeBoutillier is well aware of the disastrous political consequences to be expected, if American POWs were to be brought out at this late date! And it's clear why many unsavory elements in government would desperately block every effort to bring the POWs home! He asks: "Who is going to take the responsibility for leaving these men there? Who is responsible for not telling the truth . . . ? What about the inevitable charges of a cover up? The CIA, DIA, State Department, and White House will have a lot of answering to do!"[64]

"It's a blot on our national honor," charges former New Hampshire Governor Thompson, "that Secretaries of State under four Presidents [Nixon, Ford, Carter, Reagan] and a host of sycophantic aides, have deceived the people of the United States about Americans still being held as Prisoners of War in Southeast Asia."[65] Some of the most scandalous behavior in America's history will be exposed when the wall of secrecy is finally cracked! And *surely it will be!* We could begin by querying, under oath, Walt Rostow, Dean Rusk, Henry Kissinger, Richard Nixon, Alexander Haig, Theodore Sorensen, and many others known to have been instrumental in the betrayal of South Vietnam to the Communist forces!

"There was such a hurry to make this truce [the surrender accords negotiated and signed by identified Soviet spy Henry Kissinger]*66* that they forgot to liberate your own Americans from captivity! They were in such a hurry to sign this document that some . . . Americans, 'Well, they have vanished . . . Part of them, indeed, can be missing in action, but the leaders of North Vietnam themselves have admitted that some of them are still being kept in prison," explains Alexander Solzhenitsyn. "And do they give you back your countrymen? No, they are not giving them back, and they are always raising new conditions! . . .They are never again shown to the world because they will tell such tales as the human mind cannot accept. A part of your returned POWs told you they were tortured. This means that those who have remained were tortured even more, but did not yield an inch. These are your best people. These are your first heroes, who, in a solitary combat, have stood the test. And today, unfortunately, they cannot take courage from our applause. They can't hear it from their solitary cells where they may either die or sit 30 years . . . "[67]

A friend of the author secretly entered Communist Occupied Laos during July-August, 1986, as part of a privately financed eight-man expedition. This team sought to verify the existence of live American military men still being held prisoner by the Communists. They were taken to a cave inhabited only weeks before by three "caucasians" and several former South Vietnamese Air Force officers. Unusual markings were found painted on the walls. These included a "T" encircled by a drawing of a heart. Above the heart was written " "85." One American POW/MIA is Thomas Hart, a pilot who was shot down in 1973! A Laotian child had previously gone into the cave after the prisoners were taken away, in early July. He found part of a silver oak leaf, the insignia worn by a U.S. Lt. Colonel.

Former POW Red McDaniel reports in 1987: "This spring, a Laotian resistance fighter wrote to the Pentagon and told them he had obtained a Major Donahue's name, date of birth, the identity of his downed aircraft, and the plane's number! . . . there was an important signal in the information that proves it came from Major Donahue. Rather than stating the correct number of the aircraft, the number turned out to be the zip code of the home Morgan left in 1968. . . But when the family asked the government what was being done to bring Major Donahue home, they were told the case was closed! Even with hard evidence, the government refuses to act! . . . Major Donahue has been in his own personal Hell for 19 long years."[68]

According to the Defense Intelligence Agency: " . . . Morgan Jefferson Donahue, date of birth May 2, 1944, airplane AC-123, No. 32931 [his hometown zip code] . . . is still alive in the prison at Phoubaytong, Muang Khamkent, province of Khammouan."[69]

Stan Cottrell, an American runner, was in Communist Occupied Vietnam on a good-will mission in February, 1988. He personally reported seeing up to 20 American POWs being held under heavy guard at a "re-education camp" (concentration camp for former South Vietnamese anti-Communist officials).

Iwanobu Yoshida, a 65-year old Buddhist monk, had been in a Hanoi prison from 1975 to January, 1989. In June of 1989, he revealed how he had been incarcerated with a minimum of three and a maximum of six American POWs, at different times.

In August, 1989, it was reported by reliable intelligence sources that men in the highest levels of the United Stated Government know American POWs are being held on a prison island near Ho Thach Bai. Known as the Alcatraz of Communist Occupied Vietnam, this jungle covered cesspool is located in the middle of a reservoir, 43 miles northwest of Hanoi. Because it was constructed in the latter part of the

1970's, it doesn't appear on charts or aerial photographs. The canopy of jungle foliage, blanketing the prison, makes it undetectable to aerial or satellite surveillance.

An officer is *never* allowed, under *any* circumstances, to abandon the men under his command! Such activity is *always* an automatic court-martial offense! And the ultimate punishment might even be death! Isn't the President of the United States also the Commander-in-Chief of America's Armed Forces? Didn't President Eisenhower inexcusably abandon the nation's fighting men in Korea? Didn't President Nixon inexcusably abandon Major Donahue and other of the nation's fighting men in Vietnam?

Has there been any substantive effort by President's Eisenhower, Kennedy, Johnson, Nixon, Ford, Carter, Reagan, or Bush to force the release of American POWs from the Korean War or the Vietnam War? The *only* thing done by a disinterested Carter Administration was to legally change the status of all MIAs to *killed in action.* This scandalous attempt to wipe the slate clean took place in 1977! Large numbers of American POWs were still being held in Southeast Asia and was officially known by Ronald Reagan since 1981. In January 1982, President Reagan said the POW issue would receive "the highest national priority." Eight years later the silence was still deafening!

Despite all this, the President of the United States, George Bush (CFR), appears to be following in the footsteps of his predecessors. In August, 1989, he addressed a meeting of POW/MIA families; and despite evidence to the contrary, contended that there was "no evidence of captivity."

A relatively recent POW case says it all. Two Swedish businessmen observed a chain gang of haggard looking men working on a road outside of Hanoi. As they passed, one of the laborers yelled: "We are American POWs! There are many of us here, many of us! Tell America not to forget us!"[70]

Chapter 16

A Potpourri of Traitorous Acts and Treasonous Deeds

Traitor: "betrayer; turncoat . . . conspirator . . . Judas."
Roget's College Thesaurus

Treason: "Disloyalty to one's country."
New Webster's Dictionary

Security risk Dean Acheson started out in government as Roosevelt's Under Secretary of the Treasury, in 1933. He'd been vigorously recommended by, and was the protégé of, leftist Felix Frankfurter (Chapter 11) of Harvard, later to be appointed an Associate Justice of the Supreme Court in 1939. Acheson, along with Communist espionage agent Lee Pressman, had been one of Stalin's attorneys in the United States, long before Communist Occupied Russia gained recognition from Washington![1]

Soviet agent Alger Hiss, Acheson's protégé, was indicted for perjury on December 15, 1949. He'd lied to a Federal Grand Jury when questioned about his spying service to Moscow as a Communist mole! Hiss should rightfully have been indicted for treason! He was instead found guilty on January 21, 1950, by Judge Henry W. Goddard, on two counts of perjury and given a five year sentence. This espionage agent was then released on $10,000 bail, pending an appeal.

Elevated to Secretary of State under Truman, Acheson stood firmly behind his intimate friend. He declared on January 25, 1950, that "whatever the outcome" of the appeal, "I do not intend to turn my back on Alger Hiss!"[2] Senator Joseph R. McCarthy (R-WI) commented: "What clearer signal could have been given to the traitors and potential traitors in government? They were assured of support from the highest officials in our government."[3]

Hiss served less than four years in prison. As could be expected, he became a martyr and a folk hero to the Communists and the so-called liberal-left element in the United States. The mystery still remains unanswered as to why Alger Hiss wasn't tried under the existing espionage laws, or better yet, tried for treason! Less than four years in a federal penitentiary is a relatively light sentence for a traitor!

Michael Straight—a fellow Red—criticized Acheson for publicly supporting Hiss! This Communist conspirator charged Acheson with "indulging in a personal luxury that could only damage the State Department and the Foreign Service."[4] His comments "infuriated" Associate Justice Felix Frankfurter,[5] one of Roosevelt's innumerable radical leftist appointees!

Straight, for many years a high level "mole" in the United States, explained: "He summoned me to his chambers in the Supreme Court building and gave me a tongue lashing for my lack of courage. 'We must never be afraid to be identified with our friends!' he cried."[6] According to Straight "friends" is a Red mole's code word for other Communists in the hierarchy.[7] Is Michael Straight implying that Justice Frankfurter considered himself to be a Communist? Yes![8] And does Straight feel Frankfurter considered Acheson to be a Red as well? Yes![9] Offers Medford Evans: "It would require more than ordinary skepticism to doubt that Frankfurter considered himself, Acheson, and Straight to be Communists."[10]

******

Sidney Hillman (Chapter 11) was a Communist conspirator and Franklin Roosevelt's right-hand man! This Kremlin espionage agent and President of the Amalgamated Clothing Workers of America was given the job of running the enforcement arm of the National Recovery Administration. The NRA was America's first experience with an officially sanctioned Gestapo-like organization! John T. Flynn recalled: "They roamed through the garment district like storm troopers. They could enter a man's factory, send him out, line up his employees, subject them to minute interrogation, and take over his books on the instant. Night work was forbidden. Flying squadrons of these private coat-and-suit police went through the district at night, battering down doors with axes looking for men who were committing the crime of sewing together a pair of pants at night."[11]

******

Notoriously pro-Communist Earl Warren, Chief Justice of the United States Supreme Court—a man who spent some of his vacations with Communist Occupied Yugoslavia's murderous dictator Tito *12—lied* when he charged the "right wing" (anti-Communist movement) with the November 22, 1963, assassination of President John F. Kennedy![13] Warren—who spent other of his vacations in the Crimea, visiting with Nikita Khrushchev, the neanderthal "Butcher of Budapest"*14*—lied again when he claimed it was "a result of the hatred and bitterness that has been injected into the life of our nation by bigots." Communist Occupied Russia's *Tass*— all the while knowing the assassin was one of their own — called it the work of "racists, the Ku Klux Klan and the Birchists." The Soviet *New Times* magazine followed suit and said it was "an act of ultra-Right political terror." The *Daily Worker* demanded that Warren be appointed to head an investigation of the despicable murder!*15* Lyndon Johnson dutifully obeyed the Communist Party organ. The New York *Daily News* editorialized: "In view of the Earl Warren Supreme Court's long-standing tenderness toward Communists, any report this commission may give birth to will be open to suspicion of pro-Communist...bias."[16]

The Warren Commission's sole task appears to have been to hide the Soviet Union's involvement in the assassination of an American President! Glossed over or ignored were a number of extremely important facts about ACLU member Lee Harvey Oswald. According to David Emerson Gumaer, Oswald "joined the ACLU shortly before his major role in the assassination of the President of the United States. Although the *Warren Report* mentions Oswald's ACLU membership . . . someone has deliberately omitted all reference to the ACLU from the *Warren Report* index."[17]

FBI Director J. Edgar Hoover called Oswald a "dedicated Communist."[18] His physically abused Russian wife, Marina, was the ward of a KGB (Soviet secret police) Colonel. Oswald had previously tried to assassinate General Edwin A. Walker but the bullet missed by inches! He wrote: "in the event of war I would kill any American who put a uniform on in defense of the American government—any American."[19] An avid Marxist as a teenager, Oswald refused to salute the flag in school. While a marine, he was jokingly referred to as "Comrade Oswaldkowich." Lee Harvey Oswald was unquestionably an assassin in the employ of Communist Occupied Russia! He had been meticulously trained in guerrilla warfare, sabotage, terrorism, and as a specialized killer in and by the Soviet Union.[20] (Chapter 9).

The biased Warren Commission did its job well! It successfully prevented evidence of a Moscow-directed conspiracy in Kennedy's assassination from reaching the American people! The deceptive *Report is* believable only by people who still wait for Santa Claus on Christmas Eve and look for the Bunny to come on Easter morning! It is widely accepted in intelligence circles to be no more than a whitewash for a major KGB operation!

Former Congressman Martin Dies (D-TX) brings forth a point to ponder: "At no time has the President or any official speaking for our government, except J. Edgar Hoover, said frankly that President Kennedy was murdered by a

Communist whose record was well-known to our intelligence agencies, but who was permitted to roam at large even when the President's car passed within a rifle shot of the place he worked."[21]

******

Lyndon Baines Johnson assumed the Presidency in November of 1963. The first person he called was the ghoulish neanderthal, Nikita Khrushchev, in Moscow.[22] This wasn't done to break diplomatic relations, as he should. joined with the Korean Reds and Chinese Communists in brutally torturing American POWs! This anti-American feculent assisted the enemy forces in obtaining fake germ-warfare confessions![25] Burchett was later allowed to again enter the United States, during the Carter Administration. Posing as a journalist, he was allowed to freely tour college campuses and lecture to young "American students on the glories of betraying one's country to the Communists."[26] When he died, it was at his home in Communist Occupied Bulgaria!

******

On June 6, 194S, career diplomat John Stewart Service (Chapter 10, 13) and five others were arrested by the FBI for violating the Espionage Act. Service had been caught red-handed giving classified government documents to Andrew Roth, Naval Intelligence-State Department Liaison Officer, and Philip Jaffe, editor of *Amerasia,* a Communist magazine![27]

Both these men were Soviet espionage agents. Others involved were Emmanuel S. Larsen, State Department China Affairs expert; Kate L. Mitchell, *Amerasia* editor; and Mark J. Gayn, contributor. These six conspirators had clearly committed treason!

In addition, the FBI raided the *Amerasia* office in New York and found 1,700 classified documents! These papers had been stolen from the Navy Department, Office of War Information, Office of Strategic Services, War Department, the State Department and other agencies.[28]

Charges were preferred against Service by Under Secretary of State Joseph C. Grew and FBI Director J. Edgar Hoover. Assistant Secretary of State Dean Acheson, himself a notorious security risk, demanded that all legal action be stopped! Grew still insisted the traitor be vigorously prosecuted! Hoover had what he called a "100 percent airtight case against Service."*29* Attorneys representing Service, however, were able to pull strings. His hearing was inexplicably switched to a new Grand Jury. Service brazenly admitted turning over sensitive documents to Kremlin spy Philip Jaffe. Yet the new Grand Jury refused to indict him! There was said to be *"insufficient evidence."* Why? Hoover's devastatingly incriminating data had been *withheld* from the Grand Jury by Attorney General Tom Clark's Justice Department![30]

Clark, the father of radical leftist Ramsey Clark (Chapter 6), was amply rewarded by Truman in 1949, when he became an Associate Justice of the Supreme Court. Incredibly, *only* Jaffe, Roth, and Larsen were indicted. Gayn was cleared despite the 200 classified documents found in his apartment!*31* Larsen was given a meager $500 fine! Kremlin spy Jaffe pleaded guilty and was let off with a mere $2,500 fine! The case against Roth, *also a Soviet spy,* was dismissed!

John Stewart Service had been given *six separate security clearances* by the State Department's three member Loyalty and Security Board!*32* Subversive Dean Acheson was a memb er of the Board! Nelson Rockefeller was another! He was later identified as a Communist by Eisenhower's CIA Director, Walter Bedell Smith!*33* Eventually, the Civil Service Loyalty Board determined Service's loyalty to be of "reasonable doubt" and he was fired in December 1951. Nevertheless, he was officially welcomed back to the State Department in 1957, after a lengthy court battle (Chapter 8). Astoundingly, he was now given another security clearance by Deputy Under Secretary of State Loy Henderson!

This subversive retired from government in 1962 on a generous tax-payer provided pension. He joined the University of California, Berkeley, where he taught, appropriately, at the Center of Chinese Studies. Now this conspiratorial traitor could freely indoctrinate college students with his anti-American, pro-Communist offal. Comrade Service visited Chou En-lai in the Fall of 1971, when he was personally invited by the Red tyrant.

******

"Most of us here were, at one time or another, active in either the OSS, the State Department, or the European Economic Administration," revealed H. Rowan Gaither, while President of the subversive, tax exempt Ford Foundation in 1953. "During those times, and without exception, *we operated under directives issued by the White House, the substance of which was to the effect that we should make every effort to so alter life in the United States as to make possible a comfortable merger with the Soviet Union. We are continuing to be guided by just such directives.34* (emphasis added).

******

On May 26, 1953, Senator William Jenner (R-IN) notified President Eisenhower about a serious breach of U.S. security. The American Communications Association was found to be under *total* Communist control! This union was responsible for servicing all communication lines to and from American military bases in the U.S. and overseas! Eisenhower and his people chose to ignore the warning!35 A report was issued which concluded: "The control that the American Communications Association, a Communist-directed union, maintains over communication lines vital to the national defense poses a threat to the security of this country."36 Still no action was taken!

A little more than three years later, the Senate Internal Security Subcommittee investigated further and issued another report. William Brucker, Eisenhower's Secretary of the Army, was questioned by Committee counsel Richard Arens.

"Arens: Are you conversant with the fact that the North Atlantic Cable which carries important messages vital to the security of our nation is now serviced by the American Communications Association, a Communist-controlled labor organization?

"Sec. Brucker: I am aware of that."[37]

Brucker offered to do nothing to correct this dangerous security problem! Eisenhower predictably acted exactly as could be expected when it came to security-related situations—he, too, did nothing! Some congressmen lacked the necessary courage to take remedial action. Others simply didn't care!

This serious breach of American security still exists today! Says former congressman William M. Tuck: "It is a shocking fact that the North Atlantic cable which day by day carries important, top-secret information to and from the Pentagon itself is being serviced right now by the American Communications Association, a Communist dominated union that was thrown out of the CIO in 1950 because of Communist content."[38]

******

Eisenhower's Attorney General Brownell publicly revealed that Truman's Assistant Secretary of the Treasury, Harry Dexter White, was a Soviet espionage agent. And that President Truman unquestionably knew of White's spying activities for the Kremlin. Brownell reported: "... Harry Dexter White was a Russian spy. He smuggled secret documents to Russian agents for transmission to Moscow. Harry Dexter White was known to be a Communist spy by the very people who appointed him to the most sensitive and important position he ever held in Government service. The FBI became aware of White's espionage activities . . . and from the beginning made reports on these activities to the appropriate officials in authority. But these reports did not impede White's advancement . . . I can now announce officially for the first time . . . that White's spying activities for the Soviet Government were reported in detail by the FBI to the White House by means of a report delivered to President Truman through his military aide, Brigadier General Harry H. Vaughan, in December of 1945."[39]

Nevertheless, White was still able to keep his influential position in the Treasury Department! And on January 23, 1946, Truman (CFR), all the while knowing White was a spy, nominated him for an even more important higher paying job! Incredible though it may seem, HST promoted a man he had been repeatedly warned was an enemy spy! And the Senate hastily confirmed this Communist agent without debate! Yes, Harry Dexter White was to become Executive Director of the International Monetary Fund! This subversive then got the President to appoint his friend, Virginius Frank Coe, another Kremlin mole, as Secretary of the IMF!

******

On January 29, 1961, President Kennedy said: "Let every public servant know . . . that this Administration recognizes the value of dissent and daring, that we greet healthy controversy as the hallmark of healthy change."[40] Yet forest ranger Don Caron was forced to resign in 1961 over a weekly anti-Communist newspaper column he was writing based on FBI reports and Congressional hearings![41] The criticism?: " . . . the editorials reflect a zealous and almost fanatical patriotism and an active effort to awake the public to the dangers of Communism . . . regardless of all else, the whole subject matter is surely controversial."[42]

******

Robert Strange McNamara (CFR) instituted the *Reuther Memorandum* as Kennedy's Secretary of Defense. This radical directive was authored by the infamous leftist labor union leader Walter Reuther, who once wrote from Communist Occupied Russia: "Carry on the fight for a Soviet America."[43] The incredible pro-Communist memorandum recommended the outright censorship of all military leaders! No further criticism of Communists or Communism in speeches or writings would be tolerated!

General Edwin A. Walker, with a well-deserved reputation as the best combat officer in Europe, was the first major military casualty. He was relieved of his West German command in 1962 for requiring that his men be taught patriotism and be well informed about the dangers of Communism! Security risk Adam Yarmolinsky, McNamara's hatchet-man, coldly axed Walker's career! His treatment was designed to serve as a warning to other patriotic, anti-Communist military officers! It showed exactly what would happen to their careers if they spoke out against, or taught anything about, the Communist enemy with whom their country was at war! Walker testified that evidently, "militant anti-Communist leadership by a division commander," was no longer to be tolerated by Communists and other subversives in government!44 At the same time, however, the leftist *Nation,* edited by Communist Carey McWilliams, *was* allowed for troop indoctrination!

McNamara (Chapter 11) and his "whiz kids" effectively enforced thought control over the opinions of military men! Joining him in muzzling anti-Communists in the Armed Forces were such outlandish security risks as Secretary of State Dean Rusk (Chapter 9, 10, 11), Under Secretary of State George Ball, and Cyrus Vance (Chapter 11). Advance texts of all speeches by military officers were required by a State Department censor board! This censorship involved the deleting from speeches and writings of all unpleasant references to Communism and Communists! Ball's illogical excuse for this traitorous activity was that "name calling" might be resented by the Communists! He gave specifics: the word "slavery" was no longer appropriate for denoting those enslaved by the Reds! Communism was not to be referred to as "the enemy"! Communist terrorist acts shouldn't be described as "brutal"![45]

The Senate Armed Services Committee collected over 200 pages of anti-Communist words and remarks deleted from some of the 1500 censored speeches on hand. In 1962, Senator Strom Thurmond (R-SC) gave examples of phrases blue lined from the material of Lieutenant General Arthur

Trudeau: "The steady advance of Communism"; "insidious ideology of Communism"; "The Soviets have not relented in the slightest in their determination to dominate the world and destroy our way of life."[46]

The *Reuther Memorandum*[47] recommended using the Internal Revenue Service to harass anti-Communist organizations and leaders! The IRS came down hard on people like anti-Communist Walter Knott, of Knott's Berry Farm, in an obvious attempt to make him an example! He was wrongly assessed a fortune in taxes on technicalities and reversals of previous IRS decisions! Tax exemptions were to be taken away from anti-Communist organizations, whenever possible! The IRS did this, for example, to anti-Communist leader Billy James Hargis and his Christian Crusade! It was also recommended that the Federal Communications Commission (FCC) be used to eliminate anti-Communist programs from the air waves! They succeeded! All anti-Communist organizations were to be classed as "subversive" and placed on the Attorney General's list! This recommendation was so outlandish that it was never implemented! And lastly, J. Edgar Hoover's anti-Communist activities were to be reined in because he was said to exaggerate "the domestic Communist menace" and stir up the public with regard to an internal Communist threat! Hoover was too widely respected and admired for the Communists to curb so easily!

******

FBI Director J. Edgar Hoover spoke on dealing with the Communist threat: "The best yardstick of the effectiveness of the fight against Communism is the fury of the smear attacks against the fighter — launched and conducted by the Reds!"[48] On December 5, 1960, delegates representing Communist Parties from 81 countries gathered in Moscow. A manifesto was issued calling for the total destruction of anti-Communism within the United States! The virulent, carefully orchestrated hate campaign started soon after.[49]

The Communist *People's World* initiated it all by attacking the anti-Communist John Birch Society.[50] Media leftists of all stripes immediately began parroting Moscow's smears! Edward Hunter, a psychological warfare expert, appeared before the SISS and explained how the Soviets had originated the vicious smear campaign against anti-Communists. *Few people listened!* The Kremlin, Hunter said, viewed the fast growth of anti-Communism in America with a great deal of alarm! *Few people listened!* The Moscow based program, explained Hunter, was specifically designed to destroy the burgeoning grass roots movement!*51 Few people listened!*

President Kennedy shamelessly ignored Hunter's warning and joined the Red-planned assault on anti-Communists! Blatantly following Moscow's directive and spouting the Communist line without deviation, JFK first attacked American anti-Communists on November 18, 1961: " . . . the discordant voices of extremism are heard once again in the land! Men who are unable to face up to the danger from without are convinced that the real danger comes from within . . . They look suspiciously at their neighbors and their leaders . . . they find treason in our finest churches, in our highest court! But you and I and most Americans take a different view of our peril. We know that it comes from without, not within. "[52]

******

John J. McCloy (CFR) became Kennedy's Special Advisor on Disarmament. On June 23, 1961, this shadowy subversive submitted the draft of a bill to create the Arms Control and Disarmament Agency! Its incredibly treasonous goals, per a McCloy (Chapter 11) letter to the President, were *to disarm the United States; turn American weapons over to a UN militia; and bring about world government!53* In September 1961, Congress actually passed the Constitutionally suicidal Arms Control and Disarmament Act! James Utt (R-CA) revealed that the plagiarized legislation was an "almost word-for-word duplication of a disarmament proposal advanced by Khrushchev in 1959."*54* The Act was later published as a 19-page report entitled

Freedom From War: United States Program for General and Complete Disarmament in a Peaceful World.55 It should have read *Freedom from War: Moscow's Program for the Disarming and Surrender of the United States.*

The plan was for the United States to disarm unilaterally! In other words, America was to disarm whether or not the Communist enemy disarms! Under McCloy's legislation, all nuclear testing was to stop! No nuclear weapons were to be produced! No missile delivery systems were to be manufactured! No systems were to be built to defend the U.S. against enemy missile attacks! Existing nuclear warheads and all U.S. military forces eventually were to be transferred to the Communist controlled UN!

Senator John Tower (R-TX) took issue with the plan: "As skeptical as I have always been of the measure of . . . loyalty within the State Department I never would have believed . . . our diplomats could so completely and unabashedly advocate the surrender of American rights and sovereignty! . . . if more American people knew about this scheme there would be a nationwide uproar that would make the reaction to the Alger Hiss scandal look like another era of good feeling by comparison!"[56]

Unfortunately, the American people were never told! Not surprisingly, the media did amazingly little to publicize this treasonous activity at the highest levels of government! Therefore, no "uproar" was ever heard from the public. This insane disarming plan and the resulting surrender of U.S. sovereignty, is still quietly being adhered to almost three decades later!

******

The Logan Act 57 is designed to stop private citizens from interfering with a President's exclusive, Constitutionally guaranteed right to conduct America's foreign policy! It's purpose is to also stop members of other branches of government—Senators, Representatives, judges— from improper interference in foreign affairs! The law is clear as to what constitutes a violation and the allowable criminal penalties. There have been numerous occasions when this law could and should have been enforced against private citizens and Congressmen, involved with enemy foreign governments in recent years. One case is that of Congressman Jim Wright (D-TX) and the nine others who signed the infamous "Dear Commandante"*58* letter of support to Madison Avenue Daniel Ortega, the dictator of Nicaragua. Other examples are Jane Fonda, Tom Hayden, Cora Weiss, David Dellinger, Rennie Davis, former Attorney General Ramsey Clark (Chapter 6, 11, 15), and hundreds of other Communists and pro-Communists who made treasonous trips to Communist Occupied Vietnam.

These traitors were illegally involved in private negotiations with the Red leadership in Hanoi! Theirs was a deliberate effort to wreck American foreign policy under the guise of ending the Vietnam War! Stopping the war to these radicals simply meant an end to all opposition to the Communists in the North! It meant letting South Vietnam fall to the enemy! These traitors were openly contemptuous of the law! They traveled abroad at will, to meet with the Communist North Vietnamese leaders. Their sole intention was to alter U.S. policy to favor the goals of the Communists! There's absolutely no question but that Fonda and others of her ilk should have been indicted and tried, at the very least, under the Logan Act! And they certainly should have been prosecuted for treason! But, unfortunately, they were not!

The Communist Party, the National Lawyers Guild, the ACLU, and other radical groups are working to have the Logan Act repealed. They falsely claim it's somehow a dire threat to free speech, free association, and all the rest of the usual leftist scare phrases. Judge for yourself! The language isn't difficult to understand: "Any citizen of the United States, wherever he may be, who, without authority of the United States, directly or indirectly commences or carries on any correspondence or intercourse with any foreign government of any officer or any agent thereof, with intent to influence the measures or conduct of any foreign government of any officer or agent thereof, in relation to any disputes or controversies with the United States, or to defeat the measures of the United States, shall be fined not more than $5,000 or imprisoned not more than three years, or both."[59]

American POWs were tortured in order to force them to meet with American traitors, who continually visited Hanoi during the Vietnam War! Those collaborators, many of them known Communists, helped their North Vietnamese comrades by checking POW "confessions" for accuracy! Why were U.S. citizens even allowed to go to Hanoi in the first place? Why didn't the government prosecute the hundreds of traitors who made these unauthorized trips to cavort with the enemy? Why were none of these pro-Communists tried for treason? The excuse generally given was that the powers that be didn't wish to make martyrs out of the collaborators! The truth is simply that the Communist and pro-Communist revolutionaries doing all the traveling were being aided and abetted and protected by their "respectable" Communist and pro-Communist revolutionary counterparts entrenched in the government!

Sybil Stockdale—wife of the highest ranking navy POW—was officially informed that the passports of these traitors "weren't stamped in North Vietnam and so there was no legal evidence that they'd been there, even when they broadcast the details of these trips on the front page of the newspapers."[60] Hogwash!

The Department of Justice refused to enforce the Logan Act during the Vietnam War. For example, Ramsey Clark (Chapter 6, 11) arrived in Hanoi *from Moscow* on July 29, 1972, "on a two week visit as a guest of the North Vietnamese Government."[61] While there he was interviewed for a propaganda broadcast on the Communist Voice of Vietnam! Upon his return to the U.S., Clark held a news conference and said he "believed that as a private citizen he had the right to go to North Vietnam and do what he could to try to bring peace and gain release of prisoners."[62] Despite Clark's open acts of treason and his flaunting of the law,

Nixon's Attorney General Richard G. Kleindienst's response was incredible: "I don't anticipate any Logan Act cases right now. No evidence of any wrongdoing has been presented to the Department yet."[63]

******

Dr. Walt Whitman Rostow (CFR)—an atrocious security risk— constantly preached surrender of U.S. sovereignty! He advocated the absorption of the United States into a world government, policed and ruled by the Communist-conceived and Communist-controlled United Nations! Benedict Arnold only tried to surrender the fort at West Point to the British and was severely punished for treason. Rostow and many clones of his ilk have tried to surrender the entire American nation! Yet, not one of these traitors has ever even been accused of treason!

Congressman and patriot James B. Utt wrote: "In January 1962, there was the secret *Rostow-Moscow Report* which called for the implementation of the 'no-win' policy through the following five points: 1. Abandon first strike weapons; 2. Refrain from encouraging revolts behind the Iron Curtain; 3. Refrain from criticizing satellite countries; 4. Deny foreign aid to countries which refuse 'coalition governments'; 5. Work toward general and complete disarmament."[64]

President John F. Kennedy was advised by Comrade Rostow (Chapter 11) that Russian leaders considered U.S. planes, missile bases and first strike weapons to be "provocative" and "worrisome." Kennedy quickly responded by stopping Cruise missile deployment! The Skybolt missile was scrapped, as was the Nike-Zeus anti-missile program for America's defense! Production of the most remarkable jet fighter plane ever produced by America, the Lockheed F-104, was halted! The Strategic Air Command (SAC) was to be eliminated! The RS-70 Bomber was canceled, while the B-52 and B-58 manned bombers were phased out! Offensive weapons were destroyed and missile bases abandoned—all in an insane effort to appease Communist Occupied Russia's slave labor dictatorship!

******

USAF General Thomas Power wrote a book after retiring as head of the Strategic Air Command (SAC). He sent the required 13 manuscript copies to the Pentagon for approval. Clearance wasn't forthcoming and Power requested their return. He received only twelve! The missing copy happened to be the one assigned to Adam Yarmolinsky (Chapter 11), Kennedy's subversive Assistant Secretary of Defense. *Yarmolinsky's copy mysteriously surfaced in Moscow.* This was discovered when Marshal Sokolovsky's *Soviet Military Strategy* was found to contain footnotes referring to Power's *unpublished* manuscript! Exactly how the General's manuscript found its way to Communist Occupied Russia hasn't ever been clarified! Why has no one dared asked Comrade Yarmolinsky?

******

Communists in the Government Printing Office have ready access to top secret military information. This facility handles upwards to 250,000 pieces of classified material annually! At least 15 suspected Reds were under investigation back in August 1953, by the Senate Permanent Investigating Subcommittee.*65* So blatant were one GPO employee's Communist activities that the FBI sent some 40 confidential reports to his superiors. Each was ignored!*66* Edward Rothschild wasn't fired until Senator Joseph R. McCarthy (R-WI) publicly exposed his Red background.

******

In 1965, the Johnson Administration was going full steam ahead in treasonously bankrolling, assisting, feeding, and arming dire Communist enemies of the U.S. (Chapter 1, 2, 3, 4, 6). Top American research facilities were regularly toured by groups of Red Bloc scientists! One such "scientific" expedition included representatives from Communist Occupied Romania, Poland, Czechoslovakia, Yugoslavia, and Hungary. Each Red dictatorship was an openly professed ally and supplier of military aid to the enemy North Vietnamese Communist forces!*67* Congressman Richard Roudebush (R-IN) revealed how these Iron Curtain experts were allowed to "lecture, conduct seminars, survey our current research, take field trips in the U.S., and conduct research of their own."*68* American taxpayers were footing the bill for their travel, lodging, food, and medical costs. The Communist Bloc scientists were even paid a salary while they were in the United States!*69*

These ludicrous trips were allowed to take place even though intelligence data proved that most Red Bloc scientists allowed to visit the U.S. are KGB agents! Even those few who aren't are given assignments by the KGB to obtain specific classified materials! FBI Director J. Edgar Hoover explained: "Upon returning, Soviet scientists who have visited the United States under the exchange program are required by the KGB to submit comprehensive reports on the technical aspects of their trip, including descriptions of installations visited, research being conducted, and the status of particular projects. They must also submit reports concerning Americans contacted, for possible future use by the KGB."*70*

******

Richard Nixon signed an agreement with Communist Occupied Russia's Leonid Brezhnev—which stated that its objectives were "general and complete disarmament." The President was well aware that a Communist *always* commanded the UN military forces, per an understanding reached many years ago between Stalin and Roosevelt's shadow, Soviet espionage agent Alger Hiss (Chapter 14)! Yet, he treasonously agreed to the establishment of an all-powerful UN militia—"land, sea and air forces"*71* — which would surpass that of the United States! Along with this travesty, Nixon also had concrete plans to declare martial law when necessary to subdue 4internal disorders" in the United States! He was rightfully accused by William

Howard (of the Newhouse newspaper chain) of "making plans for a dictatorship in America."[72]

******

"The Chinese Communists . . . are international criminals!" said the candidate in 1968.[73] He wouldn't agree to let Red China join the UN! Nor would he allow trade with them! By 1971, Nixon, the President, had done away with all trade restrictions regarding these "international criminals." He enthusiastically endorsed Red China's admission to the UN. Nixon, the President, then engineered a stunning reversal of long standing U.S. policy. He and his subversive shadow — the sinister Kremlin agent, Henry Kissinger— made a traitorous pilgrimage to Communist Occupied China in 1972. This visit will forever stand as one of the most monstrous sellouts in all history. Here a leader of the greatest nation the world has ever known was toasting one of the worst atheistic mass-murderers of the era!

Nixon obsessively sought a new relationship with Communist Occupied China's maniacal despots! The President cold-bloodedly served up for sacrifice South Vietnam, in a graceless show of treachery! He ruthlessly plunged a knife in the back of America's old friend and long-term ally, the Nationalist Chinese Government on Taiwan. Chou En-lai required these things as tribute, before he would allow Nixon to visit his Red slave dictatorship. All of this and more was part of the sordid package deal identified Soviet spy Henry Kissinger [74](Chapter 6) had previously arranged with Chou.

Now the U.S. and Communist Occupied China were cozy partners in crime. America's new policy was to (at all cost) avoid offending the sensitive Chinese butchers! Uncomplimentary terms such as planned famines, forced abortions, slave labor, genocide, terrorist acts, mass murderers, etc., were to be avoided! The upwards of 50 million people killed in Red China since 1957 were no longer attributed in Washington circles to murderous atrocities. Mass murder was now politely referred to as a "population setback!"

******

Carter further betrayed America's dependable Free Chinese allies by canceling the Mutual Defense Treaty! Taiwan was denied the purchase of jet fighter planes and other military goods essential to their survival. One of Carter's most despicable acts was to more closely ally the United States with Peiping's mass-murderers. He granted Diplomatic Recognition in 1979 to a regime known to have methodically eliminated perhaps as many as 64 million of its own people in the three short decades since the Communist enslavement of this hapless nation, in 1949. Most Favored Nation (MFN) trade status was also given to a dictatorship presently maintaining over 7,500 concentration camps, with 23 million or more slave laborers!

******

Carter developed and utilized a pretentious "human rights" scheme throughout his term of office. It was an efficient means of undermining and destabilizing the governments of long-term anti-Communist allies! *Only* anti-Communist countries were made the butt of America's animosity! Included were such friends as Nicaragua, Argentina, Brazil, Guatemala, Paraguay, Uruguay, and Chile. All of these pro-American nations were under siege by Soviet-and Cuban-supported Red terrorists! Any reasonable and necessary military response to terrorist violence was called by Carter a violation of "human rights." The same is true when Communist revolutionaries were jailed for kidnapping, bombings, and murder! The horrendous terrorist acts themselves were completely and deliberately overlooked!

On April 1, 1977, as if participating in a monstrous April Fool's joke, Communist Occupied Russia *demanded* a stop to all criticism of them regarding "human rights"! They audaciously charged it was "interference in Soviet internal affairs."75 Carter meekly obeyed! On the other hand, an arms embargo was ordered against America's ally, South Africa, on October 27, 1977! Carter, the consummate hypocrite, claimed there was a "blatant deprivation of basic human rights."[76] Ironically, warranted censure of the slave labor, concentration-camp-filled Russian dictatorship ceased! And unwarranted criticism intensified of a free, non-slave labor republic without concentration camps'

******

While Americans were fighting and dying in the no-win Vietnam War, Communist Occupied China was supplying the North Vietnamese enemy with light weapons, military equipment, at least 4,000 battle hardened officers, and 320,000 combat veterans! Yet, a Georgia newspaper headline revealed this shocker: "RED CHINESE SOLDIERS TO TRAIN AT FORT BENNING."[77] Yes, Americans being ordered to train the soldiers of a deadly Communist adversary they may one day face in battle! Who could possibly have approved such leftist lunacy?

A Defense Department spokesman offered a ludicrous rationalization for training soldiers from Communist Occupied China. He said: "The United States Government now regards China as a 'friendly, non-allied' country. This policy is based upon the assessment that a modernizing, more secure China—which shares with the United States a common threat [the Soviet Union]—can be an increasing force for peace and stability in East Asia [As China has been in Cambodia, Vietnam, Tibet, Korea, etc.?]."[78] Strangely enough, the Department of Defense still secretly listed Communist Occupied China as *"hostile to the United States"*.[79]

This was the same lame excuse used years ago by leftists regarding Communist Occupied Russia. Americans were then told the snarling Russian Bear must be aided and appeased to make it "feel more secure." The Soviets had to be fed and armed because "a common threat" was shared. At that time, the "common threat" was supposedly Communist Occupied China. Suffice to say, Communist Occupied Russia saw fit in 1985 to sign a very friendly $14 billion trade agreement with America's new found Red Chinese "ally."[80]

******

Allan C. Brownfeld declares: "The Soviet Union clearly seeks to destroy the current government of South Africa and replace it with a Marxist regime similar to those now in existence in Mozambique, Angola and Ethiopia."[81] Let's take a closer look at America's involvement in the South African situation. Would there really be any difference if Brownfeld had said "United States" instead of the "Soviet Union?" Shockingly, the answer is no! Both nations have identical goals in mind— Communist occupation of one of the most valuable pieces of real estate of the globe!

Dr. John L. Grady charges: " For the United States to undermine South Africa is unfair and unreasonable! We have no legal or moral right to meddle in the internal affairs of another stable and friendly nation. Nevertheless, past presidents, administrations and congresses have done so under the pretext of human rights. At the same time, they have totally overlooked the more than one hundred million people starved, murdered, and executed by the Communists in Russia and China and conveniently ignored the vicious black genocide which has occurred in the majority of the other black ruled [Communist occupied] nations of Africa such as Uganda, Angola, Congo, Nigeria, Biafra and others."[82] Who's behind this traitorous folly? Which people in our government are fomenting the incredible stampede toward the destruction of America's strategically important South African ally and friend?

******

CIA agent Richard Welch was ambushed and assassinated in Athens, Greece, when he was traitorously exposed by a subversive Washington-based group called OC-5. One of OC-5's advisors is CIA turncoat Philip Agee, a self-proclaimed Communist. An attorney for the CIA explained how anyone "could walk into the Soviet Embassy and hand over a complete list of our agents and nothing

335

could be done about it!"*83* Incredibly, it isn't against the law to reveal the identity of U.S. intelligence agents to the Communist enemy! Yet it's a crime to detain a federal pigeon; to give out the police record of a Communist terrorist; or to reveal the name of a federal welfare recipient!

The late Congressman Larry McDonald said this: "Picture in your mind an organization in Moscow consisting of Soviet citizens who specialize in 'fingering' Moscow's agents for assassination. Imagine such an organization demanding—and receiving—highly sensitive information from the government it is betraying. And as a crowning absurdity, imagine this group demanding that the government grant its financial supporters a tax deduction."*84* This is exactly what has been taking place in Washington!

******

The Strategic Arms Limitation Treaties (SALT) are ballyhooed around the world, the propaganda barrage so intense that hardly anyone dares to raise a voice to protest. Yet, exactly how do these treaties come about? And what is the sinister role being play-acted out by Kremlin master spy Henry Kissinger?*85* According to Admiral Chester A. Ward: "Every single provision of both SALT agreements originated with the Soviet strategic experts and planners in the Kremlin, was approved by Leonid Brezhnev and his closest associates in the Politburo, and was passed — usually by Soviet Ambassador Anatoly F. Dobrynin — to Henry Kissinger, who then provided the rationalization for it and 'sold' it. . . That is to say, he was working with the Soviets and against the United States of America."[86]

The results of such duplicity are far-reaching and disastrous to the security of the United States. Scott Stanley, Jr., reveals: "The results are that the Kissinger SALT agreements have formally granted the Soviets a 41 percent superiority in land-based missiles; a 34 percent superiority in sea-based missiles; a 50 percent superiority in numbers of submarines; a four-to-one advantage in missile payloads; and, a three-to-one advantage in total number of missiles

deployed. In no area covered by the agreement is the United States permitted to so much as maintain parity with the USSR"[87] J. Kesner Kahn charges: . 'Kissingerism' is simply what does not conflict with Communist interests, which gives him the power of one serving the Communists while negotiating w
hat U.S. policy will be![88]

******

Both Houses of Congress have been blessed with their share of volatile anti-American misfits! Some of the illustrious Congressional elite envision tyrants of the totalitarian left as poor misunderstood neurotics or wayward juvenile delinquents. Still others consider an appeasement-minded pro-Communist foreign policy and no win wars as in Korea and Vietnam to be in the national interest!

Why are known Communists, who vow to destroy America, allowed to run for public office? Why are known Communists, who vow to destroy America, allowed to be members of Congress? Why is a Communist allowed to take the oath for the House or the Senate and swear to "support and defend the Constitution of the United States against all enemies, foreign and domestic" when, in fact, they are the enemy? The oath of office for a Senator ends with "So help you (Representative—'me') God." What meaning can this possibly have to a Communist who is, by his very conditioning, a professed atheist?

Yet, out and out Communist Party members do hold seats in today's Congress! One example is Representative Augustus F. Hawkins (D-CA). He was identified as a Red by John L. Leech, former organizer and State Committee member of the California Communist Party![89]

Another is Representative Charles Hayes (D-IL) who was named by two witnesses during the 1950s as a Party member! This Red was formerly vice-president of the United Food and Commercial Workers Union.90 No one knows how many more there may be!

Yes, some members of Congress have been and are a part of the international Communist conspiracy! This is an unpleasant but undeniable fact! A number of Representatives and Senators—through ideology, blackmail, or sheer opportunism—have allowed their names and position to be used to aid Communism through front organizations and subversive activities.

Adam Clayton Powell (D-NY), Congressman from Harlem for 12 terms, was affiliated with over 100 Communist Fronts. He was also the featured speaker at many Communist Party fund raising gatherings![91] Emanuel Cellar (D-NY) served 25 Congressional terms, despite nearly 40 Communist Front affiliations and ventures![92]

Congresswoman Bella S. Abzug (D-NY) was director of the New York branch of the Communist National Lawyers Guild. The NLG was cited as never having "failed to rally to the legal defense of the Communist Party and individual members thereof, including known espionage agents."[93] Abzug was also affiliated with a multitude of Communist Fronts! She helped found the International Association of Democratic Lawyers, which is directly under the control of the KGB and the Central Committee of the Communist Party in Moscow![94]

Some House members boldly allow Communist revolutionaries to use their office space. The Red conspirators then organize activities against the best interests of the United States! The distinguished historian Otto Scott reveals: "There are men in Congress whose staffs are in constant touch with the Soviet Embassy; there are others in Congress whose careers have been based upon close associations with Communists and Communist causes . . . [95] For the first time in our history we see an American Congress that regards an American President as a worse enemy than an implacable foreign power that is already unloading troops and weapons on our own continent and that openly declares it seeks our defeat."[96]

Read that again! It's unbelievable, but true!: "For the first time in our history we see an American Congress that regards an American President as a worse enemy than an implacable foreign power that is already unloading troops and weapons on our own continent and that openly declares it seeks our defeat."

Few Communists in the United States have so openly served the cause of the Red conspiracy as has Congressman Ronald Dellums (D-CA)! He let revolutionaries use his office space for planning the Communist May Day demonstrations in Washington!97 Dellums provided committee Rooms to "Hanoi" Jane Fonda (Chapter 6) and radical leftist Tom Hayden (Chapter 6), in which to hold hate-filled anti-U.S. seminars.98 He calls himself a Marxist! Dellums sponsored, endorsed, or cooperated with every major pro-Hanoi, anti-American organization during the Vietnam War! This leftist even pushed legislation to give veteran's benefits to Americans who fought for the Communists during the Spanish Civil War!

Representative John Conyers (D-MI) served on the Executive Board of the National Lawyers Guild, America's Moscow-run Communist front for attorneys! He was featured with fugitive Weather Underground terrorist bomber, Bernadette Dorn, at the NLG's 31st annual meeting. This radical leftist has belonged to or associated with innumerable Communist Fronts! He also participated in Red activities with Communist Party official Angela Davis and Communist attorney Mark Lane![99]

George W. Crockett (D-MI) is yet another Congressional member of the Communist National Lawyers Guild. He has been intimately associated with the Communist Party, Communists, Communist Front organizations, and Communist causes for some 40 years! This subversive attorney defended 11 Communist Party leaders who were tried and convicted under the Smith Act. So outrageous was Crockett's courtroom behavior that Judge Harold Medina sentenced him to four months in jail for contempt![100]

Senator Howard Morton Metzenbaum (D-OH) was once an official in the National Lawyers Guild, the legal arm of the Communist Party in the U.S. He was formerly associated with quite a number of other subversive Front groups. Metzenbaum has shown a devotion to Communist causes over the years.[101]

Senator Claude D. "Red" Pepper, charges investigative journalist John Rees, "carried the torch for Stalin in the U.S. Senate and amassed a never equaled record as the most openly pro-Communist member in the History of that august body."[102]

Senator Alan Cranston (D-CA) began his career as a protégé of Communist spy Louis Adamic. He knowingly hired Communist Party organizer David Karr (formerly Katz) and other Reds while working for the heavily infiltrated Office of War Information.[103] Cranston was denied a security clearance by Army Intelligence in July of 1944, yet he edited Army Talk, while working for Communist Major Julius Schreiber.[104] The propaganda Cranston wrote for U.S. troops was so blatant that it was reprinted by the Daily Worker! Cranston's entire adult life has been one of close association with Communists and Communist goals.[105]

Senator Mike Gravel (D-AK) gained a well-deserved reputation as being politically to the left of Karl Marx! Gravel once sponsored a showing of Brazil: A Report on Torture in the Senate Office Building auditorium. The purported "documentary" attacked the anti-Communist pro-U.S. Brazilian Government. The movie was actually all shot in Chile, not Brazil, and it starred 70 Cuban trained terrorists! Propaganda printed by the SDS was distributed to the viewers. Here a United States Senator knowingly sponsors a Communist propaganda movie; the film stars terrorists trained by Communist Occupied Cuba; it was produced by Reds in Communist Chile; and the "documentary" is accompanied by Communist literature handed out by Communist revolutionaries! Is Comrade Gravel a Communist? He's never been officially identified as one!

******

Who would have believed the Soviet KGB and their Communist Bloc counterparts would be able to place spies in at least nine Congressional offices?[106] And that Communist espionage agents operate on a number of Congressional committee staffs?[107] Or that a leftist Senator— Christopher J. Dodd (D-CT) (CFR)—would reputedly share jet-setter Bianca Jagger's sexual favors with Tomas Borge, the animalistic mass-murdering butcher who runs Communist Occupied Nicaragua's secret police organization?[108]

Who would have dreamed that 249 members of the House would vote against giving the Judiciary Committee $300,000 to investigate Communist activities in the United States?[109] And that many members of Congress were on Soviet espionage agent Orlando Letelier's "contact list?"[110] That leftist Senator James Abourezk (D-SD) and socialist Congressman Michael Harrington (D-MA) would have taken money from Communist Letelier, a dangerous KGB man?[111] Or that 10 radical members of the House would arrogantly sign the traitorous "Dear Commadante" letter in support of Nicaragua's Communist dictator, Daniel Ortega?[112]

These are but a few of the traitorous shenanigans openly taking place in America! Security risks, Communist agents, terrorists, and those who actively aid and abet them, operate confidently throughout government and society. There's little fear of exposure! There's even less fear of prosecution! All of this is the direct result of America having been quietly stripped of any internal security apparatus (Chapter 7, 8). There is no official or congressional committee left that is willing to investigate, spotlight, and punish the brazen acts of treason taking place daily in and out of government!

Epilogue: Communism's Inherently Evil Nature

"I would think that if you understood what Communism was, you would hope, you would pray on your knees that we would someday become Communist."*1*

Jane Fonda

"While the persecutions, arrests, massacres, mass starvations, and forced resettlements of people take place, those most capable of exposing such atrocities—the Western governments, the media ... at best sit by quietly hoping not to embarrass the totalitarians," charges Vilius Brazenas who fled Communist Occupied Lithuania. "When the nauseating stench of rotting corpses invades their nostrils; when their eyes witness the emaciated political prisoners; when they look about and discover that the totalitarians have destroyed the last vestiges of civilization, the people of the Free World will repeat the question others asked countless times before: 'How could we have allowed this to happen?'"2

Americans should be aware of what to expect were the New World Order conspirators to achieve their avowed goal of world domination. At this point in America's glorious history, the enemies of freedom are on the march. Our government treasonously ships them wheat. soybeans, and other foods on credit! The world's worst deadbeats are given low and no interest loans that nobody expects them to repay! These terrorist-run slave states are supplied with factories, nuclear plants, and industrial equipment! And these same diabolical monsters are being developed into superpowers, with the most advanced American weapons and technology!

If America is occupied by the forces of darkness, America will see a brutal dictatorship forcibly installed. The general population will be methodically terrorized. Women up to 80 and girls down to baby-age will be raped and tortured and killed! Men and boys will be horribly brutalized and maimed and murdered! Innocent babies will be hacked to pieces! All these horrors and more will be undertaken to create a climate of fear in the minds of those who are left.

All told, a substantial percentage of the people are to be immediately and methodically eliminated. Those selected have been predetermined long before the fall of America. Others will be rounded up and taken by trucks and railroad cars to inhuman slave labor camps run by barbaric sadists! Prisoners will die like flies due to beatings, starvation, torture, and filth! Young girls and boys will be prostituted! Life in such camps will be horrendous! Little said can come close to accurately describing such a Hell.

Rebellious segments of the American citizenry will be isolated and deliberately starved to death. United Nations troops will be sent in to "scorch the earth" -- to deliberately destroy or to confiscate all crops. All other food will be confiscated in house to house searches! Wells and other water supplies will be poisoned! Then the community or area will sealed off by the military. This has happened time and time again in such Communist occupied countries as the Ukraine, Cuba, Ethiopia, Hungary, Cambodia, Afghanistan, China, Romania and Nicaragua.

Slumbering Americans must be awakened to the possibility of such a disaster. By such an arousal, the high treason in Washington can and will be forced to a screeching halt! When the treason is stopped and the traitors imprisoned, then hanged, the problem orchestrated by the New World Order conspirators will cease to exist! For as previous chapters clearly show, the enemy is aided, financed, fed, and armed by traitors in the U.S.A!

Slave Labor In A "Workers Paradise"

Communist Occupied Russia's Gulag Archipelago is no secret. This atrocity consists of well over 2,000 known slave labor concentration camps! They're always filled with at least 15 million prisoners and sometimes with as many as 30 million! Better than 40 percent of Soviet industry is totally dependent upon slave labor. It's also no secret that Communist Occupied China runs more that 7,600 slave labor concentration camps! They have an incredible 23 million slaves incarcerated in them! This same inhumane Chinese dictatorship runs the world's largest single concentration camp. Close to 10 million slave-labor prisoners are held in Chinghai, the northeastern province of Tibet. Expect the same in America if the New World Order conspirators have their way!

"These victims—men like you and me—work out the days or years until they are no longer worth famine-rations to their captors," explained the late Robert Welch, a courageous, patriotic American. "As we sit in our warm homes, after a happy meal with our families, and turn on our television sets or radios, it is hard for us to think of a man just like ourselves always half-starved, always half-frozen, haggard and hopeless, remembering the days when he too was free, as he is brutally driven to finish up the literal exhaustion of his body in labor for the benefit of the very tyrant who has enslaved him."3

During the years Stalin ruthlessly ruled Communist Occupied Russia (1924-1953), the average number of slave laborers in the gulag was estimated to be well over 15 million! The annual replacement rate exceededed an astounding 50 percent! Over half the prisoners died of malnutrition, torture, freezing, overwork, and murder.

Nothing has never changed in this regard,. not even when another despicable dictator named Mikhail Sergeyvich Gorbachev, a man portrayed as a kindly more lovable gentleman, was running the show. And all of this is what Americans can expect unless the American people join together and battle the traitors in Washington.

Professor David Dallin tells what happened to a shipment of slave laborers on the way to Siberia: "The Dzhurma . . . sailed from Vladivostok . . . to Ambarchik (over 4,00 miles) carrying . . . about 12,000 prisoners.... the ship reached the Arctic Ocean too late in the season, and was caught in packed ice ... near Wrangel Island.... the Dzhurma, when it finally arrived in Ambarchik . . . did not land a single prisoner. . . . However, what mattered for the government was not the loss of prisoners . . . but the fact that the valuable ship was saved."4

"The Soviet government uses prisons and labor camps to crush . . . those who oppose official ideology and policies," charges Anatoly T. Marchenko. "The Soviet government views this as its sovereign right and a purely internal affair."5

Much slave labor used in Russia, for example, is not Russian by citizenship. For example, Communist Occupied Russia and Nazi Germany jointly invaded Poland in 1939. A million-and-a-half Poles were deported to slave-labor camps in Central Asia and Siberia! The same thing happened when the hungry Russian Bear gobbled up Latvia, Estonia, and Lithuania. Says Michael F. Connors: "Of the approximately three million inhabitants of Lithuania in 1939 . . . fully 500,000 ended up in Siberian slave-labor camps! This was done in pursuance of a policy of systematic depopulation as a prelude to colonization by more 'reliable' Russians."6

Unknown numbers of American servicemen were held in German POW camps at the end of World War II. These men were seized by our Russian "allies" and sent to labor camps within the Soviet Union. None were ever heard from again! Over 3,500,000 German troops were captured by the Soviets and only 1,500,000 returned. Approximately 2,000,000 German civilians were shipped to Communist Occupied Russia. All those who survived the travel hardships ended up in atrocious slave labor camps, deep inside the USSR!

After the ruthless enslavement of South Vietnam was completed, the Soviet Union obtained 500,000 "Siberian volunteers" from Hanoi! According to Doan van Toai, a former Vietcong who defected, the age of these slave laborers ranged from 17 to 35 years. A half-million hapless

Vietnamese were shipped to horrifying Soviet concentration camps, unmatched by any the world has ever known! 7 They were exported to Communist Occupied Russia as partial payment for the trucks, anti-aircraft guns, surface-to-air missiles, and other war goods their Soviet benefactor so willingly supplied during the Vietnam conflict. Inhuman arrangements of this type have been undertaken with every country the USSR has assisted, militarily or otherwise, in a Communist takeover!

Cronid Lubarsky is an astronomer who spent five years in Russian labor camps and prisons. Now residing in the West, he reveals: "Essentially, there is not a significant area of the Soviet economy in which prison labor is not exploited. Metals processing, the chemical industry, the manufacture of clothing and of machinery, agriculture, mining— forced labor is used in all of them."8 David Satter of the Wall Street Journal agrees: "Forced labor is by no means exceptional in the Soviet Union. It is an integral part of the economic system, and it is extremely doubtful whether the current Soviet economy could function without it."9

Former gulag resident Georgy Davydov describes life in a slavelabor camp: "Using Regular Women's Camp UTs-267/10 as an example (in Gornoye in Maritime Kray) . . . There are 2,000 women in a camp designed for 500. Water is brought in from the outside and is therefore in short supply. Baths are rare . . . The laundry has only 20 tubs . . . for 2,000 women! There are only two paramedics (and no physician) in the medical unit . . . the possession of medicine by inmates is prohibited. Fungus infections, dysentery, and jaundice are rife in the camp . . . "[10]

Julia Voznesenskaya was arrested by the KGB in Leningrad and tried for "anti-Soviet slander." She was convicted and quickly sent to a Siberian slave labor camp. Says Joseph Harriss: "Shifts stretched to 12 hours to meet impossibly high production quotas. Those who failed to meet them had their meager food ration cut. With gallows humor, she and her fellow laborers called the thin, half-putrid fish broth served every day 'graveyard soup'—it contained nothing but bones. Prisoners with tiny children often looked on helplessly as the toddlers sickened and died."[11]

One former slave-labor camp inmate tells how some prisoners acted after six months of constant hunger: "You could hardly think about anything except a piece of bread.... I witnessed a few prisoners who cut open a vein in order to dip bread in their blood as a means of satisfying their hunger. I once saw a prisoner who cooked a piece of flesh that he had cut from his own leg."[12]

Terrible implements of torture are commonplace in Soviet slave labor camps. Instruments are always readily available for ripping off the finger and toe nails! There are special bone crushers and testicle smashers! There are sole piercers for the victim's feet! And there are a variety of electrical shockers! Slave labor camp OTs-78/7 is located in Riga, the capital of Latvia. A former prisoner told Avraham Shifrin:

"Worst of all was RGB Captain Elmar Zaul, head of the operations section at the camp. A real Gestapo type . . . In his office he had rubber hoses, boxing gloves and even handcuffs attached to electrical wiring. . . Zaul thus often beat the prisoners himself; it was not unusual to hear the cries of his victims from his office."[13]

Typical Atrocities Committed by the Communists

Joseph Stalin alone was responsible for the massacre of at least 17 million persons between 1929 and 1939. Roughly 15 million people— more than the combined populations of over a dozen States including Idaho, Rhode Island, Alaska, Delaware, and Vermont—were deliberately starved to death in Ukraine. This ungodly deed transpired between 1932-1933 under the direction of Stalin's reprehensible, neanderthal henchman, Nikita S. Khrushchev.[14] When resistance to the planned famine developed, the Communists deliberately infected the women of entire villages with venereal diseases! Medical treatment was denied unless these women informed on everyone who was involved in the anti-Russian movement.

Terror has always been a major element in the Communist psyche. Lenin was obsessed with the use of terror. He spoke of it often, saying such things as "terror must be encouraged," and "we can achieve nothing unless we use terror." Moscow still honors Felix Dzerzhinsky, the dreaded chief of the old secret police and master terrorist. Terror was a daily event when Communist Occupied Russia invaded Estonia, Latvia, and Lithuania. People suspected of being anti-Russian were severely punished! Nicolai Tolstoy tells how they were "tied to trees, and there the guards experimented with various methods of prolonging death. Some had their eyes slowly gouged out. Others were scalped and had their brains squeezed out of their skulls. Men had their tongues torn out, their sides and legs slowly cut open, or had bayonets slowly thrust into their mouths down their throats."[15]

Where else other than under Communist sanctioned terrorism has the world witnessed the consistent gang rape and torture of nuns?; the brutalization and mutilation of Christian missionaries?; the burning of churches, with the entire congregation locked inside?; the use of the Red Cross insignia on hospital roofs, for bombing and strafing practice?

Who other than the diabolical Communist military are ordered to butcher prisoners, after wiring their hands behind their backs?; to decapitate political leaders, impale their heads on wooden posts, and place the posts on all roads coming into a village?; to laughingly massacre mothers and their children with flame throwers?; to bury people alive in ant hills?

What kind of demonic mentality enjoys tying defenseless women to stakes and inserting burning coals into the vagina?; obtains gratification from slowly skinning people alive?; delights in disemboweling pregnant women and bayoneting unborn babies?; relishes cutting the nose and ears off prisoners and then forcing the person or family members to eat them?

Communist bestiality knows no limitations! Communist ruthlessness has no conscience! Communist action precludes no morality! Here is a perfect example of how a typical Communist leader blandly views murder, deceit, and immorality. William C. Bullitt was the American Ambassador to the Soviet Union in 1934. He was seated at dinner one evening between Marshal Budenny and General Kliment Voroshilov. Referring to Budenny, Voroshilov turned to Bullitt and said: "I think the most extraordinary thing we ever did together was to capture Kiev without fighting . . . there were 11,000 Czarist officers with their wives and children in Kiev and they had more troops than we had . . . we told them that they would be released and allowed to go to their homes with their families and treated as well as possible by our army, and they believed us and surrendered."

"What did you do then?" Bullitt asked.

"Oh," responded Voroshilov, "we shot all the men and boys and we put all the women and the girls into brothels for our army."

"Do you think that was a very decent thing to do?" Bullitt queried in astonishment. "My army needed women," said Voroshilov matter of factly, "and I was concerned by my army's health and not with the health of those women; and it didn't make any difference anyhow, because they were all dead within three months.[16]

Immediately following the takeover of China in 1949—with the assistance of traitors in the U.S. government—Mao Tse-tung and his Communist thugs orchestrated a massive orgy of death and destruction. Approximately 64 million unarmed Chinese civilians were methodically slaughtered! Time reported: "These are figures that stagger the imagination. In no previous war, revolution or human holocaust . . . have so many people been destroyed in so short a period."[17]

Professor Richard L. Walker, foremost China scholar, explains how Moscow-trained Mao and his vengeful comrades handled things after gaining power: "Many of the executions took place after mass public trials in which the assembled crowds, whipped up to a frenzy by planted agitators, called invariably for the death penalty and for no mercy for the accused . . . Mao and colleagues made no effort to conceal the violent course being followed. On the contrary, the most gruesome and detailed accounts were printed in the Communist press and broadcast over the official radio for the purpose of amplifying the condition of mass terror the trials were clearly intended to induce."[18]

Mao's highly touted Great Leap Forward (1958-1960) was directly responsible for an incredible 27 million more murders! Amnesty International cites recent evidence of a continuing policy of "mass executions." Comrade Wang-Jingrong matter-of-factly brushes it all off: "We have a population of 1 billion and those executed only comprise a small number comparatively!"[19]

Missionary Raymond J. DeJaegher tells of a typical atrocity committed by Communist Chinese gangsters in Ping Shan. Those who participated thoroughly enjoyed their sadistic task: "The son was held . . . and forced to watch the awful process and listen to his father's screams of agony . . . The Reds poured vinegar and acids over the man's body so that the skin would come off quickly and make the job a quick and easy one . . . He began at the back, peeling from the shoulders down in long strips. The man was skinned entirely, except for his head. He died within a few minutes after the peeler had completed his gruesome task."[20]

DeJaegher recalls how Communist Chinese soldiers brought 13 young prisoners to a school playground. The teachers and their students were called outside to observe. The tightly bound men were forced to kneel while false accusations were made! The school children were told to sing patriotic songs. All 13 captives were quickly decapitated. "Several . . . among the group rushed forward now and pushed the corpses over on their backs . . . each soldier bent down with a sharp knife and made a quick, circular incision in the chest. He then jumped on the abdomen with both feet, or pumped on it over and over with one foot, forcing the heart out of the incision. Then he swooped down again, snipped and plucked it out. When they had collected the thirteen hearts, they strung them all on a pointed marsh reed . . . which they tied together to make a . . . carrying device."[21]

The Red Chinese were totally ruthless in dealing with unwanted segments of their society. Reverend Shih-ping Wang reveals one aspect of the horror: "All the elderly people 60 years of age and above who cannot work are put in the old people's 'Happy Home!' . . . they are given shots. They are told these shots are for their health. But after the shots are taken they die within two weeks. After they die, the corpses are placed in vats. When the bodies decay and maggots set in, the maggots are used to feed the chickens! The remainder of the body is used for fertilizer!"[22]

The Romanian police state's hatred for Christians is unmatched in its intensity! Reverend Richard Wurmbrand was a prisoner in Communist Occupied Romania for 14 years. He tells how a group of priests were "tied to crosses for four days and nights. The crosses were put on the floor and hundreds of prisoners had to fulfill their bodily necessities over the faces and bodies of the crucified ones. Then the crosses were erected again and the Communists jeered and mocked: 'Look at your Christ!How beautiful he is! What fragrance he brings from heaven!' " One priest almost lost his mind while undergoing such blasphemous punishment. As an added indignity reveals Wurmbrand, the priest's Romanian guards forced him "to consecrate human excrement and urine and give Holy Communion to Christians in this form!"[23]

Wurmbrand was put through living hell. He describes his horrifying "refrigerator cell" experience: "I was thrown into one with very little clothing on. Prison doctors would watch through an opening until they saw the symptoms of freezing to death, then would give a warning and the guards would rush in to take us out and make us warm. When we were finally warmed, we would immediately be put back in the ice-box cells to freeze—over and over again! Thawing out, then freezing to within just one minute or two of death, then being thawed out again. It continued endlessly. Even today sometimes I can't bear to open a refrigerator."[24]

Dr. Fernando Penabaz was a prominent Havana attorney when the Castro terrorists took control of Cuba. Two men he knew were placed in a small sealed cell. Penabaz explains: " . . . they felt that their feet were sinking into something soft. The impression is that you're sinking in dust . . . almost immediately, you hear a whirring sound . . . of high-powered fans. What you have sunk into is not dust; it is ground glass. . . The glass . . . begins to permeate . . . your nose . . . your ears . . . your mouth. You try desperately to breathe, and then you begin to hemorrhage —blood from the ears, blood from the nose, blood from the throat."[25]

The Communists were handed control of North Korea by traitors in the United States Government. Kyung Rai Kim, a religious editor in Seoul, told of these atrocities: "An evangelist . . . was killed by the Communists . . . The Red police stripped him naked, bound him, and put him in an empty water pool. It was 17 degrees below zero that day. They filled the pool solid. My friend froze to death in 30 minutes.... A lady evangelist . . . was tied between two horses. Then the horses were sent running in different directions . . . 250 pastors were killed by the Communists on the same day in the same place . . . The Red police made holes through the pastors' hands with an ax and bound them with wire rope, and then they shot them . . . at Wong Dang church, Red soldiers burned 83 Christians to death with gasoline." [26]

According to General Mark W. Clark, more than 5,000 young American POWs—arms tied harshly behind with wire—were murdered with a bullet in back of the head. This was done on direct orders from China's Mao! Many others were dumped into huge pits and buried alive![27] A former POW described how the Korean Communists treated 800 helpless wounded American prisoners: " . . . they bayoneted them! The wounded were screaming. They couldn't do anything."[28] Said Deputy Secretary of Defense Roger M.

Kyes: "The prisoners were shot down in cold blood, were burned alive in prison buildings, were beaten to death..."[29]

Sergeant Glen J. Oliver explains what happened to American boys in Prison Camp Five: "Men in poor condition were placed outdoors with little or no clothing and eaten by flies and worms. I saw at least 15 men given injections of an unknown type of fluid and they would die within five minutes."[30] General Mark W. Clark, Commander of the UN military in Korea revealed: "There was evidence that the Communists used POWs as human guinea pigs for medical experiments . . . chicken livers and other parts of animals were implanted beneath the skin of sick prisoners as experiments in healing techniques."[31]

It was reported in 1954: "American prisoners of war who were not deliberately murdered at the time of capture, or shortly after capture, were beaten, wounded, starved, and tortured . . . Some torture methods included "perforating the flesh of prisoners with heated bamboo spears, burning prisoners with cigarettes and inserting a can opener into a prisoners open wound."[32]

Sergeant Wendell Treffrey told of weak, fly and maggot covered POWs, who were denied medical attention. The Senate Report said: "Sergeant Treffrey experienced treatment from his Communist captors equally as horrible. His toes, which were rotting, having been frozen when his combat boots were confiscated, were amputated with a pair of garden shears by a Chinese nurse without benefit of anesthesia. Later, in order to avoid being sent to a hospital where many of the seriously wounded were sent to die, he broke off the remaining two toes with his fingernails."[33]

Psychological warfare expert Edward Hunter reveals torture methods used on American POWs by the Korean Reds: " . . . In 'flying an airplane,' the victim is hoisted by the thumbs, then doused with cold water to revive him whenever he passes out. In the 'diamond-mine treatment, 'he is forced to crawl back and forth on a plank covered with bits of broken glass. Sometimes he is roped and rolled back and forth over a plank studded with sharp nails. Innumerable variations of the 'ice bath' were used in Korea. In one version, the POW was stripped from waist down and put outside in subzero weather with his feet in a basin that soon froze."[34]

The Communists operate identically in every country they subjugate. Vietnam was no different than Korea. When the Communist North Koreans invaded South Korea, they simply annihilated their opposition. Robert Leckie reports: "At Sachon the North Koreans burned the jail and 280 South Korean police, government officials and landowners who were inside it! At Anui, at Mokpo, at Kongju, and at Hamyang and Chonju, United Nations soldiers uncovered trenches stuffed with the bodies of hundreds of executed civilians, many of them women and children! Near Taejon airstrip 500 ROK soldiers lay with their hands bound behind their backs and bullet holes in their brains!"[35]

The USS Pueblo was captured by Communist Occupied North Korea on January 23, 1968. Commander Lloyd Bucher tells of an incident he witnessed while a prisoner of the bestial Reds: "A South Korean was . . . strapped to the wall . . . he was a South Korean spy. He was alive, but had been through a terrible ordeal. He had a compound fracture of the upper right arm. The bone was sticking out. He was stripped to the waist. He had completely bitten through his lower lip, and his lower lip was hanging down from the side of his mouth. His right eye had been put out. His head was hanging down. There was a lot of . . . black matter which had run out of his eye and down his right cheek . . . "[36]

Robert E. Lee reveals: "In 1946, after Ho chi Minh established his troops in Hanoi, there were two indigenous Vietnamese sects in the area which, because they were also fervently anti-Communist, represented a future potential threat to Ho's plans. So he decided to have them exterminated. Since routine murder would have fallen short of the desired impact on others, he resorted instead to burying members of the two sects alive in fields, so that only their heads were above the ground, then having harrows driven back and forth across the fields, as one report later described it, to 'scratch and tear and chop those living heads like so many small tree stumps as the harrows went over them."[37]

Tom Dooley was an American missionary who witnessed extensive Communist brutality. In one instance, North Vietnamese soldiers visited a school. The teacher and seven students were dragged outside and bound. " . . . the Viet Minh accused these children of treason . . . As a punishment they were to be deprived of their hearing . . . two Viet Minh guards went to each child and . . . rammed a wooden chopstick into each ear . . . The stick split the ear canal wide and tore the ear drum. The shrieking of the children was heard all over the village . . . Since their hands were tied behind them, they could not pull the wood out of their ears. They shook their heads and squirmed about, trying to make the sticks fall out. Finally they were able to dislodge them by scraping their heads against the ground.

"As for the teacher . . . One soldier held his head while another grasped the victim's tongue with a crude pair of pliers and pulled it far out. A third guard cut off the top of the teacher's tongue with his bayonet. Blood spurted into the man's mouth and gushed from his nostrils . . . When the soldiers let him loose he fell to the ground vomiting blood."[38]

Priests are commonly selected for special treatment by the Communists. Many of the most hideous atrocities are reserved for "treason"—teaching about Jesus and God. Dr. Dooley reports: . . . there was an old man lying on straw on the floor. His head was matted with pus and there were eight large pus-filled swellings around his temple and fore-head . . . Eight nails had been driven into his head, three across the fore-head, two in the back of the skull and three across the dome.... When the unbelievable act was completed, the priest . . . walked from his church to a neighboring hut, where a family jerked the nails from his head."[39]

"I well remember a little twelve-year old girl the Communists had dragged off a bus," offered Sergeant Alan L. Davidson in 1968. "They had pulled her around to the side where all the passengers could look on in horror as one V.C.

held her arm and another chopped it off with a machete . . . I remember wondering what the will to resist would be like in(say) California if in but one year, more than two thousand Mayors and City Councilmen were shot, beheaded, or eviscerated in the main street of their communities and left with their blood to pool in the gutter. Precisely that happened in Vietnam . . . the Vietcong has systematically butchered some fifteen thousand local officials. The Communists have no regard for that life if its elimination will further the aims of the International Conspiracy in the slightest way."[40]

John Dryden was a Green Beret in Vietnam. He tells of the horror he witnessed upon returning to a village after the Communists had come and gone: "When I arrived at the outpost, it was impossible not to see my friends. Their bodies were on one side of the highway, laid out as if for inspection, their heads on the other side. It was all militarily neat and orderly. Their wives and children, as befitting mere civilians, were not in ranks. They lay where they had been shot or bayoneted—haphazardly. Every single living thing in that community was dead—water buffalo, pigs, and dogs!"[41]

West Point graduate Lieutenant Colonel Paul G. Erickson tells this horror story: "Before I left Saigon, I visited a government photo lab. There they had more than 600,000 photographs of Communist atrocities against the Vietnamese people. I saw pictures of the charred bodies at Dak Son, where the Vietcong had turned flame throwers on several hundred defenseless men, women, and children! . . . Many were of mutilated priests and nuns and hamlet chiefs, since the village leaders were always a major target of the Communists. There were thousands of photographs of men who had been disemboweled, their eyeballs popped out, and their throats cut in front of the entire populace! Nuns had been raped repeatedly by the Communists, and then Christian villagers were forced at gunpoint to participate before the Sisters were murdered!"[42]

Identified Soviet spy Henry Kissinger,[43] as Nixon's subversive Secretary of State, assured Americans that there'd be no bloodbath in South Vietnam! So did Tom Wicker of the New York Times and numerous other wild-eyed leftists! Mary McGrory, for example, had the unmitigated gall to declare: "The new leaders of South Vietnam are far too busy to draw a bloodbath . . . They are behaving more like missionaries than conquerors."[44]

Syndicated columnist Paul Scott reports on the fall of Saigon in the Spring of 1975: "The most vicious bloodbath in modern history is now going on in South Vietnam . . . the total number of persons killed or executed outright since the Communists started their takeover . . . has soared to more than . . . 250,000 . . . In one instance, more than 400 helpless orphans and at least five nuns . . . were put to death at the Sacred Heart Catholic Orphanage in DaNang and at an orphanage in China Beach . . . Aerial photographs taken of the China Beach area in early April showed more than 30,000 bodies of South Vietnamese executed by the Communists. The region appears to be one of the main execution sites."[45]

John Hubbell gives one horrifying example of an atrocity committed by the North Vietnamese Reds. This tragic episode transpired in a small hamlet near Da Nang: "All were herded before the home of their chief. While they and the chief's pregnant wife and four children were forced to look on, the chief's tongue was cut out. Then his genital organs were sliced off and sewn inside his bloody mouth. As he died, the V.C. went to work on his wife, slashing open her womb. Then, the nine year old son: a bamboo lance was rammed through one ear and out the other. Two more of the chief's children were murdered the same way. The V.C. did not harm the five year old daughter—not physically; they left her crying holding her dead mother's arm."[46]

Yes, this is the same place the New York Times headlined: "INDOCHINA WITHOUT AMERICANS/FOR MOST A BETTER LIFE."[47]

The North Vietnamese did a variety of ghastly things to their captives, while consolidating their control of South Vietnam. Blood extraction was a favorite! Castro carried out an identical program in Communist Occupied Cuba called

"Operation Blood Plasma." Blood was extracted from Cuban prisoners and then sold to help finance his Communist dictatorship! Dr. Russell Kirk explains what happened to many South Vietnamese captives: "Officials, military officers and other opponents of the Communists were sent to hospitals—but not for the pretended 're-education' that Radio Hanoi and Radio Saigon propagandized about. In those Saigon hospitals . . . the captives 'give' blood . . . thus atoning for their former ways . . . But they are bled excessively; in a few days they are bled to death deliberately."[48]

These are the murderous fiends so glorified by Jane Fonda. She enthusiastically called them "the conscience of the world!" This traitor spoke of the ungodly Vietcong barbarians as being "driven by the same spirit that drove Washington and Jefferson!" So enthralled was Fonda with the atheistic mass-exterminators that she jubilantly told her youthful listeners: "I would think that if you understood what Communism was you would hope, you would pray on your knees that we would someday become Communist!"[49]

The people responsible for the fall of Cambodia in April 1975 have much for which to answer. The demonic murder spree carried out by the Khmer Rouge even surpassed that which took place in Vietnam. Over 1.2 million Cambodians were slaughtered in the first nine months! In early 1976, orders went out to execute anyone with a seventh-grade education or above! A "blood debt" was to be settled by murdering all military and civilian government workers and their families! Jean Lacouture wrote: "What Oriental despots or medieval inquisitors ever boasted of having eliminated in a single year, one-quarter of their own population?"[50]

The Khmer Rouge inflicted unbelievable atrocities on the Cambodian people! Entire families—men women and children—had to be "purified" by the Communists, because the father had worked for the enemy: "With military orderliness, the Communists thrust each official forward one at a time and forced him to kneel between two soldiers armed with bayonet-tipped AK-47 rifles. The soldiers then stabbed the victim simultaneously, one through the chest and the other through the back. Family by family, the Communists pressed the slaughter, moving methodically down the line. As each man lay dying, his anguished, horror-stricken wife and children were dragged up to his body. The women, forced to kneel, also received the simultaneous bayonet thrusts. The children and babies, last to die, were stabbed where they stood.

"Saray Savath tried to escape. He was caught and given a first-degree execution. That meant he was to die slowly . . . First the Red Khmers cut off his nose and ears; then they cut a deep gash into his arm. Thus, as he was bleeding to death, his arms were tied behind his back and attached to a tree. The rope was long, so the colonel could dance around the tree with pain . . . For two days and two nights the colonel called for help . . . nobody was allowed to go near him. On the third day he died."[51]

Robert G. Mugabe is the blood-thirsty Red fanatic who runs the police state called Zimbabwe (Communist Occupied Rhodesia). Terrible atrocities were committed daily by Mugabe terrorists. The London Times reported: "Another case of brutality by guerrillas operating in Rhodesia's north-eastern border area . . . A tribesman . . . had his ears cut off and

was forced to eat them. Then most of his toes and fingers were hacked off . . . Last December a tribesman has his nose, ears, lips and chin hacked off and his wife was forced to eat them."[52]

Russian-backed terrorists pulled a violent, blood-drenched coup in Afghanistan, April 1978. The Soviets soon after invaded the country and occupied it with 120,000 soldiers. Felix Ermacora of Austria wrote of the Communist atrocities in a report to the United Nations: "A former officer of the security police . . . listed the following . . . types of torture: giving electric shock, generally to the genitals in men and the breasts of women; tearing out nails . . .; sticking pieces of wood in the men's anus . . .; pressing on the prisoners' throats to force them to open their mouth while the guards urinate into them; . . . raping women, tying their hands and feet and introducing a variety of objects into the vagina."[53]

Former Russian Army Sergeant Igor Rykov explained how the Soviets treated their POWs in Afghanistan: "As soon as we caught them, the officers ordered us to slaughter them!" Rykov's commander, Lieutenant Gevorkian, felt his men had to be taught to kill without flinching! According to Rykov: "One day he brought in a boy, an Afghan kid about 14 years old. There was one soldier in our unit, Oleg Sotnik, who could not stand the sight of blood. Then Gevorkian took out a sort of bayonet . . . He gave this knife to Sotnik and told him to kill the boy. Sotnik's face was unbelievable. He was planted to the ground, shaking all over his body. The boy was sitting peacefully on the ground. Finally Sotnik got control of himself, went up to the boy, and stuck the knife in his chest. The boy started to shriek, and he grabbed onto Sotnik's hands. Then Gevorkian started yelling. 'You idiot! What do you think you're doing? Watch how it should be done!' He pulled out the knife, kicked the boy in the face, and when the boy fell backwards, he stuck the knife in his throat, once, twice."[54]

Helsinki Watch tells of the plight of Afghanistan children. The Soviets bomb them "in their schools and during religious instruction in the mosques. They are burned alive in locked rooms, their charred bodies unrecognizable to their grieving parents. Village children are shot while fleeing to caves in the mountains or enroute to refuge in Pakistan or Iran . . . unborn children are bayoneted in their mother's wombs."[55]

The above accounts of Communist barbarianism, brutality, inhumanity, and wanton slaughter are not isolated by any stretch of the imagination! Such demonic activity is the rule rather than the exception in Communist occupied areas of the world. In unconscionable acts of immorality, American leaders turn their heads and ignore the truth. They pretend these atheistic tyrants are worthy friends. America builds them factories! America arms their military!

America feeds their masses. Yes, the fact remains that many of our leaders are, and have been in the past, conscious, willing traitors, men who commit treason a regular basis. They deliberately take action designed to strengthen the governments of our enemies and to weaken the government of America. They devote their treasonous energies toward destroying our Republic and installing a socialist New World Order dictatorship on our shores.—a tyranny to be policed by United Nations "peacekeepers." As the heroic American patriot, Robert Welch, rightly said: "May God forgive us."

References

Preface

1. Somoza, *Nicaragua Betrayed*, 1980.
2. McKinney, Nicaragua: A New Captive Nation, *The New American*, July 14,1986, p. 21.
3. Capell, *Henry Kissinger: Soviet Agent* 1974.
4. Speech, Lehman, Annapolis graduating class, May 25, 1983.
5. Duplantier, Sanctimonious Sanctions, *The New American*. February 3, 1966, p. 18.
6. Gatsis, Planning for Defeat, *The New American*, August 11, 1986, p. 27.
7. Sutton, *The Best Enemy Money Can Buy*, 1986.
8. Irvine, Time to Encourage Accuracy in Academia. *Conservative Digest*, July 1986, p. 78.
9. *United States Constitution, Article III, Section 3.*

Part 1—Massive Doses of Treason

Chapter 1: Arming America's Communist Enemies

1. Hoar, ·The Soviets are Preparing for War, *American Opinion*, November 1978, p. 21.
2. Wood, The Betrayed: Our Men in Uniform want to Win in Vietnam, *American Opinion*, January 1969, p. 8.
3. Allen, *The Great Pretense*, 1969, p. 2.
4. Sennholz, More Vietnam, *American Opinion*, June 1967, p. 101.
5. Hospers, ·Bullets, *Conservative Digest*, June 1987, p. 118.
6. Stang, ·Red Traders: Aid and Comfort to the Enemy, *American Opinion*, January 1972, p.2.
7. Ibid.

8. Sutton, *National Suicide: Military Aid to the Soviet Union,* 1973, p. 13.
9. Ibid.
10. Drummey, The Captive Nations,. *The New American,* July 14,1986, p. 30.
11. Ibid.
12. East-West Trade, Report of the Senate Permanent Sub-Committee on Investigations of the Committee on Government Operations, July 1956, p. 46.
13. Speech, Tito, State visit to Communist Occupied Russia, June 7, 1956.
14. Presidential Determination, No. 81-11, July 8, 1981. Presidential Determination, No. 83-1, October 1, 1982.
15. Report, Proposed Shipment of Ball Bearing Machines to USSR, Senate Internal Security Sub-Committee, February 28, 1961.
16. *New York Times,* March 9, 1971.
17. Capell, *Henry Kissinger: Soviet Agent,* 1974.
18. Joiner, The USSR was made in the USA, *The New American,* July 14, 1986, p.37.
19. Hoar, After Helsinki, *American Opinion,* Mary 1977, p. 89.
20. Hoar, Soviet Military, *American Opinion,* November 1981, p. 85.
21. Huck, The Ford Foreign Policy, *American Opinion,* October 1976, p. 9.
22. Drummey, Stop Helping Communism, *The New American,* December 5, 1988, p. 25.
23. Hoar, After Helsinki, *American Opinion,* March 1977, p. 87.
24. Stang, Red Traders: Aid and Comfort to the Enemy,' *American Opinion,*
    January 1972, p. 17.
25. Lee, How America is being Taken in Trade, Conservative Digest, June 1986, p. 58.

26. Allen, 'The Looters: How Our Economy is being Destroyed, *American Opinion,* May 1974, p. 73.
27. AFL-CIO Executive Council, August 8, 1978.
28. Stang, Red Traders: Aid and Comfort to The Enemy, *American Opinion,* January 1972, p. 19.
29. Mr. Candidate, The *New American,* December 21, 1987, p. 5.
30. Hoar, Soviet Military, *American Opinion,* November 1981, P. 86.
31. Briefly Stated, *The New American,* April 7, 1986, p. 4.
32. Time, July 16, 1973.
33. Speech, Hoover, Daughters of the American Revolution, April 22, 1954.
34. 1980 Republican Party Platform.
35. Jasper, Ronald Reagan: Should This Man be so Popular?, *The New American,* July 28, 1986, p. 32.
36. Sutton, *National Suicide: Military Aid to the Soviet Union,* 1973.
37. Hoar, Soviet Military, *American Opinion,* November 1981, P. 18.
38. Hoar, ·The Right Answers, *Conservative Digest,* April 1987, p. 124.
39. Teller, They Paused to Remark, *American Opinion,* September 1983, p. 42.
40. Schlafly and Ward, *Kissinger on the Couch,* 1975, p. 378.
41. Interview, Reagan, 1980 Presidential campaign, *Los Angeles Times.*
42. Ibid.
43. They Paused to Remark, *American Opinion.* February 1964, p. 12.
44. *Knoxville News Sentinel,* January 27, 1988.
45. Speech, Deng Xiaoping (Teng Hsiao-ping), July 1977.

46. Kidwell, ·Goldwater Blasts White House Red China Policy,. *The New American,* April 21, 1986, p. 12.
47. Gerstenzang, China's Military Tries to March Out of the Dark Ages—with US Help, Los Angeles Times, November 27, 1986, p. 29.
48. US to Arm China, *Insight* December 2, 1985.
49. Reagan, *Presidential Order,* June 12,1984.
50. Perloff, ·Free China under Attack *The New American,* October 13, 1986, pp. 24, 25.
51. Joiner, ·Aid and Trade—Stop Financing Communism, *The JBS Bulletin,* November 1986, p. 25.
52. Perloff, ·Free China Under Attack, *The New American,* October 13, 1986, p. 25.
53. Interview, Reagan, Red Chinese journalists, April 17, 1984.
54. Drummey, The Captive Nations, *The New American,* July 14, 1986, p. 32.
55. Kidwell, Reagan and the Red Dragon, *The New American,* June 16, 1986, pp. 9-10.
56. Genstenzang, ·China's Military tries to march our of the Dark Ages—with U.S. Help. *Los Angeles Times,* November 27, 1986, p. 29.
57. Hoar, The Right Answers, *Conservative Digest,* June, 1987, p. 124.
58. Reagan Administration announcement to Congress, April 8, 1986.
59. Genstenzang, China's Military tries to march out of the Dark Ages—with U.S. Help, *Los Angeles Times,* November27, 1986.
60. Pierre, Pending Legislation, *The JBS Bulletin,* May 1986, p. 27.
61. Kidwell, Reagan and the Red Dragon, *The New American,* June 16, 1986, p. 8.
62. Joiner, Pending Legislation, *The JBS Bulletin,* July 1986, p. 20.

63. *Knoxville News Sentinel,* January 27, 1988.
64. Speech, Reagan, during Goldwater Presidential campaign, 1964.
65. Editorial, *Barron's,* January 16, 1967.

Chapter 2: Treason and Big Business

1. *AIM Report,* December 1987.
2. Ibid.
3. Joiner, 'The U.S.S.R. was Made In the U S A, *The New American,* July 14, 1986, p. 37.
4. Abraham, If this is Moscow, Why Ain't I Dead? *Conservative Digest,* March 1987, p. 73.
5. *Human Events,* July 22, 1967.
6. Drummey, The Captive Nations, *The New American,* July 14, 1986, p. 29.
7. Ibid.
8. Ibid
9. Ibid
10 Ibid
11. Allen, Calling it Conspiracy—Part II, *American Opinion,* April 1983, p. 106.
12. Stang, Red Traders Aid and Comfort to the Enemy, *American Opinion*, January 1972, p. 8.
13. Ibid.
14. Ibid, p. 9
15. Ibid, pp. 9,11
16. Allen, Mr. Nixon The Candidate versus *the* President, *American Opinion,* April 1972, p. 30.
17. *Ford Engineering,* May 1967.
18. Ibid
19. Ward, Western Europe, *American Opinion,* July-August 1983, p. 121.
20. Error

21 Allen, 'The Looters: How our Economy is being Destroyed, *American Opinion,* May 1974. p. 63.
22. *Business Week,* December 8, 1973
23. Ashbrook, *Congressional Record*
24. Abraham, If this is Moscow, Why ain't I Dead? *Conservative Digest,* March 1987, p. 73.
25. *US. News & World Report,* December 18, 1978.
26. McDonald, ·A Talk with Major General George Keegan on Defense, *American Opinion,* September 1977, p. 77.
27. *Time,* July 16, 1976.
28. Sutton, *National Suicide: Military Aid to the Soviet Union,* 1973, pp. 207-208.
29. Rees, Following the Presidential Scenario, *American Opinion,* October 1979, p. 87.
30. *Time,* July 16, 1973.
31. Allen, 'The Red Traders Aid and Comfort to the Enemy, *American Opinion,* April 1984, p. 108.
32. *United Press Intentional,* September 18,1973.
33. Allen, 'The Looters: How Our Economy is being Destroyed, *American Opinion,* May 1974, p. 59.
34. Pierre, Funding Communism is treason, *The JBS Bulletin* March 1986, p.3.
35. Allen, 'The Looters How Our Economy is being Destroyed,' *American Opinion,* May 1974, p. 69.
36. Drummey, George P. Shultz Continuing the Policies of Appeasement,. *The New American,* May 19,1986, p.32.
37. *American Opinion,* November 1982, p. 20.
38. *The Review of the News,* June 24, 1981, p. 12.
39. Pierre, Funding Communism is Treason,' *The JBS Bulletin,* March 1986, p. 3.
40. Bullets,' *American Opinion,* October 1974, p. 31.

41. 'Verity in Veritas' *The New American,* December, 21,1987, p. 39.
42. Ibid
43. Hoar, The Continuing Machinations of the Trilateral Commission, *American Opinion,* February 1984, p. 49.
44. Private Boycotts vs. The National Interest, *Document 8117, U.S. Department of State,* August 1966.
45. Allen, The Looters - How Our Economy is being Destroyed, *American Opinion,* May 1974, *p. 69.*
46. Ibid
47. Ibid, p 71.
48. *Christ Und Welt,* 1956.
49. Hoar, After Helsinki, *American Opinion,* March 1977, p. 91.
50. *New York Times,* January25, 1977.
51. Ward, Jeane J. Kirkpatrick—America's Ambassador, *Conservative Digest,* January
    1986, p. 52.
52. Allen, 'The Looters - How Our Economy is being Destroyed, *American Opinion,*
    May 1974, p. 71.
53. *Ibid.*
54. Ibid
55. Pierre, Ex-Im Bank Pays for Angola's War,' *The New American,* June 30,1986, p. 14.
56. Angola, *The Review of the News,* September 23,1981, p. 75.
57. Ibid
58. Kidwell, *The New American,* July 14, 1986, p. 9.
59. Duplantier, Sanctimonious Sanctions,' *The New American,* February 3,1986, p. 18.
60. Hoar, 'Captive Europe, *American Opinion,* July-August 1983, *p. 122.*
61. Evans, 'Delibris,' *American Opinion,* May 1984, p. 65.

62. Joiner, 'The U.S.S.R. was Made in the U S A,' *The New American,* July 14, 1986, p. 37.
63. Capell, *Henry Kissinger: Soviet Agent,* 1974.
64. Allen, The Looters: How Our Economy is being Destroyed, *American Opinion,* May 1974, p. 71.
65. DuBerrier, The World,' *American Opinion,* July-August 1974, p. 113.
66. Allen, ·The Looters - How Our Economy is being Destroyed, *American Opinion,* May 1974, p. 75.
67. *Los Angeles Times,* May 20, 1973.
68. Allen, The Looters - How Our Economy is being Destroyed, *American Opinion,* May 1974, p. 73.
69 Joiner, Aid and Trade—Stop Financing Communism, *The JBS Bulletin,* May 1986, p. 13.
70. Copper, ·How Communist China Floods our Markets, *Conservative Digest,* September 1986, p. 94.
71. McManus, Red China Myths, *The New American,* August 25, 1986, p. 47.
72. Pierre, Who Sold Out to Red China? *The New American,* June 2, 1986, p. 49.
73. Drummey, Stop Helping Communism, *The New American,* January 16,1989, p. 28.
74. Pierre, Who Sold Out to Red China *The New American,* June 2, 1986, p. 49.
75. *USA Today* March 11, 1988.
76. Kidwell, Goldwater Blasts White House Red China Policy,. *The New American,* April 21, 1986, p. 12.

Chapter 3: Financial Assistance for the Reds

1. *The New American,* January 8,1988,p 15
2. Delinquent International Debt Owed to the United States. *United States House of Representatives,* 1974

3. Drummey, The Council on Foreign Relations, *The New American,* April 7,1986, p 8
4. Allen, ·Insiders *of* the *Great Conspiracy, American Opinion,* September 1982, p 42
5. Allen, Think Tanks: Where the Revolution is being Planned, *American Opinion,* March 1971, p 5
6. Allen, Insiders of the Great Conspiracy, *American Opinion,* September 1982, p 42
7. Senator Jesse Helms(R-NC), *The New American,* January16, 1989,p 29.
8. McManus, CFR Media Clout, *The New American,* January 16, 1989, p 17.
9. Stang, Its Time to Expose the Conspiracy, *American Opinion,* December 1980, p 76.
10. Allen, The Looters: How Our Economy is being Destroyed, *American Opinion,*
 May 1974, p. 59.
11. Ibid.
12. Kidwell, U.S. and Allies Finance Soviet Empire, *The New American,* May19, 1986,p. 13.
13. Editorial, Nowak, *Washington Post,* 1986.
14. Kerrison, Crazy Ways We give help to our Enemies, New *York Post,* September 22, 1986.
15. Hoar, Soviet Military, *American Opinion,* November 1981, p. 77.
16. Buchanan, Let's Freeze the Debt Bomb, *Conservative Digest,* October 1985, p. 107.
17. Lipscomb, *Congressional Record,* September 2, 1965.
18. Ibid.
19. Speech, Tito, June 11, 1956.
20. Evans, *The Politics of Surrender.* 1966, p. 164.
21. Lipscomb, *Congressional Record,* September2, 1965.
22. Lee, The Big Banking Giveaway, *American Opinion,* May 1984, p. 81.

23. *The Indianapolis News,* January 8, 1966.
24. Benoit, Captive Nations Week, *The JBS Bulletin,* April 1986, p. 16.
25. Dispatch, *Mobile Register,* August 17, 1978.
26. Down a Rathole, *Barron's,* September 25,1978.
27. Lee, The Big Banking Giveaway, *American Opinion,* May 1984, p. 81.
28. Pierre, Ex-Im Bank Pays for Angola's War, *The New American,* June 30,1986, p. 14.
29. Angola, *The Review of the News,* September 25, 1981, p. 75.
30. Drummey, The Council on Foreign Relations, *The New American,* April 7, 1986, p. 9.
31. Buchanan, Let's Freeze the Debt Bomb, *Conservative Digest,* October 1985, p. 108.
32. Lee, The Big Banking Giveaway, *American* Opinion, May 1984, p. 81.
33. Drummey, The Captive Nations, *The New American, July* 14, 1986, p. 34.
34. Drummey, The Council on Foreign Relations, *The New American,* April 7,1986, p. 9.
35. McAlvany, ·Revolution and Betrayal, *The New American,* August 11, 1986, p. 3.
36. Roth, letter to fellow House members, March 1986.
37. Lee, 'The Big Banking Giveaway, *American Opinion,* May 1984, p. 81.
38. Hoar, Captive Europe, *American Opinion,* July-August 1983, p. 115.
39. Lee, The Big Banking Giveaway, *American Opinion,* May 1984, p. 84.
40. Hoar, Captive Europe, *American Opinion,* July-August 1983, p. 122.
41. Pierre, Funding Communism is treason, *The JBS Bulletin,* March 1986, p.6.

42. Allen, Megabank$Megadebt$, *American Opinion,* September 1983, p. 26.
43. Ibid.
44. Stang, Latin America, *American Opinion,* July-August 1983, p. 25.
45. Pierre, Arming Communists Continues, *The New American,* June l6, 1986,p. 14.
46. Pierre, Ex-lm Bank Pays for Angola's War, *The New American,* June 30,1986, p. 14.
47. Ibid.
48. Lee, The Big Banking Giveaway, *American Opinion,* May 1984, p. 83.
49. Joiner, Aid and Trade—Stop Financing Communism, *The JBS Bulletin,* February 1986, p. 9.
50. Pierre, Funding Communism is Treason, *The JBS Bulletin,* March 1986, p. 6.
51. Editorial, Nowak, *Washington Post,* 1986.
52. Kerrison, Crazy Ways we give help to our Enemies, *New York Post,* September 22, 1986.
53. *Wall Street Journal,* February 5,1986.
54. Kidwell, *The New American,* July 14,1986, p. 9.
55. Pierre, Arming Communists Continues, *The New American,* June 16, 1986, p. 14.
56. Drummey, Captive Europe and the Soviet Union, *The New American,*
    January 5, 1987, p. 41.
57. Buchanan, Let's Freeze the Debt Bomb, *Conservative Digest,* October 1985, p. 113.
58. Allen, Betraying China, *American Opinion,* October 1971, pp. 27, 28.
59. Pierre, Arming Communists Continues, *The New American,* June 16, 1986, p. 14.
60. Kidwell, Reagan and the Red Dragon, *The New American,* June 16, 1986, p. 9.

61. Lee, The Big Banking Giveaway, *American Opinion,* May 1984, p. 77.
62. Ibid.
63. Ibid, p. 81.
64. Hoar, The Right Answers, *Conservative Digest,* August 1986, p. 124.
65. Drummey, Correction Please, *The New American,* October 13, 1986, p. 55.
66. *Albuquerque Journal,* November 19, 1986.

Chapter 4: Trade with and Aid to America's Enemies

1. Speech, Solzhenitsyn, AFL-CIO dinner, July 30, 1975.
2. Bullets, *American Opinion,* June 1974, p. 77.
3. Drummey, Captive Nations, *The New American,* July 14, 1986, p. 29.
4. Senator William Armstrong, They Paused to Remark, *American Opinion,*
    July-August 1982, p. 44.
5. Drummey,·The Evil Empire is Still Evil, *The New American,* July 18, 1988, p. 8.
6. Belair, President is Told Tariff Barriers Threaten West, *New York Times,* January 8, 1962.
7. Dies, ·The Smear: It Goes On, and On, and On, *American Opinion,* March 1965, p. 87.
8. Kidwell, ·Stalin's Legacy, *The New American,* December 8, 1986, p.4.
9. Latta, *Human Events,* August 4, 1961, p. 506.
10. Statement, Dodd, September 9, 1965.
11. Ibid, October 1, 1963.
12. Mehrten, The Solution to Barbarism, *Crusade to Stop Financing Communism, 1983.*
13. Evans, *The Politics of Surrender,* 1966, pp. 153-154.
14. Ward, Jeane Kirkpatrick—America's Ambassador, *Conservative Digest,*

January 1986, p. 52.
15. Statement, Department of Agriculture, March 1964.
16. Allen, *The Great Pretense,* 1969, p. 8.
17. Allen, The Unelected, *American Opinion,* June 1968, p. 102.
18. Armour, ·A Message from your President, *The JBS Bulletin,* October 1986, p. 30.
19. Stang, Red Traders: Aid and Comfort to the Enemy, *American Opinion,*
    January 1972, p. 20.
20. Capell, *Henry Kissinger: Soviet Agent,* 1974.
21. Allen, The Looters: How Our Economy is being Destroyed, *American Opinion,*
    May 1974, p. 75.
22. Stang, A Man Who Won't Quit, *American Opinion,* December 1976, p. 22.
23. Allen, The Looters: How Our Economy is being Destroyed, *American Opinion,*
    May 1974, p. 75.
24. Ibid.
25. Ibid.
26. *Congressional Record,* June 16,1974.
27. Reagan, first Presidential news conference, 1981.
28. *New York Times,* October 2, 1981.
29. Drummey, George P. Shultz: Continuing The Policies of
    Appeasement, *The New American* May 19, 1986, p.32.
30. Costick, *The Economics of Detente and U S.-Soviet
    Grain Trade* monograph, Heritage Foundation, 1981.
31. Kidwell, 'The New Farm Bill: More Bad News for
    American Agriculture, *The New American*, January 20,
    1986, p. 14.
32. McManus, Reagan's Wheat Charity, *The New American,* September 15, 1986, p. 11.
33. *Dallas Morning News,* July 13,1961.
34. D.C. Favors Soviet Trade, *Baltimore Sun,* December 14, 1962.

35. Congressman John Ashbrook, August 31, 1961.
36. Wood, It's Treason: Aid and Comfort to the Vietcong, 1968, p. 13.
37. Speech, Khrushchev, Bucharest, Romania, June 19, 1962.
38. Report, *The Many Crises of the Soviet Economy,* United States Senate, 88th Congress, Committee of Judiciary.
39. 'Bullets', *American Opinion,* January 1975, p. 33.
40. Derwinski, *Congressional Record,* July 1, 1965.
41. Evans, *The Politics of Surrender,* 1966, p. 176.
42. *Journal of Commerce,* October 13, 1970.
43. Allen, The Looters: How Our Economy is being Destroyed, *American Opinion,*
    May 1974, p. 71.
44. Roberts, *Missing In Action,* 1980, p. 49.
45. Pierre, Funding Communism is Treason, *The JBS Bulletin,* March 1986, p. 3.
46. Roth, Time to Act Against Ethiopian Holocaust, *Conservative Digest,* April 1987, p. 86.
47. State Department briefing paper, January 1985.
48. 'Tis Passing Strange, *The Review of the News,* November 25, 1981, p. 34.
49. Hermann, ·U.S. Foreign Aid to Red China Urged Here, *The Indianapolis News,*
    January 11, 1966.
50. Russia, China, Cuba to get Food Credits, *Los Angeles Herald,* Examiner, July 27, 1973.
51. Allen, The Looters: How Our Economy is being Destroyed, *American Opinion,*
    May 1974, p. 77.
52. Dispatch, Hong Kong, August 22, 1973.
53. Allen, The Looters: How Our Economy is being Destroyed, *American Opinion,*
    May 1974, p. 73.
54. *Kansas City Times,* August 21, 1973.
55. *New York Times,* August 28, 1984.

56. Isaacs, ·Red Traders and Ugly Sisters, The New American, August 11, 1986, p. 43.
57. Kidwell, Reagan and the Red Dragon, *The New American*, June 16, 1986, p. 9.
58. Briefly Stated, *The New American*, June 2, 1986, p. 7.
59. Perloff, Free China Under Attack, *The New American*, October 13, 1986, p. 25.
60. Rowe, *Ally Betrayed: The Republic of China*, Western Goals monograph.
61. Benson, *Principles and National Survival*, 1964. p. 287.
62. Capell, ·They Paused to Remark, *American Opinion*, January 1974, p. 34.
63. Kidwell, Goldwater Blasts White House Red China Policy, *The New American*,
    April, 21, 1986.
64. Pierre, Pending Legislation, *The JBS Bulletin*, November 1985, p. 28.
65. Letter, Kowalski, *Conservative Digest*, February 1984, p. 2.
66. Wood, *It's Treason: Aid and Comfort to the Vietcong*, 1968, p. 12.
67. Editorial, *The New American*, July 14, 1986.

Chapter 5: Illegally Importing Communist Slave-made Goods

1. Shifrin, *The First Guidebook to Prisons and
    Concentration Camps of the Soviet Union*, 1982.
2. Dalin, *Forced labor in Soviet Russia*, 1948.
3. Allen, The Looters: How Our Economy is being
    Destroyed, *American Opinion*,
    May 1974, p. 73.
4. Allen, 'The Red Traders: Aid and Comfort to the Enemy,
    American Opinion,
    April 1984, p. 99.
5. Harriss, Reader's *Digest*, September 1983.

6. Report, Heritage Foundation, 1984.
7. Shifrin, *The First Guidebook to Prisons and Concentration Camps of the Soviet Union*, 1982.
8. Report, *Heritage Foundation*, 1984.
9. Report, Department of State, February 1983.
10. Allen, 'The Red Traders: Aid and Comfort to the Enemy, *American Opinion*, April 1984, p. 103-4.
11. Hoar, The Right Answers, *Conservative Digest*, November 1985, p. 125.
12. Allen, The Red Traders: Aid and Comfort to the Enemy, *American Opinion*, April 1984, p. 102.
13. Solzhenitsyn, *The Gulag Archipelago*, 1985.
14. MacKenzie, Ed & Op-Ed, *Conservative Digest*, December 1986, p. 52.
15. Testimony, Sharegin, *International Sakharov Hearings on Human Rights in Russia*, September 27, 1979.
16. The News, *The Review of the News*, October 10, 1979, p. 11.
17. Slave Labor Study, Free Trade Union Committee, American Federation of Labor.
18. Allen, *The Red Traders: Aid and Comfort to the Enemy*, April 1984, p. 102.
19. Stang, Slaves, *American Opinion*, May 1981, p. 50, 51.
20. Allen, The Red Traders: Aid and Comfort to the Enemy, April 1984, p. 4.
21. *Chicago Tribune*, December 3, 1974.
22. Ward, The Presidential Colorado Senator William Armstrong, *Conservative Digest*, September 1 986, p. 1 0.
23. Reagan, Captive Nations Proclamation, July 21, 1986.
24. *St. Louis Post* Dispatch, October 7, 1962.
25. How to Free Nicaragua, *Conservative Digest*, April 1985, p. 6.
26. *Washington Post*, February 8, 1982.
27. Allen, *The Red Traders: Aid and Comfort to the Enemy*, April 1984, p. 106.

28. Jasper, Ethiopian Patriot Speaks Out, *The New American*, February 10, 1986, pp. 15, 17.
29. Hoar, Captive Europe, *American Opinion* July-August 1983, p. 119.
30. Drummey, Stop Helping Communism, *The New American*, January 16, 1989, p. 28.
31. Cooper, How Communist China Floods our Markets, *Conservative Digest*,
September 1986, p. 91.
32. Allen, *The Red Traders: Aid and Comfort to the Enemy*, April 1984, p. 106.
33. Ibid.
34. Hoar, Change in Red China, *American Opinion*, January 1985, p. 99.
35. Ingbretson, Out Contribution to the Slave Trade, *The New American*, July 14, 1985, p. 43.
36. Joiner, Aid and Trade—Stop Financing Communism, *The JBS Bulletin*, September 1986.
37. Federal Law 19 U.S.C. 1307—Section 307, *Smoot-Hawley Tariff Act* of 1930, pp. 11,11.
38. Allen, *The Red Traders: Aid and Comfort to the Enemy*, April 1984, p. 4.

Chapter 6: Vietnam—A Classic Example of Wholesale Treason

1. Wood, The Betrayed: Our Men in Uniform want to Win in Vietnam, *American Opinion*, January 1969, pp. 11, 12.
2. Robert S. Allen and Paul Scott, Red Trade Pushed to Businessmen, *The Indianapolis News*, December 16, 1964.
3. Wood, *It's Treason! Aid and Comfort to the Vietcong*, 1968, p. 12.
4. Pamphlet, *No Substitute for Victory*, n.d., pp. 3,4.
5. *People's World*, November 5, 1966.

6. Rowe, They Paused to Remark, *American Opinion*, February 1985, p. 20.
7. Lipscomb, *Congressional Record*, September 2, 1965.
8. *Izvestiya*, December 27, 1966.
9. Wood, *It's Treason: Aid and Comfort to the Vietcong*, 1968, p. 13.
10. Evans, *The Politics of Surrender*, 1966, p. 176.
11. Wood, The Betrayed: Our Men in Uniform Want to Win in Vietnam, *American Opinion*, January 1969, p. 15.
12. Wood, Vietnam: While Brave Men Die, *American Opinion*, June 1967, p. 11.
13. Lipscomb, *Congressional Record*, September 2, 1965.
14. Evans, *The Politics of Surrender*, 1966, p. 162.
15. Thurmond, *Congressional Record*, July 26, 1965.
16. Speech, Johnson, National Conference of Editorial Writers, October 7, 1966.
17. Wood, Vietnam: While Brave Men Die, *American Opinion*, June 1967, p. 8.
18. Ibid.
19. Ibid, p. 9.
20. Speech, Mundt, National Convention of the American Legion, August 1967.
21. Commerce Department, 68-page commodity list, October 12, 1966. For complete list see *Congressional Record*, March 26,1967, pp. 3543-3547.
22. Ibid.
23. *New York Times*, October 27, 1966.
24. *Chicago Tribune*, December 26, 1966.
26. Comments on national television, Harriman, November 2, 1966.
26. Stockdale, *In Love and War*, 1984.
27. Wood, It's Treason—Aid and Comfort to the Vietcong, 1968, p. 7.
28. Wood, Vietnam: While Brave Men Die, *American Opinion*, June 1967, p. 10
29. *The Reporter*, January 1967.

30. Wood, Vietnam: While Brave Men Die, *American Opinion,* June 1967, p. 10.
31. Sennholz, *More Vietnam,* 1967, p.103.
32. *Associated Press,* September 13, 1967.
33. *Register of Shipping of the USSR,* published in Leningrad.
34. Soviet communique, September 23, 1967.
35. Speech, Johnson, National Conference of Editorial Writers, October 7, 1966.
36. *Congressional Record,* April 13, 1967, p. H4107.
37. *Human Events,* July 22, 1967.
38. Letter, Derwinski, August 14, 1967.
39. Speech, Katzenbach, National Association of Manufacturers, December 9,1967.
40. Wood, *It's Treason—Aid and Comfort to the Vietcong,* 1968, p. 7.
41. Ibid, pp. 12-13.
42. Presidential Executive Order, July 29, 1968.
43. Nationwide radio speech, Nixon, October 24,1968.
44. Allen, Mr. Nixon: The Candidate versus the President, American Opinion,
April 1972, p. 33.
45. Hoar, Jimmy Carter, *American Opinion,* September 1976, p. 85.
46. Guidry, Who is Afraid of Bay Jane, *Conservative Digest* December 1985, p. 55.
47. Letter, Day, November 1987.
48. McManus, Hanoi Jane Feeling Heat, *The New American,* August 1, 1988, p. 17.
49. Guidry, Who is Afraid of Baby Jane, *Conservative Digest,* December 1965, pp. 55, 57.
50. Stang, The Code, *American Opinion,* June1973, p.4.
54. Guidry, Hanoi Jane, *American Opinion,* June 1979, p. 105.
55. Ibid.

56. Ibid.
57. Ibid.
58. Ibid, p. 104.
59. Guidry, Who is Afraid of Baby Jane, *Conservative Digest,* December 1985, p. 57.
60. Capell, Entertainment, *American Opinion,* May 1973, p. 86.
61. Gumaer, Sabotage: The Guerrilla Warfare has Begun, *American Opinion,* June 169, p. 59.
62. Stang, Kent State, *American Opinion,* June 1974, pp. 1, 2.
63. Ibid, pp. 5, 15.
64. Guidry, ·Hanoi Jane, *American Opinion,* June 1979, p. 105.
65. Letter, Day, November 1987.
66. Ibid.
67. Hanoi Jane, *American Opinion,* June 1979, p.109.
68. *Boston Herald Traveler,* December 12, 1971.
69. Vien told to POW Medal of Honor winner James Bond Stockdale in 1966.
70. Hoar, John Forbes Kerry—The most Peculiar Man in the Senate, *Conservative Digest,* February 1987, p. 25.
71. *Action News No. 5.*
72. Hoar, Reviewing the Carter Administration Personnel, *American Opinion,*
    October 1980, p. 91.
73. Rees, Who's Watching the Store? *American Opinion,* November 1977, p. 27.
74. Ibid, p. 29.
75. Ibid.
76. Hoar, Reviewing the Carter Administration Personnel, *American Opinion,*
    October 1980, p. 91.
77. Ibid.
78. *Associated Press,* March 19, 1980.
79. Capell, *Henry Kissinger: Soviet Agent,* 1974.

80. Stang, Watergators, *American Opinion,* September 1973, p. 7.

Part II—Are There not Traitors Among Us?

Chapter 7: A Peek at Internal Security

1. Dies, The Court: How It Supports The Communists, *American Opinion,* January 1967, p.99.
2. Speech, Hoover, *The Faith To Be Free,* NBC-TV, December 1961.
3. Capell, Since F.D.R.: Some Not So Ancient History, *American Opinion,* March 1971, p.49.
4. Ibid, p.51.
5. Barmine, The New Communist Conspiracy, *Reader's Digest,* October 1944, p.32.
6. Capell, Since F.D.R.: Some Not So Ancient History, *American Opinion,* March 1971, p.55.
7. Gumaer, former FBI undercover operative in the Communist Party.
8. Gitlow, *The Whole Of Their Lives,* 1948, pp.254-255.
9. Hoar, The K.G.B. On Capitol Hill, *American Opinion,* June 1976, p.3.
10. Gumaer, Sabotage: The Guerrilla Warfare Has Begun, *American Opinion,* June 1969, p.51.
11. Testimony, Trudeau, May 24, 1967.
12. Speech, Nelson, Industrial Management Club, Lockport, New York, 1969.
13. Rees, The Disasterous Foreign Policy of Jimmy Carter, *American Opinion,* May 1980, pp.38, 39.
14. Gumaer, ·Sabotage: The Guerrilla Warfare Has Begun, *American Opinion,* June 1969, pp.57, 58.
15. Dies, Treason: The Fantastic Perfidy, *American Opinion,* May 1964, p.70.

16. Dies, None So Blind As Those Who Will Not See, *American Opinion,* February 1965, p.57.
17. Dies, America: How It Is Being Communized, *American Opinion,* July-August 1964, p.102.
18. Special Report, *House Committee to Investigate Communist Propaganda,* 71st Congress [Fish Report], January 17, 1931.
19. Guide To Subversive Organizations And Publications, House Committee On Un-American Activities, December 1, 1961, p.121.
20. ABC Television, Mike Wallace Show, March 4, 1958.
21. Grey, The Cyrus Eaton Story, *American Opinion,* March 1959, p.13.
22. Huck, The Operation, *American Opinion,* May 1975, p.26.
23. Rees, McGoverning, *American Opinion,* February 1979, p.51.
24. Dies, The H.C.U.A.—Committee Under Attack, *American Opinion,* March 1966, p.105.
25. *Parade,* July 24, 1988.
26. Capell, The Left: Collectivists In The Congress, *American Opinion,* July-August 1974, p.71.
27. Schuyler, Pastorniks, *American Opinion,* May 1967, p.27,28.
28. Hoar, Secret Police: Watching The K.G.B. And C.I.A, *American Opinion,* April 1975, p.36.
29. Capell, *Henry Kissinger: Soviet Agent,* 1974.
30. Huck, ·The Operation, *American Opinion,* May 1975, p.26.
31. Speech, Anderson, House of Representatives, December 9, 1970.
32. Can A Congressman Afford A Conscience? *Look* April 20, 1971.
33. *New York Times Magazine,* April 25, 1971.
34. Speech, Boggs, House of Representatives, April 5, 1971.

35. Oliver, Marxmanship In Dallas, *American Opinion,* February 1964, p.25.
36. United States Senate, April 14, 1971.
37. *The Guardian,* April 17,1971.
38. American Civil Liberties Union, *1970-1971 Annual Report*
39. Matthews, January 1955.
40. Special Report, *House Committee to Investigate Communist Propaganda,* 71st Congress [Fish Report] January 17, 1931.
41. Stang, The Price Of Honor, *American Opinion,* June 1984, p.85.
42. Hoar, ·Secret Police: Watching the KG.B. and C.I.A, *American Opinion,* April 1975, p.31.
43. Stang, National Security Mousetrap, *American Opinion,* November 1976, p.43.
44. McDonald, On Defense, *American Opinion,* September 1977, p.73.
45. *McDonald-Ashbrook Bill,* (House Resolution 48), January 4, 1977.
46. How Liberals Weakened U.S. Internal Security, *Conservative Digest,* February 1984, p.15.
47. Rees, Internal Security, *American Opinion,* December 1983, p.49.
48. Rees, Time To Restore The Internal Security Committee, *American Opinion,* January 1981, p.40.
49. McHugh, They Paused To Remark, *American Opinion,* June 1973, p.78.
50. Capell, McCarthyism: Still The Fight For America, *American Opinion,* January 1973, p.75.
51. Evans, Bullets, C*onservative Digest,* December 1985,p.67.
52. Allen, *Kissinger The Secret Side Of The Secretary Of State,* 1976, p.131 .

53. Stang, National Security Mousetrap, *American Opinion*, November 1976, p.44.
54. Ibid, p.54, 103
55. Rees, Internal Security, *American Opinion*, December 1983, p.43.
56. Improved Intelligence Is The Key, *Conservative Digest*, February 1984, p.16.
57. Dies, Communists—The Menace Within, *American Opinion*, April 1966, p.97.
58. Benson, *Prophets, Principles and National Survival* 1964, p.251.
59. Huck, Founding Of The Society, *American Opinion*, March 1985.
60. Drummey, McCarthy: The Truth, The Smear, And The Lesson, *American Opinion*, May 1964, p.9.
61. They Paused To Remark, *American Opinion*, May 1964, p.18.
62. Hoover, letter to law enforcement officials, March 1, 1960.
63. Hoar, The K.G.B. On Capitol Hill, *American Opinion*, June 1976, p.79.
64. Ibid.
65. Ibid.
66. From The Hopper, *The Review of the News*, April 11, 1984. p.53.
67. Stacy and Lutton, Without A Shot Being Fired, *The New American*, June 2, 1986, p.11.
68. Ibid.
69. Stang, ·Immigration, *American Opinion*, January 1979, p.105.
70. Huck, The Operation To Destroy America's Internal Security, *American Opinion*,
    May 1975, p.32.
71. McDonald, ·Internal Security, *American Opinion*, February 1976, p.9.
72. Wood, ·The Betrayed: Our Men In Uniform Want To Win In Vietnam, *American Opinion*, January 1969, p.8.

Chapter 8: Internal Security—The Supreme Court and the President

1. Benson, *National Program Letter,* November 1970.
2. Malkin, *Return To My Father's House,* 1972.
3. Rees, ·Save The Logan Act, *American Opinion,* October 1982, p.47.
4. Evans, *The Liberal Establishment,* 1965, pp.192-193.
5. Dies, ·The Court And Our Security Laws, *American Opinion,* April 1967, p.99.
6. Dies, ·The Court: How It Supports The Communists, *American Opinion,* January 1967, p.107.
7. *Congressional Record,* May 2, 1962, p.7028-31.
8. Oliver, 'The Warren Gang, *American Opinion,* December 1963, p.27.
9. Senate Hearings on the Jenner Bill to limit the appellate jurisdiction of the Supreme Court, 1958.
10. Allen, ·Harry Bridges: How The Communists Control Our Shipping, *American Opinion,* March 1967, p.13.
11. Ibid.
12. Ibid.
13. Malkin, *Return To My Father's House,* 1972.
14. *Pennsylvania* vs. *Nelson,* 350 U.S. 497, (April 3, 1956).
15. *Slochower* vs. *Board of Education* of New York 350 U.S. 551, (April 9, 1956).
16. *Cole* vs. *Young,* 351 U.S. 536, (June 11, 1956).
17. *United States* vs. *Witkovich,* 353 U.S. 194 (April 29, 1957).
18. *Schware* vs. *Board of Bar Examiners of the State of New Mexico,* 353 U.S. 232
    (May 6, 1957).
19. Dies, The Court: How It Supports The Communists, *American Opinion,*
    January 1967, p.105.
20. *Jencks* vs. *United States,* 353 U.S. 657, (June 3, 1957).

21. Rose, Coincidence Or Treason, *American Opinion,* April 1962, p.36.
22. Hoover, *Masters Of Deceit,* 1958, pp.68-69.
23. Cohn, *McCarthy, 1968,* p.24.
24. Hoover, *Masters Of Deceit,* 1958, p.69.
25. Hearings, *Scope Of Soviet Activity In The United States,* Senate Internal Security Subcommittee, November 21, 1956.
26. *Yates* vs. *United States,* 355 U.S. 66 (June 17, 1957).
27. *Watkins* vs. *United States,* 354 U.S. 178, (June 17, 1957).
28. *Sweezy* vs. *New Hampshire,* 354 U.S. 234, (June 17, 1957).
29. *Service* vs. *Dulles,* 354 U.S. 363 (June 17, 1957).
30. Dies, The Court And Our Security Laws, *American Opinion,* April 1967, p.103.
31. Ibid, p.99.
32. Speech, Hall, Eugene Dennis funeral, February 1961.
33. Report, *Communist Activities Among Aliens And National Groups,* Senate Subcommittee on Immigration and Naturalization, September 7-29, 1949, part 2, p.800.
34. Ibid.
35. Dies, 'Treason: The Fantastic Perfidy, *American Opinion,* May 1964, p.17.
36. Drummey, The State Department, *The New American,* May 19, 1986, p.17.
37. *Congressional Record,* September 22, 1950, p.A6832.
38. Malkin, *Return To My Father's House,* 1972.
39. McCarthy, *The Fight For America,* 1952.
40. Cohn, *McCarthy,* 1968, p.104.
41. Schlafly, *A Choice Not An Echo,* 1964, p.64.
42. Lee, Confirming the 'Liberal' Establishment, *American Opinion,* March 1981, p.89.
43. Cohn, *McCarthy,* 1968, p.61.
44. Benson, *Prophets, Principles And National Survival,* 1964.
45. Cohn, *McCarthy,* 1968, p.95.

46. Drummey, *Setting The Record Straight: Senator Joseph R. McCarthy,*
 n.d., p.14.
47. Campaign speech, Eisenhower, 1952
48. Allen, Mr. Nixon: A Hard Look At The Candidate, *American Opinion,*
 September 1968, p.8.
49. *Executive Order,* Eisenhower, Friday May 17, 1954.
50. Cohn, *McCarthy,* 1968, p.64.
51. Drummey, Remembering McCarthyism, *American Opinion,* November 1984, p.81.
52. Former CIA official Tom Braden admitted this on *Crossfire,* television program, Fall 1983.
53. *Presidential Order,* Eisenhower, December 29, 1954.
54. Allen, Mr. Nixon: A Hard Look At The Candidate,
 American Opinion,
 September 1968, p.8.
55. *Associated Press,* October 17, 1956.
56. Statement, Nixon, Rock Island, Illinois, October 14, 1956.
57. Allen, Mr. Nixon: A Hard Look at The Candidate, *American Opinion,* September 1968, p.8.
58. Stang, ·Since Camelot, *American Opinion,* October 1973, p.25.
59. Allen, Mr. Nixon: A Hard Look at The Candidate, *American Opinion,* September 1968, p.8.
60. Ibid, p.19.
61. *Allen-Scott Report,* March 6, 1964.
62. Capell, *Henry Kissinger: Soviet Agent* 1074.
63. Schlafly, *A Choice Not An Echo,* 1964, p.15.
64. Campaign speech, Nixon, October 13, 1968.
65. *Wall Street Journal,* January 6, 1969.
66. *New York Times,* April 24, 1969.
67. *The Hatch Act of 1939.*
68. *Communist Control Act of 1954,* (Public Law 637).

Chapter 9: Security Risks in the State Department

1. Memorandum, Senate Appropriations Committee, June 10, 1947.
2. Ibid.
3. Gill, *The Ordeal Of Otto Otepka, 1969.*
4. Ibid.
5. Memorandum, Senate Appropriations Committee, June 10, 1947.
6. Capell, Carter's Radical Personnel At State, *American Opinion,* July-August 1980, p.69.
7. Ibid, pp. 65, 67.
8. *Plain Talk* November 1946.
9. Capell, Carter's Radical Personnel At State, *American Opinion,* July-August 1980, pp.65, 67.
10. Ibid.
11. Ibid.
12. *Senate Report 2050 On The Institute Of Pacific Relations,* Senate Judiciary Committee, July 2, 1951, pp.223, 225.
13. Capell, Canter's Radical Personnel At State, *American Opinion,* July-August 1980, pp.65, 67.
14. Drummey, McCarthyism: Forty Questions And Answers About Senator Joseph McCarthy, *The New American,* May 11, 1987,
15. Evans, *The Politics Of Surrender,* 1966, p.62.
16. Speech, Rusk World Affairs Council, University of Pennsylvania, June 14, 1951.
17. *New York Times,* February 7, 1969.
18. Allen, Betraying China, *American Opinion,* October 1971, p.7.
19. Dispatch, Klosson, U.S. Department of State, July 11, 1961.
20. Capell, *Henry Kissinger: Soviet Agent,* 1974.

21. Barron, The Burners: Security Files Are Being Destroyed, *American Opinion,*
November 1964, p.2.
22. *Allen-Scott Report,* September 25, 1964.
23. Dies, Invasion: Moscow's Secret Army In America, *American Opinion,*
November 1964, p.77.
24. Senate Report 2050 *On The Institute Of Pacific Relations,* Senate Judiciary Committee,
July 2, 1951, pp.223, 225.
25. Oshinsky, *A Conspiracy So Immense: The World Of Joe McCarthy,* 1983.
26. Hearings, *Institute Of Pacific Relations,* Senate Internal Security Subcommittee, 1952.
27. Gannon, *Biographical Dictionary Of The Left,* 1969.
28. Capell, No Intelligence: A Worried Look At The C.I.A, *American Opinion,*
January 1971, p.57.
29. Drummey, The State Department, *The New American,* May 19, 1986, p.20.
30. Huck, Otto Otepka: Will President Nixon Keep His
Promise, *American Opinion,* March 1969, p.33.
31. House Committee On Un-American Activities, September 21, 1950.
32. Letter, Clark to Loyalty Review Board, released April 27, 1949.
33. *Plain Talk,* November 1946.
34. Capell, Carter's Radical Personnel At State, *American Opinion,*
July-August 1980, pp.57, 58.
35. Capell, McCarthyism Still The Fight For America,
American Opinion, January 1973, p.73.
36. Capell, *Henry Kissinger Soviet Agent,* 1974.
37. Capell, Carter's Radical Personnel At State, *American Opinion*, July-August 1980, p.69.

38. Capell, McCarthyism Still The Fight For America, *American Opinion,* January 1973, p.73.
39. Hoar, *Shakedown, American Opinion,* January 1975, p.32.
40. Capell, *Henry Kissinger: Soviet Agent,* 1974.
41. Otto Otepka, former Chief Security Evaluator at the Department of State, December 22, 1972.
42. Stang, A Man Who Won't Quit, *American Opinion,* December 1976, p.19.
43. Case No 41, presented to the United States Senate by Senator Joseph R McCarthy (R-WI), February 20, 1950.
44. Capell, McCarthyism Still The Fight For America, *American Opinion,* January 1973, p.71.
45. Capell, Foreign Policy The Department of State, *American Opinion,*
July-August 1972, p.34.
46. Case No 43, presented to the United States Senate by Senator Joseph R McCarthy (R-WI), February 20, 1950.
47. Capell, McCarthyism Still The Fight For America, *American Opinion,*
January 1973, p.71, 72. 48. Capell, Foreign Policy The Department of State, *American Opinion,*
July-August 1972, p.37.
49. Capell, Carter's Radical Personnel At State, *American Opinion,* July-August 1980, p.63.
50. Capell, *Henry Kissinger: Soviet Agent,* 1974.
51. Allen, *Kissinger,* 1976, pp.127, 128.
52. Capell, Foreign Policy The Department of State, *American Opinion,*
July-August 1972, p.39.
53. Capell, Carter's Radical Personnel At State, *American Opinion,* July-August 1980, p.59.
54. Ibid, p.61.
55. Hoar, Carterized, *American Opinion,* March 1979, p.11.

56. Capell, *Henry Kissinger: Soviet Agent,* 1974.
57. Capell, Carter's Radical Personnel At State, *American Opinion,* July-August 1980, p.63.
58. Speech, Lincoln, Springfield, Illinois, 1838

Chapter 10: Misdeeds of the Subversive State Department

1. Dies, America How It Is Being Communized, *American Opinion,* July-August 1964, p.101.
2. *United States Government Organization Manual.*
3. Allen, Betraying China, *American Opinion,* October 1971, p.21.
4. Utley, *The China Story,* 1951.
5. McCarthy, *The Fight For America,* 1952.
6. Drummey, The Captive Nations, *The New American,* July 14, 1986, p.33.
7. Hearings, *Institute Of Pacific Relations,* Senate Internal Security Subcommittee, 1952.
8. Drummey, The Captive Nations, *The New American,* July 14, 1986, p.33.
9. Allen, Betraying China, *American Opinion,* October 1971, p.9.
10. Ibid, p.10.
11. Ibid, p.9.
12. Ibid, p.10.
13. Kubek, *How The Far East Was Lost,* 1963.
14. Penkovsky, *The Penkovsky Papers,* p.206.
15. *Congressional Record,* August 31, 1960, p.17407.
16. *Christopher News Notes,* No. 119, April 1962.
17. Senator Thomas Dodd (D-CT), Southern California School of Anti-Communism, Los Angeles, August 28, 1961.
18. Hearings, *Soviet Total War,* House Committee On Un-American Activities,

September 30, 1956.
19. Ibid.
20. Hoar, High Cost Of Liberalism, *American Opinion,* June 1985, p.101.
21. Hearings, *Communist Threat To The United States Through The Caribbean,* Senate Internal Security Subcommittee, 1960-1961, Parts 1-12, p.683.
22. Ibid, p.746.
23. Ibid, p.736.
24. Lamphere, *The FBI-KGB War,* 1986, p.100.
25. Report, *Institute Of Pacific Relations, Senate* Internal Security Sub-committee, 1952, p.153.
26. Hearings, *Communist Threat To The United States Through The Caribbean,* Senate Internal Security Subcommittee, 1960-1961, Parts 1-12, p.736.
27. Ibid, p.756.
28. Ibid, pp. 793, 797, 800.
29. Ibid, p.798.
30. Rousselot, Disarmament, *American Opinion,* February 1963, p.13.
31. Hearings, *Communist Threat To The United States Through The Caribbean,* Senate Internal Security Subcommittee, 1960-1961, Parts 1-12.
32. Ibid, p.738.
33. Hoar, High Cost of Liberalism, *American Opinion,* June 1985, pp. 101, 103.
34. Kennedy, Presidential press conference, January 24, 1962.
35. *New York Times News Service,* January 25, 1962.
36. Drummey, The State Department, *The New American,* May 19, 1986, p.20.
37. Barron, Treason Facts The State Department Hides, *American Opinion,* June 1964, p.6.
38. Eisenhower, April 26,1963.
39. Welch, September 1958.

40. Hearings, *Communist Threat To The United States Through The Caribbean,* Senate Internal Security Subcommittee, 1960-1961, Parts 1-12, p.806.
41. Ibid, p.725.
42. Hunt, *The Untold Story Of Douglas MacArthur.*
43. Allen, 'Betraying China, *American Opinion,* October 1971, p.21.
44. McCarthy, *America's Retreat From Victory,* 1965.
45. Lee and Hensel, *Douglas MacArthur,* 1952.
46. Willoughby and Chamberlain, *MacArthur, 1941-1951,* 1954, pp. 401,402.
47. U.S. *News & World Report,* February 11, 1955.
48. Hoar, The Forgotten War In Korea, *American Opinion,* November 1977, p.18.
49. Ibid,pp.17, 18.
50. Ibid, p.14.
51. New York Times, June 17, 1956.
52. Drummey, Remembering McCarthyism, *American Opinion,* November 1984, p.82.
53. Evans, Tito's Freedom Of Maneuver, *National Review Bulletin,* July 10, 1962.
54. Cohn, *McCarthy* 1968, p.3.
55. Drummey, The State Department, *The New American,* May 19, 1936, p.20.
56. Barron, Otto Otepka And The State Department American Opinion, January 1964, p.5.
57. U.S. Code, Title 5, paragraph 652(d).
58. Barron, Otto Otepka And The State Department, *American Opinion,* January 1964, p.3.
59. Huck, Otto Otepka: Will President Nixon Keep His Promise?, *American Opinion,* March 1969, p.34.
60. Drummey, The State Department, *The New American,* May 19, 1986, p.20.
61. Hoar, Carterized, *American Opinion,* March 1979, p.15.
62. *Granna,* July 20, 1975.

63. Thompson, They Paused To Remark, *American Opinion*, November
    1977, p. 32.
64. Smoot, They Paused To Remark, *American Opinion*, March 1972, p.72.
65. Stang, The Panama Canal Sellout, *American Opinion*, November 1977, p.97.
66. Rees, The Left, *American Opinion*, July-August 1984, p.30.
67. Robertson, Presidential campaign literature, 1988.
68. *American Opinion*, November 1981, p.54.

Chapter 11: Those Close to the President

1. Report, *Interlocking Subversion In Government Departments*, Senate Internal Security Sub-committee, July 30, 1953.
2. Allen, Betraying China, *American Opinion*, October 1971, p.15.
3. Allen, Supreme Court, *American Opinion*, May 1969, p.9.
4. Hearings, *Institute Of Pacific Relations*, Senate Internal Security Sub-committee, 1952.
5. Hoar, F.D.R., 1932-1940, *American Opinion*, December 1978, p.100.
6. Hoar, The Amazing John J. McCloy, American Opinion, March 1983, p.26.
7. Allen, The Unelected, *American Opinion*, June 1968, p.109.
8. Straight, *After A Long Silence*, 1983.
9. Gumaer, The AC.L.U., *American Opinion*, September 1969, p.63.
10. Hoar, F.D.R., 1940-1945,- *American Opinion*, January 1979, p.31.
11. Van Gorder, *Ill Fares The Land*, 1966, p.7.
12. Republican Party Platform, 1952.

13. Gumaer, Apostasy: The National Council of Churches, *American Opinion,*
   February 1970, p.61.
14. Capell, Foreign Policy: The Department of State, *American Opinion,*
   July-August 1972, p.25.
15. Citation, House Committee On Un-American Activities, September 21, 1950.
16. Hearings, *Institute Of Pacific Relations,* Senate Internal Security Sub-committee, 1952.
17. Tansill, Retrospect On The Kennedy-Johnson Administration, *American Opinion,* October 1964, p.63.
18. Allen and Scott, McNamara Refutes Own Testimony on Arms, *The Indianapolis News,* September 2, 1964.
19. Stang, Rockefeller: Remember Who Called the Shots, *American Opinion,*
   November 1974, p.43.
19b. Allen, The Unelected, *American Opinion,* June 1968, p.82.
20. Allen, Insiders Of The Great Conspiracy, *American Opinion,* September 1982, p.78.
21. Allen, Our Military, *American Opinion,* September 1971, p.23.
22. Schlesinger, They Paused To Remark, *American Opinion,* October 1962, p.41.
23. *Daily Worker,* January 30, 1944.
24. Oliver, The Warren Gang, *American Opinion,* December 1962, p.32.
25. *Guide To Subversive Organizations,* House Committee On Un-American Activities, December 1, 1961, p.121.
26. Straight, *After A Long Silence,* 1983.
27. *San Francisco Examiner,* January 9, 1967.
28. Evans, Openers, *American Opinion,* October 1968, p.85.
29. Hearings, *Institute Of Public Relations,* Senate Internal Security

Sub-committee, 1952.
30. *Appendix IX,* House Committee On Un-American Activities, 1944, p.804.
31. Senate Internal Security Sub-committee, 1956.
32. Evans, Openers, *American Opinion,* October 1968, p.83.
33. House Intelligence Committee, 1978.
34. Allen, The Unelected, *American Opinion,* June 1968, p.117.
35. Allen, America, 1968, *American Opinion,* July-August, 1968. p.1.
36. Dies, America: How Communist Are We?, *American Opinion,* July-August 1966, p.113.
37. Shearon, *Wilbur J Cohn: The Pursuit Of Power.*
38. *USA Today,* April 27,1988, p.3a.
39. House Committee On Un-American Activities, 1939.
40. Ibid, 1944.
41. Capell, *Henry Kissinger: Soviet Agent,* 1974.
42. Evans, ·DeLibris, *American Opinion,* November 1974, pp.50, 51.
43. Capell, No Intelligence: A Look At The C.I.A, *American Opinion,* January 1971, p.57.
44. Capell, *Henry Kissinger: Soviet Agent,* 1974.
45. Column, Scott, June 1974.
46. Acheson to Walter Cronkite, September 28, 1969.
47. Report, *Military Cold War Education And Speech Review Policies,* Senate Armed Services Committee, Part IV, October 19, 1962, p.1491.
48. Allen, Second Term: New Nixon and Agnew Circus, *American Opinion,* March 1973, p.73.
49. The Inside Page, *Conservative Digest,* April 1986, p.3.
50. Capell, *Henry Kissinger: Soviet Agent* 1974.
51. Lee, Al Haig At State, *American Opinion,* February 1981, p.82.
52. Hoar, DeLibris, *American Opinion,* June 1964, p.59.
53. Capell, *Henry Kissinger: Soviet Agent,* 1974.

54. Press conference, Hyatt House, Birmingham, Alabama, August 14, 1975.
55. Ibid.
56. Smith, *OSS: The Secret History of America's First Central Intelligence Agency,* 1972, p.367.
57. *New York Times,* January 11, 1964.
58. Allen, Gerald Ford and his Domestic Policy, *American Opinion,* October 1976, p.79.
59. Capell, *Henry Kissinger: Soviet Agent,* 1974.
60. Smith, *OSS: The Secret History of America's First Central Intelligence Agency,* 1972.
61. Gumaer, Montreal: The Vietcong's Hemispheric Conference, *American Opinion,* February 1969, p.5.
62. Capell, *Henry Kissinger: Soviet Agent,* 1974.
63. Smith, *OSS: The Secret History of America's First Central Intelligence Agency,* 1972.
64. Capell, *Henry Kissinger: Soviet Agent,* 1974.
64a. Stang, Mr. Jimmy, *American Opinion,* December 1977, p.85.
64b. Brzezinski, *Between Two Ages,* 1970, p.70.
64c. Rees, Who's Watching the Store, *American Opinion,* November 1977, p.20.
65. Hoar, Jimmy Carter, *American Opinion,* September 1976, p.83.
66. Capell, *Henry Kissinger: Soviet Agent* 1974.
67. Ibid.
68. Allen, The Looters: How Our Economy Is Being Destroyed, *American Opinion,* May 1974, p.55.
69. Capell, *Henry Kissinger: Soviet Agent,* 1974.
70. Stang, The Canal Treaties Are Illegal, *American Opinion,* October 1973, p.82.
71. Dies, America: How It Is Being Communized, *American Opinion,* July-August 1964, p.101.

Chapter 12: Presidential Words and Deeds

1. Anderson, They Paused To Remark, *American Opinion,* September 1974, p.29.
2. Dies, The H.C.U.A: Committee Under Attack, *American Opinion,* March 1966, p.101.
3. Speech, Crane, *Nature of the Beast,* address to the World Anti-Communist League, Taipei, Republic of China August 1981.
4. Crocker, *Roosevelt's Road to Russia,* 1959.
5. Ibid.
6. Mikolajczyk, *The Rape of Poland,* 1948.
7. Colby, *'Twas A Famous victory,* 1974.
8. Ibid, p.29.
9. Baciu, *Sell-Out To Stalin,* 1985
10. St. John, ·Lent-Lease: A Lethal Web, *The New American,* March 17, 1987, p.44.
11. Pegler, Yellow Dog Democrats, *American Opinion,* March 1963, p.12.
12. Dies, Treason: The Fantastic Perfidy, *American Opinion,* May 1964, p.67.
13. Epstein, *Operation Keelhaul,* 1973.
14. Pegler, Yellow Dog Democrats, *American Opinion,* March 1963, p.12, 13.
15. Flynn, *The Roosevelt Myth,* 1948.
16. Article, Adam Lapin, *Daily Worker,* July 27, 1944.
17. Senator Hugh Scott (R-PA), reported in the *New York Times,* September 26, 1948.
18. McCarthy, *The Fight For America,* 1952.
19. Hoar, Welch and Eisenhower, *American Opinion,* March 1985, p.61.
20. Ibid.
21. Capell, Since F.D.R.: Some Not so Ancient History, *American Opinion,* March 1971, p.61.
22. Hearings, *The Crimes of Khrushchev,* House Committee on Un-American Actvities, 7 vols.

23. *Illinois State Journal,* Springfield, Illinois, September 29, 1959.
24. Interview, Eisenhower, Walter Cronkite, CBS, February 15,1962.
25. Larson, *Eisenhower: The President Nobody Knew.*
26. Eisenhower, *Reader's Digest,* April 1969.
27. Drummey, ·Remembering McCarthy, *American Opinion,* November 1984, p.82.
28. Welch, *The Politician,* 1963, p.134.
29. Hoar, Beware Summitry, *American Opinion,* May 1984, p.46.
30. Interview, Russell, WSB-TV, Atlanta, Georgia, December 12, 1962.
31. Speech, Johnson, to Senior Citizens at the White House, January 15,1964.
32. Allen, ·America: How Communist Are We?, *American Opinion,* July-August 1967, p.4.
33. Atomic Energy Commission, June 12, 1954.
34. Borden, letter to the FBI, November 7, 1953.
35. Gumaer, The A.C.L.U., *American Opinion,* September 1969, p.90.
36. Ibid.
37. Telegram, Johnson to Baldwin, January 20, 1964.
38. *Guidance On Dissent* issued by the Pentagon, May 1969.
39. Ibid.
40. Paul Scott, syndicated column, May 30, 1969.
41. Capell, *Henry Kissinger: Soviet Agent* 1974.
42. Foreign Affairs, October 1969.
43. *Time,* November 15, 1976.
44. Rees, The Council Is Watching, *American Opinion,* January 1984, p.24.
45. Singlaub, They Paused To Remark, *American Opinion,* October 1984, p.36.
46. Berrier, Bullets, *American Opinion,* April 1984, p.37.
47. Rees, The War On Intelligence, *American Opinion,* December 1980, p.82.

48. Ibid.
49. Drummey, Profile, *The Review of the News,* April 11,1984, p.51.
50. Hoar, ·The Soviets Are Preparing For War, *American Opinion,* November 1978, p.25.
51. Hoar, Carterized, *American Opinion,* March 1979, p.109.
52. *The JBS Bulletin,* July1986, p.7.
53. Stang, Latin America, *American Opinion,* July-August 1983, p.41.
54. Reagan, June 11, 1985.
55. Speech, Ashbrook, October 4, 1967.
56. Rousselot, Civil Rights, *American Opinion,* February 1964, p.5.
57. *Time,* January 3, 1964.
58. Stang, ·Senator Scott: The Little Man Who Isn't There, *American Opinion,*
January 1970, p.31.
59. Hoar, Inside FBI Files On The Reverend Martin Luther King, *Conservative Digest,* January 1987, p.39.
60. Stang, Senator Scott: The Little Man Who Isn't There, *American Opinion,*
January 1970, p.31.
61. Lee and Ferguson, Mysteries Of Korean Air Lines Flight 007, *Conservative Digest* October 1985, p.86.
62. Rees, One Man, One Year, *American Opinion,* February 1978, p.53.
63. Speech, Reagan, National Association of Evangelicals, March 8, 1983.
64. Barker, *The JBS Bulletin,* April 1986, p.22.

Chapter 13: Miscellaneous Subversion In Government

1. *Congressional Record,* February 23, 1954, p.2014ff.

2. Allen, Mr. Nixon: The Candidate Versus The President, *American Opinion,*
April 1972, p.40.
3. Special Report, *House Committee to Investigate Communist Propaganda,* January 17, 1931.
4. Ibid.
5. Report, *Interlocking Subversion In Government Departments,* Senate Internal Security Subcommittee, July 30, 1953.
6. Ibid.
7. Bloor, *We Are Many.*
8. Toledano, *Seeds Of Treason,* 1965, p.34.
9. Capell, Entertainment, *American Opinion, May* 1973, p.81.
10. Toledano, *Seeds of Treason,* 1965, pp.32, 33.
11. Report, *Interlocking Subversion In Government Departments,* Senate Internal Security Sub-committee, July 30, 1953, p.44.
12. Ibid.
13. Hoar, F.D.R. 1932-1940, *American Opinion,* December 1978, p.101.
14. Report, *Interlocking Subversion in Government Departments,* Senate Internal Security Sub-committee, July 30, 1953.
15. Capell, Agriculture: How The Communists Sowed the Seeds, *American Opinion,* March 1973, p.17.
16. Van Gorder, *Ill Fares the Land,* 1966, p.4.
17. Ibid, p.6.
18. Capell, Agriculture: How The Communists Sowed the Seeds, *American Opinion,* March 1973, p.21.
19. Speech, Brownell, to Executive Club Luncheon, Chicago, November 6, 1953.
  Also see Chapter 16.
20. *One Man's Opinion,* November 1956.

21. Allen, Stop the Bank Gang, *American Opinion*, February 1979, p.13.
22. Hoover *Master's of Deceit*, 1958, p.275.
23. Lamphere, *The FBI-KGB War*, 1986.
24. Skousen, *The Naked Capitalist*, 1970, p.1.
25. Capell, Since F.D.R.: Some Not So Ancient History, *American Opinion*, March 1971, p.59.
26. *New York Daily News*, August 3, 1948.
27. Philbrick, *I Led Three Lives*.
28. Welch, *May God Forgive Us*, 1952, p.38.
29. Gumaer, The Killers: Assassination Made to Order, *American Opinion*
    February 1971, p.47.
30. Evans, James V. Forrestal, *American Opinion*, October 1967, inside back cover.
31. Capell, Since F.D.R.: Some Not So Ancient History, *American Opinion*,
    March 1971, pp. 57, 58.
32. Toledano, *Seeds of Treason*, 1965, p.83.
33. *The Sentinel Star*, Orlando, Florida Editorial reprinted in *Human Events*,
    August 11, 1961, p.525.
34. Allen, Mr. Nixon: A Hard Look at the Candidate, *American Opinion*,
    September 1968, pp.3, 4.
35. Roosevelt, *My Day*, August 16, 1948.
36. Reprinted in *Human Events*, September 15, 1961, p.619.
37. Testimony, Bentley, Senate Internal Security Subcommittee, May 29, 1952.
38. Drummey, The State Department, *The New American*, May 19, 1986, p.17.
39. Hoover, *Master's Of Deceit*, 1958, p.200.
40. Report, *Interlocking Subversion in Government Departments*, Senate Internal Security Subcommittee,
    July 30, 1953.
41. Capell, McCarthyism, *American Opinion*, January 1973, pp. 67, 69.

42. Report, *Interlocking Subversion in Government Departments,* Senate Internal Security Sub-committee, July 30, 1953.
43. Ibid.
44. Ibid.
45. Ibid.
46. Gitlow, *The Whole of Their Lives,* 1948, p.359.
47. Skousen, *The Naked Capitalist,* 1970, pp.79, 80.
48. Hearings, *Scope of Soviet Activities in the United States,* Senate Internal Security Sub-committee, June 14, 1956.
49. Drummey, McCarthy: The Truth, The Smear, and the Lesson, *American Opinion,* May 1964, p.5.
50. Barron, Otto Otepka: And the State Department, *American Opinion,* January 1964, p.10.
51. Rees, Moles Burrowing To High Places in U.S. Intelligence Agencies, *Conservative Digest,* November 1985, p.6.
52. Drummey, The State Department, *The New American,* May 19, 1986, p.17.
53. FBI Report, House Intelligence Committee, 1982.
54. Dispatch, Bullitt to Hull, April 20, 1936.

Chapter 14: The United States In the United Nations

1. Allen, Get US Out: The UN Threatens the United States, *American Opinion,* January 1972, p.65.
2. Ibid.
3. Ibid, p.68.
4. Scott, syndicated column, October 7, 1971.
5. The News, *The Review of the News,* October 10, 1979, p. 15.
6. Berner, Bullets, *American Opinion,* February1984, p.23.
7. Skousen, *The Naked Capitalist,* 1970, p.119.
8. *Postwar Foreign Policy Preparation 1939-1945,* U.S. Department of State Report, 1950.

9. Capell, Since F.D.R.: Some Not So Ancient History, *American Opinion,* March 1971, p.54.
10. *Time,* April 16, 1945.
11. Allen, Supreme Court, *American Opinion,* May 1969, p.10.
12. Allen, ·Insiders of the Great Conspiracy, *American Opinion,* September 1982, p.49.
13. Report *Institute of Pacific Relations,* Senate Internal Security Sub-committee, 1952, pp.223-225.
14. Evans, *The Politics of Surrender,* 1966, p.338.
15. Report, *Institute of Pacific Relations,* Senate Internal Security Sub-committee, 1952, p.224.
16. Lee, *The United Nations Conspiracy,* 1981, p.35.
17. *Time,* May 18, 1953.
18. Skousen, *The Naked Capitalist,* 1970, p.119.
19. Bush letter in response to a concerned citizen, The Candidacy of George Bush, *The New American,* January 18, 1988, p.43.
20. Hiss to Senator Karl Mundt (R-SD) before a Congressional Hearing, 1948.
21. *Time,* April 16, 1945.
22. Browder, *Victory and After.*
23. Allen, Get US Out!: The UN Threatens the United States, *American Opinion,* January 1972, p.61.
24. Toledano, *Seeds of Treason,* 1965, p.82.
25. Hearings, Senate Internal Security Sub-committee, March 4,1957.
26. Speech, Kornfeder, *The Communist Pattern in the U.N.,* Congress Of Freedom, San Francisco, April 1955.
27. *Nationalities In The USSR,* UNESCO, distributed throughout Latin America Africa and Asia
28. Internal Security Annual Report for 1954 Senate Internal Security Sub-committee, March 4, 1957, pp.213, 214.

29. The World Assembly At San Francisco, *Political Affairs,* April 1945,
   pp.289 300.
30. *Life,* July 16, 1945.
31. *Chicago Tribune,* July 11, 1945.
32. Allen, Get US Out!: The UN Threatens the United States, *American Opinion,*
   January 1972, p.61.
33. Testimony of Colonel Jan Bukar before the House Committee on Un-American Activities.
34. *Associated Press, Los Angeles Times,* April 7, 1970.
35. *New York Daily News,* May 26, 1954.
36. Hearings, *Activities Of U S. Citizens Employed by the UN,* Senate Internal Security Sub-committee, December 1952.
37. Ibid, pp.407, 408.
38. Statement, Eastland, December 17, 1952.
39. Speech, Kornfeder, The Communist Pattern in the UN, Congress of Freedom, San Francisco, April 1955.
40. Statement, McCarran, January 28, 1953.
41. Lie, *In The Cause of Peace,* pp.45, 46.
42. Grfffin, *The Fearful Master,* 1964, p.85.
43. Mahoney, The Tragedy of Southeast Asia, *The New American,* February 1, 1988, p.29.
44. Report, Dr. E. Van den Haag, *War In Katanga,* American Commission to
   Aid Katanga Freedom Fighters.
45. *New York Times,* December 31, 1961.
46. *St. Louis Post Dispatch,* December 31, 1962.
47. Report, Dr. E. Van den Haag, *War In Katanga,* American Commission to
   Aid Katanga Freedom Fighters.
48. Vleurinck, *46 Angry Men,* 1962, pp.91, 92.
49. *The Tidings,* Los Angeles, January 11,1963, p.1.
50. *Santa Ana Register,* March2, 1964.

51. Speech, Eisenhower, Wichita, Kansas, 1949.
52. Allen, Get US Out!: The UN Threatens the United States, *American Opinion,* January 1972, p.68.
53. Stanley, United Nabobs—Watergate To World Government, *American Opinion,* February 1974, p.22.
54. *Newsweek,* May 14, 1973.
55. Stanley, United Nabobs—Watergate To World Government, *American Opinion,* February 1974, p.20.

Chapter 15: Betrayal of the Prisoners of War— Korea and Vietnam.

1. Speech, Eisenhower, Presidential campaign, 1952.
2. Stang, The Prisoners: Why Does American Abandon Her Own, *American Opinion,* March 1970, p.9.
3. Clark, *From The Danube to the Yalu,* 1954.
4. Stang, The Prisoners: Why Does America Abandon Her Own, *American Opinion,* March 1970, p.2.
5. Letter, Lee, January 6,1965.
6. Stang, ·The Prisoners: Why Does American Abandon Her Own, *American Opinion,* March 1970, p.2.
7. Singlaub, *The American Legion,* August 1980.
8. Noble, *New York Times,* April 5, 1955.
9. Stang, The Prisoners: Why Does America Abandon Her Own, *American Opinion,* March 1970, p.2.
10. Stang, The Code, *American Opinion,* June 1973, p.16.
11. Ibid.
12. Ibid, p.15.
13. Homecoming 11 Newsletter, April 1986.
14. Interview, Smith, August 12, 1986.
15. Kidwell, America's Missing In Action, *The New American,* June 16,1986, p.12.
16. Ibid.
17. Ward, Our Men Are Still Out There And The Government Knows It,

Conservative Digest, August 1986, p.12.
18. *New York Times,* January 29, 1973.
19. *Wall Street Journal,* October 15,1985.
20. Becker, Americans In Captivity, *The New American,* July 14, 1986, p.18.
21. Roberts, *Missing In Action,* March 1980, p.55.
22. Ward, Our Men Are Still Out There and the Government Knows It,
Conservative Digest, August 1986, p.6.
23. Testimony, Hopper, Senate Veterans Affairs Committee, January 1986.
24. Ibid.
25. *The Union Leader,* Manchester, New Hampshire, December 12, 1987.
26. Becker, Americans In Captivity, *The New American,* July 14, 1986, p.18.
27. Testimony, *Smith,* Senate Veterans Affairs Committee, April 1984.
28. Ibid.
29. Ibid.
30. Ibid.
31. Ward, Our Men Are Still Out There And The Government Knows It,
Conservative Digest, August 1986.
32. Testmony, Shinkle, House Sub-committee on Asian and Pacific Affairs, reported in Roberts' *Missing In Action,* March 1980, pp.51, 52.
33. Ibid.
34. Ibid.
35. Ibid.
36. *The Review of the News,* October 10, 1979, p.51.
37. Hoar, The Missing, *American Opinion,* December 1980, p.91.
38. Ibid, p.18.
39. Ibid, p.89.

40. Ibid, p.18.
41. Thompson, The Scandal of the Abandoned Americans, *Conservative Digest,*
December 1985, p.50.
42. Capell, An Intelligence Report, *The Review of the News,* October 10, 1979, pp.51, 52.
43. Ibid, p.51.
44. Thompson, ·The Scandal of the Abandoned Americans, *Conservative Digest,*
December 1985, p.48.
45. McManus, Americans in the Gulag, *The New American,* December 8, 1986, p.21.
46. Letter, *The Honorable John LeBoutillier,* Skyhook 11 Project, 1988.
47. Interview, *Smith,* August 12, 1986.
48. LeBoutillier, Ed 8 Op-Ed, *Conservative Digest,* February 1986.
49. Letter, *The Honorable John LeBoutillier,* Skyhook 11 Project, 1988.
50. Ward, Our Men Are Still Out There And The Government Knows It,
Conservative Digest, August 1986.
51. Becker, Americans In Captivity, *The New American,* July 14, 1986, p.18.
52. Press Conference, National Vietnam Veterans Coalition, Washington, D.C.,
November 1986.
53. Kidwell, Rescuing The POWs, *The New American,* December 8, 1986.
54. Paul, *Wall Street Journal,* August 1986.
55. Anderson, *Washington Post,* September 18, 1985.
56. Turtle to the Honorable John LeBoutillier, reported in *Conservative Digest,*
February 1986.
57. Ward, Our Men Are Still Out There And The Government Knows It,
Conservative Digest, August 1986, p.6.

58. Ibid.
59. Ibid, p.11.
60. Singlaub, *The American Legion,* August 1980.
61. Ward, Our Men Are Still Out There and the Government Knows It,
    Conservative Digest August 1986, p.7.
62. Hoar, The Missing, *American Opinion,* December 1960, p.17.
63. Letter, *The Honorable William M. Hendon,* July 13, 1987.
64. Thompson, The Scandal of the Abandoned Americans, *Conservative Digest,*
    December 1985, p.45.
65. Ibid.
66. Capell, *Henry Kissinger: Soviet Agent* 1974.
67. Speech, *Solzhenitsyn,* AFL-CIO dinner, July 30, 1975.
68. Letter, *Eugene B. McDaniel,* Captain, USN Retired, September 17, 1987.
69. Ron Martz, *The Atlanta Journal,* September 1,1987.
70. Letter, *The Honorable John LeBoutillier,* Skyhook II Project, 1988.

Chapter 16: A Potpourri of Traitorous Acts and Treasonous Deeds

1. Capell, Since F.D.R.: Some Not So Ancient History,
   American Opinion, March 1971, p.54.
2. Capell, McCarthyism: Still The Fight For America,
   American Opinion, January 1973, p.64.
3. Ibid.
4. Editorial, Straight, *New Republic.*
5. Straight, *After a Long Silence,* 1983.
6. Ibid.
7. Ibid.
8. Ibid.

9. Ibid.
10. Evans, DeLibris, *American Opinion,* December 1983, p.64.
11. Hoar, F.D.R., 1932-1940, *American Opinion,* December 1978, p.100.
12. Oliver, Marxmanship In Dallas, *American Opinion,* February 1964, p.25.
13. Stang, Since Camelot, *American Opinion,* October 1973, p.11.
14. Oliver, Marxmanship In Dallas, *American Opinion,* February 1964, p.25.
15. *Daily Worker,* November 26, 1963.
16a. *New York Daily News,* January 3, 1964.
16b. Gumaer, The AC.L.U.- Lawyers Playing the Red Game, *American Opinion,*
    September 1969, p.89.
17. Barron, The Burners: Security Files Are Being Destroyed, *American Opinion,*
    November 1964.
18. Letter, Oswald, to his brother after defecting to Communist Occupied Russia
19. Oliver, Marxmanship In Dallas, *American Opinion,* February 1964, p.13.
20. Dies, Invasion: Moscow's Secret Army in America, *American Opinion,*
    November 1964, p.76.
21. Capell, Since F.D.R.: Some Not So Ancient History, *American Opinion,*
    March 1971, p.67.
22. Ibid.
23. Capell, *Henry Kissinger: Soviet Agent,* 1974.
24. Hoar, How The Far Left Writes, *American Opinion,* February 1985, p.75.
25. Stang, Mr. Jimmy, *American Opinion,* December 1977, p.91.

26. Capell, Since F.D.R.: Some Not So Ancient History, *American Opinion,* March 1971, p.54. The Amerasia, case was thoroughly covered in a series of articles by Frederick Woltman in the *New York World-Telegram,* and published as a booklet by the newspaper in 1950.
27. Allen, Betraying China, *American Opinion,* October 1971, p.8.
28. Ibid.
29. Ibid, p.9.
30. Welch, *May God Forgive Us,* 1952, p. 18.
31. Drummey, The State Department, *The New American,* May 19, 1986, p.19.
32. Smith, *OSS: The Secret History of America's First Central Intelligence Agency,* 1972.
33. Statement to Norman Dodd, Research Director of the Special House Committee to Investigate Tax Exempt Foundations, December 1953.
34. Report, *Interlocking Subversion In Government Departments,* Senate Internal Security Sub-committee, July 30, 1953, p. 43, 44.
35. Ibid.
36. Hearings, *Scope of Soviet Activities In The United States,* Senate Internal Security Sub-committee, part 49, November 21, 1956.
37. Tuck, They Paused To Remark, *American Opinion,* November 1967, p.24.
38. Speech, Brownell, Executive Club Luncheon, Chicago, November 6, 1953.
39. Kennedy, State of the Union Address, January 29, 1961.
40. NBC News, Three Star Extra, September 14, 1961.
41. Letter, J. Herbert Stone, Regional Forester to Forest Supervisor, Okanogen National Forest, July 12, 1961.
42. Letter, Reuther to Melvin Bishop, January 30, 1934.
43. Evans, Dean Rusk: Is He The Insiders' Quarterback?, *American Opinion,* March 1968, p.81.

44. Report, *Military Cold War Education And Speech Review Policies,* Senate Armed Services Committee, October 19, 1962, p.203.
45. Ibid.
46. Reuther, Walter and Victor, *Reuther Memorandum,* written to Attorney General Robert Kennedy.
47. Speech, *J. Edgar Hoover*, June 16, 1959.
48. Report, *New Drive Against the Anti-Communist Program,* Senate Internal Security Sub-committee, July 11, 1961.
49. *People's World,* February 25, 1961.
50. Report, *New Drive Against The Anti-Communist Program,* Senate Internal Security Sub-committee, July 11, 1961
51. Speech, Kennedy, *New York Times,* November 19, 1961.
52. Letter of transmittal, McCloy, June 23, 1961.
53. Allen, Disarmament: They're Promoting Peace of the Grave, *American Opinion,* June 1970, pp.10, 11.
54. *Document 7277*, U.S. Department of State, September 1961.
55. Tower, *Congressional Record,* January 29, 1962.
56. Drafted in 1799.
57. Letter to Nicaragua's Communist tyrant, March 20, 1984, signed by 10 members of the U.S. House of Representatives.
58. Rees, Save the Logan Act, *American Opinion,* October 1982, p.46.
59. Stockdale, *In Love And War,* 1984.
60. Rees, Save the Logan Act, *American Opinion,* October 1982, p.79.
61. Ibid.
62. Ibid.
63. Utt, *Congressional Report,* September 24, 1969.
64. *The World Almanac and Book of Facts For 1954,* p.115.
65. Donovan, *Eisenhower, The Inside Story,* p.246.
66. Evans, *The Politics of Surrender,* 1966, pp.159-161.
67. Statement, Roudebush, January 1, 1966.
68. Evans, *The Politics Of Surrender,* 1966, pp.159-161.

69. Testimony, *Hoover*, before the House Sub-committee on Appropriations, March 4,1965.
70. *Los Angeles Examiner,* October 28, 1950.
71. Allen, The Merger: Planning For World Government, *American Opinion,* October 1973, p.66.
72. Nixon, Presidential Campaign, 1960.
73. Capell, *Henry Kissinger: Soviet Agent,* 1974.
74. Rees, Following The Presidential Scenario, *American Opinion,* October 1979, p.10.
75. Ibid, p.79.
76. *The Herald,* Albany, Georgia, June 25, 1985.
77. Joiner, Aid and Trade—Stop Financing Communism, *The JBS Bulletin,* November 1986, p.14.
78. *Knoxville News Sentinel,* January 27, 1988.
79. Joiner, Aid and Trade—Stop Financing Communism, *The JBS Bulletin,* November 1986, p.14.
80. Brownfeld, *South Africa's Importance To The Free World—An Untold Story,* 1984, p.8.
81. Grady, *U.S. Leaders Undermine South Africa Enroute to Destruction of America,* American Pistol & Rifle Association, pamphlet, p.3.
82. McDonald, Internal Security, *American Opinion,* February 1976, p.14.
83. Ibid, p.9.
84. Capell, *Henry Kissinger: Soviet Agent,* 1974.
85. Huck, The Ford Foreign Policy, *American Opinion,* October 1976, p.9.
86. Stanley, *The Review of The News,* June 23, 1976.
87. Bullets, *American Opinion,* April 1974, p.77.
88. Capell, The Left: Collectivists In The Congress, *American Opinion,* July-August 1974, p.68.
89. The Inside Page, *Conservative Digest,* January 1986, p.4.
90. Capell, The Left: Collectivists In The Congress, *American Opinion,* July-August 1974, p.68.

91. Ibid.
92. Citation, House Committee On Un-American Actvities, 1950.
93. Rees, How They Nearly Destroyed U.S. Intelligence, *American Opinion*, November 1981, p.27.
94. Scott, Let Reagan Beware Of The Revolution, *Conservative Digest*, June 1987, p.49.
95. Ibid, p.50.
96. The Communist *Daily Worker*, February 6, 1971.
97. Capell, The Left: Collectivists In The Congress, *American Opinion*, July-August 1974, p.68.
98. Ibid p.69.
99. Rees, Kook Left Given Power In Congress, *Conservative Digest*, June 1987, p.68-70.
100. Hoar, The Embarrassing Case of Senator Howard Metzenbaum, *Conservative Digest*, March 1987, p.51.
101. Rees, The Left, *American Opinion*, July-August 1984, p.99.
102. Hoar, California's Alan Cranston Astounds Voters, *Conservative Digest*, August 1986, p.88, 89.
103. Hearings, *Investigation Of Major Julius Schrieber*, Senate Internal Security Sub-committee, 1954.
104. Ibid, p.77.

105. Rees, Time To Restore The Internal Security Committee, *American Opinion*, January 1981, p.49.
106. Ibid.
107. The Inside Page, *Conservative Digest*, March 1987, p.3.
108. Huck, Gambling With Subversion, *American Opinion*, May 1977, p.13.
109. Ibid.
110. Ibid.

111. Rees, The Left, *American Opinion,* July-August 1984, p.30.

Epilogue

1. Speech, *Fonda,* Michigan State University, November 22, 1969.
2. Drummey, The Evil Empire Is Still Evil, *The New American,* July 18, 1988, p.6.
3. Graves, May God Forgive, *American Opinion,* March 1985, p.50.
4. Dallin, *Forced Labor In Soviet Russia,* 1948.
5. Marchenko, They Paused To Remark, *Conservative Digest,* December 1986, p.40.
6. Connors, Atrocities Which The Liberals Hide, *American Opinion,* January 1965, p.65.
7. Ingbretson, Our Contribution To The Slave Trade, *The New American,* July 14,1986, p.43.
8. Ibid.
9. Allen, The Red Traders, *American Opinion,* April 1984, p.2.
10. Davydov, testimony before Congress, 1983.
11. Harriss, *Reader's Digest,* September 1983.
12. Shifrin, *The First Guidebook To Prisons And Concentration Camps of the Soviet Union,* 1982.
13. Ibid.
14. Hearings, *Crimes of Khrushchev,* House Committee On Un-American Activities, 7 vols.
15. Allen, The Red Traders, *American Opinion,* April 1984, p.96.
16. *The Great Pretense: A Symposium On Anti-Stalinism And The 20th Congress Of The Soviet Communist Party,* House Committee on Un-American Activities, May 19,1956, pp.18, 19.
17. *Time,* March 5, 1956.

18. Walker, 1971 study for Congress, Institute Of International Studies at the University of South Carolina.
19. Hoar, Changes In Red China, *American Opinion,* January 1985, p.100.
20. DeJaegher, *The Enemy Within.*
21. Ibid.
22. Hearings, *Communist Persecution Of Churches In Red China and Korea,* House Committee on Un-American Activities, p.3.
23. Wurmbrand, *Tortured For Christ,* 1969.
24. Ibid.
25. Lee, The Nature Of Communism, *American Opinion,* November 1983, p.87.
26. Hearings, *Communist Persecution Of Churches In Red China And Korea,* House Committee On Un-American Activities, p. 31, 32.
27. Allen, Detente With Monsters, *American Opinion,* September 1975, p.105.
28. *New York Times,* April 30, 1953.
29. *New York Times,* November 29, 1953.
30. Stang, The Prisoners: Why Does America Abandon Her Own?, *American Opinion,* March 1970, p.1.
31. Ibid, p.6.
32. Senate Permanent Sub-committee On Investigations, 1954.
33. Ibid.
34. Hunter, *Brainwashing,* 1958.
35. Leckie, *Conflict,* 1962.
36. Stang, 'The Prisoners: Why Does America Abandon Her Own?, *American Opinion,* March 1970, p.1.
37. Lee, 'The Nature Of Communism, *American Opinion,* November 1983, p.88.
38. Dooley, *Deliver Us From Evil,* 1956, p.98.
39. Ibid.

40. Davidson, Vietnam: When Terror Is Not Statistics, *American Opinion*
    February 1968, p.80,81,83.
41. Mahoney, The Tragedy Of Southeast Asia, *The New American,* February 1988, p.32.
42. Wood, The Betrayed, *American Opinion,* January 1969, p.10.
43. Capell, *Henry Kissinger: Soviet Agent,* 1974.
44. McGrory, syndicated column, August 19, 1975.
45. Hoar, The Human Cost Of Betrayal, *American Opinion,* October 1977, p.77,79.
46. Ibid, p.77.
47. *New York Times,* April 3, 1975.
48. *Twin Circle,* July 27, 1975.
49. Speech, Fonda, Michigan State University, November 22, 1969
50 Lacouture, *New York Review Of Books,* 1977.
51 Barron and Paul, *Murder Of A Gentle Land,* 1977.
52. *London Times,* February 19, 1976.
53. Shams, *In Cold Blood,* 1987.
54. Rykov to Helsinki Watch Investigators, 1986.
55. *To Win The Children: Afghanistan's Other War,* Helsinki Watch Committee,
    December 1986.

INDEX

A

Aaron, David L., 236
Abourezk, James,, 349
Abraham, Larry, 31
Abzug, Bella S.,, 346
Acheson, Dean, 165, 174, 178, 183, 198, 199, 200, 207, 221, 224, 231, 273, 285, 286, 287, 322, 327
Acheson, George, Jr., 199
Adamic, Louis, 348
Adams, John G., 166
Adams, Sherman, 166
Adler, Solomon, 276, 285
Agee, Philip, 343
Aiping, Zhang, 24
Alcibiades, 248
Alien Registration Act, 158
Alinsky, Saul, 45
Amendment, Wylie, 67
Amerasia, 176, 193, 326, 420
American Allied Drug and Chemical Company, 32
American Cyanamid, 34
Amin, Idi, 226
Andropov, Yuri V., 62, 72
Aptheker, Herbert, 123
Arens, Richard, 135, 329
Armco Incorporated, 38
Armour, Charles R., 75
Armstrong, William L.,, 93, 107
Arthur G. McKee Company, 33
Arthur J. Brandt Company, 12
Ashbrook, John,, 31, 35, 258, 383
Austin Company, 11

B

Baciu, Nicholas, 243
Baker, James, 86

Baldridge, Malcolm, 41
Baldwin, Roger, 135, 220, 250
Ball, George, 72, 185, 331
Barker, Clifford, 260
Barmine, Alexander, Gen., 131, 218
Barnes, Scott, 310
Barnet, Richard, 140, 186
Barnett, Robert W., 188
Barron, Bryton, 206
Barry, Marion, 47
Batista, Fulgencio, 203
Battle Act of 1951, 13
Bay of Pigs, 179, 223
Beam, Jacob Dyneley, 184
Bechtel Corporation, 34, 35
Becker, Yvonne, 316
Bell, Griffin, 149
Belov, Yuri, 92
Bendjedid, Chadli, Col., 61
Bennett, John C., 135
Benson, Ezra Taft, V, 74, 87, 110, 145, 166
Bentall,, David J., 226, 227
Bentley, Elizabeth, 221, 245, 269, 270, 291
Berger, Samuel David, 187
Berle, A.A., 242
Berle, Adolph, 162
Bethancourt, Romulo Escobar, 213
Biddle, Francis, 155
Black, Justice, 154
Block, John, 77
Bloor, Ella Reeva, 265
Boeing, 15, 39, 46
Boggs, Hale, 138
Bohmrich, Louis, 84
Bokassa, Jean-Bedel, 301
Borden, William L., 250
Borge, Thomas, 214
Bourne, Peter G., 125
Boussarath, Kham-Mou, 314
Braden, Carl, 135
Breckinridge, John, 9

Brennan, William J., Jr., 220
Brezhnev, Leonid, 40, 77, 112, 256, 339, 344
Bridges, Harry, 155, 161, 394
Bridges, Styles,, 132
Brockman,Orville, 259
Brodsky, Joseph R., 227
Browder, Earl, 161, 165, 271, 291
Brown, Archie, 161
Brown, Samuel Winfred, 125, 317
Browne, Malcolm W., 43
Brownell, Herbert, 166, 222
Brownell, Herbert, Jr., 166, 222
Brownfeld, Allan C., 343
Bryant Chucking Grinder Company, 14, 15
Brzezinski, Zbigniew, 235, 236, 263
Buchanan, Patrick, 63, 126
Buckley, James L., Senator, 147
Budenny, Marshal, 357
Budenz, Louis, 145, 184, 199, 218, 219, 245, 271, 287
Bullitt, William C., 282, 357
Bunche, Ralph, 294, 295
Bundy, McGeorge, 224
Bundy, Theodore, 224
Bundy, William P., 165
Bunker, Ellsworth, 186
Burch, J. Thomas, 309
Burnham, James, 223
Burns, John F., 60
Burton, Phillip, 135, 137
Bush, George, 26, 290, 321, 413

C

C.E. Lummus Company, 38
Capell, Frank, 87, 131, 238
Carillo, Santiago, 149
Carmichael, Stokely, 125, 228
Caron, Don, 330
Carter, Jimmy, 20, 212, 254, 388, 390, 406
Casey, William J., 52, 238
Castro, Fidel, 179, 202, 203, 204, 206, 212, 238
Caughlan, John, 137

Ceausescu, Nicolae, 16, 83, 101, 112
Cellar, Emanuel, 346
Chambers, Whittaker, 162, 229, 242, 245, 269, 272, 274, 275, 277
Chancellor, John, 182
Chevron-Gulf, VI, 44, 45, 64
Chi, Harriet Levine, 177
Chicago Seven, 127
Chissano, Joaquim, 301
Church, Frank, 148
Cicero, 10, 151
Clark, J. Reuben, 288
Clark, Mark W., Gen., 303, 360, 361
Clark, Ramsey, 120, 228, 317, 327, 335, 336
Clark, Tom, 186, 327
Cleveland, Harlan, 185, 298
Coe, Virginius Frank, 51, 63, 180, 269, 285, 330
Cohen, Wilbur J., 229
Cohn, Roy, 158
Colbert, Evelyn, 192
Coleco, 103
Coler, Jack, 144
Communist Control Act, 172, 396
Conlan, Don, 63
Connors, Michael F., 353
Control Data Corporation, 19, 34, 36, 44, 252
Conyers, John, 135, 347
Cooper, John F., Professor, 102
Coplon, Judith, 192
Cottrell, Stan, 320
Crane, Philip M., 241
Cranston, Alan, Senator, 348, 423
Crockett, George W., 347
Crockett, William J., 187
Currie, Lauchlin, 163, 169, 183, 198, 221, 263, 275

D

D'Amato, Alfonse, Senator, 94
d'Aubuisson, Robert, 257
Dallin, David, 352
Davies, John Paton, 183, 186, 198, 199
Davies, John Paton, Jr., 183, 186, 198, 199

Davis, Angela, 347
Davis, Rennie, 127, 335
Davydov, Georgy, 354
Day, George E., Cal., 120, 123
Dean, Vera Micheles, 177
Debs, Eugene V., 229
DeJaegher, Raymond J., 358
Dellinger, David, 335
Dellums, Ronald, Congressman, 347
Denton, Jeremiah, Senator, 147
DePorte, Anton William, 191
Derwinski, Edward J., Congressman, 117
Dikeos, Victor H., 192
Dimitroff, Georgi, 277
Dobrynin, Anatoly F., 344
Dodd, Christopher J., Senator, 349
Dodd, Thomas, Senator, 14, 73, 202, 400
Dodd, William E., 184
Dohrn, Bernadine, 123
Domestic Terrorist Digest, 144
Dominick, Peter H., 118
Donahue, Morgan Jefferson, 320
Dong, Pham Van, 308
Donner, Frank J., 138
Dooley, Tom, 363
Dorn, Bernadette, 347
Doty, Madeline, 250
Dresser firm, 18
Drinan, Robert, 137
Drummey, James J., 26, 71
Dryden, John, 364
Duarte, Napoleon, 257
duBerrier, Hilaire, 254, 285
Duggan, Lawrence, 184, 203, 232
Dulles, Allen, 165, 263
Dulles, John Foster, 13, 177, 273, 287
Dzerzhinsky, Felix, 356

E

Eagleberger, Lawrence S., 93
Eaker, Ira, 255

Eastland, James O., 141
Eaton, Cyrus Stephen, 134
Eduardo, Jose, 59, 64, 101
Edwards, Donald, 135
Edwards, Willard, 208
Ege, Ismail, Cal., 277
Eisenhower, Milton, 204, 300
El Paso Natural Gas Company, 34
Electric Boat Company, 12
Elegant, Robert S., 46
Ellsberg, Daniel, 128, 223
En-lai, Chou, 22, 276, 328, 340
Erickson, Paul G., 364
Ermacora, Felix, 367

F

Fallows, James Mi, 233
Farmer, James, 135
Feinglass, Abe, 149
Felt, Mark, 226, 227
Ferguson, Isaac E., 177, 183, 198
Field, Frederick Vanderbilt, 117
Findley, Paul, 139, 264
Fish, Hamilton, Congressman, 191, 192
Fishback, Sam, 271, 287, 294, 295
Flato, Charles, 229
Flynn, Elizabeth Gurley, 139, 220
Flynn, Errol, 291
Flynn, John T., 243, 244, 324
Fonda, Jane, 120, 121, 122, 123, 335, 347, 350, 366
Ford Foundation, 165, 328
Ford Motor Company, 11, 33
Ford, Gerald, 15, 233, 252, 253, 406
Ford, Henry, 11
Foreign Assistance Act, 147
Foreign Intelligence Surveillance Act, 150
Forrestal, James V., 273, 282, 411
Fortas, Abe, 218, 226, 227, 267, 286
Foster, William Z., 220
Fowler, Henry, 228
Frankfurter, Felix, 220, 226, 232, 245, 322, 323

Frechtling, Louis Earl, 182
Freedom of Information Act, 147
Freeman, Fulton, 199
Froines, John, 127
Fulbright, William, Senator, 12, 26, 35, 36, 52, 93, 107, 112, 138, 144, 163, 165, 166, 169, 171, 172, 175, 182, 184, 185, 186, 187, 190, 198, 203, 205, 206, 217, 218, 220, 222, 226, 227, 238, 250, 255, 262, 269, 277, 282, 285, 291, 307, 312, 328, 329, 339, 357, 381, 385, 418
Furskins, 112

G

Gallagher, Leo, 227
Galvin, Robert, 47
Garn, Jake, Senator, 15, 16
Garwood, Robert 230,, 307, 314
Gatsis, Andrew J., Brig. Gen., VI
Geer, Will, 265
Gelb, Leslie, 128
Gerstacker, Carl, 34
Gerstenzang, James, 24
Gill, William J., 175
Gilman, Benjamin A., 82
Ginzburg, Alexander, 92
Gitlow, Benjamin, 132, 279
Glasser, Harold, 190, 220, 232, 269, 274, 285
Gleason Works, 16
Goddar, Henry W., 322
Goldberg, Arthur, 226
Goldsmith, Arthur J., 271
Goldwater, Barry, 23, 47, 87, 110, 124
Goleniewski, Michael M., Col., 137, 170, 230
Gorbachev, Mikhail Sergeyvich, 11, 20, 71, 91, 352
Gravel, Mike, Senator, 348
Gray, L. Patrick, 149
Greenberg, Michael1, 180, 221
Grew, Joseph C., 327
Guild, Eugene, Capt., 304
Guthrie, Woody, 229

H

Habib, Philip C., 193

Haig, Alexander, 232, 263, 319
Hall, Gus, 161
Hall, Jack, 159
Halperin, Morton, 128
Hammarskjold, Dag, 294
Hammer, Armand, 32, 34, 35, 52, 54, 237, 238
Hammer, Julius, 237
Hansen, Clifford P., Senator, 112
Hargis, Billy James, 332
Harman, Sidney, 236
Harriman, Averill 27,, 32, 115, 183
Harrington, Michael,, 349
Harrington, Sir John, 107
Harris, Jack Sargent, 295
Harriss, Joseph, 92, 354
Hart, Thomas, 319
Hasbro, 103
Hatch Act of 1939, 172, 396
Hawkins, Augustus F., 345
Hayden, Tom, 120, 121, 123, 125, 127, 133, 140, 233, 335, 347
Hayes, Charles, 345
Helms, Jesse, Senator, 27, 39, 378
Henderson, Loy, 327
Hendon, William M.,, 312, 418
Hercules Motor Corporation, 12
Heritage Foundation, 41, 93, 382, 385
Hertzberg, Hendrick, 127
Hill, Robert, 202
Hillman, Sidney, 52, 219, 230, 324
Hiss, Alger, 54, 136, 162, 165, 169, 171, 177, 178, 180, 183, 184, 185, 190, 192, 195, 198, 200, 205, 208, 215, 219, 220, 227, 230, 231, 232, 234, 242, 243, 245, 263, 267, 268, 269, 273, 274, 275, 285, 286, 288, 289, 290, 292, 293, 294, 295, 297, 322, 323, 334, 339
Hiss, Donald, 221, 268, 286
Hoar, William P., 35
Hodges, Luther, 72
Hoffman, Abbe, 127
Hoffman, David, Lt.Cmdr, 120
Hoffman, Paul G., 166
Holland, Wade, 37
Homer, 277

Honecker, Erich, 66, 98
Hoover, J. Edgar, 19, 123, 130, 135, 137, 143, 144, 146, 158, 159, 163, 181, 245, 270, 279, 283, 325, 327, 332, 339, 421
Hopkins, Harry, 51, 161, 163, 220
Hopper, Earl P., Col., 309
Howard, Hungerford B., 199
Howard, William, 340
Hsiao-ping, Teng, 23, 24, 25, 372
Hua,Huang, 284
Hubbell,John, 365
Huber, Robert J.,, 122
Huck, Susan, Dr., 84, 142, 145
Hughes, Howard, 40
Hull, Cordell, 282
Humphrey, Hubert H., 72
Hunter, Edward, 333, 361
Husak, Gustav, 63, 100

I

IBM, 17, 19, 36, 37, 39, 43, 252
Ickes, Harold L., 219, 230
Immigration and Nationality Act, 148
Inderfurth, Karl F., 236
Internal Security Act, 160

J

Jackson, Jesse, 259
Jaffe, Philip, 326, 327
Jaffee,Philip J.., 177
Jagger, Bianca, 349
Jaruzelski, Wojciech, Gen., 83
Javits, Jacob, 187
Jencks, Clinton, 157
Jenner, William E.,, 277
Jessup, Philip C., 183, 191, 287
John Birch Society, 332
John K Calder Company, 33
Johnpoll, Alexander, 189
Johnson, Joseph E., 231
Johnson, Lyndon Baines, 134, 249, 326
Johnson, Manning, 294

Johnson, Sam, 120
Joiner, Herb, 65
Jones, Jim, 59
Jones, Leroi, 249
Joseph, James A., 126

K

Kadar, Janos, 43, 56, 62, 66, 113
Kahn, Albert, 11
Kahn, J. Kesner, 345
Kai-shek, Chiang, 85, 178, 179, 184, 186, 197, 204, 209, 218, 221, 245, 276
Kama River, 17, 18, 36, 52, 53, 118
Kaplan, Irving, 229, 269, 286
Karr, David, 348
Kastenmeier, Robert W., 135
Keegan, George, Maj. Gen., 37, 375
Kelley, Clarence, 144
Kendall, Donald, 30
Kennedy, John F., 205, 219, 299, 324, 337
Kennedy,.Robert, 224, 421
Khrushchev, Nikita, 73, 79, 201, 209, 241, 247, 324, 326
King, Cora Weiss, 227
King, Martin Luther, Jr., 136, 193, 228, 258, 259, 409
King, Mary, 125
Kirkpatrick, Jeane J., 44, 74, 376
Kissinger, Henry, VI, 14, 45, 75, 119, 128, 137, 170, 181, 188, 189, 192, 193, 230, 232, 233, 234, 235, 238, 263, 276, 308, 319, 340, 344, 364, 370, 371, 377, 382, 389, 391, 396, 397, 398, 399, 400, 405, 406, 408, 418, 419, 422, 426
Klein, Lawrence R., 236
Kleindienst, Richard G., 337
Klosson, Boris, 181, 188
Koppers Corporation, 33
Kornfeder, Joseph Zack, 139
Kosygin, Aleksei N., 34
Kramer, Charles, 267, 268
Krivitsky, 268
Kuan-hua, Chiao, 284
Kubek, Anthony, 200
Kyes,Roger M., 361

L

Lacouture, Jean, 366
Lane, Arthur Bliss, 221
Lane, Mark, 347
LaPasionaria, 122
Larsen, Emmanuel S., 326
Larson, Arthur, 247
Laski, Harold, 52, 187
Latta, D.L.,, 73
Lattimore, Owen, 177, 183, 198, 209, 218, 219, 227, 245, 287
Laughton, Raymond A., 232
Lausche, Frank J.,, 79
Lawton, Kirke B., Maj. Gen., 167
Leech, John L., 345
Lehman, John, VI
Lehrer, Jim, 182
Lena Goldfields Ltd, 32
Lessiovski, Viktor M., 259
Letelier, Orlando, 236, 349
Letson, William N., 36
Leuer, Kenneth C., Maj. Gen., 311
Levi, Edward H., 143, 234
Levison, Stanley David, 259
Lewis, John, 236
Lie, Trygve, 296
Lincoln, Abraham, 194
Lindstrom, Paul,, 306
Linowitz, Sol, 213, 263
Lodge, Henry Cabot, 166
Logan Act, 124, 334, 335, 336, 394, 421
Lonigan, Edna, 265
LoPresti, Robert G., Lt, 109
Ludden, Raymond P., 199
Lumumba, Patrice, 185
Lunning, Just, 190

M

M'ba, Leon, 301
MacArthur, Douglas, 207, 297, 402
Mack Truck, 32
MacKenzie, Ross, 95

MacKnight, Jesse, 192
Magdoff, Harry, 229
Makarenko, Mikhail, 39, 71, 78
Malkin, Maurice, 152, 155
Maltsev, Yevdokin Yegorovich, Gen., 78
Marchenko, Anatoly T., 353
Margolies, Daniel Franks, 190
Marshall, George Catlett,, 52, 174, 197
Marshall, Thurgood, 227
Martin, Edwin M., 188, 263
Martin, Joseph W., Jr., 208
Martinez, Arabella, 126
Marx, Karl, 53, 236, 249, 264, 348
Mattel, 103
Matthews, J.B., 139
McCarran Act, 160
McCarran, Pat, 148, 296
McCarran-Walter Act, 148, 149
McCarthy, Joseph, 191, 247, 397
McClosky, Frank, 307
McConnell, John P., 116
McDonald, Larry, 19, 140, 146, 150, 223, 259, 344
McFarlane, Robert C., 308
McGovern, George, 148
McHenry, Donald, 193, 259
McLeod, Scott, 175, 176, 177, 188, 191, 192, 195, 211, 281
McNamara, Robert Strange, 222, 330
McWilliams,Carey, 331
Meany, George, 54
Mecure, Alex P., 126
Medina, Harold, 347
Metzenbaum, Howard, 423
Michalowski, Jerzy, Madam, 184
Mindszenty, Jozsef Cardinal, 189
Minh, Ho Chi, 123, 125, 127, 212, 246
Mobutu, Joseph, 301
Mondale, Walter, 236, 260, 263
Monroe Doctrine, 251
Montenegro, Arturo, 203
Montgomery, Ed, 226
Moody, L.B., Col., 197

Morris, Robert, 57, 145
Moynihan, Daniel P., 249
Mugabe, Robert G., 60, 367
Mundt, Karl E., Senator, 118
Murphy, Frank, 155
Muskie, Edmund, 128, 138

N

Nagy, Imre, 200
Nelson, Eleanor, 190, 267
Nelson, O.W., Jr., 133
Nelson, Steve, 156
New Deal, 131, 260
Nicholas II, Czar, 242
Niles, David K, 220
Nixon, Richard, 54, 81, 82, 85, 222, 230, 231, 253, 263, 275, 319, 339
Nkoloso, Edward Mukuka, 302
Nkrumah, Kwame, 187
Noble, John H., 305
Noriega, Manuel Antonio, 213
Nowak,Jan, 55, 65
Nyerere, Julius, 256

O

O'Connor, John J., Congressman, 161
Occidental Petroleum, 32, 34, 35
ODRA, VI, 230, 234
Oliver, Glen J., Sgt., 361
Olson, Carl, 38
Ortega, Daniel, 54, 65, 202, 255, 335, 349
Oswald, Lee Harvey, 179, 181, 253, 325
Otepka, Otto, 172, 175, 176, 180, 185, 189, 205, 210, 212, 397, 398, 399, 402, 412

P

Panuch, J. Anthony, 279
Panuch, Joe, 190
Pasquini, Guiseppe, 149
Pastor, Robert, 236
Pasvolsky, Leo, 288, 293
Patterson, Leonard, 294

Paul, Bill, 315
Pauling, Linus, 226
Pawley, William D., 198
Peek, George N., 266
Peng, Li, 88
Pentagon Papers, 128, 223
PepsiCo, 30
Perlo, Victor, 54, 267, 269, 270, 285
Peterson, Esther, 226
Philbrick, Herbert A., 272
Philby, Kim, 168
Pillion, John R., 182
Ponomarev, Boris N., 132
Pope John, 299
Popper, David Henry, 176, 178, 180, 183
Powell, Adam Clayton, 346
Power, Thomas, Gen., 338
Pressman, Lee, 54, 180, 220, 227, 232, 267, 268, 286, 322
Privacy Act, 148
Prosten, Jesse, 135
Puhan, Alfred, 189, 190
Pullman Incorporated, 36

Q

Qaddafi, Muammar, 54
Quynh, Hoang Huu, 317

R

Raskin, Marcus, 140
Ray, James, 121
Reagan, Ronald, 13, 22, 28, 77, 238, 256, 259, 261, 321, 372
Reeva, Ella, 122, 265
Refugee Relief Act, 149
Resor, Stanley R., 251
Reuther, Walter, 330
Rhee,Syngman, 304
Rice, Edward E., 199
Richardson, Elliot L., 232
Rimestad,Idar, 171
Ringwalt, Arthur, 199
Rizo, Julian Torres, 133

Robinson, Roger W., Jr., 55
Rockefeller, David, 52, 53, 60, 91
Rockefeller, Nelson, 234, 235, 327
Rockwell, W.F., Jr., 88
Rogers, William P.,, 166, 171, 172, 186, 222
Roosevelt, Eleanor, 187, 245, 249
Roosevelt, Theodore, 220
Rosenberg, Alan, 190
Rosenberg, Anna, 52
Roth, Toby, 50, 61
Rothschild, Edward, 338
Roudebush, Richard, Congressman, 339
Rouge, Khmer, 299, 366
Rowe, David Nelson, Professor, 111
Rubin, Sam, 140
Rubottom, Roy, 206
Ruraz, Zdzislaw M., 83
Rusk, Dean, 72, 80, 171, 172, 178, 179, 180, 185, 205, 210, 224, 319, 331, 420
Russell, Richard, 249
Rustin, Bayard, 258
Rykov, Igor, 368

S

Saga, 133
Santos, Jose Eduardo dos, 59, 101
Savath,Saray, 367
Schlesinger, Arthur, 225
Schmidt, Robert D., 19
Schreiber, Julius, 348
Schware, Rudolph, 157
Scott, Otto, 346
Sears, 104, 105, 155
Sedition Act, 122
Service, John Stewart, 160, 183, 186, 198, 199, 281, 326, 327
Shah of Iran, 254
Shearon, Marjorie, 229
Shevchenko, Arkady N., 284
Shifrin, Avraham, 21, 90, 93, 355
Shultz, George, 237, 263
Silverman, George, 267, 269, 285

Silvermaster, Nathan Gregory, 163, 180, 182, 222, 270, 285
Singlaub, John K., 254
Slochower, Harry, 156
Smith Act, 153, 158, 159, 160, 219, 347
Smith, Earl E.T., VI, 202
Smith, Horace, 199
Smith, Mark, Maj., 311, 314
Smith, Walter Bedell, 234, 327
Snow, Edgar, 186
Sokolovsky, Marshal, 338
Solzhenitsyn, Alexander, 70, 95, 319
Somoza, Anastasio, VI, 62, 214
Son, Hoang, 318
Sorensen, Theodore C., 223
Sotnik, Oleg, 368
Spiegal, Jack, 135
Spock, Benjamin, 135, 136
Sprouse, Philip D., 199
Stalin, Joseph, 241, 355
Standard Oil, 33, 46
Stans, Maurice, 119
Stark, Peter, 110
Stassen, Harold E., 13
Stettinius, Edward R., 274, 291
Stewart, Maxwell, 198
Stockdale, James, 115
Stokes, Rose Pastor, 186
Straight, Michael, 323
Stratemeyer, Albert, 207
Stratemeyer, George, 298
Stripling, Robert, 272
Strong, Anna, 186
Sulzberger, C.L., 14
Summary Suspension Act, 156
Sutton, Anthony, VI, 21
Swain, Robert C., 34
Sweezy, Paul, 160
Swerdlow, Irving, 185
Symans, Edward, 184
Symms, Steven D., 40, 147
Szulc, Ted, 214

T

Tabankin, Margery A., 125
Taft, Robert, 166
Taylor, Henry J., 213, 284
Thomas, J. Parnell, 164
Thompson, James, 122
Thurmond, Strom, Senator, 112, 211, 331
Tito, Josef Broz, 209
Tolstoy, Nicolai, 356
Toure,Sekou, 226
Tower, John, 334
Treverton, Gregory, 236
Trojan horse, 277, 285
Trumbo, Dalton, 291
Tse-tung, Mao, 179, 269, 297, 357
Tshombe, Moise, 185, 298
Turtle, Jerry, Adai, 316

U

Ullman, William, 291
Ulyanov, Vladimir Ilich, 30
Unger, Leonard, 187, 189
United Aircraft, 16
Utley, Freda, 198
Utt, James B., 118, 337

V

Valaurs Actuelles, 128
Vance, Cyrus, 128, 232, 331
Vaughan, Harry H., 330
Vien, Nguyen khac, 124
Vincent, John Carter, 183, 189, 198, 199, 285, 287
Volker, Paul, 18
Voroshilov, Kliment, Con., 357

W

Wald, Royal Jules, 193
Walker, Richard L., 357
Wallace, Henry, 227
Wallop, Malcolm, 281
Walter, Francis E., 135, 169

Ward, Chester A., 344
Ward, Harry F., 139
Ware, Harold, 122, 264, 265, 266, 270, 288
Warnell, W. Raymond, 143
Warnke, Paul, 128, 232
Warren Commission Report, 182
Warren, Earl, 152, 153, 159, 324
Warsaw Pact, 77
Waskow, Arthur, 140
Watch, Helsinki, 368, 426
Watkins, James D., 26
Watkins, John, 159
Watson, Barbara, 187
Weaver, Robert, 230
Webster, William H., 144
Weinberg, Sidney, 166
Weinberger, Caspar, 21
Weiss, Cora, 227, 335
Weiss, Peter, 140
Welch, Richard, 126, 343
Westinghouse, 33, 36, 44, 45
White, Harry Dexter, 51, 63, 98, 162, 163, 169, 183, 203, 208, 219, 220, 227, 232, 234, 263, 269, 276, 286, 291, 329, 330
White, Lincoln, 210
Wieland, William Arthur, 203, 206
Wiesner, Louis A., 190
Wilkinson, Frank, 135, 136
William Sellers Company, 12
Williams, Aubrey, 136
Williams, James, 316
Williams, Ronald, 144
Wilson, John B., 306
Wilson, Woodrow, 220
Wirtz, Robert, 226
Wirtz, Willard, 226, 237
Witt, Nathan, 227, 267, 268
Wright, Jim, 335
Wurmbrand, Richard, 359

X

Xiaoping, Deng, 47, 372

Y

Yaobang, Hu, 68
Yarmolinsky, Adam, 223, 231, 249, 263, 331, 338
Yau-bang, Hu, 86
Yilin, Yao, 87
Yoshida, Iwanobu, 320
Yost, Charles Woodruff, 180, 205
Young, Andrew, 193, 258, 259, 263
Young, Coleman A., 235
Young, William, 255

Z

Zaul, Elmar, 355
Zhivkov, Todor, 81, 100, 113
Ziannian, Li, 88
Zinchenko, Konstantin E., 297
Zinoviev, Alexander, 66

Printed in the United States
67461LVS00003B/71